Goa

Goa Handbook
Second edition
© Footprint Handbooks Ltd 2000

Published by Footprint Handbooks
6 Riverside Court
Lower Bristol Road
Bath BA2 3DZ. England
T +44 (0)1225 469141
F +44 (0)1225 469461
Email discover@footprintbooks.com
Web www.footprintbooks.com

ISBN 1 900949 45 8
ISSN 1368-4272
CIP DATA: A catalogue record for this
book is available from the British Library

In USA, published by
NTC/Contemporary Publishing Group
4255 West Touhy Avenue, Lincolnwood
(Chicago), Illinois 60712-1975, USA
T 847 679 5500 F 847 679 2494
Email NTCPUB2@AOL.COM

ISBN 0-658-00015-2
Library of Congress Catalog Card
Number on file

Credits

Series editors
Patrick Dawson
Rachel Fielding

Editorial
Editor: Stephanie Lambe
Maps: Sarah Sorensen

Production
Pre-press Manager: Jo Morgan
Typesetting: Richard Ponsford and
Emma Bryers
Maps: Kevin Feeney, Robert Lunn
and Claire Benison
Proof reading: Howard David

Design
Mytton Williams

Photography
Front cover: Art Directors & Trip Photo
Library
Back cover: Travel Ink
Inside colour section: Robert Harding
Picture Library; Ian Large; Art Directors
& Trip Photo Library; Eye Ubiquitous;
Mike McQueen

Illustrations by Shane Feeney and
Robert Lunn

Printed and bound
in Italy by LEGOPRINT

Every effort has been made to ensure
that the facts in this Handbook are
accurate. However, travellers should still
obtain advice from consulates, airlines
etc about current travel and visa
requirements before travelling. The
authors and publishers cannot accept
responsibility for any loss, injury or
inconvenience however caused.

Goa

Footprint Handbook

The travel guide

Robert & Roma Bradnock

My village has shores and waving dunes,
hillocks and springs, shadows of palm trees,
chapels and devalayas, paddy fields and ponds
resting under red and white lotuses.

My village is a plot of land stretched along the
mountain, and is fringed with surf.
My village is a corner of calm and restfulness.

Telo de Mascarenhas, *When the mango trees blossomed*

Contents

Left: a garlanded statue of Christ is testimony to the continuing Portuguese imprint on the Old Conquests of Goa.

A foot in the door

Since Afonso de Albuquerque established the first Portuguese toehold in Goa, the lush coastal region of India has captured the western imagination. Yet while many today think of Goa almost as an extension of a Mediterranean culture grafted onto Indian stock, the image is misleading.

Certainly Goa has an often magical coastline, for three quarters of the year bathed in sunshine yet never suffering the gruelling heat of the Indian interior. The state also has a relaxed and easy going feel, where the decaying buildings, not of the British Raj but of the Portuguese, have created a wholly distinctive atmosphere. The coastal villages all have beautifully white painted churches and piazzas and wayside crosses, which create a startling impression against the clear blue sky. Yet inland Goa remains predominantly Hindu, and its position right on the border between north and south India, has meant that these influences have made their own mark on Goa's identity. Within the tiny state, barely 100 km from north to south and 60 km from west to east, it is possible to see in microcosm something of the astonishing diversity of India beyond. Indeed, within two or three days you can easily visit the neighbouring Indian states, tracking back into some of India's great empires and kingdoms.

Goa today is an integral, if still highly distinctive, part of India. And that indeed is part of its welcoming charm.

Highlights

Beaches For the first Portuguese sailors to land in Goa it was the golden land, not because of its magnificent beaches but because of the legendary wealth they believed lay in its hinterland. Yet in recent years it is Goa's golden sands themselves that have become legendary. The sea however does remain a vital source of livelihood for fishing communities up and down the west coast of India, colourful fishing boats and the occasionally powerful smell of drying fish demonstrate that for thousands of Goans these beaches are their own workplace.

Sheltered by rocky headlands in the north they form small bays, picturesquely semi-enclosed by huge boulders and craggy cliffs, sometimes topped with the remains of a Portuguese or a Maratha Fort. The discovery of Goa's easy life by westerners in the late 1960s brought with it an alien "hippy" culture and Anjuna became a destination of its own. Its weekly flea market and full moon raves have been a highlight for backpackers for years. A stunning stretch of sand runs all the way south from the Baga River to the old Portuguese fort of Aguada which commands the northern approach to the Mandovi estuary. Between the pockets of development which have sprung up, remain beaches which are rarely visited. Beyond Vagator, which has the northernmost hotel development, is the tiny Tiracol Fort that looks south along a completely undeveloped - and protected - expanse of forest-backed sand.

The beaches of the south have a quite different character from those of the north. Here too, clusters of beach shacks in places such as Colva or nearby Benaulim, provide excellent cheap meals, with seafood a speciality. Goa's largest luxury resorts have been built on the flat sandy shoreline from Cansaulim to Majorda and the estuary of the Sal River. Mostly landscaped, low rise and largely concealed under a canopy of trees, none encroach on the extraordinary unbroken silver sands along which you can walk uninterrupted for nearly 20 km. Beyond Cabo da Rama, one of the most starkly romantic of all Portuguese forts in Goa, is Palolem. Along with the much less visited bay of Agonda, the stunningly picturesque palm fringed bay here matches the most romantic portraits of a tropical paradise.

Goa's beaches must still rank as among the most beautiful and sparsely populated in the world.

Left: the striking lamp tower - deepmal - of the Sri Mangesh Temple near Ponda gives a distinctively Goan feel to the temple courtyard.
Below: fishing on the broad slow flowing rivers - still more a way of life than a recreation.

Above: women sort out the early morning catch for sale on Colva beach.
Left: the remarkable Shri Shantadurga Temple at Queula (1738), built by a grandson of then great Maratha leader Shivaji, is dedicated to the Goddess Durga in her peaceful aspect.

Right: palm leaf mats for sale in Mapusa market.
Below: the quiet back lanes of Panaji retain
their Portuguese atmosphere.

Above: cycle hire may be informal but it
offers a great way of getting about.
Right: crowded ferries still cross many of Goa's
unbridged rivers and estuaries, as at Siolim.

As the chief centre of Portuguese economic, political and religious ambitions in India, Goa retains the most vivid reminders of its distinctive colonial past. White painted churches are the universally recognised hallmarks of Portugal's Catholic impact, but remarkable seminaries, country houses and minor memorials continue to give the territories of the Old Conquests - Ilhas, Bardez and Salcete - a unique character.

The Portuguese inheritance

Panaji's Church of the Immaculate Conception dominates the square in the town centre from the top of a high flight of steps. In Bardez, Saligao's late 19th-century parish church of Our Lady the Mother of God commands a huge expanse of open land, its nave and tower surmounted by strikingly ribbed pinacles. Nearby Mapusa's 16th-century Our Lady of Miracles is the centre of both Christian and Hindu pilgrimage. Salcete, to the south, also has its share of churches such as the impressive Baroque Church of the Holy Spirit in Margao, while the great seminary of Rachol, established in 1580, stands out as a still active centre of training and worship. Wayside crosses along many of the major and minor roads in effect claimed the land of the Old Conquests for its Christian masters.

At the heart of 'Portuguese' Goa is Old Goa itself, one of the finest collections of Portuguese colonial churches and a World Heritage site. The dominant influence on Goan Christian architecture was that of the Italian late Renaissance and of the early Baroque imported by the Jesuits. The most striking features of the latter are best captured in Old Goa, in the ornately decorated interiors where a profusion of gilded wood covers the whole of the reredos behind the altar.

Old Goa

Old Goa's historical connections are themselves richly coloured, centering on the life and work of St Francis Xavier, whose tomb in the Basilica of Bom Jesus is still the object of pilgrimage from around the world. Across the square where the court of the Inquisition once carried out its gruesome business is the Se Cathedral, possibly the largest church in Asia, with an astonishingly gilded and painted main altar. Surrounding the core of Old Goa are the splendid domed baroque Church of St Catejan, the tower of St Augustine and many other notable shrines, churches and monuments.

Standing apart from the white painted churches – in Portuguese times they were the only buildings that were allowed to be painted white – are the few remaining estate houses. Goa's elite (who were predominantly Indian) expressed their nobility and wealth by building grand houses within large grounds. The long airy verandas, tiled terracotta roofs, oyster shell windows in wooden frames shaded by wide eves – all of these protected the rooms from the worst of the strong summer sun and torrential monsoon rains. The formal salons of these 18th-century family houses were appropriately fitted out with beautifully carved rosewood furniture, imported crystal chandeliers, gilded Belgian mirrors, and fine Chinese porcelain while the private rooms and kitchen were set around the traditional inner courtyard. One of the best known is the Menezes Braganza House. Partly dating from the 16th century and set in large grounds, the house reflects the lifestyle of Portuguese families who established substantial plantations and used the profits to sustain a lifestyle which linked Goan and Portuguese societies. The early 18th-century Miranda House in Loutolim is another example, giving a glimpse of a way of life now largely consigned to the past.

Estate houses

The Portuguese influence was not restricted to its buildings. Church festivals, which are such a enriching aspect of the life of the Christian community in Goa, brought a new dimension to the social life of the country. The Feast of the Three Kings celebrated at Cansaulim, Chandor and Reis Magos on 6th January and special feasts in honour of St Anthony on 13th June to ensure the onset of the monsoon, or the almost unique Procession on All Saints at Goa Velha before Easter, illustrate the continuing role of the

Festivals

Christian Church in Goa's richly woven culture. The wider community eagerly await the highly colourful, and often boisterous carnival held in Panaji before Lent in February-March , with its brilliantly designed costumes and a parade of floats conjured up by an imagination let loose. Hindu festivals are interwoven with those of the Christian community. Shigmotsav, the spring festival celebrated as Holi across northern India at the March-April full moon, is marked by the same vigorous – sometimes riotous – loosing of inhibitions. Families and friends spray each other with implausibly coloured powders and liquids. Temple festivals have similarly noisy and colourful celebrations for temple deities through the year.

The Hindu heartland Away from the Portuguese dominated coastal districts of the Old Conquests is the pulsating heart of Hindu Goa. At Tambdi Surla, in the foothills of the Ghats, is the tiny gem of the 12th-13th century Mahadeva Temple, the only remaining example of pre-Portuguese Hindu architecture. Much closer to the coast are the remarkable living temples of the Ponda region such as the 18th-century Shri Mangesh at Mardol or the Shri Shantadurga at Queula. These newer Hindu temples may lack the brilliance of fine stone carving seen in other parts of India but here they are marked out by their distinctive design influenced by Christian, and to a lesser extent Muslim, religious architecture. Often sited along a river valley, screened from view by dense foliage and tall palms, the white or colour washed temples with their unusual domes, open sided pavilions, tall lamp towers and large water tanks lined with laterite blocks, take the visitor by surprise. Set in picturesque forest clearances, they breathe the life of another world.

Spice plantation The forests are not only the homes of shrines and spirits but of spices, nuts and a huge variety of valuable trees. The spice plantation at Savoi Verem which is over 200 years old has much else besides spices. In its shady groves on the hillside, it offers a window to the variety of terrain which produces many of Goa's richest harvests, from cashew nuts to pepper, nutmeg, jack fruit, bread fruit and cocum. The eye-opening guided tour reveals the mystery of the healing properties of many plants, apart from their traditional use in flavouring curries.

Dudhsagar Falls The spectacular waterfalls on the eastern edge of Goa, on the border with Karnataka, is a special delight in the winter months when it cascades down 600m, its foaming froth giving it its name - the "Sea of milk". Part of the fun is getting there. The newly-widened broad gauge line runs due east of Margao, crossing tributaries of the Zuari and Mandovi River to Colem before beginning a steep climb up the forested scarp of the Western Ghats, still with a powerful sense of their isolation and remoteness. Rich in birdlife, and with a hint of freshness in the air, the walk down to the beautiful bathing pool or up the steep climb to the head of the falls makes a wonderfully refreshing break. It will be accessible once again by train if the Dudhsagar station re-opens on schedule in 2,000.

Essentials

2

Essentials

Planning your trip

A week in Goa allows time to see a major site like Old Goa and some Hindu temples around Ponda as well as to laze on a beach. But all of Goa is highly accessible and it is easy to travel from north to south in a day by car, motorbike or bus. With a fortnight in hand, you could sample different stretches of coastal Goa from Tiracol in the far north to Palolem in the south, visiting Portuguese forts and churches on the way. You would also have time to take in some of the sights inland, perhaps choosing the ancient temple at Tambdi Surla, Dudhsagar Falls, a spice plantation, or wind down to Chandor and Loutolim to see the traditional Portuguese mansions. If you have three to four weeks, you can experience something of the fascination of India beyond, by choosing to go on a couple of three or four day excursions into neighbouring Karnataka or Maharashtra.

Essentials

Where to go

Goa's beaches lie all along its magical coastline with sandy coves and estuaries to the north and long palm-fringed quieter stretches to the south. You can choose a beach for its character – from crowded, lively, party-going **Anjuna** and **Chapora**, through to the quieter and more sedate **Candolim** and **Mobor**, to the relative isolation and beauty of **Arambol** in the extreme north, or **Palolem** to the far south.

Beaches

Wherever you stay, on Wednesdays all roads (as far as foreign visitors are concerned) lead to the much publicized **Anjuna Flea market** though many would find a lot more local colour in **Mapusa** on Fridays.

Markets

Along the rocky headlands are remains of small Portuguese forts which are great to explore – tiny **Tiracol** in the northernmost part of Goa, has been renovated to become a 'Heritage' hotel, while **Cabo de Rama**, to the south holds an aura of its historic past.

Forts

By venturing a short distance away from the coast you can explore the richness of Goa's cultural heritage. Goa's Portuguese Catholic history is best-captured in **Old Goa**. In addition, a trip to **Chandor** allows a visit to the Menezes Braganza House which gives you an insight into the opulent lifestyle once enjoyed by the old Portuguese families. Nearby is **Rachol**, the seminary which is well worth visiting and adjoined to it is the Museum of Christian Art.

Cultural heritage

Predominantly Hindu inland Goa has its best preserved ancient temple at **Tambdi Surla**. The vibrant, living temples dotted around **Ponda** give an insight into the strong religious tradition of the majority of its population.

Temples

A walk around the spice plantation near **Savoi Verem** is really rewarding and although Goa's national parks are rather disappointing as far as wildlife is concerned, they are situated in picturesque forest-rich areas. One has the famous **Dudhsagar Falls** within its boundaries, which is a spectacular sight in the wet months.

Walks & waterfalls

To see something of the astonishing diversity of India beyond Goa, take a short two or three-day excursion and travel east into Karnataka to the ruins of the fabulous capital of the Vijaynagars at **Hampi,** or go through **Belgaum** with its Muslim past, or visit **Gokarna** on the coast to the south, alive and crowded with its present-day Hindu pilgrims. You can also easily wander across the northern border near Tiracol to cross into Maharashtra to see a Maratha fort ruin at **Redi** which also has a beautiful deserted beach, and then climb the Ghats, up to the minor hill station of **Amboli.**

Beyond Goa

Mumbai to Goa   If **Mumbai** is your entry point, you will see a flourishing Indian regional capital in sharp contrast to the much smaller state capital of Goa. The road journey along the NH17 allows a night halt at the hill station of **Mahabaleshwar** after seeing the Maratha Sivaji fort at **Pratapgarh**. Or you can stop at **Chiplun**, which enjoys picturesque river views, before continuing to Goa via Sivaji's coastal fort at **Sindhudurg**.

When to go

Goa is warm throughout the year but its position on the coast means that it never suffers the unbearable heat of India's northern plains. However, from mid-April until the beginning of the monsoon in early June both the temperature and the humidity rise sharply, making the middle of the day steamy hot and the beach sand almost untouchable. The monsoon itself makes June and July very wet months. On the coast, the heavy rain often comes as torrential storms accompanied by lashing winds, while up in the cooler Ghats, if it is not raining, the hill tops are often wrapped in swirling cloud and mist – it's a good time to see the waterfalls! Heavy showers can persist in August and September and humidity can remain unpleasantly high, but by October rainfall drops significantly. The beautiful, warm, clear and dry weather of Goa's tropical winter from mid-October to March, makes it justifiably the best time for foreign visitors. It is also the period when charter flights operate direct to Goa and tourist facilities are in full swing. Going outside this main tourist season means that many eating places, especially on the beach, are closed.

What to take

It is always best to keep luggage to a minimum. A sturdy rucksack or a rigid suitcase covers most eventualities. Light cotton clothes are useful in Goa at any time of year. It is a good idea to have some very lightweight long sleeve cotton shirts and trousers for the evenings, preferably light in colour, as they also give some protection against mosquitoes. Some find open shoes or sandals best in hot weather but it is also important to guard against blisters, cuts and bruises which are common problems with unprotected feet. Comfortable canvas shoes or trainers are good options. Women should dress modestly (it is worth shopping locally for cotton items as these are very good value). Even on the beach, very revealing swimwear attracts unnecessary attention. Toiletries, including tampons and barrier contraceptives, may not be available in smaller towns. Camera film is available in all major cities and tourist centres, though to be assured of quality it is best to take rolls of films from home and certainly any specialist camera batteries. If you have to buy film in Goa only buy from a reputable shop since hawkers and roadside stalls may not be reliable– also check the carton carefully as well as the expiry date. We list here some items you might find particularly helpful in Goa:

Checklist   International driving licence; nailbrush; photocopies of essential documents; short
See page 44 for a   wave radio; spare passport photographs; student card (ISIC); sun hat and sunglasses;
medical checklist   sun protection cream (factor 15 plus); Swiss army knife; torch; wet wipes; zip-lock bags.

Budget travellers may also want to take the following:
Cotton, sheet sleeping bag; earplugs; eyeshades; mosquito net (impregnated, ideally); padlock (for room and baggage); soap; string (washing line); towel; washbasin plug.

Indian tourist offices

Australia Level 1, 17 Castlevegh St, Sydney, NSW 2000, T02-2321600, F02-2233003.

Austria Opernring 1, 1010 Vienna, T1-5871462.

Canada 60 Bloor St, West Suite No 1003, Toronto, Ontario, T416-9623787, F416-9626279.

France 8 Blvd de la Madeleine, 75009 Paris, T42658386.

Germany Baserler Str 48, 60329 Frankfurt 1, T069-235423, F234724.

Italy Via Albricci 9, Milan 20122, T8053056.

Japan Pearl Building, 9-18 Chome Ginza, Chuo Ku, Tokyo 104, T03-5715062, F5715235.

The Netherlands Rokin 9-15, 1012 Amsterdam, T020-608891.

Singapore 20 Kramat Lane, 01-01A United House, Singapore 0922. T2353800, F2358677.

Sweden Sveavagen 9-11 1st Flr, S-III 57 Stockholm 11157, T468-215081, F210186.

Switzerland 1-3 rue de Chantepoulet, 1201 Geneva, T022-321813.

Thailand 3rd Flr, Singapore Airlines Bldg, 62/5 Thaniya Rd, Bangkok, T2353800.

UK 7 Cork St, London W1X 2AB, T020-74373677/8, F4941048.

USA 3550 Wiltshire Blvd, Room 204, Los Angeles, California 90010, T213-4773824, F3806111; 1270 Ave of the Americas Suite 1808, New York, NY 10020,

Essentials

Finding out more

You may choose to try an inclusive package holiday or let a specialist operator quote for a tailor-made tour. Out of season these can be worth exploring. The lowest prices quoted for 1999 from the UK vary from about US$500 for a week (flights, hotel and breakfast) in the low season, to over US$3,000 for three weeks during the peak season. Otherwise, be adventurous and make your own arrangements.

Tours & tour operators

ACE Study Tours, T01223-835055, F837394, ace@study-tours.org; **Banyan Tours**, T01672-564778, BanyanUK@compuserve.com; **Andrew Brock**, T01572-821072; **Cox & Kings** (now of the Taj Group), T020-78735001, F76306038; **Dragoman**, T01728-86113, www.dragoman.co.uk; **Greaves Tours**, T020-74879111, F74860722, sbriggs@greavesuk.com; **Indian Magic**, T0208-4274848, sales@indiamagic.co.uk; **Mysteries of India**, T020-85742727, F85710707, vo43@dial.pipex.com; **Myths and Mountains**, USA T800-6706984, travel@mythsandmountains.com; **North South Travel**, T01245-492882 (which gives its profits to charity); **Spirit of India**, USA T888-3676147, inquire@spirit-of-india.com; **STA Travel**, T020-73616161, www.statravel.co.uk; **Western & Oriental**, T020-73136611, F73136601, enquiries@westernoriental.com

Tour companies

Before you travel

In early 2000 the following visa rules applied: **Transit**, for passengers *en route* to another country; **Tourist**, one month (entry must be within a month of issue), or six month visa, from the date of issue with multiple entry. Same fee; **Business**, up to one year from the date of issue (a letter from company giving the nature of business is required); **Five year**, for those of Indian origin only, who have held Indian passports; **Student**, valid up to one year from the date of issue (attach a letter of acceptance from Indian institution, and an aids test certificate – allow up to three months for approval).

Visas & permits
Visa fees vary according to nationality

Visa extensions Applications should be made to the Foreigners' Regional Registration Offices at New Delhi, Mumbai, Kolkata or Chennai, or an office of the Superintendent of Police in the District Headquarters. After six months, you must leave India and apply for a

Essentials

 Indian embassies & consulates

Australia 3-5 Moonah Place, Yarralumla, Canberra T6273-3999; Sydney T9223-9500 Melbourne T9386-7399.

Austria Kärntner Ring 2, A-1015 Vienna, T50-58666669, F50-59219.

Bangladesh House 120, Rd 2, Dhanmondi RA, Dhaka-2, T503606, Chittagong T211007.

Belgium 217-Chaussée de Vleurgat, 1050 Brussels, T6409802, F6489638. Consulates: Ghent T091-263423, Antwerp T03-2341122.

Bhutan India House Estate, Thimpu, T2162.

Canada 10 Springfield Rd, Ottawa, Ontario K1M 1C9, T613-7443751. Consulates: Toronto T416-9600751, Vancouver T9266080.

Denmark Vangehusvej 15, 2100 Copenhagen, T3918-2888, F3927-0218.

Finland Satamakatu 2 A8, 00160 Helsinki-16, T608927.

France 15 Rue Alfred Dehodencq, Paris, T40-507070.

Germany Adenauerallee, 262/264, 5300 Bonn-1, T0228-54050. Consulates: Berlin T8817068, Frankfurt T069-271040, Hamburg T338036, Munich T089-92562067, Stuttgart T0711-297078.

Ireland 6 Lesson Park, Dublin 6, T01-9470843.

Israel 4 Kaufmann St, Sharbat, Tel Aviv 68012, T0368-580585, F510143.

Italy Via XX Settembre 5, 00187 Rome, T4884642. Consulates: Milan T02-8690314, Genoa T54891.

Japan 2-11, Kudan Minami 2-Chome, Chiyoda-ku, Tokyo 102, T03-2622391, F03-2344866. Consulate: Kobe T078-2418116.

Korea 37-3, Hannam-dong, Yongsan-Ku, Seoul, T7984257, F7969534.

Malaysia 20th Flr Wisma Selangor Dredging, West Block, 142-C, Jl Apang, 50450 Kuala Lumpur, T03-2617000.

Netherlands Buitenrustweg 2, The Hague (2517KD), T070-3469771.

Maldives Mafabbu Aage 37, Orchid Magu, Male 20-02, T323015.

Nepal Lainchour, PO Box No 292, Kathmandu, T410900.

New Zealand 10th Flr, Princess Tower, 180 Molesworth St (PO Box 4045) Wellington, T4736390.

Norway 30 Niels Jules Gate, 0272 Oslo-2, T443194.

Pakistan G5 Diplomatic Enclave, Islamabad, T050-8144731, Karachi T021-814371.

Singapore India House, 31 Grange Rd, Singapore 0923, T7376777.

Spain Avda Pio XII 30-32, 28016 Madrid, T457-0209. Consulate: Barcelona T93-2120422.

Sri Lanka 36-38 Galle Rd, Colombo 3, T421605 Kandy T446430.

Sweden Adolf Fredriks Kyrkogata 12, Box 1340, 11183 Stockholm, T08-107008, F08-248505.

Switzerland 17 Weltpoststrasse 17, 3015 Berne, T031-44019.

Thailand 46 Soi 23 (Prasarn Mitr) Sukhumvit 23, Bangkok 10110, T2580300.

UK India House, Aldwych, London WC2B 4NA, T020-78368484. Consulates: The Spencers, 19 Augusta St, Hockley, Birmingham, B18 6DS, T0121-2122782; 6th Flr, 134 Renfrew St, Glasgow 3 7ST, T0141-3310777, F3310666. (Send SAE for postal applications).

USA 2107 Massachusetts Ave, Washington DC 20008, T202-9397000. Consulates: New Orleans T504-5828105, New York T212-8797800, San Francisco T415-6680662, Chicago T312-781680, Cleveland T216/696.

new visa. **Registration** No foreigner needs to register within the 180 day period of their tourist visa. **Income tax clearance** All foreign visitors who stay in India for more than 180 days are required to get an income tax clearance exemption certificate from the Foreign Section of the Income Tax Dept in Delhi, Mumbai, Kolkata or Chennai. In Goa, contact Directorate of Employment (Enforcement, Foreign Exchange Regulation Act), Shanta Building, Second floor, St Inez, Panaji.

Duty Free allowance Tourists are allowed to bring in all personal effects, 'which may Customs reasonably be required', without charge. The official customs allowance includes 200 cigarettes or 50 cigars, 0.95 litres of alcohol, a camera with five rolls of film and a pair of binoculars. You may be asked to register valuable personal effects or professional equipment on a Tourist Baggage Re-Export Form (TBRE), including jewellery, special camera equipment and lenses, lap-tops, sound and video recorders. These forms require the serial numbers of such equipment. It saves considerable frustration if you know the numbers in advance and are ready to show the serial numbers on the equipment. In addition to the forms, details of imported equipment may be entered into your passport. Save time by completing the formalities while waiting for your baggage. It is essential to keep these forms for showing to the customs when leaving India, otherwise considerable delays are very likely at the time of departure. **NB** Duty free shops in Goa and Mumbai are extremely limited.

Currency regulations There are no restrictions on the amount of foreign currency or travellers' cheques a tourist may bring into India. If you are carrying more than US$2,500 or its equivalent in cash or travellers' cheques you will need to fill in a currency declaration form.

The **import** of dangerous drugs, live plants, gold coins, gold and silver bullion and **Prohibited &** silver coins not in current use, ivory, skins of all animals, snake skin and articles made **restricted items** from them, are either banned or subject to strict regulation. Similarly, the **export** of antiquities and art objects over 100 years old, and gold jewellery purchased in India costing over Rs 2,000 and other jewellery (including settings with precious stones) costing over Rs 10,000, are either banned or subject to strict regulation. It is illegal to import firearms into India without special permission.

Money

Indian currency is the **Rupee**. It is not possible to purchase this currency overseas. The Currency Rupee is divided into 100 Paise. New notes are printed in denominations of Rs 500, *See inside front cover for* 100, 50, 20 and 10. Coins are minted in denominations of 50, 25, 20, 10, 5, 2 and 1 *a list of exchange rates* although coins below 50 paise are rarely seen. **NB** It can be difficult to use torn or very worn notes. Check notes carefully when you are given them and refuse any that are damaged. The Rs 500 and Rs 100 notes are easy to confuse. Always double check.

On arrival at the airport you should change money while waiting for your luggage since Money you will need some Rupees to pay for transport to the hotel. This is generally easy and changing fairly quick. If you are booked into a large resort hotel and have free transfer arranged, *A list of banks can be* you can usually change money (often 24 hours) at their desk. In the major resort areas, *found in each town's* banks, hotels and private dealers all offer exchange services. **NB** If you cash sterling, make *individual directory* certain you are given Rupees at the sterling and not at the dollar rate.

It is best to take travellers' cheques into India, rather than cash, since the latter can't be Travellers' replaced if lost or stolen. Travellers' cheques are widely accepted in the major resorts in cheques Goa. Many private dealers (often doubling up as travel agents) offer competitive rates and are generally much quicker than banks. They usually have long opening hours though some banks in Goa have now extended their opening times. Exchange desks in the large hotels may be open 24 hours but they often offer a poorer rate of exchange. To save time, it is worth changing enough to last for some days. It is essential to show your passport when exchanging travellers' cheques. In a large number of shops and travel agents, travellers' cheques are accepted for direct purchases.

Take care to follow the advice given about keeping proof of purchase slips and make a note of travellers' cheque numbers separately from the cheques. In the case of loss, you will need to get a police report and inform the travellers' cheque company. Replacement cheques may only be given by authorized agents. In Panaji, Thomas Cook deal with claims efficiently whereas the Amex agent in town is not authorized to issue cheques.

Unscrupulous dealers may offer a premium of 40-50 percent on the face value of your travellers' cheques in order to cash them with false signatures, and ask you to get replacements. Do not be tempted.

Credit cards Major credit cards are increasingly acceptable in the main centres. Payment by card for purchases can sometimes be more expensive than payment by cash because of the premium the shop may have to pay to the credit card company. *Master Card* and *Visa* are widely accepted, though not consistently and not by all. Railway reservation centres in some major cities are now accepting *Visa* card. Remember that it often takes a long time to check authorization.

ATMs Automatic Telling Machines that accept major foreign credit cards are being introduced in the main towns by *HDFC* and *Times Bank*, which have recently merged. (The frequently seen ATM signs at many banks are for local account holders only.) *Mastercard*, *Visa* and *Amex* cards are usually accepted. The minimum withdrawal is Rs 100, maximum Rs 10,000 per day (3 x Rs 3000 plus 1 x Rs 1000). One worry though – what happens if there is a power cut whilst your card is in the machine?

Encashment certificates These are given free whenever you exchange foreign currency (cash, travellers' cheques, etc) and allow you to change Indian Rupees back to your own currency so you should retain enough certificates to reconvert Indian Rupees upon departure. The certificates also enable you to use Rupees to buy airline tickets or Foreign Tourist Quota rail tickets (not applicable at Margao), and to pay bills in some upper category hotels where tourists must pay in foreign exchange. **NB** When receiving cash through a bank draft or transfer, insist on a certificate since you cannot purchase travellers' cheques without them. However, ATM machines do not give these certificates.

Black market There is no black market in Goa now, since premiums are small. However, it is worth carrying one or two small denomination currency notes (eg £10 or US$10 notes) for emergencies since it is easy to find someone to change them. **NB** Changing money through unauthorized dealers is illegal.

Transferring money *Thomas Cook*, *American Express* and *ANZ Grindlays* can make instant transfers to their offices in India but charge a high fee (about eight percent). *State Bank of India* branches abroad charge less but can take two to three days. A bank draft (up to US$1,000) which may be posted (three to five days by *Speedpost*) is the cheapest option (*Lloyds Bank* charge about 1.5 percent).

Cost of living The Indian cost of living remains well below that in the industrialized world. Most food, accommodation and public transport, especially rail and bus, are exceptionally cheap. There is a widening range of moderately priced but clean hotels and guest houses and good, inexpensive beach restaurants, making it possible to get a great deal for your money. Budget travellers (sharing a room) can expect to spend about Rs 350-400 (about US$8 or £6) a day to cover cost of accommodation, food and travel. Those planning to stay in fairly comfortable hotels and use taxis for travelling to sights should expect to spend at least Rs 2,000 (about US$45 or £30) a day. During a visit to Mumbai you will spend more than when in Goa. **NB** Prices in the *Handbook* are quoted in Rupees as these are used exclusively throughout India. Very few people are familiar with international currencies, including dollars. Visitors do best to think in Rupee terms.

Carry only enough to cover your daily budget in a purse (a good way to prevent overspending!). Keep larger amounts of money in a belt worn under clothing, or use the hotel safe if you intend to spend the day on the beach. Try to avoid taking large amounts of money out of your money belt or bag in public as this may attract unwelcome attention. Keep a supply of small denomination notes, especially useful for tipping.

Carrying money

Getting there

Air

There are a limited number of direct scheduled *Indian Airlines* flights to Goa's Dabolim Airport from the Middle East. The airport is owned by the Indian Navy and consequently no scheduled flights from Europe are allowed to land. A new international airport is being proposed at Mopa in North Goa but it has faced local objections. Even if permission is given it will be several years before direct scheduled flights are allowed. Scheduled flights to Mumbai, from Europe, USA, Canada, Australasia and the Far East are an alternative.

Scheduled flights

Several tour operators from Europe, especially from Britain (eg *First choice*, *JMC*, *Jewel in the Crown*, *Manos*, *Somak*, *Tropical Places*) flying from Gatwick and Manchester, offer package holidays between October and April. They are often exceptional value (especially in November and from mid-January to mid-March). Flights arrive at the airport at Dabolim, across the bay from Panaji and are only allowed to land in daylight and on certain days of the week. **The following rules apply to charter flights:** they are not available to Indian nationals; the deal must include accommodation; officially, charter passengers can only stay for a maximum of 45 days, although this restriction can be bent somewhat if you have a valid visa to cover the duration of your proposed extension. For details, contact Davidair, The Old Post House, Escrivao, Main Road, Candolim, T277000, F276509, davidgoa@goa1.dot.net.in Open 0900-1800.

Charter flights

Campus Travel, *Trailfinders* and *STA* have over 100 offices worldwide and they offer special deals for students and under-26s. *General Sales Agents* (GSAs) for specific airlines can sometimes offer attractive deals. *Jet Airways*, 188 Hammersmith Rd, London W6 7DJ, T020-89701500, for *Gulf Air*, *Kuwait Airways* etc. *Welcome Travels*, 58 Wells St, London W1P 3RA, T020-74363011, for *Air India*. *Orient International (Travels) Ltd*, 91 Charlotte St, London W1P 1LB, T020-76371330, 76370037, F73239755, offer good discounts. It is also possible to book some internal flights on *Air India* (see page 29).

Ticket agents

The best deals are offered from the UK. Direct charter flights which operate during the winter months take just over 10 hours. Alternatively, you can pick up attractive deals on *Air India* which flies direct to Mumbai throughout the year, with a transfer to Goa, usually after an overnight stop. A few European airlines (eg *Lufthansa*, *KLM*) and several from the Middle East (eg *Emirates*, *Gulf Air*, *Kuwait Airways*, *Royal Jordanian*) offer good discounts to Mumbai (and other Indian regional capitals) from London, but fly via their hub cities, so adding to the journey time.

From the UK, Continental Europe & the Middle East

Quantas, Singapore Airlines, Thai Airways, Malaysian Airlines, Cathay Pacific and Indian Airlines are the principal airlines connecting the continents, flying to one of the Indian regional capitals. From there you will need to get onward flights or rail connections to Goa. At present, there are no direct charter flights to Goa from this part of the world. *STA* and *Flight Centres* offer discounted tickets from their branches in major cities.

From Australasia via the Far East

Essentials

Essentials

From North America Direct charter flights to Goa do not operate from North America. From the east coast, it is best to fly direct to Mumbai from New York via London by *Air India* (18 hours) and then transfer to Goa. Alternatively, try a direct charter from UK to Goa but this will usually involve a stopover in London. Discounted tickets on *British Airways*, *KLM*, *Lufthansa*, *Gulf Air* and *Kuwait Airways* are sold through agents although they will invariably fly via their country's capital cities. From the west coast, it is best to fly via Hong Kong, Singapore or Bangkok to Mumbai using one of those countries' national carriers. *Hari World Travels* and *STA* have offices in New York, Toronto and Ontario. Student fares are also available from *Council Travel* with several offices in the USA and *Travel Cuts*, in Canada.

Touching down

Airport information

For details of arrival in Goa by rail or road see pages 97 & 67 respectively

Goa's Dabolim airport is south of Panaji, across the Mormugao Bay. There are counters at the airport for car hire, foreign exchange and tourist information, all of which are normally open to meet flights, usually 1230-1530.

Transport to town Package tour companies and luxury hotels usually arrange courtesy buses for **hotel transfer**. Other options are to take a taxi, bus or car hire. The **pre-paid taxi** counter immediately outside the arrivals hall has rates clearly displayed (eg Panaji Rs 340 which takes 40 mins; North Goa beaches from Rs 450; Tiracol Rs 750; south Goa beaches from Rs 240; Palolem Rs 700). State your destination at the counter, pay and get a receipt which will give the registration number of your taxi. Keep hold of this receipt until you reach your destination. There is no need to tip the driver since the pre-paid rate is already generous by local standards. **Warning** The taxi driver may insist that the hotel you have asked for has closed down or is full and will suggest another in order to get a commission from the hotel. To avoid this problem, say that you have a reservation (booking) at the hotel of your choice (even if you don't!). *Indian Airlines* sometimes have a **bus** for transfer to Panaji to meet their incoming flights (Rs 30), although this was not running in early 2000. The public bus stop on the far side of the roundabout outside the airport gates (left after leaving the arrivals hall), has regular buses to Vasco da Gama (Rs 3), from where there are connections to all major places in Goa. If you want to go straight to the nearest beach, go to the right of the roundabout, cross the road, and you will find a bus stop for buses to Bogmalo (Rs 3). **NB** The possible closure of the Zuari Bridge for repairs may greatly increase the transfer time by road from the airport, to Panaji and North Goa via Ponda. The new *Hotel Airport*, 1 km away is listed under Panaji 'sleeping'.

Security International airlines vary in their arrangements and requirements, in particular the carrying of equipment like radios, tape-recorders, lap-top computers and batteries. It is advisable to ring the airline in advance to confirm what their current regulations are. **NB** Internal airlines often have different rules from the international carriers. You are strongly advised not to pack valuables in your luggage (there have been several reports of vandalism and theft from luggage, particularly on *Air India*) and avoid having to repack at the airport.

Immigration formalities in Mumbai can be particularly slow

Documentation Despite recent improvements, 'Arrival' can be a slow process. Disembarkation cards, with an attached customs declaration, are handed out to passengers during the inward flight. The customs slip should be handed over when leaving the baggage collection hall.

Touching down

Electricity 220-240 volts AC. Some top hotels have transformers. There may be pronounced variations in the voltage, and power cuts are common. Socket sizes vary so you are advised to take a universal adaptor (available at most airports). **NB** Many hotels even in the higher categories don't have electric razor sockets. During power cuts, diesel generators are often used in the medium and higher category hotels to provide power for essential equipment but this may not always cover air-conditioning.

Emergency numbers Police 100, Fire 101, Ambulance 102.

Hours of business Banks: 1030-1430, Monday-Friday; 1030-1230, Saturday. Top hotels sometimes have a 24-hour service.

Post offices: Usually 1000-1700, Monday-Friday; Saturday mornings.

Government offices: 0930-1700, Monday- Friday; 0930-1300, Saturday (some open on alternate Saturdays only).

Shops: 0930-1800, Monday-Saturday. Bazaars keep longer hours.

IDD 91. A double ring repeated regularly means it is ringing. Equal tones with equal pauses means engaged.

Official time GMT +5½ hours throughout the year (USA, EST +10½ hours).

Weights & measures The metric system has come into universal use in the cities. In remote rural areas local measures are sometimes used.

Airport tax Rs 500 is the tax for all international departures but this is usually included in the price of the international air ticket; check this when buying.

Tourist information

There are Government of India and State Government Tourist offices in Panaji. The Goa Tourism Development Council, which has its own office runs modest hotels and dormitories in over a dozen locations. **NB** Don't take advice from unofficial 'tourist offices' at airports or railway stations.

See individual town and city directories for details of tourist offices

Full time students qualify for an ISIC (International Student Identity Card) which is issued by student travel and specialist agencies (eg *Campus*, *STA*) at home. A card allows certain travel benefits (eg reduced prices) and acts as proof of student status within India allowing ticket concessions into a few sites.

Student travellers

The country isn't geared up towards providing for the physically handicapped or wheelchair-bound traveller. Access to buildings, toilets (sometimes 'squat' type), pavements and kerbs and public transport, can prove frustrating but it is easy to find people to give a hand with lifting and carrying. Provided there is an able-bodied companion to scout around and arrange help, and so long as you are prepared to spend on at least mid-price hotels or guest houses, private car-hire and taxis, Goa should be rewarding, even if on a somewhat limited scale.

Disabled travellers

Compared with many other countries it is relatively easy and safe for women to travel around India, even on their own, though most people find it an advantage to travel with at least one companion.

Women travellers

Children of all ages are widely welcomed, being greeted with a warmth in their own right which is often then extended to those accompanying them. However, care should be taken when travelling to remote areas where health services are primitive since children tend to become more rapidly ill than adults.

Travelling with children

It is best to visit India in the cooler months since you need to protect children from the sun, heat, dehydration and mosquito bites. Cool showers or baths help, and avoid being out during the hottest part of the day. Diarrhoea and vomiting are the most common problems, so take the usual precautions, but more intensively. Breastfeeding is best and most convenient for babies. In the big cities you can get safe baby foods and formula milk. It doesn't harm a baby to eat an unvaried and limited diet of familiar food carried in packets for a few weeks if the local dishes are not acceptable, but it may be an idea to give vitamin and mineral supplements. See also under Health on page 44. Wet wipes are always useful and sometimes difficult to find in India, as are disposable nappies. The biggest hotels provide babysitting.

Rules, customs and etiquette

Customs Most travellers experience great warmth and hospitality. With it comes an open curiosity about personal matters. You should not be surprised if total strangers ask for details of your job, income and family circumstances, or discuss politics and religion.

Appearance Respect for the foreign visitor should be reciprocated by a sensitivity towards local customs and culture. To create a good first impression dress sensibly. Cleanliness, modest clothes and a smile go a long way. Scanty, tight clothing draws unwanted attention. Nudity is not permitted on beaches in India. It is illegal, and although there are some places where this ban is ignored, it causes widespread offence.

Courtesy It takes little effort to learn and use common gestures of courtesy but they are greatly appreciated by Indians. The **greeting** when meeting or parting, used universally among the Hindus across India, is the palms joined together as in prayer, sometimes accompanied with the word *namaste*. Muslims use the greeting *assalām aleikum*, with the response *waleikum assalām*, meaning 'peace be with you'. "**Please**" is *mehrbani-se* and "**thank you**" is often expressed by a smile and *abrigaad* in Goa, or with the somewhat formal *dhanyabad, shukriya* (Urdu).

Conduct You may at times be justifiably frustrated by delays, bureaucracy and inefficiency, but displays of anger and rudeness will not achieve anything positive, and may in fact make things worse. We suggest you remain patient and polite. The concept of time and punctuality is also rather vague so be prepared to be kept waiting. Indian law forbids homosexual acts for men (but not women) and carries a maximum sentence of life imprisonment. Although it is common to see young males holding hands in public, it doesn't necessarily indicate a gay relationship and is usually an expression of friendship. Overt displays of affection between homosexuals and heterosexuals give offence, and should be avoided.

Hands & eating Traditionally, Indians use the right hand for eating, cutlery being alien at the table except for serving spoons. In rural India, don't expect table knives and forks though you might find small spoons. Use your right hand for giving, receiving, eating or shaking hands as the left is considered to be unclean since it is associated with washing after using the toilet.

Visiting religious sites Visitors to all religious places should be dressed in clean, modest clothes; shorts and vests are inappropriate. Always remove shoes before entering (and all leather items in Jain temples). Take thick socks for protection when walking on sun-baked stone floors. Non-Hindus are sometimes excluded from the inner sanctum of **Hindu temples** and occasionally from the temple itself. Look for signs or ask. In certain temples, and on special occasions, you may only enter if you wear unstitched clothing such as a *dhoti*. Menstruating women are considered 'unclean' and should not enter places of worship. In **Muslim mosques**, visitors should only have their face, hands and feet exposed; women should also cover their heads. Mosques may be closed to non-Muslims shortly before formal prayers. Some temples have a register or a receipt book for **donations**. In general, if you wish to leave a donation, put money in the donation box.

*A Goa **government ban** on smoking and spitting in public places within the state came into effect on the first day of the millennium. Offenders will be fined Rs1,000.*

Begging

Beggars are often found on busy street corners in large Indian cities, as well as at bus and train stations where they often target foreigners for special attention. Visitors usually find this very distressing, especially the sight of severely undernourished children or those displaying physical deformity. You may be particularly affected when some persist on making physical contact; say a very firm "*Jaao*" (go away). Yet those seeking alms near religious sites are another matter, and you may see Indian worshippers giving freely to those less fortunate than themselves, since this is tied up with gaining 'merit'. How you deal with begging is a matter of personal choice but it is perhaps better to give to a recognized charity than to make largely ineffectual handouts to individuals. It is not helpful to hand out sweets, 'school pens' (which are often sold), and money, indiscriminately to open-palmed children who tag on to any foreigner.

Charitable giving

A pledge to donate a part of one's holiday budget to a local charity would be an effective formula for 'giving'. Some visitors like to support self-help co-operatives, orphanages, refugee centres, disabled or disadvantaged groups; Chapora has an orphanage. Others prefer international charities like *Oxfam*, *Save the Children* or *Christian Aid* which work with local partners, either by making a donation or by buying their products – http://www//India charitynet.com is useful. You may contact *Oxfam* at Sushil Bhawan, 210 Shahpur Jat, New Delhi 110049, T0116491774 or at 274 Banbury Rd, Oxford OX2 7D2, UK, oxindia@giasdl01.vsnl.net.in (400 grassroots projects). *SOS Children's Villages* is based at A-7 Nizamuddin (W), New Delhi 110013, T0114647835, http://www//pw2. netcom/sanjayd/sos.html (over 30 poor and orphaned children's projects in India).

Tipping

Children sometimes offer to do 'jobs' such as call a taxi, carry shopping or pose for a photo. You may want to give a coin in exchange. A tip of Rs 10 to a bell boy carrying luggage in a modest **hotel** (Rs 20 in a higher category) would be appropriate. In up-market **restaurants**, a 10 percent tip is acceptable (when service is not already included), while in places serving very cheap meals, round off the bill with small change. Indians don't normally tip **taxi drivers** but a small extra amount over the fare is welcomed. **Porters** at airports and railway stations often have a fixed rate displayed but will usually press for more. Ask fellow passengers what the fair rate is – they will nearly always advise.

Tour companies sometimes make recommendations for 'suitable tips' for **coach drivers** and **guides**. The figures may seem modest by western standards but are very inflated if compared with normal Indian earnings. A tip of Rs 50 per day from each member of the group can safely be regarded as generous.

Photography

Many monuments now charge a camera fee ranging from Rs 10 to Rs 50 for still cameras, and may be as high as Rs 500 for video cameras and much more for professionals. Special permits are needed from the Archaeological Survey of India for photographing monuments using tripods and artificial lights. **NB** Photography of airports, military installations, bridges, and in tribal and 'sensitive border areas', is not permitted.

Drugs These are widely available from local and foreign dealers at most resorts in Goa, especially at the northern beaches of Anjuna and Chapora. All night beach 'parties' are heavily involved with drug-taking. Some police have been suspected of planting drugs on likely looking travellers and then arresting them, hoping for substantial bribes for their release. Usually, 'stop and search' tactics are carried out at entrance and exit roads to the all night parties. Police are also known to search cheap accommodation, particularly in the Anjuna to Chapora area. The bribe demanded may run into hundreds of dollars and some foreigners are detained in local police cells until the necessary funds are raised. **Warning** Anyone charged with the illegal possession of drugs risks facing a fine of Rs 100,000 and 10 years' imprisonment. In the 18 months after 25 November 1995 over 50 were imprisoned for drugs related offences, 21 among them were foreigners.

Safety

Compared to Western holiday resorts, Goa is still very safe in terms of personal safety, although with more tourist dollars coming into the state, the temptation for opportunist thieves is growing.

Theft Theft is becoming more common especially in cheap budget accommodation, although more upmarket hotels are not immune. Budget travellers should use their own, strong padlock (those with a numbered code are recommended!). Don't leave anything of value close to windows; better to keep them hidden when leaving your room. Make photocopies of all important documents and keep them in a safe place apart from the originals. Make sure you get a detailed receipt when leaving valuables in hotel safes. Some of the top range hotels are beginning to install personal safes in rooms. 'Safety deposit packets' are available at the *Bank of Baroda* in Calangute and Anjuna. Money belts worn under clothing or a waistcoat with zipped internal pockets are good options for deterring pickpockets, but keep some cash easily accessible in a purse. After changing money, put it in a safe place before leaving the bank or private dealer. Thieves on motorbikes or scooters have been known to snatch bags from unsuspecting travellers. Even after taking all reasonable precautions people do have valuables stolen. You can minimize the inconvenience caused by keeping a record of vital documents, including your passport number and travellers' cheque numbers in a separate place from the documents themselves. If you have items stolen, they should be reported to the police as soon as possible. Larger hotels will be able to assist in contacting and dealing with the police.

Personal In general the threats to personal security for travellers in India are remarkably small.
security However, incidents of petty theft and violence directed specifically at tourists have been on the increase. The police have also been involved in extorting money from tourists. Basically follow the same precautions you would when at home. Avoid wandering alone outdoors late at night. If you must, make sure that you have a clear head! During daylight hours be careful in out of the way places, especially when alone. If you are under threat scream loudly or better still carry a whistle to blow into with force. **Never** accept food or drink from casual acquaintances.

Safety on Roads in the main tourist areas are usually quite narrow with no pavements to speak
roads of so walking along them can be extremely hazardous, especially given the often devil-may-care attitude of most Goan drivers and motorbike riders. It is better to walk in single file rather than two abreast. At night carry a bright torch and wear light coloured clothing.

It can be difficult to protect your valuables if travelling alone by train. First class air conditioned and first class compartments are self-contained and normally completely secure, although nothing of value should be left close to open train windows. Two-tier air conditioned compartments, which have much to recommend them especially in the summer, are larger, allowing more movement of passengers and are therefore not so secure. Attendants may take little notice of what is going on, so luggage should be chained to a seat for security overnight. Locks and chains are easily available at main stations and bazaars. Travelling bags and cases should be made of tough material, if possible not easily cut, and external pockets (both on bags and on clothing) should never be used for carrying either money or important documents. Strong locks for travelling cases are invaluable. Use a leather strap around a case for extra security. Pickpockets and other thieves do operate in the big cities. Crowded areas are particularly high risk, and it is impossible to travel far on railways without being in crowded areas from time to time. Keep valuables as close to the body as possible.

Security on trains

Essentials

There are some problems for women to watch out for and some simple precautions to take which make it possible to avoid personal harassment.

Women travelling alone

Seats for women are set aside in buses, while separate compartments in trains try and get around the problem of "eve teasing", a euphemism for physical harassment. There has been an increasing number of incidents of harassment reported committed by local men who follow and touch women or behave indecently. Modest dress for women is always advisable: loose-fitting, non-see-through clothes when not swimming or sunbathing. Topless bathing is not permitted (one Goan hotelier advises women not to dress like Madonna!). Occasionally, police beach patrols will tell topless bathers to cover up or even issue an on-the-spot fine.

Goa is also a popular destination for Indian tourists for whom the glimpse of bare flesh is often a highlight of their visit. Women are often asked to pose for photographs (usually by rowdy groups of young students from Mumbai). Fuelled by images from cheap western movies and the overt intimate behaviour between western couples, some Indian men assume that all foreign women are fair game for sexual contact and may make unwanted advances, in the form of stroking the hair or skin or touching private parts of the body. Unfortunately, rape also occurs on a few isolated occasions each season. Although these incidents are rare compared to Europe and America it is sensible to take the same precautions as you would at home. Be 'beachwise' in Goa as you would be streetwise home.

It is best to be accompanied by a friend to avoid any chance of being molested while being measured for clothing in tailors' shops or when having an ayurvedic massage. At night it is advisable to walk in large groups especially when attending late nightclubs and parties, and not to take taxis or rickshaws unaccompanied. Be prepared to raise an alarm if anything unpleasant threatens.

Avoid drinking sessions with groups of Indian men and don't get drunk in their company. One tip is to say that you are married (wearing a 'wedding' ring may help); having children also raises your level of respect. Another good tip when the going gets too hot is to quietly explain that you have stomach pain because you are having your period, since in India, women are widely regarded as 'unclean' during their menstrual cycle.

A recent scam is for respectable looking Indian men to sweet-talk unaccompanied women (usually middle-aged with high-powered jobs) into giving them large loans for a short time. Don't expect to see these men again after parting with your money!

Goa has introduced a number of Tourist Police (easily identifiable in their blue and white uniforms) who are seen patrolling the major beaches. However, they mainly tend to hassle the beach vendors during the day, except on Wednesdays when they descend on Anjuna hoping to collect 'baksheesh' from foreign motorcyclists who are

Police

not carrying the correct documents. However, it is rare to be stopped by the police for traffic violations except at Anjuna and on the roads leading to and from parties and popular night spots.

A more profitable occupation of the Goan police is to extort money for possession of drugs. Although punishments for drug offences are severe, the number of convictions is small compared to the amount of drugs consumed in Goa. It is believed that individual policemen have to pay a large sum to secure a posting in the tourist belt of Goa for the rich pickings the area promises by way of 'baksheesh'. They are increasingly targeting better-dressed tourists and travellers in the hope of greater rewards. Demands often run into hundreds of dollars.

Dealings with the police can be very difficult. The paper work involved in reporting losses can be time-consuming and irritating, and your own documentation (eg passport and visas) may be demanded. It is essential to ensure that you have a valid international driving licence and insurance documents and ownership papers with you when driving a car or motorbike. If you face a demand for a fine, insist on a receipt. If you have to go to a police station, try to take someone with you. If you face really serious problems, for example in connection with a driving accident, you should contact your consular office as quickly as possible. However difficult it may seem, if you are faced with unlawful detention by the police, the best policy is to keep calm and patient. Insist on seeing the senior officer and on reporting the matter to the Chief of Police.

Confidence
tricksters
These are particularly common where people are on the move, notably around railway stations or places where budget tourists gather. A common plea is some sudden and desperate calamity; sometimes a letter will be produced in English to back up the claim. The demands are likely to increase sharply if sympathy is shown.

Where to stay

Accommodation is represented on the town maps with a symbol: ■
Like the rest of India, Goa has a wide range of accommodation. You can stay safely and very cheaply by western standards in resorts, towns and villages. There are also high quality hotels, offering a full range of personal and business facilities. Prices at the top luxury resorts are sometimes comparable with the west.

See inside front cover for a quick guide to hotel price codes
Prices and categories The price for each category is a guide to what you would pay for the standard double room in high season. Prices over Christmas and New Year rise dramatically, in some cases almost double. However, generous reductions are offered during the off-season. Many hotels are prepared to discount their listed price by at least 10 percent to independent travellers who ask for it since the hotel saves the commission to an agency. Taxes can add considerably to the basic price (see below). The price categories are not star ratings, and individual facilities vary considerably. Normally the following facilities will be found as standard in the given classes.

Most **LL, L, AL** and some **A** and **B** category hotels charge foreigners, except those working in India, and NRIs (non-resident Indians), a 'dollar price', about 50 percent more than the 'rupee price'. All hotels in Class **C** and above, and some below, accept payment by credit card. There are some excellent value hotels in the **E** and **F** categories, though they can vary in quality. Many **F** hotels (and some **D** or **E**) have very cheap rooms and/or dormitory beds. These are always very basic, but can be clean and adequate; occasionally dormitories have only four or six beds and are very good value. There is a youth hostel at Miramar near Panaji. Long-stay visitors often rent cheap rooms on a monthly basis. An extra bed in a room is usually available at an attractive rate. However, sometimes only a mattress will be provided. Clarify when reserving.

For people travelling off the beaten track outside Goa there are several cheap options. Railway stations often have *retiring rooms* or 'rest rooms'. These may be hired

Hotel categories

LL and **L** (US$150+) These are exceptional hotels. They are in the metropolitan cities or in exclusive locations such as a commanding coastal promontory, a lake island or a scenic hilltop, with virtually nothing to fault them. They have high class business facilities, specialist restaurants and well-stocked bars, several pools, sports.

AL (US$100-150) and **A** (US$50-100) Most major towns have at least some in the these categories which also reach high international standards but are less exclusive. Many quote an inflated 'dollar price' to foreigners.

B (US$25-50) Comfortable but not plush, choice of restaurants, pool, some have a gym. These are often aimed at the business client.

C (Rs 750-1200) In many small towns the best hotel is in the **C** category, but they are not necessarily the best value. Some charge higher prices for a flash reception area

usually provide central air conditioning, restaurant, satellite TV, foreign exchange and travel desk.

D (Rs 400-750) hotels, often offer very good value though quality and cleanliness can vary widely. Most have some air conditioned rooms with bath, satellite TV, restaurants.

E (Rs 200-400) Simple room with fan (occasionally air-cooler or air conditioning), often shared toilet and shower. May not have a restaurant or provide bed linen, towel etc. **F** (Under Rs 200) Very basic, shared toilet (often 'squat'), bucket and tap, variable cleanliness and hygiene. **E** and **F** category hotels are often in busy parts of town. They may have some rooms for under Rs 100, and dormitory beds for under Rs 50. **D** hotels may have some rooms in this price range, so if you are looking for good but cheap accommodation, start there!

for periods of between one and 24 hours by anyone holding an onward train ticket. They are cheap and usually provide a bed and a fan. Some stations have a couple of air conditioned rooms, but they are often very heavily booked. They can be very convenient for short stops if travelling extensively by train, although some can be very noisy. The old domestic airport at Mumbai has similar facilities.

Taxes In Goa, a range of taxes (including Business Turnover Tax or BTT) applies to different categories of hotels. In the cheapest hotels no extra tax is normally chargeable. A tax of five percent is charged on rooms costing up to Rs 500; 10 percent for Rs 500-800, rising to 15 percent for over Rs 800. An additional five percent to 10 percent service charge may apply. When a luxury tax applies in the higher category hotels in India, these are added to bills presented at the end of your stay which usually includes meals. To avoid the extra charge, if you eat in the hotel restaurant, it is worth paying the meals bill separately to ensure that tax is not added to food as well as room charges.

Bills Some visitors have complained of **miscalculations**, even in the most expensive hotels. The problem particularly afflicts those who are part of groups, when last-minute extras sometimes appear mysteriously on some guests' bills. Check at the desk the evening before departure, and keep all receipts. It is essential to check carefully again when paying your bill.

Facilities You have to be prepared for difficulties which are uncommon in the west. It is best to inspect the room and check that all equipment (air conditioning, TV, water heater, flush) works before checking in at a modest hotel.

Air conditioning is usually only available in category **C** and above. Elsewhere air conditioned rooms are cooled by individual units and occasionally by large 'air-coolers' which can be noisy and unreliable. When they fail to operate tell the management as it is often possible to get a rapid repair done, or to transfer to a room where the unit is working. Fans are provided in all but the cheapest of hotels.

Where staff training is lacking, the person who brings up your cases may proceed to show you light switches, room facilities, TV tuning, and hang around waiting for a tip. Room boys may enter your room without knocking or without waiting for a response to a knock. Both for security and privacy, it is a good idea to lock your door when you are in the room. It is worth noting these in the comments book when leaving as the management may then take action.

Apart from the **AL** and **A** categories, 'baths' do not necessarily refer to bathrooms with Western bathtubs. Other hotels may provide a bathroom with a toilet, basin and a shower. Power cuts mean hot water may be restricted to certain times of day. The largest hotels have their own generators but it is best to carry a good torch. In the lower priced hotels and outside large towns, a bucket and tap may replace the shower, and an Indian 'squat' toilet instead of a Western WC. Even medium sized hotels which are clean and pleasant do not always provide towels, soap and toilet paper. In some Goan village homes, the toilet raised off the ground is not connected to a sewer, but is cleaned out by pigs which are allowed to roam underneath. As for water supply, this is rationed periodically (especially in the dry season), occasionally even in the better hotels. Keep a bucket filled to use for flushing the toilet during water cuts. Occasionally, tap water may be discoloured, simply due to rusty tanks. Electric water heaters may provide enough for a shower but not enough to fill a bath tub! **NB** For details on drinking water see page 38.

At some times of the year and in some places mosquitoes can be a real problem. In cheap hotels you need to be prepared for a wider range of insect life, including flies, cockroaches, spiders, ants, and geckos (harmless house lizards). Poisonous insects, including scorpions, are extremely rare in towns. Hotel management are nearly always prepared with insecticide sprays. Many small hotels in mosquito-prone areas supply nets. Remember to shut windows and doors at dusk. Electrical mat and pellets are now widely available, as are mosquito coils which burn slowly. At night, fans can be very effective in keeping mosquitoes off.

Hotels close to temples can be very noisy, especially during festivals. Music blares from loudspeakers late at night and from very early in the morning, often making sleep impossible. Mosques call the faithful to prayers at dawn. Some find ear-plugs helpful.

Laundry can be arranged very cheaply (eg a shirt washed and pressed for Rs 10-20 in **C-D** category; Rs 50 in luxury hotels) and quickly in 12-24 hours. It is best not to risk delicate fibres, though luxury hotels can usually handle these and also dry-clean items.

Checkout time in most places is 1200. You may usually ask to leave your bags at the reception for some time after that if you wish. Some hotels expect you to vacate your room by 0900 (ask at the time of checking in), while others operate a convenient 24-hour checkout system, meaning you can stay 24 hours from the time of check-in.

Some hotels and restaurants close between Jun to Sep – the beach assumes a deserted look as the shacks disappear one by one

Seasons Many hotels in Goa charge the highest room-rate over Christmas and New Year (between mid-December to mid-January), but also offer large discounts from mid-June to mid-September.

In the peak season (November to March) bookings can be extremely heavy so it is best to reserve accommodation well in advance, which you can do by fax either from abroad or in India itself. However, double check re-confirmation details, and always try to arrive as early as possible in the day, or your reservation may be cancelled. If you travel out from the major centres (eg spending a night away from your booked hotel, when touring), be prepared to accept much more modest accommodation.

In the low season (May to Mid-September) when foreign package tours cease with the last charter flight out, some of the larger resort hotels turn their attention to attracting Indian business conventions and conferences; these take on quite a different character. Some hotels offer three to four day special weekend bargains for Indian tourists which throw in a few excursions, a complimentary massage, a bottle of wine etc, and are often not great value. You may prefer to take advantage of a genuine discount of 20 percent to 50 percent on the room price. During the low-season, hotel restaurants may offer a different menu with more spicy dishes, to suit the change in clientele.

Getting around

Air

In addition to *Indian Airlines* (the nationalized carrier) which connects Goa with Bangalore, Chennai, Delhi, Mumbai, Pune and Tiruchirapalli, private airlines operate on some of these routes (eg *Gujarat Airways*, *Jet Airways*, *Sahara*). It is essential to book as early as possible, especially in the peak season. Since buying tickets on *Indian Airlines* can be time-consuming and frustrating, it is best to use a reputable travel agent. Details of flights are given under Dabolim and Mumbai.

See individual towns and cities for further details of getting there and around

Some travel agents will make reservations for internal flights abroad if the international ticket is booked through them on a major carrier. Alternatively, try a *GSA of Indian Airlines* (eg SD Enterprises, 103, Wembley Park Drive, Wembley, Middlesex HA9 8HG, England, T020-89033411, F89030392, they are also agents for *Jet Airways)*.

Foreigners buying air tickets in India must use foreign exchange and pay the 'Dollar rate'. Competing airlines charge virtually the same price. Major credit cards, travellers' cheques and cash (with encashment certificate) are accepted. *Indian Airlines* offer a 25 percent discount for passengers under 30 years of age.

Be prepared for delays and cancellations. For long journeys flying saves time – but often not as much as you may hope! Despite the improvements in air travel it can be a very frustrating experience. If you do not have a confirmed booking it pays to arrive early at the airport and to be persistent in enquiring about your position in the queue. **NB** *Indian Airlines* do not allow passengers to carry batteries in hand luggage; confiscated batteries may not be returned.

Train

Trains offer a unique experience, and are often an excellent alternative way of getting to and from Goa. The Konkan Railway allows you to reach Margao (Madgaon) from either Mumbai or Mangalore on a comfortable modern train although the journey times are still slow. Equally, the broad gauge service from Vasco and Margao to Londa allows easy connections to the Indian interior. Since it is such a small state, it is rarely worth taking rail journeys within Goa. The exception to this is for a visit to Dudhsagar Falls. Indian railways are divided into regions, and despite a computerized booking system, it can often prove difficult to book train tickets across the country. It is worth asking a travel agent to book your tickets for a small fee. Tourists have special quotas on many trains. When tickets are not available over the general sales counter, it may still be possible to travel on a tourist quota ticket. *Indian Railways* also offer discounts on Indrail passes for foreign tourists which can mean a considerable saving. Payment must be in foreign exchange or in Rupees as long as you have your foreign currency encashment certificate.

Schedules change so check timings locally

A/c First Class, available only on main routes and cheaper than flying, is very comfortable (bedding provided). *A/c Sleeper* two and three-tier, are clean and comfortable and good value. *A/c Executive Class*, with wide reclining seats are available on many *Shatabdi* trains at double the price of the ordinary *a/c Chair Car* which are equally comfortable. *2nd Class* (non-a/c) two and three-tier, provides exceptionally cheap travel but can be crowded and uncomfortable, and toilet facilities can be unpleasant. It is nearly always better to use the Indian style toilets as they are better maintained.

Road

Roads offer the only way of reaching many sites of interest within Goa and the neighbouring states. For the uninitiated, travel by road can be a worrying experience, since drivers appear to follow few of the traffic rules which apply in the west.

Bus

Avoid the back half of the bus if possible – the ride is often very uncomfortable

Although the buses in Goa are not up to western standards they are a fascinating way of getting around and experiencing some of the local colour which is missed when travelling exclusively by car. They are also extremely cheap! Special tourist '**luxury**' **coaches**, which may be air conditioned, are the most comfortable. Overnight **sleepers** have bunks but since two often have to share, they are not ideal unless you are travelling with a companion. '**Video coaches**' can be unbearably noisy and so are best avoided – or take earplugs! Road speeds are very slow and express buses rarely average more than 40 km per hour. Despite advertised timetables the fastest bus from Mumbai to Goa takes at least 16 hours.

Government run and private buses connect with virtually all of Goa and it is rare for more than one change to be required to reach any particular destination unless travelling from north to south or vice versa. It is usually possible to get a seat on most buses, but if the bus is full just wait for the next one. On local routes they are generally quite frequent. There are now regular non-stop minibuses plying between the major towns. Buy tickets before boarding the bus at the easily located booths – prices and destinations are usually clearly stated. Bear in mind that some towns have different bus stations for different destinations, eg Margao. If your destination is only served by a local bus it may be wise to take the express bus and 'persuade' the driver/conductor in advance to stop at the place you want to get off with a tip. You have to pay the full fare to the first scheduled stop after your intended destination, but you will get there faster and more comfortably. Booking on major routes, particularly for travelling to other states is now computerized, and it is worth booking in advance for longer journeys where possible.

Car

A car provides a chance to travel off the beaten track, and gives unrivalled opportunity to see something of Goa's interior villages and small towns. However, the roads are often in poor condition. Furthermore, the most widely used hire car, the Hindustan Ambassador, is often unreliable. For a similar price, Marutis are a better bet in terms of reliability, though the small Maruti 800 has very limited space for luggage.

Find out what happens in case of a break down. Get telephone contact numbers

Car hire A two or three-day trip around Goa can give excellent opportunities for sightseeing in reasonable comfort and very economically (especially when shared by three or four people), though prices rise dramatically in the high season, especially Christmas/New Year, and in luxury resorts. Check beforehand if fuel and inter-state taxes (if you are taking the car out of Goa) are included in the hire charge. Occasionally drivers are forced to pay small bribes to police to be allowed to continue their journey. For self-drive car hire, foreign nationals must hold a valid International Driving Permit and leave a security deposit of at least Rs 5000. Daily hire charges vary from Rs 700 per day for a non air conditioned 800cc Maruti, up to Rs 1650 per day for the Maruti Esteem. Insurance is included in the price. *Amex*, *Mastercard* and *Visa* credit cards are accepted. Point to point can be arranged but is liable to an extra charge for the return of the vehicle elsewhere. Rates vary according to whether the car is hired for a city trip or an out of town trip. A car with driver rate is given in the box over page and is meant as a guide.

The rules of the road?

Vehicles drive on the left – in theory. Routes around the major cities are usually crowded with lorry traffic, and the main roads are often poor and slow. National highways are rarely dual carriageway, and many main roads are single track. Some district roads are quiet, and although they are not fast, they can be a good way of seeing country and village life if you have time. Asking the way can be very frustrating as you are likely to get widely conflicting advice each time you stop to ask, and map-reading is an alien concept in India. Goa's signposting can be frustrating since along the minor roads they are often absent or old, rusty and difficult to read. On the main roads, 'mile' posts periodically appear in English and can help. Elsewhere, it is best to ask directions often. Fortunately Goa is small, so you can't get too lost for too long!

There are many hazards when driving, and particularly motorcycling around Goa where each season a large number of visitors receive the 'Goan Road Tattoo' whilst some are more seriously injured or killed. It is essential to take great care.

Road sense as we know it in the west is virtually unknown amongst local drivers and riders. They may emerge from side roads without looking, stop or turn without signalling, and the larger vehicles may overtake on blind corners. Expect the unexpected and use your horn regularly to alert other road users (including pedestrians), especially when overtaking. Cows, dogs, chickens, goats and pigs are unpredictable road users and roam at will. Pigs have a nasty habit of running across roads at great speed from behind bushes and are big enough to cause substantial damage. People can often prove to be equally obstructive in the absence of pavements. Riding at night only adds to

this mayhem. Bikes often have inadequate lights, whilst the lights on some scooters are directly connected to the throttle which means you have to speed up to see (or be seen) by which time you are too late to slow down to avoid hazards! Many lights are badly adjusted and Goan drivers rarely dip their headlights and it is impossible to see when faced with full beam headlights. Prepare to slow down, turn in and stop until they have passed. Do not assume that a single light is another motorcyclist. Many trucks, buses and cars have only one light working. If the non-functioning light is on your side it may be too late to realize that you are driving straight towards a speeding truck! On a motorcycle there are the following additional concerns. It is impossible to avoid being hit by countless insects especially at dusk. At speed, the larger ones can be quite painful, especially if they hit the eye. Some Goans prefer to wear a visor to avoid this problem. Most roads in Goa are poorly constructed and are repaired irregularly. After the monsoon, a new generation of potholes emerge, causing motorcyclists to treat the roads as a slalom course. Hitting a pothole at high speed can throw even the most experienced biker off balance. New roads are generally covered with a layer of gravel. Take care and slow down when passing these sections, especially with small-wheeled scooters; on sandy tracks it can be like riding on ice. Take care and use both feet for balance. Speed bumps are increasingly being introduced at approach roads leading to villages and beaches. There are usually unmarked and crudely constructed. Keep your eyes peeled for a tower of rocks – sometimes used to mark the spot. The latest bone-shakers though, the triple speed bumps, are usually signed!

Chauffeur driven cars Chauffeur driven cars from *GTDC* start at a rate of Rs 7 per kilometre. *Sai Service* rates are similar, although work out cheaper over a longer period. A car with driver (including fuel) may be hired for varying numbers of hours with a specified kilometre allowance, eg four hours or 50 km, eight hours or 80 km, 12 hours or 120 km. Drivers may be helpful in being able to communicate with local people and

Essentials

👉 *Car hire rates with driver*

	Economy	Regular A/C	Premium A/C	Luxury A/C
	Maruti 800 Ambassador	Maruti 800 Ambassador	Maruti 1000 Contessa	Esteem Opel etc
Mumbai				
8 hrs/80 km	Rs 700	Rs 900	Rs 1,300	Rs 1,800
Extra km	Rs 7	Rs 9	Rs 13	Rs 18
Extra hour	Rs 40	Rs 50	Rs 70	Rs 100
Out of town				
Per km	Rs 7	Rs 9	Rs 13	Rs 18
Night halt	Rs 160	Rs 200	Rs 250	Rs 250

also make a journey more interesting by telling you about the places and local customs. If you hire the services of a driver for more than a day it is usual for the driver to sleep in the car overnight if the hotel you stay in doesn't provide a bed for them. They are responsible for all their expenses, including their meals. A tip at the end of the whole tour of Rs 50-100 per day (if you wish to give one), in addition to their inclusive daily allowance, is perfectly acceptable.

Self-drive car hire This is still in its infancy though the rates are attractive when compared to 'with driver' rates, especially for out-of-town travel. **Drivers must have third party insurance.** This may have to be with an Indian insurer, or with a foreign insurer who has a national guarantor.

When reserving the car emphasize the importance of good tyres, brakes, headlamps and general roadworthiness. Check the car (scratches, dents etc) before driving away. On main roads across India, petrol stations are reasonably frequent, but parts of Goa are poorly served. Some service stations only have diesel pumps though they may have small reserves of petrol, so always carry a spare can. When buying petrol at a petrol station, make sure that the meter is set at zero before filling up. Carry adequate food and drink, correct documentation (especially for inter-state travel) and a basic tool set in the car. Accidents can produce large and angry crowds very quickly. It is best to leave the scene of the accident and report it to the police as quickly as possible. The Automobile Association office in Goa is at the Tourist Hostel in Panaji (in Mumbai, Lalji Narainji Memorial Building, 76, Veer Nariman Rd).

Taxi   Taxis are readily available at major resorts. They usually wait outside the larger hotels or at recognized taxi stands. Bargaining is required although they don't reduce the asking rate much in the tourist areas. In some areas they have a list of agreed prices, whilst larger hotels usually have a taxi desk with listed fares. Before travelling in an unmetered taxi, ask at the hotel desk for an estimated price. Whatever fare you agree, you are paying a very good rate by local standards so it is unnecessary to tip. Try to insist on the taxi meter being 'flagged' in your presence. In some cities taxis refuse to use the meter – the official advice is to call the police! At railway stations, and at Mumbai and Dabolim airports, it is often possible to share a taxi to a central point. It is worth looking for fellow passengers who may be travelling in your direction. When travelling from Mumbai airport at night always have a clear idea of where you want to go and insist on being taken there. Many Mumbai taxi drivers will do everything possible to convince you that the hotel you have named was 'closed three years ago' or is 'completely full'. It may be necessary to insist that you have an advance reservation.

The paperwork

It is illegal to ride a motorbike of any kind in Goa without the appropriate documents. This means an **International Driving Permit**, **valid insurance** (check that the bike's insurance papers are valid for "Any driver"), the **vehicle's registration document** and a **valid pollution certificate** if the bike is over one year old. Police are happy to relieve you of some of your rupees if you are not carrying any of the above. The Wednesday Flea Market in Anjuna is a popular place for the police to supplement their income by stopping likely looking law breakers (ie just about everyone on a motorbike or scooter!).

Essentials

Auto-rickshaw

Auto-rickshaws – autos – are cheap and convenient for getting about. Using them for short journeys will usually cost a minimum Rs 8, Rs 4 per kilometre thereafter. In some areas younger drivers often speak some English and know their local area well. You can hire them by the hour (about Rs 30), half day, or full day (about Rs 200). You pay a surcharge if you do a single journey out of the city limits; for luggage pay Re 1 per piece. **NB** Remember, rickshaw, and taxi, drivers often earn commissions from hotels, restaurants and gift shops, so their advice is not always impartial.

Motorcycle taxi

Motorcycle taxis are peculiar to Goa and offer the cheapest means of covering short distances, although they are also the least safe and can be quite tiring if you have a heavy rucksack. Official motorbike taxis are black and yellow. Agree a price in advance before sitting astride the machine. Minimum fare is Rs 6, Rs 4 per kilometre thereafter. **NB** Your insurance policy may not cover you if you are involved in an accident.

Cycling

Cycling is an excellent way of seeing the quiet by-ways of Goa. Indian cycles are heavy and without gears, but on the flat they offer a good way of exploring comparatively short distances outside towns. All cyclists should take bungy cords (to strap down a backpack) and good lights from home. Take care not to leave your machine parked anywhere with your belongings though. Repair shops are universal and charges are nominal.

Cycle hire is widely available and costs around Rs 3-5 per hour; Rs 20-40 per day, depending on the town/resort, season and age of the cycle. It is possible to tour more extensively and you may then want to buy a cycle. There are shops in the larger towns and the local *Raleighs* are considered the best, with *Atlas* and *BSA* as good alternatives. Expect to pay around Rs 1,200-1,500 for a second-hand Indian one but remember to bargain. At the end of your trip you can usually sell it quite easily at half that price. Imported bicycles have the advantage of lighter weight and gears, but are more difficult to get repaired, and carry the much greater risk of being stolen. If you wish to take your own, it is quite easy if you dismantle it and pack it in its original shipping carton.

Be sure to take all essential spares and a pump. Recent travellers found it was comfortably possible to cover 50 to 80 km a day, – "the National Highways are manic but country roads, especially along the coast, can be idyllic, if rather dusty and bumpy". You can even put your cycle on a boat for a backwater trip, or on top of a bus. Should you wish to take your bike on the train, allow plenty of time for booking it in on the brake van at the parcels office, and for filling in forms. It is best to start a journey early in the morning, stop at midday and resume cycling in the late afternoon. Night-riding, though cooler, can be hazardous because of lack of lighting and poor road surfaces. Try to avoid the major highways as far as possible. Fortunately foreign cyclists are usually greeted with cheers, waves and smiles and truck drivers are sometimes happy to give lifts to cyclists. This is a good way of taking some of the hardship out of cycling round India. Suggested reading: **Richard Ballantyne's** *Richard's New Bicycle Book*, London, Pan, 1990; **Rob van den Plas**, *The Bike Touring Manual*, Sierra Club, Bicycle Books, 1993.

Motorcycling One of the most popular and convenient way of exploring Goa is to hire a motorbike or scooter. These are easily available at all the major resorts although a number of hazards accompany this seemingly carefree form of transport (see boxes). Many small guest houses have one or two bikes for hire, or will arrange one. A few enterprising locals have built up small fleets of old (and often beaten up) vehicles. The most commonly available are the automatic Kinetic Honda, Yamaha or Suzuki 100cc and the highly desirable 350cc Enfield Bullet. On the Kinetic Honda, the headlight is directly connected to the throttle so that it dims whenever you slow down. But help is at hand in the form of a 'Hi-Beam' attachment, which connects the headlight directly to the battery and costs just over Rs 100. If you opt for a KH, ask your dealer to fit the attachment or get one from the local repair shop. Tourist pressure may result in all KHs for hire being fitted with a 'Hi-Beam' before long.

Motorcycle hire rates are generally consistent across Goa. Scooters (eg Kinetic Honda, TVS Scooty) are about Rs 150-200 per day, larger, 125cc motorbikes (eg Honda, Yamaha) cost between Rs 200-300 per day while the popular 350cc Enfield Bullet comes in the Rs 300-400 price range. Discounts are given for long-term rental so it pays to bargain. Some bike hirers require a large deposit or passport for security against damages to the bike and to ensure that the bike is returned (some lazy travellers have hired a bike in Colva and abandoned it in Palolem!). Others are more relaxed and allow you to take a bike with no deposit and pay upon return. Bikes rarely come with crash helmets since these are not compulsory in Goa. It may be worth asking if you can borrow one to increase your chances of avoiding serious injury. When hiring a motorbike, check it carefully to see that everything is in working order, especially brakes, tyres, lights and the horn (which is usually your first line of defence against accidents). If there is any damage to the bodywork of the bike, point it out to the hirer and agree that it already exists. Otherwise you may face a repair bill. Except when the bike is covered by fully comprehensive insurance (rare) and that you are legally allowed to ride the bike (even rarer), any damages are expected to be paid for. It may be better to get damages repaired yourself rather than pay an inflated estimate, or at least insist that you accompany the owner to the garage to ensure a fair price is agreed for damages. Hired bikes come with very little petrol in the tank. This is because the owners sell off unused petrol when the bike is returned. Estimate the amount of petrol you will need and ignore advice by owners to fill the tank up if you have any problem with the vehicle.

There are a few companies who cater for those who would prefer to travel by motorcycle on an organized tour. *Peter and Friends Classic Adventures*, an Indo-German company at Casa Tres Amigos, Socol Vado 425, Assagao, west of Anjuna, T0832273351, F276124, run motorbike tours. *Syndicate Tours & Travels*, organize 15-day 'adventure tours' starting with two days of familiarization in Goa followed by a tour through Karnataka and Tamil Nadu ending in Chennai (Madras), Rs 1,500 (including good hotel accommodation and support vehicle). Similar touring with good back up is offered by Blazing Trails, T01293 533338, jewel@jewel holidays.com

Hitchhiking Hitchhiking is rare in India, partly because public transport is so cheap. You are likely to spend a very long time on the roadside, although lorries sometimes give lifts. In general it is not recommended, especially for women. In Goa, locals often hitch rides on motorbikes/scooters and generally give lifts over short distances. It is good to reciprocate if you have room on your bike and are confident of your riding.

The email explosion

As the Internet shrinks the world, travellers are increasingly using emails to keep in touch with home. Their free accounts are invariably with **hotmail.com**, **yahoo.com**, **email.com** or **backpackers.com**; usually the less common the provider, the quicker the access.

India has its own set of problems which can be frustrating: few machines, many of which are outdated; untrained staff and poor technical support; unreliable servers; a system clogged with users, especially during day; frequent power cuts... There are exceptions, of course.

New offices are opening weekly and new towns are getting connected. To track down the most reliable and best value Internet service, ask other travellers. The length of the queue can be a good indicator. On the web, you can get a list from **http://www.netcafeguide.com**. Don't always head for the cheapest since they may also have the oldest and slowest

equipment. Rates vary, but in mid-1999, it cost around Rs 50 for 30 minutes.

Hot Tips

■ Use the folder facility to save mail
■ Keep your in-box clear to reduce loading time
■ Avoid junk mail by not giving your address to on-line companies
■ Avoid downloading and using scanned pictures and documents
■ Save files and back up regularly

The system can be efficient and satisfying but it can also become an expensive habit with more than its fair share of frustrations. As one sending an email to us mused, "many a hard-up traveller will wax lyrical about 'getting away from it all' and escaping 'the pressure of western society'. They will then spend hours and several hundred rupees a week slaving over a computer keyboard in some hot and sticky back street office."

Essentials

Keeping in touch

The post is frequently unreliable, and delays are common. It is best to use a post office to hand over mail for franking across the counter. Valuable items should only be sent by Registered Post. Government Emporia or shops in the larger hotels will send purchases home if the items are difficult to carry. Airmail service to Europe, Africa and Australia takes at least a week and a little longer for the Americas. Speed Post (which takes about four days to UK) is available at major towns. Specialist shippers deal with larger items, charging about US$150 per cubic metre.

At some main post offices you can send small packages under two kilograms as Letter Post which is much cheaper at Rs 220 (rather than Parcel Post). 'Book Post' (for printed papers) is cheaper still, about Rs 170 for five kilograms. Book parcels must be sewn in cloth (best over see-through plastic) with a small open 'window' slit for contents to be seen.

The parcel process can take up to two hours. Check that the post office holds necessary customs declaration forms (two/three copies needed). 'Packers' outside post offices will do all necessary cloth covering and wax sealing for Rs 20-50. Write 'No commercial value' if returning used clothes, books etc. Address the parcel, stick stamps (after weighing at a separate counter) and one customs form to the parcel with the available glue (the other form/s must be partially sewn on). Post at the parcels counter and get your registration slip (receipt). Maximum dimensions: height 1m, width 0.8m, circumference 1.8m. Air mail is expensive (Rs 775 for the first kilogramme and Rs 200 for each subsequent kilogramme); sea mail is slow but reasonable (Rs 775 for the first kilogramme and Rs 70 for each extra kilogramme).

Postal services
Local post offices are listed under individual towns

Essentials

 Best short-wave frequencies

BBC World service: *Signal strength varies throughout the day, with lower frequencies better during the night. The nightly "South Asia Report" offers up to the minute reports covering the sub-continent. Try 15310, 17790 or 1413, 5975, 11955, 17630, 17705. More information on www.bbc.uk/*

worldservice/sasia
Voice of America: *1400-1800 GMT; 1575, 6110, 7125, 9645, 9700, 9760, 15255, 15395 Mhz. www.voa.gov/sasia*
Deutsche Welle: *0600-1800 GMT; 6075, 9545, 17845; other frequencies include 17560, 12000 and 21640.*

Poste restante facilities are available in even quite small towns at the GPO, where mail is held for one month. Ask for mail to be addressed to you with your surname in capitals and underlined. When asking for mail at 'Poste Restante' check under your Christian as well as your surname. **NB** Any special issue foreign stamps are likely to be stolen from envelopes in the Indian postal service and letters may be thrown away. Advise people who are sending you mail to India to use only definitive stamps (not commemorative).

Courier services Well known companies (eg *DHL*) operate from the larger towns. Documents take a minimum of four days to the UK and cost Rs 1313 up to 500g, Rs 265 for each additional 500g. Other parcels take an extra day; Rs 1575 up to 500g.

Telephone services
For a quick guide to area codes and useful numbers see inside front cover

International Direct Dialing is now widely available in privately run call 'booths', usually labelled on yellow boards with the letters 'PCO-STD-ISD'. You dial the call yourself, and the time and cost are displayed on a computer screen. They are by far the best places from which to telephone abroad. Varying cheaper rates operate from 2100-0600, which means long queues may form outside booths in the evening. Telephone calls from hotels are usually more expensive. Ringing tone: double ring, repeated regularly; Engaged: equal length, on and off. Both are similar to UK ringing and engaged tones. **NB** One disadvantage of the tremendous pace of the telecommunications revolution is the fact that millions of telephone numbers go out of date every year. Current telephone directories themselves are often out of date and some of the numbers given in the *Handbook* will have been changed even as we go to press. Directory enquiries, 197, can be helpful but works only for the local area code. The international phone code is 0091. The whole state now has 0832 as its code. **Fax** services are available from many PCOs and larger hotels, who charge either by the minute or per page. **Internet/email** access is becoming increasingly available in the larger cities as '*Cyber Cafés*' mushroom. Elsewhere a large hotel or travel agent may allow you to use their system.

Media India has a large English language press. In Goa itself there are three local English language newspapers, *The Herald* (probably the best written and the most popular), the *Gomantak Times* and the *Navhind Times*. The major papers now have internet sites: *The Hindu*, http://www.hinduonline.com/today/index.html; *The Hindustan Times* http://www.hindustantimes.com/default.html; *The Indian Express* http://www.expressindia.com/; *The Times of India* http://www.timesofindia.com/; and *The Statesman* http://www.thestatesman.org/ *The Economic Times* is possibly the best for independent reporting and world coverage. *The Telegraph* (published in Kolkata, has good foreign coverage. *The Asian Age* is now published in the UK and India simultaneously and gives good coverage of Indian and international affairs. Most of these are difficult to get hold of, even in Margao or Panaji. The weekly/fortnightly magazines, *Sunday, India Today* and *Frontline*, are widely read current affairs journals. There are newagents and bookshops in Margao, Panaji, Mapusa and Colva.

India's national radio and television network, *Doordarshan*, broadcasts in national and regional languages. Many Indians have now switched off 'DD', as it is known, to watch satellite TV, including the BBC World, CNN and others. Some international channels are currently relayed through the Star Network. BBC World Service radio has a large Indian audience in both English and regional languages.

There are few reminders of the Portuguese which was once spoken by Goa's élite. Konkani and Marathi now are the most common languages, while English is widely understood in towns. Hindi is India's official language and is commonly understood. The use of English is also enshrined in the Constitution for a wide range of official purposes, notably communication between Hindi and non-Hindi speaking states.

Language
See the glossary for a list of useful words and phrases

Essentials

Food and drink

Most visitors are surprised – and often delighted – at the enormous variety of delicious food on offer, some bearing little relation to the various 'curries' available outside India. Furthermore, there is a remarkable range of delicious savoury snacks and sweets. Restaurants and beach cafés in the main tourist centres offer Goan food as well as a good range of dishes from other parts of India. To suit the unaccustomed palate, they also have some Western, Chinese and sometimes even Thai and Tibetan options.

See inside front cover for restaurant price codes

Although Goan food has similarities with that in the rest of India – rice, vegetable curries and *dal*, for example – there are many local specialities. Common ingredients in Goan cooking include rice, coconut and cashew (*cazu*) nuts, pork and a wide variety of seafood. Not surprisingly, the food in this region is hot, making full use of the small bird's-eye chillies that are grown locally. Chilli was only introduced to Goa by the Portuguese, adding just one more ingredient to the already richly flavoured, and spiced diet. One recipe for the popular *sorpotel* suggests that in addition to other spices you should use 20 dry chillies for 1kg pork plus liver and heart, with four green chillies thrown in for good measure! Goa's Christians have no qualms about using pork (not eaten by Muslims and most Hindus). A state dominated by its coastline, Goa freely uses the harvest from its seas. The standard "fish curry and rice", the common Goan meal, has become a catch phrase. Most beach shacks offer a good choice (depending on the day's catch), and will usually include preparations of king fish, tuna, mackerel, prawns and shark. You will find lobsters, baked oysters, boiled clams and stuffed crabs as specialities.

Goan
See also the glossary, 'Eating out'

Vegetarians are well provided for in Goa. South Indian Brahmin food for example is wholly distinctive with tamarind and coconut being typical ingredients. Three of its snacks – *dosai*, *idli* and *vadai* – are good vegetarian options.

South Indian

North Indian cooking is often called *Mughlai*, hinting at the Muslim influence on North Indian diet over the last six centuries. Cream and *ghee* are favourite cooking mediums, and spices, herbs, nuts and fruit are all ingredients added to dishes which usually have meat as the main focus of the meal. Several different kinds of *kebab*, meat balls and minced meat preparations are served alongside *biriyani* or *pulao*. *Tandoori* dishes, marinated meat cooked in a special earthen oven, come from the far northwest, but are widely popular.

North Indian

One of the intriguing features right across the country is *paan*, which rounds off a main meal. The *paan* leaf is the vehicle for a succession of pastes and spices, the making of which is regarded as an art. Areca nuts, lime, tobacco and a number of sweetened and scented ingredients will go into the bright green leaf, to be carefully folded and then chewed, seemingly endlessly.

Paan

Thali A thali is a complete meal served on a plate or stainless steel tray, or more traditionally, on a banana leaf. Several preparations, placed in small bowls, surround the central serving of wholewheat *puris* and rice. A vegetarian *thali* basically includes chapati, rice, *daal*, two vegetable curries and poppadum, although there are regional variations. Fish, mutton or chicken curries are popular non-vegetarian dishes, which can be quite hot and spicy. A variety of sweet and hot pickles are offered – mango and lime are two of the most popular. These can be exceptionally hot, and are designed to be taken in minute quantities alongside the main dishes. Plain *dahi* (yoghurt) is usually included, which acts as a bland cooling dish to accompany highly spiced food. You may wish to order a sweet to end the meal.

European Many hotel restaurants and beach cafés offer European options, eg toasted sandwiches, stuffed pancakes, apple pies, crumbles and cheese cakes. Italian favourites (eg pizzas and pastas) are well established, while Mexican and Jewish dishes are newcomers. Western confectionery, in general, is disappointing. Ice creams, on the other hand, can be exceptionally good (eg *Cadbury's*, *Dollops*, *Kwality's*, *Walls*).

Fruit & nuts Home of one of India's most famous mangoes, the *alfonso*, Goa has a wide range of fruit. Some are highly seasonal – mangoes in the hot season, for example – while others (eg bananas) are available throughout the year. The extremely rich *jackfruit* is common, as are papaya and watermelons. Cashew nuts and pineapples (brought from South America) and papaya (brought from the Philippines), were introduced to Goa by the Portuguese.

Water
Don't add ice cubes to any drink – the water used may be contaminated
Drinking water used to be regarded as one of India's biggest hazards. It is still true that water from the taps or wells should never be regarded as safe to drink. Public water supplies are nearly always polluted and unsafe. Bottled mineral water is now widely available although not all bottled water is mineral water; some is simply purified water from an urban supply. Buy from a shop or stall, check the seal carefully (some are now double sealed) and avoid street hawkers; when disposing of bottles, puncture the neck which prevents misuse but allows recycling for storage. Water sterilization tablets can be bought from many chemists within Goa. This method reduces the amount of plastic bottles used throughtout the trip and so is a 'greener' option. Always carry plenty with you when travelling. **NB** It is important to use pure water for cleaning teeth.

Tea & coffee Tea and coffee are safe and widely available. If you wish to order it 'black' say 'no sugar', 'no milk' when ordering. At a roadside stall, however, *chai* or *chaa* is milky and sweet. *Nescafe*, *espresso* and *capuccino* coffee are sometimes on offer but may not turn out as you would expect in the West.

Soft drinks There is a huge variety of bottled soft drinks, including well known international brands (eg *Coca-Cola*, *Pepsi*, *Fanta*), which are perfectly safe. Popular and safe Indian brands include *Limca* or *Teem* (lime and lemon), *Thums Up* (cola) and *Mirinda* (orangeade), but some find them too sweet. Fruit juice is available in cartons, including mango, pineapple and apple; the best known brands are *Frooti* and *Jumpin'*. Prices of pre-packed drinks range from Rs 8-15.

Fruit juice Fresh fruit juice (prepared hygienically) is a better option; fresh lime-soda (plain, sweet or salty) is popular. Cool and refreshing fruit-flavoured milk-shakes and yoghurt based *lassis* cost around Rs 20-25. Plain *lassi* is cheaper at about Rs 10.

Alcohol A wide range of alcoholic drinks is available in Goa including some foreign brands in the major centres. Despite recent price increases, drinks in Goa remain relatively cheap

A cup of chai!

Not long ago, when you stopped at a road side tea stall nearly anywhere in India and asked for a cup of chai, the steaming hot sweet tea would be poured out into your very own, finely handthrown, beautifully shaped, clay cup! Similarly, whenever a train drew into a railway station, almost any time of day or night, and you heard the familiar loud call of "chai garam, garam chai!" go past your window, you could have the tea served to you in your own porous clay cup.

True, it made the tea taste rather earthy but it added to the romance of travelling. Best of all, when you had done with it, you threw it away and it would shatter to bits on the road side (or down on the railway track) – returning 'earth to earth'. It was

the eco-friendly "disposable" cup of old – no question of an unwashed cup which someone else had drunk out of, hence unpolluted and 'clean'. And, of course, it was good business for the potter.

But, time moves on, and we have now advanced to tea stalls that prefer thick glass tumblers (which leave you anxious when you glance down at the murky rinsing water). A step ahead – those catering for the transient customer, now offer the welcome hot chai in an understandably convenient, light, hygienic, easy-to-stack, thin plastic cup which one gets the world over, sadly lacking the biodegradability of the earthen pot. With the fast disappearing terracotta cup we will lose a tiny bit of the magic of travelling in India.

compared to elsewhere in India. The increase in alcoholism (especially among Goan men) has led certain groups to call for prohibition.

The fermented juice of cashew apples, distilled for the local brew *cazu feni* (*fen*, froth), is strong and potent. Coconut or *palm feni* is made from the sap of the coconut palm. *Feni* is an acquired taste so it is often mixed with soda. It can also be taken "on the rocks" (poured on ice), as a cocktail mixed with fruit juice (bottle, about Rs 25) or pre-flavoured (eg with ginger). Don't drink this on an empty stomach. Sip slowly and avoid taking more than a couple of 'tots' when you are new to it.

Beer is usually available in three popular brands– *Kingfisher, Kings Pilsner* (brewed with imported German hops) and the stronger *Arlem* (brewed on the outskirts of Margao). All three come in large bottles (650 ml) and cost Rs 30-40; the latter two also come in half-size bottles and cost Rs 15-25. Another lager, *Belho*, is sold in half-litre cans and two strengths, 'strong' and 'extra strong'.

Goan wines tend to be of the fortified variety and are sweet. 'Port' (a legacy of Portuguese rule), is a very sweet red wine with an alcohol content of around 14 percent. Some cheaper brands resemble sweet sherry, although the better ports are very easy to drink in quantity! A good bottle sells for Rs 50-60 in a wine shop, though beach shacks will charge Rs 40-80 depending on quality, or Rs 60 for a large peg, and quarter bottles for Rs 20-25. Dark rum is cheap (eg *Old Monk*, Rs 80 a bottle) and *Honey Bee* brandy is popular.

Shopping

Handicrafts from all over India make their way to the streets and beaches of Goa to satisfy the hunger of the foreign travellers ready to indulge in exotic purchases. Shopping can be fun and rewarding since you would pay a fraction of the price charged for similar gifts and goods at home through the many fashionable stores with an eye on attractive 'ethnic' products from the East. However, Goa itself produces little to attract the foreigner to take home, other than excellent cashew nuts and attractive packets of spices, some of which are grown locally.

Bargaining Bargaining can be fun and quite satisfying. It is best to get an idea of prices being asked by different stalls for items you are interested in, before taking the plunge. Some beach hawkers and stall holders will happily quote twice the actual price to a foreigner showing interest, so you might well start by halving the asking price. On the other hand it would be inappropriate to do the same in an established shop with price-tags, though a plea for the "best price" or a "special discount" might reap results even here. Remain good humoured throughout. Walking away slowly might be the test to ascertain whether your custom is sought and you are called back!

Kashmiri Kashmiri salesmen are renowned for their success in spreading across the country to find outlets for their excellent products. Starting with small items of hand-crafted papier maché lacquerware, 'silver' bangles and necklaces, walnut wood bowls, tables and trays, they will offer much more pricey embroidered wool shawls and scarves (remember, the export of pashmina wool is banned) and tempt you with exquisite hand-knotted rugs using old Persian designs in wool or silk. Colourful crewel-work cushion covers and floor coverings are attractive and more affordable.

Himalaya Traders from the Himalaya sell chunky 'silver' jewellery often set with semi-precious stoles, religious metalwork, thick pile Tibetan style wool carpets, wood carvings, rustic jackets and shoulder bags.

Craft items You are also likely to find craft items from Gujarat and neighbouring Karnataka fashioned out of tribal embroidery, as well as inlaid marble pieces from Agra inspired by the Taj Mahal. 'Mughal' miniatures, sometimes using natural pigments on old paper and new silk, and traditional string puppets make their way from Rajasthan, while attractive wood and metal figures of Hindu deities from South India also make good souvenirs. Whatever the claim, the latter are not always carved out of sandalwood or cast in bronze and are very unlikely to be genuine antiques (which are banned from export in any case).

Textiles Goa offers a window for India's treasure house of textiles. Handlooms produce rich shot silk from Kanchipuram, skilful ikat from Gujarat, Orissa and Andhra, silk brocades with gold zari work from Varanasi, printed silks and batiks from Bengal. Sober handspun khadi, colourful Rajasthani block-printed cottons using vegetable dyes, and tie-dye Gujarati bandhni are easier on the pocket.

Clothing It is worth looking out for ready made clothing (Indian and western styles) and leather sandals. Fabrics are exceptional value so if you don't find what you want, you can get an expert tailor to copy your own garment quickly and cheaply.

Markets The much talked of Anjuna "Flea Market" can be a great disappointment since the goods are often shoddy and poor value. You would do better to look around the shops near where you are staying or in the larger stores in Panaji or Margao. The government handicrafts emporia are generally the safest bet for guaranteed quality at fixed prices, but you will be expected to bargain elsewhere. The bazaars (as at Mapusa), are full of colour, and because they are for the local population, are competitively priced. They are often a great experience.

Pitfalls Taxi/rickshaw drivers and tour guides sometimes insist on recommending certain shops where they expect a commission, but prices there are invariably inflated. Some shops offer to pack and post your purchases but they can't always be trusted. Only make such arrangements in government emporia or a large store. **Warning** Don't enter into any arrangement to help 'export' marble items, jewellery etc which a shopkeeper may propose by making tempting promises of passing on some of the profits to you. Travellers have been cheated through misuse of their credit card accounts, and have been left with unwanted purchases. Make sure that credit cards are not run off more than once when making a purchase. Traders sometimes pass off fake marble, ivory, silver, semi-precious stones, coral etc, as real. Watch out for artificial silk (as fabric, as well as in carpets). Export of certain items such as **antiquities**, **ivory**, **furs and skins is controlled or banned**, so it is essential to get a certificate of legitimate sale and permission for export.

Sport and special interest travel

Essentials

Soccer

India's greatest popular entertainment has become sport, soccer being one. It is played from professional level to kickabout in any open space. Professional matches are played in Panaji and Margao in large stadia attracting vast crowds; the latter holds 40,000 spectators. The season is from October to March and details of matches are published in the local papers. The top class game tickets are Rs 25, but they are sold for much more on the black market. The crowds generate tremendous fervour for the big matches, and standards are improving. African players are now featuring more frequently with Indian teams and monthly salaries have risen to over Rs 40,000 per month, a very good wage by Indian standards.

Cricket

Cricket is the other. Reinforced by satellite TV and radio, and a national side that enjoys high world rankings and much outstanding individual talent, cricket has become a national obsession. Stars have cult status, and you can see children trying to model themselves on their game on any and every open space.

Watersports

The watersport industry is still a fledgling enterprise. Agents offer a number of options (parasailing, wind surfing, water skiing etc) within easy reach of the major resorts, including a choice of boat trips. Popular trips to view dolphins are available from most areas. Some guarantee sighting of usually two species, the bottle-nosed and the hump-backed dolphins. Fishing trips usually set off in the early morning or late evening returning with a catch of kingfish, snappers, Goafish or cat fish. Watersport facilities on the beaches are generally limited to isolated westerners at various locations with no guarantee that they will be there the following year. There is a good chance of finding a choice on Candolim and Colva beaches. Splash in Bogmalo is reasonably well established, while the Taj at Aguada near Panaji, and the resort hotels at Mobor in the south, offer several options but at a price. The only recognised scuba diving centre here at present is on Vainguinim Beach. You can check for PADI recognised courses in Goa before arriving, by contacting PADI International Head Office, Unit 6, Unicorn Park, Whitby Road, Bristol, BS4 4EX. T0117 9711717, F0117 9721821, general@padi.co.uk, or PADI Europe, Oberwilerstrasse 3, CH-8442, Hettlingen, Switzerland, T52 3041414, F52 3041499, admin@padi.ch

Ayurveda & meditation

Ancient ayurvedic therapy, yoga and meditation have been made accessible to foreign visitors at some of the up-market resorts. At a more down-to-earth level, Passive-Active Tourism encourages visitors at their Shanti Nature Resort at distant Tambdi Surla, or you can sample simple living at Bhakti Kutir in Palolem to the south.

Birdwatching

Even a short visit can be very rewarding with ample opportunity for a keen visitor to spot 150 to 200 species in a fortnight's stay. The varied terrain, from the sea shore to the hillslopes of the Western Ghats rising to about 1000 metres, provide diverse habitats from wetland, grassland, scrub to forest cover. The Bondla and Bhagwan Mahavir Sanctuaries, Chorao Island, Mayem and Carambolim Lakes are well worth visiting. Nearer the beach resorts, Baga river, the area around Aguada and Morjim/ Siolim are rich in bird life. Further reading: **Krys Kazmierczak and Raj Singh** *A Birdwatchers' Guide to India*, Sandy, Beds, UK, 1998. Excellent coverage with helpful practical information and maps.

Entertainment

Despite the economic boom in cities like Mumbai and Delhi and the rapid growth of a young business class, India's night life remains meagre, focused on club discos in the biggest hotels. In Goa, beach raves and parties (associated with Goa Trance and the drug scene) which often take place in make-shift venues, continue to attract large groups of young foreigners to the state, particularly during Christmas and the New Year. More traditional, popular village entertainment takes the form of folk drama, dance and music. The hugely popular Hindi film industry comes largely out of this tradition. It's always easy to find a cinema, but prepare for a long sitting with a standard story line and set of characters and lots of action. See page 240 for further details.

Holidays and festivals

National
holidays

A few national holidays count as full public holidays throughout India:
26 January: *Republic Day*
15 August: *Independence Day*
2 October: *Mahatma Gandhi's Birthday*
25 December: *Christmas Day*

In addition to the widespread celebration of Hindu festivals, with Goa's significant Christian population and the small minority of Muslims, the corresponding religious festivals are also widely observed. Hindu and Muslim festivals fall on different dates each year, depending on the lunar calendar so check dates with the tourist office.

January

Feast of the Three Kings (6 January)   Celebrated in Cansaulim (Cuelim), Chandor and Reis Magos where a big fair is also held. See page 164.
Makarashankranti   A kite flying festival when Hindus distribute sweets among friends and relatives.

February

Mahasivaratri or *Sivaratri*   A Hindu festival that marks the night when Siva danced his celestial dance of destruction (*Tandava*) celebrated with feasting and fairs at Siva temples, but preceded by a night of devotional readings and hymn singing. Special ceremonies are held at some temples for example Arvalem, Fatorpa, Mangesh, Nagesh, Queula, Shiroda.
The Carnival   A non-religious festival celebrated all over Goa in February or March. On the first day (*Fat Saturday*), 'King Momo' leayant costumes as they wind through the towns' main streets. Dances are held in clubs ands a colourful procession of floats with competing 'teams' dressed in flambod hotels through the three days and traffic comes to a halt on some streets from time to time.

March

Shigmotsav   A Hindu spring festival (Holi) held at full moon in the month of *Phalgun* and celebrated all over Goa but particularly in Panaji, Mapusa, Vasco da Gama and Margao on successive days starting at around 1600. The festivities are accompanied by percussive music on drums and cymbals and the usual throwing of colourful powder and water at each other (the 'fun' can sometimes get out of hand).
Procession of all Saints   In Goa Velha, on the Monday of Holy Week. See page 70.
The Carnival, a non-religious festival celebrated all over Goa in February or March (listed above).

Muharram (17 April 2000) Anniversary of the killing of the Prophet's grandson   April
Hussain, is commemorated with Ashoura procession of Shi'a Muslims beating their
chests to express their grief. Shi'as fast for 10 days.
Ramnavami Celebrated by Hindus. It is the birthday of Lord Rama (the seventh in-
carnation of Vishnu), hero of the epic *Ramayana*.
Feast of Our Lady of Miracles, on the nearest Sunday, 16 days after Easter. See page 133.

Music Festival (pop, beat and jazz) At the Kala Academy, Panaji.   May
Goa Statehood Day (30th) An official holiday when all Government offices and many
shops are closed.

Feast of St Anthony (13th) Songs in honour of the saint requesting the gift of rain.   June
Feast of St John the Baptist (*Sao Joao*) (24th) A thanksgiving for the arrival of the
monsoon. See page 151.
Festival of St Peter (29th) Held at Fort Aguada. A pageant on a floating raft.

Nagpanchami (4 August 2000) The *Naga* (Cobra/snake) is worshipped in the form of   July –
the thousand headed *Shesha* and *Ananta*, on which Vishnu reclined.   August

Raksha Bandhan (literally 'protection bond') (15 August 2000) A Hindu festival   August –
which commemorates the wars between *Indra*, the King of the Heavens, and the   September
demons when his wife tied a silk amulet (*rakhi*) around his wrist to protect him from
harm. The festival symbolizes the bond between brother and sister, and is celebrated
at full-moon. A sister says special prayers and ties a *rakhi* around her brother's wrist to
remind him of the special bond. He in turn gives a gift and promises to protect and
care for her. Sometimes glittering *rakhis* (which today can reach extraordinary size and
shape!) are exchanged as a mark of friendship.
Janmashtami (Birth of Lord *Krishna*) (22 August 2000) A Hindu festival where mass
bathing in the Mandovi River off Divar Island takes place. Hymns are sung and
night-long prayers are held.
Harvest Festival of Novidade (21st and 24th) The first sheaves of rice are offered to
the priests, the Governor and Archbishop, and placed in the Cathedral on the 24th.
The festival includes a re-enactment of one of the battles between Albuquerque and
the Adil Shah on the lawns of the Lieutenant Governor's Palace.
Ganesh Chaturthi (1-2 September 2000) The elephant headed deity, the God of
good omen is shown special reverence. The five-day Hindu festival follows after harvest. On the last day, clay images of *Ganesh* (*Ganpati*) are taken in procession with
dancers and musicians playing drums and cymbals (not always very tunefully) and are
immersed in the sea, river or pond. The skies light up with fireworks displays and the
air turns smoky from firecrackers.

Dasara (*Dussera*) (7 October 2000) A Hindu festival celebrated in honour of minor   October
deities. The celebrations continue for nine nights (*Navaratri*) when various episodes of
the Ramayana story are enacted and recited, with particular reference to the battle
between the forces of good and evil.
Fama of Menino Jesus (16 October 2000) Commemorates the miraculous figure in
Colva. See page 147.
Narkasur (25 October 2000) On the eve of Diwali, Goan Hindus remember the victory of Lord *Krishna* over the demon *Narkasur*. In Panaji there are processions and
competitions.
Diwali (*Deepavali*) (26 October 2000) The Hindu festival of lights when homes are
decorated with lines of earthen lamps, candles or tiny electric bulbs. Fireworks have
become an integral part of the celebration, which are often set off days before Diwali.

November *Ramadan* (30 November 2000) Start of the month of fasting when all Muslims (except young children, the very elderly, the sick, pregnant women and travellers) must abstain from food and drink from sunrise to sunset.

December *Liberation Day* (17th) Commemorates the end of Portuguese colonial rule and is a public holiday marked by military parades.

Christmas (25th) Observed with Midnight Mass in churches across the state and usual family get-togethers and involves every community. Special Goan sweets made with ground rice and sugar are prepared.

Id-ul-Fitr (the "small feast") (28 December 2000) The 3-day festival to mark the end of Ramadan determined by the sighting of the new moon Id-ul-Azha /Bakr-Id (the "great feast")–(8 March 2001) Muslims commemorate Ibrahim's sacrifice of his son according to God's commandment; the main time of pilgrimage to Mecca (the Hajj). It is marked by the sacrifice of a goat, feasting and alms giving.

Health

With the following advice and precautions, you should keep as healthy as you do at home. In India the health risks are different from those encountered in Europe or the USA but the region's medical practicioners have particular experience in dealing with locally occuring diseases.

Before you go

Take out medical insurance. Have a dental check up if you are taking an extended trip, get a spare glasses prescription and, if you suffer from a long-standing condition such as diabetes, high blood pressure, heart/lung disease or a nervous disorder, arrange for a check up with your doctor who can at the same time provide you with a letter explaining details of your disability. Check the current practice for malaria prevention.

Medical care Good hotels can often provide a list of recommended doctors. There are many well qualified doctors in Goa, a large proportion of whom speak English. However, the quality and range of medical care are much lower in rural areas. Traditional systems of medicine are common and local practitioners have a lot of experience with the particular diseases of their region. If you are a long way away from medical help, a certain amount of self medication may be necessary.

Medicines Many drugs available in the west are available from chemists. However, always check the date stamp and buy from reputable pharmacies because the shelf life of some items, especially vaccines and antibiotics, is markedly reduced in hot conditions. Locally produced drugs are not subjected to quality control procedures and can be unreliable.

Medical checklist Anti-acid tablets; anti-diarrhoea tablets; anti-infective ointment; anti-malaria tablets; disposable needles; dusting powder for feet; first aid kit; insect repellent (*Mosiguard* is recommended by MASTA); sachets of rehydration salts; travel sickness pills.

Vaccination & immunization The following vaccinations are recommended:

Typhoid (monovalent): one dose followed by a booster in one month's time. Immunity from this course lasts two to three years. An oral preparation is currently being marketed in some countries and a one dose injectable vaccine is also available but is more expensive than monovalent: Typhim-Vi (Mevieux).

Polio-myelitis: this is a live vaccine generally given orally and a full course consists of three doses with a booster in tropical regions every three to five years.

Tetanus: one dose should be given with a booster at six weeks and another at six months; 10 yearly boosters thereafter are recommended.

Meningococcal Meningitis and **Japanese B Encephalitis (JVE)**: immunisation (Japanese or Korean vaccine: effective in 10 days) gives protection for around three years. There is an extremely small risk, though it varies seasonally and from region to region. Consult a travel clinic.

Hepatitis A: many travellers contract Hepatitis A. Protection is very strongly recommended. Havrix, Havrix Monodose and Junior Havrix vaccine give protection for 10 years after two injections (10 days to be effective). Alternatively, one gamma globulin injection to cover up to six months' travel is effective immediately and is much cheaper.

Hepatitis B: this is a sexually transmitted disease, also passed on from blood transfusions or infected needles. A vaccine is available – three shots over six months. Regular travellers should have a blood test first to check whether they are already immune to Hepatitis A or B.

Rabies Rabies is endemic in India. Pre-exposure vaccination gives anyone bitten by a suspect animal time to get treatment (so particularly helpful to those visiting remote areas) and also prepares the body to produce antibodies quickly. If you are bitten by a domestic or wild animal, don't leave things to chance. Scrub the wound with soap and water/or disinfectant, try to have the animal captured (within limits) or at least determine its ownership where possible and seek medical assistance at once.

Small-pox, cholera and yellow fever Vaccinations are not required. You may be asked for a certificate if you have been in a country affected by yellow fever immediately before travelling to India.

Children should, in addition, be properly protected against **diphtheria**, **whooping cough**, **mumps**, **measles** and **HIB**. Teenage girls should be given **rubella** (German measles) vaccination if they have not had the disease. Consult your doctor for advice on BCG inoculation against **tuberculosis**; the disease is still common in the region.

On the road

Almost everyone suffers upset stomachs. Most of the time, intestinal upsets are due to the insanitary preparation of **food**. Under-cooked fish, vegetables or meat (especially pork), fruit with the skin on (always peel your fruit yourself) or food that is exposed to flies (especially salads) are all highly risky.

Intestinal upsets

All unbottled **water** is probably unsafe, as is ice. Do not put ice cubes in drinks. If you have no choice but to drink dirty water, strain it through a filter bag (available from camping shops) and then boil or treat it. At high altitude you have to boil the water for longer than normally to ensure that all the microbes are killed. Various sterilising methods can be used and there are proprietary preparations containing chlorine or iodine compounds.

Drinking water

Pasteurised or heat treated **milk** is now widely available, as is ice cream and yoghurt produced by the same methods. Unpasteurized milk products, including cheese, are sources of tuberculosis, brucellosis, listeria and food poisoning germs. You can render fresh milk safe by heating it to 62°C for 30 minutes, followed by rapid cooling or by boiling it. Matured or processed cheeses are safer than fresh varieties.

This is usually the result of food poisoning, occasionally from contaminated water. There are various causes – viruses, bacteria, protozoa (like amoeba), salmonella and cholera organisms. It may take one of several forms, coming on suddenly, or rather slowly. It may be accompanied by vomiting or by severe abdominal pain and the passage of blood or mucus when it is called dysentery. If you can time the onset of diarrhoea to the minute, then it is probably **viral** or **bacterial** and/or the onset of

Diarrhoea
Any diarrhoea continuing for more than 3 days should be treated by a doctor

dysentery. If the diarrhoea has come on slowly or intermittently, then it is more likely to be **protozoal**, ie caused by amoeba or giardia and antibiotics will have no effect.

Treatment The linchpins of treatment for diarrhoea are rest, fluid and salt replacement, antibiotics for the bacterial types and special diagnostic tests and medical treatment for amoeba and giardia infections. All kinds of diarrhoea, whether or not accompanied by vomiting respond favourably to the replacement of water and salts taken as frequent small sips of some kind of rehydration solution. There are proprietary preparations, consisting of sachets of powder which you dissolve in water, or you can make your own by adding half a teaspoonful of salt (3.5 grams) and four tablespoonfuls of sugar (40 grams) to a litre of boiled water. For viral and bacterial diarrhoea, rehydration plus Ciprofloxacin, 500 milligrams should be given every 12 hours. The drug is now widely available and you should seek medical help. The following protozoal diarrhoea rehydration drugs may help if there are severe stomach cramps: Loperamide (Imodium, Arret) and Diphenoxylate with Atropine (Lomotil). Fasting, peculiar diets and the consumption of large quantities of yoghurt have not been found useful in calming travellers' diarrhoea or in rehabilitating inflamed bowels. Alcohol and milk may prolong diarrhoea and should be avoided during and immediately after an attack.

Heat & cold Full acclimatization to high temperatures takes about two weeks. Drink plenty of water (up to 15 litres a day can be needed if taking vigorous exercise), use salt on food and avoid extreme exertion. Tepid showers are more cooling than hot or cold ones.

Insects Insects can be a great nuisance and some carry serious diseases. To ward off mosquitoes sleep off the ground with a mosquito net and burn Pyrethrum mosquito coils. Sprays and insecticidal tablets, heated on a mat plugged into the wall socket, are effective, as are personal insect repellents. The best contain a high concentration of Diethyltoluamide. Liquid is best for arms and face (take care around eyes and make sure you do not dissolve the plastic of your spectacles).

Aerosol spray on clothes and ankles deters mites and ticks. Liquid DET suspended in water can be used to impregnate cotton clothes and mosquito nets. New style mosquito nets are wider-meshed and impregnated with permethrin (an insecticide). If you are bitten, itching may be relieved by cool baths and anti-histamine tablets (care with alcohol or driving), corticosteroid creams (great care – never use if any hint of sepsis). Calamine lotion and cream have limited effectiveness and anti-histamine creams have a tendency to cause skin allergies and are, therefore, not generally recommended.

Bites which become infected (common in the tropics) should be treated with a local antiseptic or antibiotic cream such as Cetrimide as should infected scratches. Skin infestations with body lice, crabs and scabies are unfortunately easy to pick up. Use Gamma benzene hexachloride for lice and Benzyl benzoate for scabies. Crotamiton cream alleviates itching and also kills a number of skin parasites. Malathion lotion 5% is good for lice but avoid the highly toxic full strength Malathion used as an agricultural insecticide.

Sunburn & heat stroke The burning power of the tropical sun is phenomenal. Always wear a wide brimmed hat and use some form of sun cream or lotion on untanned skin. Always use high protection factor suntan lotions, designed specifically for the tropics or for mountaineers or skiers. Glare from the sun can cause conjunctivitis so wear sunglasses, especially on tropical beaches.

There are several varieties of 'heat stroke'. The most common cause is severe dehydration. Avoid dehydration by drinking lots of non-alcoholic fluid. Put extra salt on your food.

Death from snake bite is very rare. If you are unlucky enough to be bitten by a venomous snake, spider, scorpion, centipede or sea creature try (within limits) to catch the animal for identification. The reactions to be expected are fright, swelling, pain and bruising around the bite, soreness of the regional lymph glands, nausea, vomiting and fever. If, in addition, any of the following symptoms occur get the victim to a doctor without delay: numbness, tingling of the face, muscular spasm, convulsions, shortness of breath or haemorrhage. Commercial snake bite or scorpion sting kits are only useful for the specific type of snake or scorpion for which they are designed. The serum has to be given intravenously. If the bite is on a limb, immobilise the limb and apply a tight bandage between the bite and the body, releasing it for 90 seconds every 15 minutes. Reassurance of the bitten person is very important because death from snake bite is, in fact, very rare. Hospitals usually hold stocks of snake bite serum. **Precautions** Do not to walk in snake territory with bare feet, sandals or shorts. It is also good to make noise (eg by tapping a stick). Snakes are more frightened of heavy animals like humans and will tend to disappear as they approach.

Bites & stings *Do not slash the bite area and try to suck out the poison; this does more harm than good*

Essentials

In India AIDS is increasing faster than in most countries. Heterosexual transmission is now the dominant mode and so the main risk to travellers is from casual sex. The same precautions should be taken as when encountering any sexually transmitted disease. The only way to determine whether you have been infected is by having a blood test for HIV antibodies at a place where there are reliable laboratory facilities. The test does not become positive for many weeks. **Precautions** Ensure that needles used for injections have been properly sterilised or that disposable needles are used. Hepatitis B is the main risk. Blood for transfusion should be screened for HIV but this cannot be guaranteed and remains a real risk. Be wary of carrying disposable needles yourself; customs officials may find them suspicious.

AIDs

Malaria is a serious disease and is prevalent in India. Certain areas are badly affected, particularly by the highly dangerous falciparum strain. Malaria prevention is becoming more complex as the malaria parasite becomes immune to some of the older drugs. Some of the preventive drugs can cause side effects, especially if taken for long periods of time, so before you travel you must check with a reputable agency the likelihood and type of malaria in the countries which you intend to visit and take their advice on prophylaxis. Be prepared to receive conflicting advice. You can catch malaria even when taking prophylactic drugs, although it is unlikely. If you do develop symptoms (high fever, shivering, severe headache, sometimes diarrhoea) seek medical advice immediately. **Precautions** Protect yourself against mosquito bites – cover up exposed skin at dusk, wear light coloured long-sleeved clothes, use mosquito repellent cream or gel and use a net to sleep under. It is now possible to buy light-weight impregnated nets such as the *Repel Trekker*. Enquire from your local travel shop, or in UK the *British Airways Travel Shop* or *Ikea*. Take prophylactic (preventive) drugs. Start taking the tablets a few days before exposure and continue to take them six weeks after leaving the malarial zone ('Paludrine' is difficult to find in India). To seek up-to-date advice contact the Malaria Reference Laboratory, T0891-600350 (recorded message, premium rate) or the Liverpool School of Tropical Medicine, T0151 708 9393. In the USA, try Centre for Disease Control, Atlanta, T404-3324555. *MASTA* (Medical Advisory Service for Travellers Abroad) based at the London School of Hygiene and Tropical Medicine, Keppel St, London WCIE 7HT, T0891-224100, publishes a strongly recommended book entitled: *The Preservation of Personal Health in Warm Climates*. Masta also sells a range of health products for travellers.

Malaria

Dengue fever is present in India. It is a virus disease, transmitted by mosquito bites, presenting with severe headache and body pains. Complicated types of dengue known as haemorrhagic fevers occur throughout Asia but usually in persons who

Dengue fever

Essentials

have caught the disease a second time. Thus, although it is a very serious type, it is rarely caught by visitors. There is no treatment, you must just avoid mosquito bites.

Other afflictions **Athlete's foot** and other fungal infections are best treated by sunshine and a proprietary preparation such as Tolnaftate. **Intestinal worms** are common and the more serious ones, such as hook worm can be contracted by walking barefoot on infested earth or beaches. **Leishmaniasis** can be a serious disease taking several forms and transmitted by sand flies. These should be avoided in the same way as mosquitoes. **Prickly heat** is a common itchy rash and may be avoided by frequent washing and wearing loose clothing. It is helped by the use of talcum powder and/or Boroline ointment. Allow the skin to dry thoroughly after washing.

When you get home

If you have had attacks of diarrhoea, it is worth having a stool specimen tested in case you have picked up amoebic dysentery. If you have been living rough, a blood test may be worthwhile to detect worms and other parasites.

The information above has been compiled for us by Dr David Snashall, Senior Lecturer in Occupational Health, United Medical Schools of Guy's and St Thomas' Hospitals and Chief Medical Adviser, Foreign and Commonwealth Office, London.

Further reading

The literature on Goa is significant and growing. Most of the material listed here is available in English though original sources were in some cases in Portuguese. There are excellent bookshops in all the major Indian cities where you will find books are generally much cheaper than outside. In Goa, Panaji has a few good shops, including the one at the *Mandovi Hotel* and *Varsha* near Azad Maidan. In Margao, *Golden Heart* has a wide (possibly the state's largest) collection. *Mapusa's Other India Bookshop* prides itself in covering contoversial issues. A few suggestions are listed here.

Art & architecture **Anand, Mulk Raj** *In praise of Christian Art in Goa*. Marg, Volume XXXII No 4, Mumbai. **Nunes, Judilia** *Monuments in Old Goa*. Delhi, 1979. **Pereira, José** *Baroque Goa, the architecture of Portuguese Goa*. Books & Books, New Delhi, 1955. A very detailed and technical analysis. **Pereira, José** *Goa Shrines & Mansions*. Knowledeable account of interesting temples and buildings. **Rajagopalan, S** *Old Goa*. Third revised edition by KV Rao. Archaeological Survey of India, New Delhi, 1994. A short history and guide to the monuments with a few plans and photos, usually available at the site (Rs 10).

Current affairs & politics **Alvares, Claude** (editor) *Fish, Curry and Rice, a citizen's report on the Goan environment*. An Ecoforum publication. Third revised edition, 1995. Mapusa, Other India Press. Full of current environmental information, written from a perspective of continuous moral outrage. **Esteves, S** *Politics and political leadership in Goa*. Cultural Patterns. New Delhi, 1981.

Early & colonial history **Basham, AL** *The Wonder that was India*. London, Sidgwick & Jackson, 1985. Still one of the most comprehensive and readable accounts of the development of India's culture. **Boyajiyan, James C** *Goa Inquisition – A new light on first 100 years (1561-1660)* in Journal of the Directorate of Archives, Archaeology and Museum, Panaji, Goa, Volume IV, No 1 pages 1-40. **Cabralesa, Mario,** *Legends of Goa*, IBH, Mumbai, 1998. A well researched collection, illustrated by Mario Miranda. **Lopes Mendes, S (Portuguese)** *A India Portugeza*. Two volumes, Imprensa Nacional, Lisbon, 1886. An indispensable source book with numerous illustrations. **Marjay, Frederic P** *Portuguese India: a historic study*. Livraria Bertrand, Lisbon, 1959. Arrival of the Portuguese and St Xavier, with copies of old maps, prints and photos. **Penrose, Boies** *Goa – Queen of the East*. Lisbon 1960. The story of Old Goa with interesting illustrations. **Saldhana, CF** *A short history of Goa*. Panaji. **Spear, Percival & Thapar, Romila** *A history of India*. Two volumes, Penguin, 1978. Compact and authoritative. **Xavier, PD** *Goa: a social history (1510-1640)*, Rajhans, Panaji, 1993. Detailed chapters on social structure and institutions (slavery, church, position of women, education) with full bibliographies.

Saksena, RN *Goa: into the mainstream*. Abhinav Publications, New Delhi, 1972. An account of Goa's political integration with India after its incorporation in 1961. **D'Souza, BG** *Goan Society in transition*. Popular Prakashan, Mumbai, 1975.

Modern history

Mascerenhas, Lambert *In the womb of Saudade*. Rupa, 1995. A collection of Goan short stories, illustrated by Mario Miranda. **Menezes, Armando** *Chords and dischords*. Poems by a Goan writing in English. **Naipaul, VS** *A million mutinies now*. Penguin, 1992. Naipaul's 'revisionist' account of India where he turns away from the despondency of his earlier two India books (*An area of darkness* and *India: a wounded civilisation*) to see grounds for optimism at India's capacity for regeneration. **Narayan, RK** has written many gentle and humourous novels and short stories of South India. *The Man-eater of Malgudi, Under the Banyan tree and other stories*, and *Grandmother's stories*, among many. London, Penguin, 1985 (India). Also a 're-telling' of the Mahabharata. **Roy, Arundhati** *The God of Small Things*. Indian Ink/Harper Collins 1997. Booker prize-winning novel about family turmoil in a Syrian Christian household in Kerala. **Rushdie, Salman** *Midnight's children*. Picador, London, 1981. A novel of India since Independence. *The Moor's Last Sigh*. Viking, 1996, is of particular interest to those travelling to Kochi and Mumbai because of the settings there. **Seth, Vikram** *A Suitable Boy*. Phoenix House London 1993, prize winning novel of modern Indian life. **Shetty, Manohar** *Ferry Crossings: short stories from Goa*. Penguin, 1998. A collection of social and political tales.

Literature

Raghara R Menon *Penguin Dictionary of Indian Classical Music*. Penguin, New Delhi 1995, comprehensive introduction.

Music

Albuquerque, Theresa *Anjuna: Profile of a village in Goa Promilla*. New Delhi, 1988. An attractive illustrated account of the history of one of Goa's most famous yet little known villages. **Angle, Prabhakar S** *Goa, Concepts and misconcepts*. Goa Hindu Association, Mumbai, 1994. An account of Goa's place in modern India emphasising the significance of its Hindu traditions. **Cabral e Sa, Mario & Da Costa Rodrigues, LB** *Great Goans*. NNAP, Piedade, Goa, 1985. Brief but interesting account of some of Goa's major modern figures. **Mascarenhas, Telo de** *When the mango trees blossomed*. Bombay, Longmans, 1976. Reminiscences of a freedom fighter. **Rémy (pseud)** *Goa: Rome of the Orient*. By Lancelot C Sheppard, London, Arthur Barker, 1957. **Shastry, BS** *Goan Society through the ages*. Ajanta, Delhi, 1987. **Singh, KS** (ed) *People of India Goa*. Volume XXI, Bombay, Anthropological Survey of India. Popular Prakashan, Mumbai, 1993. A traditional anthropological description of some of the major groups in Goa.

People & places

Eck, DL *Darshan: seeing the divine image in India*. Chambersburg, Pennsylvania. **Gomes Pereira, Rui** *Goa*, Volume 1, *Hindu Temples and Deities*. Translated from the original in Portuguese by Antonio Victor Couto. Panaji, Printwell, 1978. Detailed listing with some interesting historical accounts and descriptions of practices. *History of Christianity in India*. Volume 1 by **Mundadan, M**, Volume 2 by **Thekkedath, J.** Theological Publications, Bangalore, 1984. **Robinson, F** (ed) *Religions in South Asia (in The Cambridge Encyclopedia of India, Pakistan, Bangladesh and Sri Lanka)*. Cambridge

Religion

University Press, 1989. An extremely well written account of India's major religions, their philosophies and development.

Travel   **Cabral e Sa, Mario** *Goa*. Lustre Press, New Delhi, 1993. Informative; attractive souvenir with colour photos by Jean-Louis Nou. **Hall, Maurice** *Window on Goa*. Quiller Press London (Second Edition) 1995. Probably the best, most comprehensively illustrated text on Goa's religious and secular sights. **Hutt, Anthony** *Goa: a traveller's historical and architectural guide*. Scorpion, 1988. Well-written though not fully comprehensive account of Goan churches, temples and major houses. **Richards, JM** *Goa*. Revised edition. Vikas Publishing House, New Delhi, 1993. Rather idiosyncratic and dated guide but still with some valuable observations.

Wildlife &   **Ali, Salim and Ripley S Dillon** *Handbook of the birds of India & Pakistan* (compact
vegetation   edition). BNHS, Mumbai. **Bole PV & Vaghini, Y** *Field Guide to the common trees of India*. OUP. Good for identifying. **Cowen, DV** *Flowering Trees and Shrubs in India*. **Grewal B** *Birds of India, Bangladesh, Nepal, Pakistan & Sri Lanka*. Odyssey. A well-illustrated (mostly in colour) and comprehensive guide based on Salim Ali's original. **Nair SM** *Endangered animals of India*. National Book Trust, New Delhi, 1992. Attractively illustrated slim volume on the species of India's wildlife most at risk and their conservation. **Prater, SH** *Book of Indian Animals*, Third edition. OUP/Bombay Natural History Society, Mumbai, 1978. *Goa: the independent birder's guide*. Eastern Publications, Lowestoft, England, 1996.

Maps   For anyone interested in the geography of India, or even simply getting around, trying to buy good maps is a depressing experience. For security reasons it is illegal to sell large scale maps of any area within 80 km of the coast or national borders.

In Goa Goa tourist offices hand out a reasonable state map (updated with the Konkan railway) in colour. *Findoll Publications* have brought out an updated Goa yellow pages accompanied by two sheets of colour maps in 1996 (Rs 60 each) aimed at the tourist market. Goa Map 1: State and towns (Panjim, Old Goa, Mapusa, Margao, Vasco, Dona Paula, Porvorim etc). Goa Map 2: Beaches covering all popular ones from Arambol in the north to Palolem in the south. Fairly detailed, including hotels, restaurants, tourist services (banks, travel agents, tailors, beach parties, etc) but not quite up to date (eg Old Goa still shows Camoes' statue at the roundabout, Aguada Sports Complex not included), and not wholly reliable in detail. The *Bartholomew* 1:4m map sheet of India is the most authoritative, detailed and easy to use map of India available. It can be bought worldwide.

Outside Goa *Stanford International Map Centre*, 12-14 Long Acre, London WC2E 9LP; *Zumsteins Landkartenhaus*, Leibkerrstrasse 5, 8 Mnchen 22, Germany; *Geo Buch Verlag*, Rosenthal 6, D-6000 Mnchen 2, Germany; *GeoCenter GmbH*, Honigwiessenstrasse 25, Postfach 800830, D-7000 Stuttgart 80, Germany; *Libreria Alpina*, Via C Coroned-Berti, 4 40137 Bologna, Zona 370-5, Italy; *Library of Congress*, 101 Independence Ave, Washington, DC 20540, USA; *Michael Chessler Books*, PO Box 2436, Evergreen, CO 80439, USA T800 654 8502, 303 670 0093; NOAA Distribution Branch (N/CG33), National Ocean Service, Riverdale MD 20737.

Websites   **www.tourindia.com**, is the official site for the Government of India Tourist Office.
See page 36 for   **www.indiacurrentaffairs.com/**, is regularly updated cuttings from Indian national
newspaper websites &   dailies. **www.nic.in/goa/**, offers the demography and general statistics of the state as
page 15 for tour   well as practical travelling information and **www.goacom.com/goatourism**, a
company websites   government undertaking with plenty of practical information from cuisine and culture to accommodation.

Panaji and Central Goa

3

Panaji and Central Goa

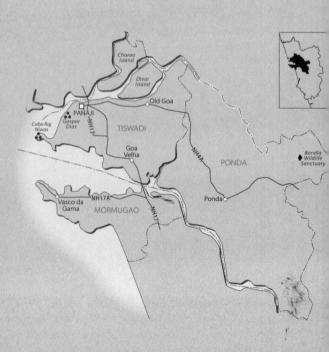

Central Goa is the state's cultural heartland. The talukas of Tiswadi, Mormugao and Ponda contain in their compact space, elements of all the features which have given Goa such a distinctive identity. It was here that the Portuguese impact was first and most profoundly felt, but Old Goa, deserted and empty today, retains the atmosphere of a powerful political and religious city. Yet immediately to the east, across the Cumbarjua Canal, a muddy crocodile infested creek, lies Hindu Ponda with a wealth of temples and Goa's only siginificant remaining mosque. Alongside the traces of colonial history in Panaji, Central Goa also has the state's largest modern town with a full range of services. Few visitors stay in Central Goa, for it has limited beaches and relatively little accommodation, but it is the axis of the state's communication and it contains much of interest to see.

Panaji (Panjim)

Occupying a narrow coastal strip between a low laterite hill – the 'Altinho' – and the mouth of the Mandovi River, Panaji, the capital, still has the feel of quite a small town. There are no great buildings or attractions which would make it a draw for a long stay, but it does retain enough character to warrant a visit. There are very pleasant walks over the Altinho and through the old district of Fontainhas.

Ins & outs
See transport directory for further details

Getting there From Dabolim airport, across Mormugao Bay, you can get a prepaid taxi or a bus. Panaji is the main arrival point for long-distance bus travellers. Most rail travellers arriving by Konkan Railway from Mumbai and the north, or from coastal Karnataka and Kerala, get to Margao, southeast of the capital; from there taxis and buses can get you to Panaji (or to your beach resort). The state Kadamba buses and private coach terminals are in Patto to the east of town. From there it is a 10 min walk, across the footbridge over the Ourem Creek to get to guest houses. The catamaran service from Bombay remains suspended. **Getting around** Auto-rickshaws are the most convenient means for negotiating the city. Motorcycle rickshaws are cheaper but can be more risky.

History

Panaji is the official spelling of the capital city replacing the older Portuguese spelling Panjim (see box on page 58). There were three principal cities in Portuguese Goa: **Old Goa** (Velha Goa), **Panjim** (New Goa), and **Margao**. Panjim was originally a suburb of Old Goa and is built on the left bank of the Mandovi Estuary. It contains the archbishop's palace, a modern port, and government buildings and shops set around a number of plazas. It is laid out on a grid and the main roads run parallel with the sea front. It was its advantageous position guarding the estuary which first attracted the Muslim ruler **Yusuf Adil Shah** to build and then fortify a palace by the river in 1500, the Idalcao Palace, as the Portuguese called it. The palace remains today as the oldest and most impressive of the lower town's official buldings, but its service to the Sultan was very short-lived, for within 10 years **Albuquerque** had seized on the strategic value of Goa's *Ilhas* site. Although Albuquerque followed the Muslims' example and occupied the site of Old Goa as his main capital, he stationed a garrison at Panaji in 1510 and made it the customs clearing point for all traffic entering the Mandovi.

The town remained little more than a military outpost, and the first Portuguese buildings after the construction of a church on the site of the present Church of Our Lady of Immaculate Conception in 1541, were noblemen's houses built on the flat land bordering the sea. It remained no more than a staging post on the way to Old Goa, used by incoming and outgoing Viceroys, but with no real settlement, until the Portuguese Viceroy finally decided to move from Old Goa to Panaji in 1759. It was a further 84 years before it was officially declared the capital, by which time the population of Old Goa had followed the Viceroy to make it the largest town in the colony.

Travel tip

Motorcycle taxis with yellow mudguards are unique in Goa. A rider takes one passenger, often dangerously, down rough/muddy roads or narrow lanes; without helmets, this can be lethal. **Warning** *Your insurance policy may not cover you if you are involved in an accident.*

Tiswadi Taluka

Panaji lies in the administrative district (taluka) named Tiswadi which stretches from the headland of Cabo de Raj Niwas in the southwest to the islands of Chorao and Divar in the Mandovi estuary to the north and is separated from Ponda taluka by the Cumbarjua Canal. It is named after the 30 (tis) island areas (wadi) that were brought under its administration.

At its centre is the thin-soiled laterite Teleigao plateau which reaches about 100m above sea level. Old Goa stands on the northern edge of the plateau while the University sits on the southern part. In places the plateau drops steeply, down to curving bays like Vanguinem or Bambolim while also forming the high ground of the Altinho in Panaji.

Some of the great sights of Portuguese Goa are on this small territory. Old Goa, the Pilar Monastery and Santana Church, represent the central traditions of the Portuguese legacy, while the beaches and bays from Miramar to Bambolim give even the area closest to the capital access to fine sand and beautiful views. In contrast, on the islands in the estuary are some of the remnants of the old estuarine marsh ecosystem.

Its central location means that all the important sites of Tiswadi can be seen relatively easily from either the northern or the southern beaches, as well as from Panaji itself. If the Zuari Bridge needs to be closed for repairs the capacity of the ferry may not meet the heavy demand and there could be very long delays. The alternative land route is via Ponda and is a long diversion but it does goes through a number of other places of interest in the Ponda taluka.

Tiswadi (or the Ilhas), where Old Goa is situated, plus the neighbouring talukas – Bardez, Mormugao and Salcete – comprise the heart of the Portuguese territory and are known as the **Old Conquests**. They contain all the important Christian churches. In contrast the **New Conquests** came into Portuguese possession considerably later, either by conquest or by treaty.

The Mandovi-Zuari estuaries reach the sea after journeys of less than 70km from their sources in the Western Ghats in a combined estuary which is one of the most important mangrove complexes in India. The sea water penetrates a long way inland, especially in the dry season, though today mangroves cover less than 20ha. However, there are approximately 20 species of mangroves, including some rare ones. The species Kandelia candel is still common despite being on the edge of extinction elsewhere. The estuary is a spawning ground for crustaceans and molluscs and many species of fish, and is host to huge numbers of migratory birds, especially ducks and shore birds. Jackals, water snakes, bats and marsh crocodiles are common.

The old & new conquests

Pernem

Bardez

Bicholim

Satari

Ilhas

Ponda

Sanguem

Salcete

Quepem

Canacona

N

Not to scale

Old conquests	New conquests
1510	1780
c1543	

Panaji & Central Goa

Sights

Riverside boulevard The boulevard (D Bandodkar Marg) runs from near the New Patto bridge, on the east side, past the jetties, to the formerly open fields of the **Campal** to the southwest, offering picturesque views across the Mandovi towards the fort of Reis Magos. When Panaji depended on boats for communicating with the rest of Goa as well as with the world beyond, this road was the town's busiest highway. Along it are some of the main administrative buildings.

Idalcao Palace Just behind the main boat terminal is the Idalcao Palace of the Adil Shahs which was once their castle. The Portuguese expanded it after capturing it in 1510 and rebuilt it in 1615. Until 1759 it was the Viceregal Palace and then it became the Viceroy's official residence. In 1918 the Governor General (as the Viceroy had become), decided to move to the Cabo headland to the southwest, now Cabo Raj Niwas, and the old Palace was used for government offices. After Independence it became the Secretariat building for the Union Territory and it now houses the Passport Office. The main entrance gate is a pilastered Romanesque arch in the south wall facing away from the river. The crest of the Viceroys which once adorned it has been replaced by the Ashokan 'Wheel of Law', the official symbol of India.

Panaji (Panjim)

Related map
A Panaji (Panjim)
centre, page 62

0 metres 100
0 yards 100

To Miramar Dona Paula (7 km) ❶   Santa Inez Church ❷ To Archives Museum of Goa (200m) ❸

■ **Sleeping**
1 Afonso *B5*
2 Blessings *B3*
3 Casa Pinho Lodge *B5*

4 Delmon *B2*
5 Frank's Inn *B3*
6 Keni's *B3*
7 Nova Goa *B3*

8 Panjim Inn, Bar & Panjim Pousada *B5*
9 Park Lane Lodge *B4*

Panaji & Central Goa

Next to the palace is an unusual and striking statue of the Abbé Faria, known in Paris as one of the discoverers of hypnotism. Abbé José Custodio de Faria was born on 30 May 1756 in Candolim, just inland of Calangute. His family claimed descent from Brahmins from Colvale, but his parents separated after his birth, his mother becoming a nun and his father a priest.

José grew up with an adopted half-sister under his father's care, but in February 1771 at the age of 15 his father took him to Lisbon – a journey that took over nine months. His father found patronage in the court and he himself was given a scholarship to study in Rome where he was ordained a priest in 1780 and later completed his doctoral thesis. Abbé Faria then went on to Paris where he got involved with the French Revolution. He made a worldwide reputation as an authority on hypnotism through publishing his book 'On the causing of lucid sleep'. However, very little is known of his subsequent career, though he gave public lectures and demonstrations of 'magnetizing power' (hypotnism) in Paris in the first two decades of the 19th century. He died at the age of 64 in 1819 in Paris, never having revisited the Goa which he had left 48 years before.

Further west, on Malacca Road, almost opposite the wharf are the central library, art gallery and public rooms of the institute. The Institute Menezes Braganza (formerly the Instituto Vasco da Gama), was established on 22 November 1871, the anniversary of the date on which Vasco da Gama sailed round the Cape of Good Hope. It was founded to stimulate an interest in

Abbé Faria
The character in Dumas' Count of Monte Christo may have been based on him

Institute Menezes Braganza

Panaji & Central Goa

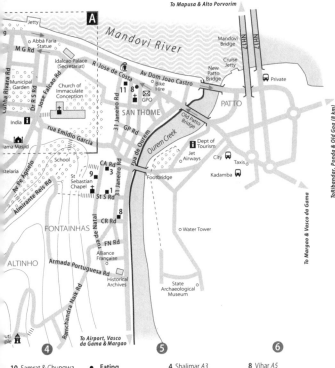

What's in a name?

The use of three languages in Goa is reflected in considerable confusion in the naming of places and the spelling of many place names, with Portuguese, Marathi and Konkani variants all in use, making it very difficult to discover the original version of many names. Pronunciation adds to the confusion. The final "im" which appears in place names indicates a nasal ending, so that the "m" is never heard. Betim, Siolim, Borlim, Cuncolim, and formerly Panjim – Goa is full of place names ending in the nasalized but otherwise silent m.

So is it Pa-na-ji or Pan-jim? PP Shirodkar has reported that the first known reference to the site can be dated precisely to 7 February 1107, when it was named on a copper plate inscription as 'Pahajanikhali', a name which refers to the starch used by fishermen to treat the threads of their fishing nets. Whatever its origins, the settlement has been known as Panjim for years, though another variant, Pangim, appears on old Portuguese maps. But in either spelling the final "m" was virtually silent, and not pronounced Pan-jim.

The modern official name, Panaji, recognised that. The central "a", appears as many Devanagari consonants have the sound "a" built into them. Thus in the Devanagari script "n" is normally pronounced "na", although the vowel sound is often so short as barely to be noticeable.

Either way you end up with a pronunciation that usually sounds to your authors' ears something like "Ponnjee" – with the "o" as in orange!

culture, science and the arts and has 24 Fellows who must all be residents of Goa. **Luis Menezes de Braganza** (1878-1938) was an outstanding social and political figure in early 20th-century Goa. (His home in Chandor, which is open to the public, gives a fascinating insight into the lives of the élite Portuguese-speaking Goan families.)

The **art gallery** upstairs includes paintings, mainly by European artists of the late 19th and early 20th centuries and Goan artists of the 20th century. There are also sculptures, coins and furniture, the last including a remarkable seven legged rectangular table used for interrogation during the Inquisition. Three legs on one side are carved to represent two lions flanking a central eagle, while the four other legs are carved into the form of human heads. The blue tiled frieze in the entrance, hand painted by Jorge Colaco in 1935, is a mythical representation of the Portuguese colonization of Goa. The *azulejos* panels, about 3m high, set against a pale yellow background should be read clockwise from the entrance on the left wall. Each picture is set over a verse from the epic poem by the great Portuguese poet **Luis Vaz de Camoes**, whose statue stood in front of the Se Cathedral until it was removed to the museum in Old Goa by the post-colonial Goa government. Camoes had served in North Africa before travelling to Goa in 1553, staying in India and the Far East for 17 years. He was a fierce critic of the Portuguese colonial enterprise, evidenced in his epic poem *Os Lusiadas.* ■ *Mon-Fri 0930-1300, 1400-1745.* The **central library** downstairs, dating from 1832, has a rare collection of religious and other texts and documents. ■ *Free. 0930-1300, 1200-1700.*

Azad Maidan Azad Maidan ('Freedom Park') is immediately to the south of the Institute Menezes Braganza. The unkempt pillared memorial in the 'park' (which is far from lush), originally housed a statue of **Albuquerque** which has been moved to the Archaeological Museum in Old Goa. It now has a black stone memorial to **Dr Tristao de Braganza Cunha**, one of Goa's most venerated freedom fighters. Tristao de Braganza Cunha was born on 2 April 1891 in Chandor village. After an education in Pondicherry and then an electrical engineering

Panaji and Goa tours

Tours can be booked at: the Tourist Hotel, M Gandhi Rd, T227103; GTDC, Trianora Apartments, Dr Alvares Costa Rd, T226515; Directorate of Tourism, Tourist Home, Patto, T225583. There are GTDC counters elsewhere including GTDC tourist hotels in other towns.

The tours run regularly in season (1 Oct-16 Jun) leave from the Tourist Hotel. Entrance are fees extra.

North Goa Tour *includes Mapusa, Mayem Lake, beaches Vagator, Anjuna, Calangute, Fort Aguada.* ***South Goa Tour*** *includes Old Goa, Loutolim, Margao, Colva, Mormugao, Pilar, Dona Paula, Miramar (with optional river cruise at extra charge); both 0930-1800, Rs 80 (Rs 100, a/c). Similar tours are offered from Margao, Colva, Vasco, Mapusa and Calangute. The* ***Village Tour*** *includes a visit to Savoi Verem spice plantation and Hindu temples at Marcela: 1000-1600, Rs 150 (includes lunch). Two-day* ***Dudhsagar***

Special (from Panaji and Margao): 1000-1800 (next day) via Old Goa, Bondla Sanctuary, Tambdi Surla. Overnight at Molem. Second class return train to the falls the following morning. Rs 350.

River cruises *by launch are organized on the Mandovi River, sometimes with live bands and sing-along entertainment (though no one seems to know the words, most are keen to join in). Evening cruises "corny but pleasant at dusk" are recommended. It is not a 'luxury' launch – metal chairs are lined upfacing the band and dancers but you are free to wander around on deck. A bar operates. The operator of one hour Sunset Cruise (1800) Rs 60; Sundown Cruise (1915), Rs 60; Full Moon Pleasure Cruise, (2030) Rs 100 (dinner available at extra cost) is GTDC at Santa Monica Jetty (east of New Patto Bridge). The private Emerald Waters Co also offers similar trips (tickets from various outlets in the city).*

Panaji & Central Goa

degree in Paris he returned to Goa in 1926. From that point, until his death in 1958, he became a leading opponent of colonialism and an advocate of full independence within India. Despite his background of conservative Catholicism rooted among the landed gentry, TB became a radical rationalist. In 1946 he was arrested by the Portuguese as a leading subversive and imprisoned, first at Fort Aguada jail and then in Vasco da Gama, in transit to jail in Portugal. Released in 1950 but under compulsion to stay in Lisbon, he escaped to Paris and then back to India in September 1953. However, India's freedom had left Goa isolated, and until his death on 26 September 1958, he struggled against widespread apathy through newspaper articles to press the case for Goan independence. Disowned by the Catholic church he was buried in a Church of Scotland cemetery in Mumbai.

Largo da Igreja

The square, or municipal garden, is south of the Secretariat. This was a marshy patch until in the mid-19th century when the area was reclaimed to create the Praca de Flores (Square of the Flowers). It is dominated by the white-washed Church of Immaculate Conception which stands at the top of a distinctive criss-cross of steps.

Church of the Immaculate Conception

The church was built in 1541 to serve the needs of arriving sailors rather than for the town population as through the 16th and 17th centuries Panaji remained no more than a marshy fishing village. The low hill offered a landmark for boats coming into the Mandovi estuary and the Portuguese established their customs post just below the hill, making it the first landing point for sailors from Europe.

In 1600 it became the parish church of the capital and in 1619 it was completely rebuilt to its present design, modelled on the church in Reis Magos

*Church of the
Immaculate
Conception*

across the estuary. Before the hill was cut and the imposing stairway built in the 1780s, access was by a narrow staircase on the west side. In 1871 the central supporting arch had to be modified and strengthened to support the great bell, which was the second largest in Goa after the bell in the Se Cathedral. Originally from the tower of the Church of St Augustine in Old Goa, it had been placed above Fort Aguada 30 years earlier but a few years later it fell and fatally wounded a member of the congregation.

Inside the church the main altar *reredos* (screens) and the altars on either side to Jesus the Crucified and to Our Lady of the Rosary, are typically ornate gilded Baroque, in turn flanked by marble statues of St Peter and St Paul. The panels in the Chapel of St Francis, in the south transept, came from the chapel in the Idalcao Palace in 1918. The *Feast Day* is on 8 December.

In 1945, the statue of Our Lady of Fatima was installed and a crown of gold and diamonds was gifted by parishioners five years later. This statue is carried in a candle light procession each year on 13 October.

The domeless Jama Masjid (mid-18th century), further along Dr Dada Vaidya Road, can be seen to the left looking from the steps in front of the church.

Mahalaxmi Temple The Hindu Mahalaxmi Temple (originally 1818, but rebuilt and enlarged in 1983), is now hidden behind a newer building. It was the first Hindu place of worship to be allowed in the Old Conquests after the ending of the Inquisition. Even then permission was slow to be granted and raised fierce opposition from Archbishop Galdino. The deity, which had been removed to Bicholim in the 16th century, was restored only after a temporary resting place was found in the house of Mahamay Kamat, near the Secretariat. However, the Archbishop did not give up his opposition to the project and in 1827 "ordered that the priests should announce that it would be a very grave sin of idolatry for anyone to engage himself in the works of Hindu temples even when ordered to do so by the Government." The *Boca de Vaca* ('Cow's Mouth') spring, is nearby.

San Thome On the eastern promontory, sandwiched between the Altinho, the Mandovi River and the Ourem Creek, is San Thome. The area takes its name from the small but historically important square in which the main post office, which was once a tobacco warehouse, stands. Hall records that public executions were held here as late as 1843 when the 15 conspirators in the Pinto Revolt lost their lives. On the east side of the square is an attractive house used briefly after 1834 as a Mint, hence its Portuguese name *Casa Moeda*. San Thome church (1849, rebuilt in 1902) stands in the corner of the square.

Fontainhas Fontainhas lies to the south of San Thome. Drained in the 18th century, the rich alluvial soil was put to coconut cultivation and came to be known as *Palmar Ponte.* In the early 19th century, when the land belonged to the Carmelites, the move to shift the Portuguese capital away from Old Goa (already in decline), put this part of Panaji under pressure for housing the new influx of people. The conjested quarter developed, sustained by the clear spring water of the *Fonte Phoenix,* which was further enhanced by a basalt reservoir built by the then Governor, and the locality gained the name

Fontainhas. You can travel back in time by taking a walk down the narrow lanes between the modest old houses. Under Portuguese rule the only buildings allowed to be painted all white were the churches, while various shades of ochre predominated for secular buildings. Features such as window or door frames were picked out in other colours or white, and the sloping tiled roofs and wrought iron fronted balconies, often covered in climbing plants, created a very picturesque urban environment.

The evocative area can be approached from several directions. Narrow lanes come down from the San Thome district, while a footbridge leads across the Ourem creek from the new bus stand and the tourist office, straight into the district. A narrow road also runs east past the Church of Immaculate Conception and the main town square down to the footbridge. However, in some ways the most attractive way to approach is by walking over the Altinho from the Mahalaxmi Temple. This route gives excellent views from the steep east side of the Altinho, a footpath dropping down into Fontainhas just south of San Sebastian. **San Sebastian Chapel** is small and attractive (built in 1818, rebuilt in 1888), and lies in the heart of Fontainhas. The chapel houses the large wooden crucifix which until 1812 stood in the Palace of the Inquisition in Old Goa, where the eyes of the Christ figure watched over the proceedings of the tribunal. For 100 years it remained in the chapel in the Idalcao's palace in Panaji before being moved to the Chapel here. The church scarcely seems large enough to house the highly ornamented altars which came originally from the Church of Mother of God in Davim, together with the statue of Our Lady of Livramento. Fontainhas is also home to the Goa State archives, a short distance south.

The Altinho

The *Altinho*, meaning hill, to the south of town offered defensive advantages; it is well worth walking up for the view over the estuary. Immediately above the Church of the Immaculate Conception was Goa's first lighthouse, but most of the buildings on the Altinho today date from the 19th or 20th centuries. The Hindu **Maruti temple** to Hanuman, established towards the end of the Portuguese period without their official approval, is still being extended. During *Shri Hanuman Jatra* in January, the deity is carried in a palanquin procession and a big fair is held.

The Campal

The broad avenue running along the sea front from the Idalcao's Palace, between the boat jetties on the seaward side and the busy commerical area of town to its south, leads to the Campal and from there to Miramar and Dona Paula. Facing across the Mandovi estuary to Reis Magos and Fort Aguada there is an area, now a pleasingly broad flat park, which was reclaimed from the

Panaji's old buildings

Panaji & Central Goa

sea in 1833. Hall records that the area's name is an abbreviation of 'Campo de Dom Manuel', Dom Manuel being the Viceroy responsible for clearing and reclaiming the ground. While his name is itself a testament to Portuguese rule perhaps the most striking relic of the colonial past is the huge 4-m long cannon. The cannon, one of the first to be made in Goa, guarded the crossing from Tiswadi to Ponda at Banastari.

Until independence the broad sweeping road which ran south along the coast to Miramar ended at a huge statue of Albuquerque, now replaced by a statue to Hindu-Christian unity. The coast road itself has been extended towards Dona Paula to bypass the narrower road that runs through the crowded villages.

Markets   Although Panaji is not a traditional Indian market town, it none the less has its own bustling municipal markets (especially fish and vegetables) just east of the Goa Medical College. They are worth visiting early in the morning for their local colour.

Museums   The **Archives Museum** ■ *Ashirwad Building, 1st floor, Santa Inez. T226006. Free. 0930-1300, 1400-1730, Mon-Fri.* The **State Archaeological Museum** is an impressive building but contains a disppointingly small collection of religious art and antiquities, both Hindu and Christian, displayed together with sculptures from the Portuguese past. ■ *Patto, south of Kadamba Bus Stand, near ADC office. T226006. Free. 0930-1300, 1400-1730, Mon-Fri.*

Panaji (Panjim) centre

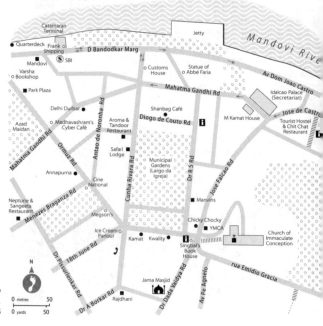

Related map
Panaji (Panjim),
page 56

Essentials

A-B *Mandovi*, D Bandodkar Marg, near Mahalaxmi Temple, T224405, F225451. 66 large a/c rooms (**A** river-facing), good restaurant, popular pastry shop, terrace bar, exchange, good bookshop, old building with hints of Art Deco, relaxing but lacks great character.

B *Delmon*, C de Alberquerque Rd. T226846, F223527. 58 a/c rooms. Modern, comfortable hotel with restaurant. **B** *Nova Goa*, T226231, F224958, novagoa@goa1.dot.net.in Large hotel, good a/c rooms with bath, some have fridge and bath tub, cheaper at rear and in annexe occupied by *Golden Goa*, good a/c restaurant and bar, clean, modern, very clean pool, pleasant staff, best in town. **B-C** *Park Plaza*, overlooking Azad Maidan, T422601, F225635. 37 modern, comfortable rooms (power showers!), most a/c, a/c restaurant and bar.

C *Fidalgo*, 18th June Rd, T226291, F225061. Once very pleasant but deteriorated, now central a/c, shabby for the price, but has a good bookshop. **C** *Panjim Inn*, E212, 31 Janeiro Rd, Fontainhas, T226523, F228136, panjiminn@goa1.dot.net.in 14 rooms with optional a/c, rooms vary in size and price so inspect first, part in 300-year-old character house kept in traditional style (period furniture, 4-posters) probably worth the erratic service, dinner overpriced, but friendly, relaxed, in-house art exhibitions.

D *Aroma*, Cunha Rivara Rd, T228310, F224330. Dim public areas, 26 cleanish rooms some with pleasant outlook over park (up to Rs 550) but lacking basic maintenance (bring a screwdriver & paintbrush!), excellent a/c restaurant (*Shere-e-Punjab Classic*) good food and very attentive service, bar. **D** *Keni's*, 18th June Rd, T224581, F435227. 38 simple though pleasant rooms, 16 a/c (Rs 650), hot water (0700-0900), restaurant. **D** *Manvins*, 4th Floor, Souza Towers, Municipal Gardens, T228305, F223231. 28 good size, clean rooms with excellent views over Municipal Gardens and River Mandovi beyond. Recommended. **D** *Palacio de Goa*, Gama Pinto Rd, T221785, F224155. Six-storey building (by no means a 'palace'), 18 decent rooms (phone, TV, some 4 or 5-bedded) and restaurant, optional a/c for extra Rs 150, top floor best for views (but take care getting in and out of lift!) check-out 0800. **D** *Panjim Pousada*, opposite, slightly cheaper sister hotel of *Panjim Inn*. 7 rooms around a permanent gallery in a courtyard, fairly attractive renovation. **D** *Rajdhani*, Dr Atmaram Borkar Rd, T235168. 20 clean rooms with bath, some a/c (Rs 100 extra), in modern Indian business style hotel, good a/c pure vegetarian restaurant (Gujarati, Punjabi, Chinese). **D** *Samrat*, Dr Dada Vaidya Rd, T224546, F224548, einteract@bom2.vsnl.net.in Some a/c rooms, a/c restaurant (Indian, Goan; *Chungwa* for good Chinese), bar, roof-garden, dimly lit public areas, unjustifiably popular Indian package hotel. **D** *Sona*, rua de Ourem, near Patto Bridge, T232281, F224425, sona@goa1.dot.net.in Clean rooms (Rs 550), with a/c and bath (Rs 770), some have good views over river but are small for the price. **D** *Tourist Hotel (GTDC)*, near the Secretariat, overlooking the river, T227103. 40 good-size rooms with balcony, some a/c (Rs 800), best views from top floor, good open-air restaurant, often full, chaotic reception area but surprisingly well-kept for a Gov't hotel, but overpriced. **D** *Virashree*, opposite Mahalaxmi Temple, Dr. Dada Vaidya Road, T226656. Brand new (Oct '99), 12 large, comfortable rooms with TV but lacking quality finish, good value (Rs 400-475). **D-E** *Blessings*, M Gandhi Rd, behind Bhatkar House, T224770, F224155. 18 ordinary rooms with TV, 2 have huge terraces instead of balconies, restaurant, often full. **D-E** *Mayfair and Rohma*, Dr Dada Vaidya Rd, T223317, F230068. Rooms with shower, some a/c with TV, single room discount, not much difference between 'standard' and 'deluxe', cheaper in *Mayfair* (non-a/c Rs 380, except around Christmas), in need of minor repairs, Goan and Continental restaurant. **D-E** *Neptune*, Malacca Rd, T224447. 37 very large rooms (Rs 350+) needing a coat of paint, some **D** a/c, all with bath, friendly but lacks character, good a/c restaurant, good value.

Sleeping
■ on maps,
pages 56 and 62
Price codes:
see inside front cover
Check out times vary;
usually between
0800 and 1200

Panaji & Central Goa

Some will accommodate a 3rd person in a double room with or without a mattress for Rs 50-100

E *Afonso*, near St Sebastian Chapel, Fontainhas, T22239. 8 rooms in a new family-run guest house, pleasant and friendly with bath and hot water. **E** *Orav's Guest House*, 31 Janeiro Rd, T426128. 16 pleasant rooms with shower, some with balcony, clean and homely, check-out 0900. Recommended. **E** *Park Lane Lodge*, rua de Natal, near St Sebastian Chapel, Fontainhas, T227154. 8 reasonable rooms (**D** over Christmas), some with bath (Rs 350), but most use clean common shower-room, rambling old house with character "but run by humourless Christian family", verandahs decorated with birdcages and plants in teapots, mediocre food, gates locked at 2230, yet popular with backpackers. **E** *Safari Lodge*, Cunha Rivera Rd, near Municipal Gardens, good value basic rooms (Rs 130). **E** *Tourist Home* (GTDC), Patto Bridge, near the Bus Station, T225715. 12 large rooms (3 beds), attached bath, dreary **F** dorm (Rs 50), standard government quality, often full, restaurant. **E-F** *Casa Pinho Lodge*, near St Sebastian Chapel, Fontainhas, simple rooms (Rs 200), dorm, pleasant roof terrace.

F *Frank's Inn*, 83 Menezes Braganza Rd, T226716. 10 rooms, shared baths, clean. **F** *Venite*, 31 Janeiro Rd, near the Tourist Hostel, T425537. 3 rooms with a common bath in an old colonial house (Rs 100-200), usually full throughout the year but arrive early as its worth a try, excellent restaurant (see below). Others nearby (usually rooms belonging to local families), include *Sonia Niwas Guest House*, with 7 ordinary rooms with bath, and *Poonam*. There are several **E** and **F** guest houses in the Fontainhas area with little to choose between them. During the high season, finding a room can be very difficult especially later in the day. Prices are usually highly inflated and bargaining fruitless. **F** *Youth Hostel* in Campal.

Dabolim airport The new **B** *Hotel Airport*, is aimed at business travellers, with 28 small but functional a/c rooms, rooftop terrace, restaurant/bar, a huge kitchen (for airlines catering!) and a pool.

Paying guests The Director of Tourism has a list of families. T226515.

Eating
• *on maps, pages 56 and 62 Price codes: see inside front cover Most restaurants here serve some alcohol*

None in the city has the atmosphere of a Mediterranean café with al fresco seating, though there are a few on rooftop terraces. Many close between 1500-1900, except for the South Indian and Goan cafés for snacks.

Expensive *Delhi Darbar*, M Gandhi Rd, T222544. Mainly North Indian, traditional Mughlai, varied seafood. A/c, excellent carefully prepared dishes (Rs 80-100 for main), impeccable service (clean toilets), very pleasant, reserve ahead for dinner, undoubtedly the very best in town. *Goenchin*, off Dr Dada Vaidya Rd. Tasty Chinese with spicy seafood options (Rs 80-140). *Mandovi*, D Bandodkar Marg. Good seafood and Goan dishes.

Mid-range *Chungwa*, in *Hotel Samrat*, Dr Dada Vaidya Rd. Authentic dishes (Rs65-80) cooked by Chinese chef. *Kwality* (Lisbon's) with a bar, Church Square. Chinese and Indian. *Le Millionaire* and bar, Padmavati Towers, 18th June Rd. Good Indian and Chinese. Pleasant atmosphere. *Quarterdeck*, near Betim ferry jetty. Goan. Pleasantly placed on the river bank, live music. *Venite*, 31 Janeiro Rd, near the Tourist Hostel, T225537. Excellent local Goan food. Rs 80+ for quality main dishes though pricier lobsters to order, menu rather limited now but mango juice is still heavenly. Arrive early to sit in 1 of 3 atmospheric narrow balconies overlooking the street on the first floor of an old colonial house, great ambience, good music, open 0800-2200 (closes in the afternoon and on Sun). Recommended.

Cheap *Annapurna*, Ormuz Rd. South Indian. Good thalis (Rs20) and dosa (Rs10) in large, clean eatery upstairs with families relaxing over chai. *Goenkar*, M Gandhi Rd, near Azad Maidan. Spicy Goan. Good choice of favourites (Rs35+), popular locally, choose a/c downstairs, or cheaper section above. **Kamat**, south of Municipal Gardens. Popular dining hall (a/c upstairs), excellent, *masala dosa* and *thalis* (Rs 30), no alcohol. **Sangeeta**, in *Hotel Neptune*, Malacca Rd. A/c, Rs 40 meals. **Shalimar**, M Gandhi Rd. Indian. Wide choice. **Shanbag Café**, opposite Municipal Garden Square, and **Sher-e-Punjab**, 18th June Rd. Generous, spicy, North Indian. **Taj Mahal**, M Gandhi Rd, opposite the Press. **Vihar**, R José de Costa. South Indian vegetarian. Well prepared tasty *thalis* and snacks, popular, convenient alternative to *Venite* when it is full.

Bakeries *A Pastelaria*, Dr Dada Vaidya Rd. Clean, glass cases, good variety of cakes, pastries and breads. *Mandovi Hotel* has a branch too (side entrance). **Simply Delicious** opposite *Hotel Sunrise*, 18th June Road, has appetizing cakes and pastries.

Cafés and fast food *Chicky Chocky* near the Church of the Immaculate Conception. Good selection of fast foods and '*Sizzle Point*' for speciality sizzlers. **Eurasia**, Dr Dada Vaidya Rd. Italian. Good pizzas, especially welcome when you are tired of curries.

Bars There is no dearth of bars in the city. Recommended for rooftop views is **Hotel Mandovi**'s, a good place for a chilled beer or wine and for meeting other travellers. *Panjim Inn* is becoming expensive but its large verandah is pleasant. For somewhere more modern and off-beat choose the *Taxi Pub* next to *Hotel Sona*.

Art gallery *Renaissance*, Rebello Mansion, 1st floor, behind FLG Garden, Campal, T225523, across the road from the Kala Academy, is an art gallery with a small café and a handicrafts shop.

Entertainment

Cultural centre *Kala Academy*, D Bandodkar Marg, Campal, T223288. The modern and architecturally impressive centre designed by Charles Correa was set up to pre-serve and promote the cultural heritage of Goa. There are exhibition galleries, a library and comfortable indoor and outdoor auditoria where performances are staged. Art exhibitions, theatre, and music programmes (from contemporary Pop, Jazz to Indian classical) are held, mostly during the winter months. In addition, courses on music and dance are offered.

Observatory *Astronomical Observatory*, 7th floor, Junta House, 18th June Rd (entrance in Vivekananda Rd) open in clear weather, 14 Nov-31 May, 1900-2100. Rooftop telescope and binoculars, plus enthusiastic volunteers. Worth a visit on a moonless night and for views over Panaji at sunset.

February: *Mahasivaratri* when Siva is honoured. The *Carnival* (3 days preceding Lent) is somewhat Mediterranean in essence, marked by feasting, colourful proces-sions and floats down streets; the procession starts near the Secretariat after midday. **March-April**: *Shigmotsav* is a spring festival held at full moon (celebrated as *Holi* else-where in India); colourful float procession through the streets often display mythological scenes. *Feast of Jesus of Nazareth*, is on the first Sunday after Easter. **November**: *Food & Culture Festival* at Miramar Beach (see below). **December**: *Feast of Our Lady of Immaculate Conception* (8 December), when a big fair is held.

Festivals

Books *Hotel Fidalgo* shop, has a reasonable selection, stocks postcards and some foreign newspapers. *Mandovi Hotel* bookshop has a good range, including foreign news magazines (Time, Newsweek etc), helpful staff. **Varsha**, near Azad Maidan, car-ries a wide stock in tiny premises, and is especially good for books on Goa, obscure titles are not displayed but ask knowledgeable staff.

Shopping
Mapusa & Margao have better municipal markets

Panaji & Central Goa

Clothes and textiles *Boutiques*, including a few on 18th June Rd, carry ready-mades. Some Indian-style clothes are sold at the Government Emporia where you can also get fabric by the metre, as you can at *Khadi Showroom*, Municipal (Communidade) Building, Church Sq.

Handicrafts Jewellery (some with a Portuguese hall-mark), particularly malachite set in gold filigree is a good buy. The bazars are worth browsing through for pottery and copper goods. Some hotel shops have jewellery, rugs and shell carvings. *Government Handicrafts Emporia*: *Goa* and *MP* at the *Tourist Hotels* and the Kadamba Bus Station; *Kashmir* and *Kerala* in *Hotel Fidalgo*, 18th June Rd; others on Dr RS Rd. *Acorn*, is near People's School, Patto Footbridge.

Photography *Fantasy*, Eldorado. *Souza Paul*, M Gandhi Rd. *Central*, *Tourist Hostel*. *Lisbon*, Church Square.

Provisions *Farm Products* outlet, north of Azad Maidan, and *Megsons*, 18 June Rd. Both are delicatessens selling cheese, cooked cold meats, Goan sausages and sweets (including *bebincas*), and ice creams. Many shops sell nuts (especially cashew) and dried fruit.

Sports **Soccer**: Professional matches are played at the stadium; season Oct-Mar. Details in local papers. **Walking**: There are some beautiful walks through the forested areas of Goa. Contact the *Hiking Assoc of Goa*, 6 Anand Niwas, Swami Vivekenanda Rd or Captain of Ports Office. **Water sports**: for para-sailing, wind surfing etc, contact *Aqua Sports*, Nizari Bhavan, T226960 with a complex has opened 2 km from Miramar beach. Some of the bigger beach resorts have windsurfing, sailing, water-skiing, parasailing etc. Diving is possible nearby from *Cidade de Goa*, Vainguinim Beach.

Tour operators *Alcon International*, D Bandodkar Marg, T/F232267. Recommended for quick, efficient and friendly flight bookings. *Citizen World Travels*, F/4 Gomes Building, 2nd floor, C de Albuquerque Rd, T227087. Friendly, helpful, efficient. *Sita*, 101 Rizvi Chambers, 1st floor, C de Albuquerque Rd, T221418. *Thomas Cook*, 8 Alcon Chambers, D Bandodkar Marg. 'Ferociously efficient' if slightly expensive. *TCI*, "Citicentre", 1st floor, 19 Patto Plaza, T224985.

Transport
See page 29 for general details
Local Bicycles: widely available for hire. *Stuart Silva*, opposite Azad Maidan, T224035, has spares. **Bus**: Main Kadamba and private bus stand are in Patto. State Kadamba Transport Corporation (KTC). Luxury and ordinary buses and private buses (often crowded) operate from the bus stand in Patto to the east of town, across the Ourem Creek, T222634. Booking 0800-1100, 1400-1630. Tourist information, 0900-1130, 1330-1700; Sun 0930-1400. The timetable is not strictly kept to as buses often wait until they are full. The minimum fare (for 3 km) is a rupee. Frequent service to **Calangute** direct from bus stand 23, 35 mins, Rs 4.50; **Mapusa**, 25 mins, Rs 3. Via Cortalim (Zuari bridge) to **Margao** 1 hr, Rs 8; **Vasco**, 1 hr, Rs 8. To **Old Goa** (every 10 mins) 25 mins, Rs 2.50, continues to **Ponda**, 1 hr, Rs 6. **Car hire**: *Sai Service* is recommended, 36/1 Alto Porvorim, just north of the Mandovi Bridge; T217065, F217064, or at airport, T514817; at Panaji T223901. They offer a good choice of Maruti cars for self drive, as well as chauffeur driven Marutis and Ambassadors. T217065, F217064. Airport Counter, T514817. *Wheels*, T224304, airport, T512138. **Private taxis**: charge similar prices. **Motorbike hire**: many beach resorts offer these. For tours, contact *Classic Bike Adventure* near New Patto Bridge (see also Mapusa), T273351, F276124. **Tourist taxis**: (white) can be hired from *Goa Tourism*, Trionora Apts, T223396, about Rs 6 per km. **Auto-rickshaws**: are easily available but agree a price beforehand (Rs 15-25). **Motorcycle-taxis**: are a bit cheaper. **Ferries**: flat-bottomed ferries charge a

nominal fee to take passengers (and usually vehicles) when rivers are not bridged. *Dona Paula-Mormugao*, fair weather service only, Sep-May, takes 45 mins. Buses meet the ferry on each side. Important ones include: **Panaji-Betim** (the Nehru bridge over the Mandovi supplements the ferry); **Old Goa-Divar Island**; **Ribandar-Chorao** for Salim Ali Bird Sanctuary; **Siolim-Chopdem** for Arambol and northern beaches; **Keri-Tiracol** for Tiracol fort. **Share-taxis**: run on certain routes; available near the the ferry wharves, main hotels and market places (maximum 5). **Mapusa** from Panaji, around Rs 10 each. Longer journeys, eg to Mumbai, are more comfortable with an overnight halt.

Air From Dabolim airport, 29 km via the Zuari bridge from Panaji, internal flights can be taken through *Air India*, T224081 to **Mumbai** and **Thiruvananthapuram**. *Indian Airlines*, T223826, reservations 1000-1300, 1400-1600, airport T0834-512788 have flights to **Bangalore**, **Delhi** and **Mumbai** daily and **Chennai**. *Jet Airways*, T221472, airport T510354, have flights to **Mumbai**. *Gujarat Airways*, T223730, to **Pune**. *Sahara*, to **Mumbai** daily, and **Delhi**.

Road NH4A, 17 and 17A pass through Goa. **Delhi** (1,904 km), **Mumbai** (582 km), **Calcutta** (2,114 km), **Chennai** (904 km), **Bangalore** (570 km), **Hyderabad** (712 km), **Mangalore** (371 km), **Pune** (505 km). **Bus**: There are long distance 'luxury' buses and 'sleepers' (with separate compartments giving a better chance of some sleep though bunks are shared.) **NB** The *Mumbai-Madgaon Express* train is cheaper, quicker and safer than taking the bus. It also allows you to see the lush environment, which you do not on the night bus. **Private operators**: *Laxmi Motors*, near Customs House, T225745; at Cardozo Building, near KTC bus stand: *Joy*, G10, T222493, *Paulo*, G1 T223059, *Saraswati*, G11; *Paulo Tours*, Hotel Fidalgo, T226291. **State buses** are run by *Kadamba TC*, *Karnataka RTC*, T225126, 0800-1100, 1400-1700; *Maharashtra RTC*, 0800-1100, 1400-1630. Buses to **Bangalore**: 1530-1800 (13 hrs), Rs 225; **Belgaum**: 0630-1300 (5 hrs); **Hospet**: 0915-1030 (10 hrs) Rs 75; **Hubli** many; **Londa**: 4 hrs on poor road, Rs 50; **Mangalore**: 0615-2030 (10 hrs) Rs 150; **Miraj**: 1030 (10 hrs); **Mumbai**: 1530-1700 (15 hrs), Rs 450 (sleeper), Rs 250; **Mysore**, 1530-1830 (17 hrs) Rs 200; **Pune**: 0615-1900 (12 hrs), Rs 250, Rs 300 (sleeper).

Check bus times and book in advance at Kadamba bus stand

Sea The fast catamaran service between Panaji and **Mumbai**, run by *Frank Shipping*, T228711 (which still carries the *Damania* logo in places), remains suspended despite schedules being printed in daily newspapers! The office in Panaji is becoming derelict, whilst the single catamaran is in a state of disrepair. Departures were from Fisheries jetty, 2 km west from Patto bus stations.

Train Rail bookings are made at Kadamba bus station, 1st floor, T225620, 232169, 0930-1300; 1430-1700. The South Central Railway service departs from Vasco; for details see the transport section for Vasco page 97.

Airline offices International *Air France*, T226154. *Air India*, 18th June Rd, T231101. *British Airways*, 2 Exelsior Chambers, opposite Mangaldeep, M Gandhi Rd, T224336. *Indian Airlines & Alliance Air*, Dempo House, D Bandodkar Marg, T224067. *KLM*, Thakkers, 205 Mahalaxmi Chamber, near Keni's Hotel, 18 June Rd, T224802. At 102 Rizvi Chambers, corner of Heliodoro Salgado and C de Albuquerque Rd *Air France* (and *Air Cananda*, *Biman*, *Gulf Air*, *Philippine Airways*, *Royal Jordanian*), T226154. *Jet Airways*, Rizvi Chambers, C de Albuquerque Rd, T221472, airport T511005. *PIA*, T226190. *Kuwait Airways*, 2 Jesuit House, Municipal Garden Sq, T224612. *Sahara*, Hotel Fidalgo, 18 June Rd, T230634.

Directory

Banks Many private agencies change travellers' cheques and cash. *Thomas Cook*, 8 Alcon Chambers, D Bandodkar Marg, T221312. Open 1 Oct-31 Mar, 0930-1800, Mon-Sat, 1000-1700 Sun; Apr-Sep, closed Sun, but open on most bank holidays except 16 Jan, 1 May, 15 Aug, 2 Oct.

Panaji & Central Goa

Recommended as the easiest and most efficient money changer in Goa. Also good for Thomas Cook drafts; money transfers from any Thomas Cook office in the world within 24 hrs. *Trade Wings*, Naik Building, M Gandhi Rd, T224576. *Wall Street Finance*, M Gandhi Rd, opposite Azad Maidan, T225399. *Amex* representative is at Menezes Air Travel, rua de Ourem, but does not cash travellers' cheques. Indian currency against certain credit cards are also given at some banks. *Central Bank*, Nizari Bhavan (against Mastercard); *Andhra Bank*, Dr Atmaram Borkar Rd, opposite EDC House, T223513, accepts Visa, Mastercard, JCB; *Bank of Baroda*, Azad Maidan, accepts Visa, Mastercard, and exchanges up to Rs 5,000 per day. ATM at *HDFC*.

Communications Couriers: *Blue Dart*, FO3 Sukerkar Mansions, T227768. *DHL*, Alcon Chambers 12, 13, D Bandodkar Marg, T226487. Open 0930-1900, Mon-Sat. *Skypak*, City Business Centre, Coelho Building, opposite Jama Masjid, T225199. **GPO:** Old Tobacco Exchange, St Thome, towards Patto Bridge, with Poste Restante on left as you enter. Open Mon-Sat 0930-1730, closed 1300-1400. Many letters are incorrectly pigeon-holed so you can do other travellers a favour by re-sorting any letters you find misplaced. **Telegraph Office:** Dr Atmaram Borkar Rd; also has STD, ISD and trunk services. *Haytechs Communications*, 6 Sujay Apartments, 18th June Rd. **Internet:** *Madhavashram's Cybercafé*, above *Café Real*, M Gandhi Rd, T224823, Rs 80 per hr, Rs 2 per min, discounted membership packages. *Pai's Cybercafé*, J Falcao Rd.

Cultural centres *Alliance Française* near Ourem Creek, T223274. *Indo-Portuguese Institute*, E-4 Gharse Towers, opposite Don Bosco School, M Gandhi Rd.

Embassies & consulates *Austria*, Hon Consul, DV Salgaonkar, 2nd floor, Kamat Centre, D Bandodkar Marg, T232011; *Germany* Hon Consul, c/o Cosme Matias Menezes Group, Rua de Ourem, T223261; *Portugal* 7-B Lake View Colony, Miramar, T224233, F44007; *UK* Agnelo Godinho, House No 189, near the GPO, T226824, F232828.

Libraries Some hotels/hostels now run 'book exchanges'; a deposit is usually required.

Medical facilities *Goa Medical College*, Av PC Lopez, west end of town, T224566, is very busy; the newer medical college is at Bambolim. *CMM Poly Clinic*, Altinho, T225918. *Sardesai Nursing Home*, near Mahalaxmi Temple off Dada Vaidya Rd, T223927, clinic 0800-1330, 1500-1630. *Dr Manu Shah's Clinic*, T/4 Shabana Chambers, near El Dourado, T227083, for acupuncture, osteopathy and naturopathy.

Tourist offices *Government of India*, Municipal Building, Church Sq, T223412. *Goa*, Directorate, Tourist Home, 1st Flr, Patto, T225583, F228819, goatour@goa.goa.nic.in Tours can be booked here but not GTDC accommodation; also Information desk at the *Tourist Hostel*, T227103, which is chaotic. There are counters at the Kadamba bus station, T225620 and Dabolim airport (near Vasco), T512644. *Goa Tourism Development Corporation* (GTDC), Trionora Apartments, Dr Alvares Costa Rd, T226515, F223926, gtdc@goacom.com, for GTDC accommodation. *Andhra Pradesh*, near *Hotel Sona*; *Karnataka*, Velho Filhos Building, Municipal Garden Sq, T224110. *Kerala*, T232168. Recommended. *Maharashtra*, near Mahalaxmi Temple. *Tamil Nadu*, Rayu Chambers, Dr AB Rd. **Guides:** for 4 persons, about Rs 250 per 4 hrs, Rs 350 per 8 hrs; excursion allowance Rs 250, overnight, Rs 800, foreign language supplement, Rs 100.

Excursions around Panaji

Chorao Island

Colour map 1, grid B3&C3 Chorao island, across the estuary from Panaji at the confluence of the Mandovi and Mapusa rivers, is rich in **wildlife**. Twenty-four hectares of the island are being adapted for fish farming. Conservationists succeeded in diverting the planned route of the Konkan Railway which was to cross the island potentially threatening its ecosystem.

    The banks along the Mandovi River are visited in the winter months by pintails, shovelers, snipes and terns. You may see blue-winged teals, maddar ducks, grey and purple herons and adjutant storks. A watchtower provides a vantage point for viewing. The mangrove forests containing 14 species (*Rhizophora, Avicennia, Bruguiera, Exocaria, Sonneratia* et cetera), form a protective habitat for coastal fauna and is now the focus of a range of conservation measures. In addition to birds, it harbours a large colony of flying foxes, some crocodiles, turtles and jackals.

The **Salim Ali Bird Sanctuary** occupies under 2 sq km of the western tip of Chorao Island. Local people are not even aware of its existence. The best way to go around the sanctuary is by boat. Find a local fisherman to row you quietly along the river for a close look at the mangroves. You may be asked for sums as high as Rs300-400 per hour but try to negotiate around Rs 50-100. Forest Department motor boats are supposed to operate but are rarely seen. You are likely to see a variety of birds according to the time of day and the season. Freshwater crabs and mudskippers are also much in evidence. Mudskippers are curious fish that slide out of the water at low tide onto the mud and are able to breathe through the mouth (in addition to their gills when in water). Their movable eyes on stalks on top of their heads help them to keep a close watch on predators and when necessary 'jump' half a metre! ■ *R 1. 0900-1700. The sanctuary is a short walk from the ferry ramp but there are no signs and there seem to be no roads or trails. Best season: Nov-Feb. No advance permission is needed.*

Buses travel along NH4A between Panaji and Ponda and stop at the Chorao ferry wharf in Ribandar. The ferry runs every 15 mins from 0600-2400, taking about 10 mins, fare Rs 2 (higher at other times).

Transport

Carambolim Lake (Karmali)

Carambolim Lake is a wide shallow lake, less than 3m deep, lying between the estuaries of the Mandovi and Zuari. The lake has a wide fauna, including 120 species of migratory and local birds similar to Chorao. Siberian pintail ducks, barbets, herons, woodpeckers, swallows, orioles, drongos and marsh harriers can be seen most of the year.

Colour map 1, grid C3
12 km east of Panaji, near the NH4A

Home to a wide range of varieties of wild rice, it has remarkably rich concentrations of detoxifying algae, some of which are believed to be responsible for the complete absence of mosquitoes in the area around the lake. The Directory of Indian Wetlands records that in winter it is host to the *Coccilellid* predator which feeds on rice pests.

Heavily silted up, the lake has been managed for many years, being emptied just before the rains for fishing and later re-filled through channels. The lake water is auctioned every April for its fish although fish numbers have deteriorated in recent years. Environmental groups suggest that a large section (nearly 20 percent) of the wetland may have been reclaimed by the Konkan Railway.

Goa Velha and Agassaim

As Richards says, **Goa Velha** means "old – being already old when the present named Old Goa (Velha Goa), was still young and flourishing". Goa Velha, once the centre of international trade along the Zuari, was destroyed by the Bahmani Muslims in 1470, although as Gopakapattana or Govapuri it had already suffered from repeated attacks and long term decline due to heavy silting.

Colour map 1, grid C3

It is difficult to imagine the splendid city here. A faded notice board standing on a pedestal by the main road, north of Agassaim, recalls Goa's ancient port capital.

In **Agassaim**, not far from the Zuari Bridge, the simple façade of 18th-century **Church of St Lawrence** hides a heavily gilded, rococo altar and reredos. **St Andrews Church**, north of the dispersed village, celebrates the *Procession of all Saints* of the Franciscan third order. On the Monday of Holy Week each year there is a procession with the church's 26 statues of saints which starts from St Andrews and winds down the main roads of Velha Goa village before returning to assemble in the dusty church square for a candle-lit service. The saints' statues remain in view in the church for two days to remind all of their good deeds. Dating from the 17th century (when the procession started from Pilar with over 60 statues), it is the only festival of its kind outside Rome. A fair is held where old fashioned hand-held fans, a local handicraft, are sold. Also actors and musicians perform in villages.

Pilar
Colour map 1, grid C3

The Pilar Seminary (Monastery) which still functions as a centre of religious instruction, is close to Goa Velha. It sits on a low hilltop which was once the site of a Siva temple. Relics of a headless *Nandi* (bull) and a rock carving of a *Naga* (serpent) among other carvings, were found here and are displayed in the museum (see below).

The seminary was founded by **Capuchin monks** in 1613, who remained here until their expulsion in 1835. The 17th-century church, dedicated to Our Lady of Pilar (brought from Spain), still shows faint remains of frescoes on the church walls, and also along the cloisters around the enclosed courtyard of the monastery. The Carmelites took over and restored the monastery in 1858, but from 1890 it became the headquarters of Missionary Society of St Francis Xavier. **Father Agnelo de Souza** (1869-1927) spent 10 years here in quiet meditation before dedicating his life to tireless service and awaits canonization. He is revered and remembered by worshippers at his tomb, especially at services on Thursdays throughout the year. The more recent extension which houses the present seminary has a small chapel with a fine marble altar and some German stained glass. Drinks and snacks are available.

The **museum** on the first floor of the seminary displays some of the finds from the Kadamba period; from the rooftop you can get good views of Mormugao harbour and the Zuari. ■ *1000-1700.*

Talaulim
Colour map 1, grid C3

Just north of the Pilar Seminary is the **Church of St Anna** (Santana) at Talaulim by the River Siridado, a tributary of the Zuari. Built around 1695, its elaborate Baroque façade is similar in design (though smaller) to the great Church of St Augustine at Old Goa (of which only part of one tower remains). The parish church once had a large congregation but it fell into disrepair when Old Goa nearby declined and had to be refurbished in 1907.

The five storeys provide an interior with great space under a high barrel-vaulted ceiling lit by two upper rows of windows which show off a profusion of stucco work. The shell-heads to the doors and niches on the lower floor attractively echo the design on the ornate façade. The church also has the unique feature of hollow side walls through which people secretly went to confession. The wooden image of St Anna above the chancel arch is particularly interesting. She appears as an elderly lady in a hat and carrying a stick, portrayed as she was reported to have appeared in separate visions to a Christian and a Hindu villager during the 17th century. The latter had also been miraculously cured by her and both said that the lady had requested a home in the village. St Anna is similarly portrayed in the choir grill and the nave.

St Anna's feast day (26 July) is celebrated by both communities who come to seek blessing from the mother of the Virgin Mary, whose intervention is traditionally sought by childless couples. It is known popularly as the *Toucheam* (or Cucumber) *Feast* because those who come to pray for a baby boy (*menino*) bring with them a *pepino* (cucumber). Unmarried boys and girls also come to pray for partners bringing with them spoons (*colher*) to plead for wives (*mulher*), and *mung* beans (*urid*) in exchange for husbands (*marido*)!

Transport

Buses travel along the NH17, the main Panaji-Margao road, and stop north of Agassaim at the bottom of the hillock. From there you can walk uphill through the new extension. It is best to take a taxi, motorbike or bike to get to Talaulim, which is 4 km north of Pilar.

Beaches and forts near Panaji

Gaspar Dias

Panaji & Central Goa

The second line of defence on this side of the estuary was a smaller fort near Miramar Beach. Built to pair with the fort at Reis Magos, it was particularly important in preventing the Dutch from gaining access into the Mandovi.

Colour map 1, grid C2

The small fortress at the point of Gaspar Dias, close to the existing fortification at Cabo, was completed at the beginning of the 17th century. The fort walls, probably made of laterite blocks which were 1½m thick and rose 5m, provided places for 16 cannons. The fort saw action when the Dutch attacked repeatedly up to the mid-17th century but its importance waned after the Maratha onslaught. The army decided to abandon Gaspar Dias after it was badly damaged during the mutiny of 1835 and although it housed recuperating soldiers for a time, by the end of the 19th century it fell into disrepair and ultimately crumbled beyond recognition.

All that remains of Gaspar Dias is the cannon at the 'Circle' in present day Miramar where it marks the possible site of the fort. The other four cannons (of the original 16) that were excavated can be found at the Directorate of Archives and the Abbé Faria monument in Panaji, and at the Farmagudi roundabout near Ponda.

Reis Magos

It is possible to visit the site of the small fort of Reis Magos to the northwest of Panaji, across the Mandovi, and the 16th-century church where the *Festival of Three Kings* is celebrated on 6 January each year (for further details see page 106).

Miramar

Miramar beach runs south along the Mandovi estuary, 3 km to the west of Panaji. It is very urban in character and since the beach is not particularly attractive it is hardly the place for a beach holiday. There can also be an undertow and the estuarine waters are polluted. Nevertheless it offers an easy escape from the bustle and heat of the city.

Colour map 1, grid C2

It is a pleasant drive from Panaji's seafront 'boulevard', along D Bandodkar Marg, the main road to Dona Paula. Most of the hotels are on, or just off this road. Take a taxi or one of the frequent buses which stop near the *Miramar Beach Resort*. Inland, the **Taleigao Church** has the image of Our Lady of Loreto. It had been moved there from its original chapel in Vainguinim to the south when it fell into disrepair after the Jesuits were evicted from Goa in 1759.

Sleeping **B** *Goa Marriott*, on Mandovi River, T237001, F237020. Big hotel, large rooms with balcony, tennis, squash etc. **C** *Blue Bay*, on Caranzalem Beach, T228087, F229735. 12 neat, modern rooms, some a/c (Rs 900), reasonable garden restaurant. **D** *Solmar*, D Bandodkar Marg (Ave Gaspar Dias), T230041, F426556, solmar@vsnl.com 34 grubby rooms (more under way), some a/c (Rs 750), 2 restaurants including *Mughal Mahal* with a bar, exchange, check-out 0900, 2 mins walk from beach. **D** *London Hotel*, T226017. 20 rooms, some a/c (Rs 700), better upstairs though not brilliantly maintained, restaurant, bar (pool tables draw large crowds at weekends), roof garden. **D** *Miramar Beach Resort*, close to the beach, T227754. 60 clean rooms, some a/c (Rs 600), better (and cheaper) rooms in newer wing by shaded groves, good restaurant, best of the GTDC hotels despite chaotic reception. Recommended. **D-E** *Bela Goa*, T224575, F224155. 11 simple rooms in an uninspiring building (Rs 525), surprisingly

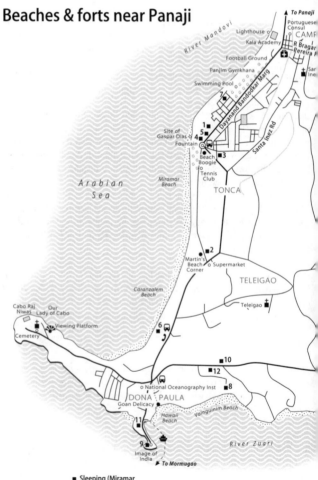

Beaches & forts near Panaji

To Panaji

River Mandovi

River Mandovi

Portuguese Consul

CAMP

Lighthouse

Kala Academy

R Bragan
Pereira P

Football Ground

Panjim Gymkhana

Sar
Ine

Swimming Pool

Dayanand Bandodkar Marg

Santa Inez Rd

Site of
Gaspar Dias

Fountain

1
5
4

3

Beach
Boogie

Tennis
Club

Miramar
Beach

TONCA

*Arabian
Sea*

2

Martin's
Beach
Corner

Supermarket

TELEIGAO

*Caranzalem
Beach*

Teleigao

Cabo Raj
Niwas

Our
Lady of Cabo

Viewing Platform

Cemetery

6
J

10

12

National Oceanography Inst

8

DONA PAULA

Goan Delicacy

Vainguinim Beach

11

Hawaii
Beach

9

Image of
India

To Mormugao

River Zuari

N

0 metres   200
0 yards   200

■ **Sleeping (Miramar
& Caranzalem)**
1 Bela Goa
2 Blue Bay
3 London
4 Miramar Beach Resort
5 Solmar & Foodland

6 Swimsea Beach Resort
7 Youth Hostel

**(Dona Paula &
Vaiguinim Beach)**
8 Cidade de Goa

9 Dona Paula Beach R
& O Pescador Resta
10 Mirabel
11 Prainha Cottages
12 Villa Sol

light and airy though no balcony, 2 a/c (Rs 900), restaurant, bar, enthusiastic staff.
F *Youth Hostel* away from the beach, T225433. 3 rooms (Rs 50 per person), 5 dorms
(separate men's and ladies', vacated during the day), maximum 3 nights, YHA members Rs 20, non-members except in Dec and Jan Rs 40, canteen, 1 day's payment for
advance reservation (not always necessary).

Mid-range *Beach Boogie*, Caranzalem Beach, towards Miramar bus stand. Garden
restaurant, varied menu, live music. *Foodland*, Miramar Beach Resort. Western, Goan.
Good fast food. *Martin's Beach Corner*, Caranzalem, near Blue Bay Hotel. Mostly seafood, open-air, uninspiring lacklustre staff but little else to choose from. *Quarterdeck*,
near Goa International. Try their South Indian fast food. **Eating**

November:*Food and Culture Festival* is organized by the Department of Tourism for
5 days at Miramar beach; visitors can sample Goan dishes and watch song and dance
performances, theatre etc. **Festivals**

Cabo Raj Niwas

*The former Portuguese fort is in a commanding position on the rocky promontory
between the two river estuaries.* *Colour map 1, grid C2*

From the roundabout by the National Oceanography Institute a road runs
600m up to Cabo Raj Niwas, now called **Raj Bhavan** (the State Governor's
House, hence not open to visitors). A platform near the entrance gives superb
views over the sweep of the coastline across the Mandovi estuary to Fort
Aguada. This is the site of the Portuguese 'Cabo' fort where only six cannons
and some sections of wall remain between the Raj Bhavan lawns and the cliff.

The first small shrine to **Our Lady of Cabo** was built in 1541 near the area
marked out for the future Cabo fort which acted as a landmark for ships at sea
and also gave the Franciscan friars, dedicated to preaching, a toehold on the territory. In 1594 the chapel had a convent added which was extended in the 17th
century. The excavated laterite for building created great hollows which were
covered to create useful rain water storage tanks. The chapel has a simple white
façade. Inside, the side altars have unusual eight-point stars (according to some,
'eight' signified regeneration and baptism); the memorial to Dona Paula de
Menezes (see Dona Paula above) is in a niche. The door to the Sacristy has carvings similar to Hindu temple art while outside, another ancient heavily carved
door leading to the back of the chapel is thought to have come from a ruined
convent in Old Goa. The *Feast* coincides with Independence Day, 15 August.

Documents of 1633 refer to the chapel and to various buildings of an
incomplete fort with only four guns. During the Napoleonic Wars British
troops garrisoned in the fort from 1799-1813 constructed more buildings for
themselves which were subsequently demolished by the Portuguese. Several
graves in the cemetery (which still has a gate and four walls), remain as stark
reminders. Around 1844, after the religious orders were abolished, the Archbishop of Goa was given the convent. It was refurbished and converted into an
impressive residence. This was later acquired by the Governor-General of Goa
and, further improved, became the Viceroy's official residence in 1918. Its
grand interior was allowed to remain untouched when the Portuguese left in
1961. The Raj Niwas's splendid glassed-in verandah on the seaward side is a
special feature

Dona Paula

Colour map 1, grid C2   *Quiet Dona Paula, 4km from Miramar, has a small palm fringed beach with casuarina groves and is very peaceful. Fisherfolk turned local vendors sell cheap seaside knick-knacks, testifying to it's popularity as a local picnic spot.*

Some say the place is named after Dona Paula de Menezes (the wife of a nobleman, Antonio de Souto Maior, and reputedly a mistress of the Viceroy), who died a young woman, in 1682. A black granite memorial stone can be found on a wall in the Chapel of Our Lady of Cabo. The family summerhouse still survives. Others link the village to a Dona Paula who reputedly jumped from the cliffs when refused permission by her father to marry Gaspar Dias, a fisherman.

The low laterite cliff forms a headland joined to the mainland by a short causeway. The platform on the highest point gives pleasant views out to the Arabian Sea and across the bay to Vasco da Gama and the very busy shipping lanes that lead to the port of Mormugao.

A white pavilion stands on the rocky islet at the end. In 1969, a sculpture by Yrza von Leistner was added to represent 'The Image of India'. The figures of a man and a woman, one looking east (or behind, and into the past) and the other west (or forward to the future), with an Asoka *chakra* (wheel) in the middle, speaks not only of India but of Goa. A Sanskrit *sloka* is inscribed below, with a translation in English: *Lead us from Untruth to the Truth, From Darkness into Light, From Death to Eternal Life.*

Entertainment   **Watersports** at the jetty are restricted to a few mins' ride in a motor boat or on a water scooter. Rs 40, 0900-1830. Popular with domestic visitors but looks hazardous.

Transport   **Bus**   Regular buses depart from Panaji to Miramar and continue to Dona Paula, Rs 5.
Ferry   A passenger ferry normally crosses over to Vasco (Mormugao) across the bay, but occasionally the jetty is hired out for private functions (eg a wedding) causing great irritation to the public. The ferry service was suspended in early 2000.

Directory   **Useful services**   Hospital T223026. Police T224488.

Vainguinim

Colour map 1, grid C2   *The beach just east of Dona Paula, in effect the private beach of the Cidade de Goa, is backed by a part of Tiswadi which the Jesuits enjoyed as highly productive land.*

The coastal strip's rich harvests of tropical fruits complemented the fish, crabs (*culleo*), tortoise and shellfish from the sea. The introduction of canal irrigation also saw a dry-season rice crop, the *vaingon*, and so the local people began to refer to the place as Culleovaingon or Curlavangni, now simply Vainguinim. After the Jesuits were ordered to leave, the government acquired all Church properties. This bit of the coast was for a time occupied by British troops sent to protect the Portuguese colony from a threat of attack by the French during the Napoleonic Wars, but they were forced to leave. The beach property was subsequently sold to a private bidder and in 1980 the *Cidade de Goa* was built to occupy the prime site.

Sleeping   **LL-AL** *Cidade de Goa*, 26 km from airport, 7 km from Panaji centre, T221133, F223303, hotelcdg@bom2.vsnl.net.in   210 rooms, 5 restaurants, pool with diving and casino (both open to non-residents), the latter with bizarre horse-racing game, Goa's only PADI course, imaginative development designed by Charles Correa, pleasant and secluded beach but unappealing at low tide. **B** *Mirabel*, opposite *Cidade de Goa*, T226879, F221397. 23 rooms, 2 restaurants, bar, pool, friendly service, partly renovated. **B** *Swimsea Beach Resort*, Caranzalem Beach, towards Raj Niwas, T227028, F224480. Medium-sized hotel, clean, airy, a/c rooms with balconies, sea-facing best (Rs 1,400), pool, very close to black sandy beach. **B** *Villa Sol*, T225852, F224155. 28 rooms with balconies, some a/c (Rs 1,750), disco/pub 'On The Rocks' (literally), good restaurant, small pool, built on high ground so a steep hike back from the beach. **B-C** *Pescador, Dona Paula Beach Resort*, T227955, F221371, pescador@goa1. dot.net.in 23 large pleasant rooms in small buildings around a garden, twice as expensive for a/c and sea-facing balcony (Rs 1,800), small garden restaurant, good pool, own little beach, quiet, pleasant, young friendly management. **B-C** *Prainha Cottages*, T227221, F229959, prainha@bom2.vsnl.net.in Range from Rs 1,200 to 2,100, 'Madeira cottages' best (a/c, nearer beach and with sea view), simple but comfortable and quiet, popular with packages, good restaurant, gardens, small pool, secluded (though not particularly clean) beach.

Eating *Cidade de Goa* has several up-market restaurants serving excellent food but at a price. The large sea-front 'coffee house' serves meals all day. *Goan Delicacy*, Hawaii Beach, southeast of National Oceanography roundabout, T224356. Tricky to find, overlooking Dona Paula and the sea, seafood, excellent menu of local dishes (Rs60-80 main courses), Tandoori Oven, bar, family-run, very friendly. *O Pescador* (Dona Paula Beach Resort) with good views over the jetty, serves seafood specialities. There is also a Punjabi *dhaba*.

Entertainment **Watersports**: *Barracuda Diving* and *Hydro Sports Club*, *Cidade de Goa*, T221133, from near the jetty.

Directory **Banks** You can change money in the larger hotels; otherwise the *State Bank of India*, 1000-1400, Mon-Fri, 1000-1200, Sun, will change TCs.

Panaji & Central Goa

Bambolim

Bambolim's dark-sand beach is secluded, free of hawkers and shaded by palms. Goa's university is nearby. It is 8 km from Panaji, off the NH17 southward bound. Close to Bambolim is **Siridao** which has a small secluded beach often good for shells. The *Feast of Jesus of Nazareth* is held on the first Sunday after Easter.

Colour map 1, grid C2
Population: 5,000

Sleeping & eating **B** *Bambolim Beach Resort* right on the beach, T230927, F230925. 120 a/c rooms, some facing the sea, simple but airy with balcony, open-air beach-side restaurant (breakfast included), bar, palm shaded terrace, pool, taxi necessary (usually available), peaceful, isolated spot. *Sand & Sea Restaurant*, down the beach will cook any kind of fish dish ordered (watch out for price quoted though).

Directory **Medical facilities** *Goa Medical College*, T223658. **Useful services** Police, T218551.

Excursions into the Portuguese past

The road to Old Goa from Panaji passes over the causeway which was built over a swamp in 1633 by the then Viceroy. It is a very attractive ride in the early morning, especially in the winter when mist often hovers over the still waters of the estuary.

Ribandar

Colour map 1, grid C3   At the end of the causeway is the attractive preserved village of Ribandar (pronounced Re-bunder) or "Royal Harbour", possibly named after the arrival of the Vijaynagar King in the 14th century. The old houses along the road, some substantial and some modest and painted in evocative colours, still conjure up an image of 17th-century Portuguese Goa. The **Church to Our Lady of Help**, originally built in 1565, gives thanks to the safe arrival of a Portuguese vessel after a fierce storm at sea. Today the ferry is in frequent use for crossing over to Chorao Island for visiting the Salim Ali Bird Sanctuary. It is the shortest route across to Mayem and Bicholim.

Old Goa

Colour map 1, grid C3
Also known as
Velha Goa

When Richard Burton, the explorer, arrived in Goa on sick leave from his Indian army unit in 1850 he described Old Goa as being a place of 'utter desolation' and the people 'as sepulchral looking as the spectacle around them'. The vegetation was dense and he had difficulty reaching the ruins. Today, Old Goa has a melancholy beauty, now revived by a steady flow of tourists and the great pilgrimage to the tomb of St Francis Xavier in the magnificent Cathedral of Bom Jesus. Visitors are mobbed by hawkers peddling postcards and souvenirs, and children selling candles.

Ins & outs   **Getting there**   From Panaji, there is a frequent bus service which takes 15-20 mins (Rs 4). Buses drop you off opposite the Basilica of Bom Jesus; pick up the return bus near the police station. Auto rickshaws charge Rs 25, taxis, Rs 150 return. **Getting around**   The major monuments are immediately around the bus stop and within easy walking distance.

Background

On the south bank of the Mandovi, Old Goa (or Velha Goa), on the crest of a low hill 8 km from Panaji, may be regarded by Christians as the spiritual heart of the territory. It owes its origin as a Portuguese capital to Afonso de Albuquerque, and some of its early ecclesiastical development to **St Francis Xavier** who was here in the mid-16th century. However, before the Portuguese arrived it was the second capital of the Bijapur Kingdom. Today, all the mosques and fortifications of that period have disappeared and only a fragment of the Sultan's palace walls remain (see also Goa Velha, page 69).

Old Goa was protected by a fortified wall. In the west lay the barracks, mint, foundry and arsenal, hospital and prison. On the banks of the river were the shipyards of Ribeira des Gales and adjacent to these was the administrative and commercial centre. To the east was the market, and the fortress of Adil Shah whilst the true centre of the town was filled with magnificent churches.

All of the churches of Old Goa used the local red laterite as the basic building material with limestone detail. The laterite exteriors were coated with a lime plaster to protect them from the weather and had to be renewed after each

Seeing the sights

Tours A visit to Old Goa is included in South Goa and Pilgrim Tours. They only spend a short time here so it may be better to arrive on your own steam a enjoy old Goa at your leisure.

Guides Official guides (with badges) are available at the major sites. Rs 100 for three churches, extra Rs 50 for each subsequent church.

monsoon. When maintenance lapsed, the buildings crumbled away. The Archaeological Survey of India is responsible for the upkeep of the churches. Some of the buildings are in ruins and thus can only be viewed from the outside.

Further reading: the ASI booklet on the monuments: *Old Goa* by S Rajagopalan, is available from the Archaeological Museum here, Rs 10. The attractive and much more extensive, illustrated books are, *Goa: a traveller's historical and architectural guide* by Anthony Hutt, 1988, and Maurice Hall's *Window on Goa: a history and guide*, second edition, 1995. They are available from several bookshops in Panaji, Margao and larger resorts.

Sights

As you approach the large central monuments you go over the 'Holy Hill' with a number of churches. The chapel (1526) belongs to the earliest period of church building and is described as Manueline. At the time of the conquest of Goa, Portugal was enjoying a period of prosperity under King Manuel I (r 1495-1521), hence the term. An architectural style evolved borrowed from Iberian decoration but also including many local naturalistic motifs as well as Islamic elements (seen on the marble cenotaph), owing to the Hindu and Muslim craftsmen employed. The church here has a two-storey entrance, a single tower and low flanking turrets. From this site Albuquerque directed the battle against the Adil Shahi forces in 1510.

Chapel of Our Lady of the Rosary

The chapel (1543), dedicated to the national saint of Portugal, and the tower of St Augustine are behind that of Our Lady of the Rosary. Although it is an uphill hike, it is very evocative and well worth the effort. St Anthony's was restored by

Royal Chapel of St Anthony

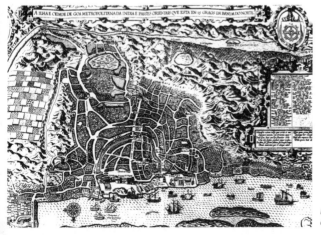

Plan of Velha Goa (north oriented downwards)

Panaji & Central Goa

the Portuguese Government in 1961. St Augustine's is now in ruins, except for the belfry. The building of St Augustine's church, which once boasted eight chapels, a convent and an excellent library, began in 1572 and was enlarged a few years later to become one of the finest in the kingdom. It was finally abandoned in 1835 because of religious persecution. The vault collapsed in 1842 burying the image, followed by the façade and main tower in 1931. Only one of the original four towers survives. The government plans to restore the tower and to make it possible for visitors to climb to the top. A heritage post box will also be placed in the tower.

Convent of St Monica (1607-27) The convent was the first nunnery in India and the largest in Asia. The huge three-storey, square building with the church in the southern part was built around a sunken central courtyard which contained a formal garden. At one time it enjoyed the status of Royal Monastery, now it is the Mater Dei Institute for Nuns, founded in 1964 for theological studies. Bishop Dom Frei Miguel Rangel in 1636 is believed to have seen a vision when the Christ figure on the Miraculous Cross here opened his eyes, as his stigmata bled and his lips quivered as if to speak. The vision was said to have been repeated later that year in the presence of the Bishop, the Viceroy Dom Pedro de Silva, and a large congregation.

The only other building on the Holy Hill is the **Church and Convent of St John of God** built in 1685 and abandoned in 1835. Descending from the Holy Hill you enter a broad tree-lined plaza with large buildings on either side. On conducted tours this is where you leave your transport and walk.

Basilica of Bom (the Good Jesus)
No photography, although this appears to be totally ignored by all
The world renowned church, a World Heritage Site, contains the body of **St Francis Xavier**, a former pupil of soldier-turned-saint, Ignatius Loyola, the founder of the Order of Jesuits. St Francis Xavier's remains form the principal spiritual treasure of the territory. The Jesuits began work on their own church in 1594 and by 1605 it was finished and consecrated. The order of Jesuits was suppressed in 1759 and its property confiscated by the state. The church, however, was allowed to continue services.

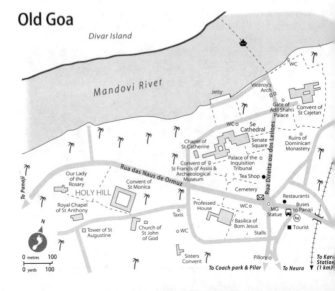

Old Goa

The church was originally lime plastered like the others but this was removed in 1956 to reveal the laterite base. The granite decorative elements have always been unadorned. The façade is the richest in Goa and also the least Goan in character. There are no flanking towers. It appears that the church was modelled on the earlier church of St Paul (now destroyed) which in turn was based on the Gesu, the mother church in Rome. There is only one tower in the building and that is placed at the east end, giving it a more Italian look. On the pediment of the façade is a tablet with IHS (Jesus in Greek or *Iaeus Hominum Salvator* – Jesus, Man's Saviour – in Latin). Apart from the elaborate gilded altars, and the twisted Bernini columns, the interior of the church is very simple.

Basilica of Bom Jesus

0 metres 20
0 yards 20

1 Chapel of the Blessed Sacrament
2 Our Lady of Hope
3 Main Altar
4 St Michael
5 Sacristy
6 Chapel of St Francis Xavier
7 St Anthony

The **Tomb of St Francis Xavier** (1698) was the gift of one of the last of the Medicis, Cosimo III, the Grand Duke of Tuscany, and was carved by the Florentine sculptor Giovanni Batista Foggini. It took 10 years to complete. It comprises three tiers of marble and jasper, the upper tier having panels depicting scenes from the saint's life. The casket containing his remains is silver and has three locks, the keys being held by the Governor, the Archbishop and Convent Administrator. The tomb lies to the right of the main chancel. There is often a fairly unruly scramble to take a photograph from the best vantage point whilst devotees offer prayers or quietly sing hymns.

You can look down onto the tomb from a small window in the art gallery next to the church

Exposition Initially after his canonization, St Francis' body was exposed for viewing on each anniversary of his death but this ceased in 1707. Since then only a few special private expositions were held until 1752 when it was again put in public view to dispel rumours that the Jesuits had removed the body. Since 1859, every 10 to 12 years on the anniversary of the saint's death, the holy relics are displayed. In 1953 it was decided that pilgrims should no longer touch the fragile relics so they were placed in a crystal urn. The last exposition was for six weeks between November 1994 and January 1995, the next is scheduled for January 2005. To enable easier viewing by the vast numbers who attend, the relics are taken to the Se Cathedral during this period. *Feast Day* is 3 December.

The body of St Francis has suffered much over the years and has been gradually reduced by the removal of various parts. Soon after his death a "small portion of the knee had been removed to show the captain of the ship on which his body was being carried" its unusually fresh condition. The neck had been broken in the Malaccas by placing the body in a grave which was too short. One devotee is reputed to have bitten off a toe in 1554 and carried it to Lisbon as a relic where it is still supposed to be kept by her family. Part of the arm was sent to Rome in 1615 where it is kept in the Gesu church. Part of the right hand was sent to the Jesuits in Japan in 1619. In 1890 a toe fell off and is displayed in an urn in the Sacristy of the Basilica.■ *Free. 0900-1230, (1030 on Sun) 1500-1830, closed Fri and during services. There is a modern art gallery next to the church.*

St Francis Xavier

The 35 year old Spanish Jesuit, Francis Xavier landed in Goa on 6 May 1542, after a journey from Portugal which had taken over a year. Called by Pope Paul III to serve as a missionary in Asia, on his arrival in Goa he agreed to join a newly established seminary as a teacher, where he remained for just under a year. He then moved to South India for two years before following the Portuguese trading route to the Malaccas. While working there he determined to take his missionary work to Japan and returned from the Malaccas to Goa. He spent a short time in Goa before re-embarking for the journey to Japan. Unable to carry out his work there because the Imperial authorities refused him a permit, he set sail to return to Goa but died on 2 December 1552 on Sancian (Chang Cheun), an island off the south Chinese coast near modern Hong Kong. His body was buried in sand, and lime was added to hasten decomposition. However, two months later when the grave was opened to transfer the bones, the body appeared fresh and totally unaffected. He was taken to Malacca for a second burial near the church of Our Lady of the Mount. The Viceroy of Goa subsequently had the body returned to Goa in 1554 when it was still found to be in an extraordinary state of preservation. The miraculous body has been venerated ever since by Catholics from all over the world.

For Roman Catholics St Francis Xavier's remains form the principal spiritual treasure of the territory. In 1613 the body of St Francis was taken from the College of St Paul in Velha Goa (Old Goa) where it had remained on being returned to Goa in 1554, and placed in the Professed House of Bom Jesus. It was moved into the Church in 1622 after his canonization, and to its present chapel in 1655 where it has remained ever since. St Francis was beatified in 1619 and declared a saint by Pope Gregory XV in 1622. In 1964 Pope Pius XII raised the church to a minor basilica.

Professed House Next to the church and connected with it, is the Professed House for Jesuit fathers, a handsome two-storey building with a typically Mediterranean open courtyard garden. It was built of plaster-coated laterite in 1589, despite much local opposition to the Jesuits. After a fire in 1633 destroyed it, it was only partially rebuilt. It now houses a few Jesuit fathers who run a small college.

Se Cathedral Across the square, the Se Cathedral is dedicated to St Catherine, on whose day (25 November) Goa was recaptured by Afonso de Albuquerque. The largest church in Old Goa, it is possibly the largest in Asia with a barrel vaulted ceiling. Built by the Dominicans between 1562-1623 in a Tuscan style on the exterior and Corinthian inside, the main façade faces east with the characteristic twin towers, one of which collapsed in 1776 when it was struck by lightning. The remaining one contains five bells including the Golden Bell (rung 0530, the 'Midday' Angelus at 1230, and 1830), cast in Cuncolim in 1652. (Resist the temptation to climb the old staircase to the top; it is unsafe.) The vast interior is divided into a nave and two side aisles. To your right is the granite baptismal font. On each side of the church are four chapels along the aisles: on the right to St Anthony, St Bernard, The Cross of Miracles and the Holy Spirit, and on the left, starting at the entrance, to Our Lady of Virtues, St Sebastian, The Blessed Sacrament and Our Lady of Life. The main altar is superbly gilded and painted with six further altars in the transept. The marble top table in front of the main altar has been used for the exposition of the relics of St Francis Xavier since 1955 in order that the large crowds could be more easily accommodated here. There is also an **art gallery**. ■ *Free. 0900-1230 (1030 on Sun), 1500-1830, closed Fri and during services.*

Se Cathedral

Panaji & Central Goa

Palace of the Inquisition Southwest of the cathedral's front door are the ruins of the Palace of the Inquisition. Over 16,000 cases were heard between 1561 and 1774. The Inquisition was finally suppressed in 1814. Beneath the hall were dungeons. In the heyday of Old Goa this was the town centre. Moving back towards the main thoroughfare you can see two other churches in the same complex as the Cathedral.

Church and Convent of St Francis of Assisi This is a broad vault of a church with two octagonal towers. The floor is paved with tombstones and the walls around the High Altar are decorated with paintings on wood depicting scenes from St Francis' life. The convent in the Portuguese gothic style was begun by Franciscan friars in 1517, and was later restored in 1762-5. It houses a **museum** and **art gallery** (see page 82).

St Catherine's Chapel The chapel was built on the orders of Albuquerque as an act of gratitude at having beaten the forces of Bijapur in 1510. The original church was built of mud and thatch, replaced two years later by a stone chapel which in 1539 became the Cathedral. Extended, possibly in 1550 (according to the inscription on the wall), and considerably renovated in 1952, the lime plaster of the simple façade sets off the exposed laterite sections.

Arch of the Viceroys (Ribeira dos Viceroys) To the northeast of the cathedral, on the road towards the Mandovi River, is the arch to commemorate the centenary of Vasco da Gama's discovery of the sea route to India. It was built at the end of the 16th century by his great-grandson, Francisco da Gama, who was Viceroy from 1597 to 1600. Built of laterite blocks, it is faced with green granite on the side approached from the river. This was the main gateway to the seat of power and on his arrival by ship each new viceroy would be handed the keys and enter through this ceremonial archway before taking office. The statue of Vasco da Gama above the arch was originally surmounted by a gilded statue of St Catherine, the patron saint of the city. The latter, however, was removed during the restoration in 1954 (now placed near the museum), together with the remains of a vaulted room which carried frescoes recording the wars fought by the Portuguese in India. A strange pair of figures appears on the back of the arch. A lady with a sword and book (possibly the Bible) stands above a lying figure of a man (a non-believer) in an awkward posture with his head resting uncomfortably on a bent arm.

Church of St Cajetan (Caetano) To the east of the arch stands the splendid domed Baroque Convent and Church of St Cajetan. A band of Italian friars of the Theatine order was sent to Golconda near Hyderabad on India's Deccan plateau by Pope Urban III to spread the Gospel but since they were not welcomed there, they moved to Goa to settle, later acquiring land to build this church around 1661, partly modelled on St Peter's in Rome.

Arch of the Viceroys

The façade with two belfries and tall Corinthian columns has four niches with figures of apostles alongside the three doorways. Inside, four enormous piers decorated with pilasters (one with a carved wooden pulpit), support the high dome above the drum, and create the aisles forming the cross. This is the last remaining domed church in Goa (others which appear domed are not). The vaulted ceiling has coffered floral decoration.

The main altar dedicated to Our Lady of Divine Providence has a free standing reredos which is elaborately decorated (as are the other six side altars), with gilded angels, cherubs, pilasters and scrolls while this rises to shafts of light beneath a golden crown. The oil paintings illustrate the life of St Cajetan whose altar is the larger one on the right. The small niches above have an attractive shell motif and along the walls there are carved wooden statues of saints. In the centre, under the dome is a curious platform which is thought to cover a 'well' which may have belonged to a Hindu temple on this site. Some think the device was incorporated into the building to provide the massive structure greater stability in difficult soil conditions!

The crypt below the main altar where the Italian friars were buried, has some sealed lead caskets containing, it is believed, the embalmed bodies of senior Portuguese officials who never returned home.

Beyond is the **Gate of the Adil Shah Palace** comprising a lintel supported on moulded pillars mounted on a plinth, probably built by Sabaji, the ruler of Goa before the Muslim conquest of 1471. The now ruined palace was occupied by Adil Shahi sultans of Bijapur who occupied Goa before the arrival of the Portuguese in 1510. It became the Palace of the Viceroys from 1554 to 1695.

Museums There is an archaeological museum and portrait gallery in the Convent of St Francis of Assisi. The collection of sculptures covers the period from before the arrival of the Portuguese. Many date from the 12th-13th centuries when Goa came under the rule of the Kadamba Dynasty. The exhibits include 'hero stones' commemorating naval battles and 'sati stones' (marking the practice of widow burning). There is also a fine collection of portraits of Portuguese Governors on the first floor which provides an interesting study in the evolution of court dress. ■ *Free. T286133 1000-1700, closed Sun.*

Sleeping & eating **E** *Tourist Hotel* (GTDC), near M Gandhi Statue Circle roundabout, T286127. 44 rooms in a poorly maintained building, mosquitoes (bring a net), adequate for an overnight stay for an early visit of the churches avoiding the crowds, friendly restaurant (limited menu). The teashop, near the Palace of the Inquisition Tribunal, is a good place for cool drinks.

Divar Island

Today Divar Island, only 9 km long by 4 km wide, is a deceptively quiet back- Colour map 1,
water. A site of great cultural significance to Hindus and of subsequent Muslim grid B3, C3
and Christian invasion, its fertile paddy fields which surround the steep wooded
hill rising to the centre of the island create a feeling of rural calm.

The island is approached by ferry from the Old Goa jetty (Arch of the Viceroys) to the **Ins & outs**
south; the Naroa ferry to the northeast; and from Ribander to the southwest. Ferries
are free and operate every 15-30 minutes. Divar comprised 4 villages, Navelim,
Goltim, Malar and Naroa.

Once an important Hindu pilgrimage place, a **Ganesh temple** stood on the hill
at Navelim in the centre of the island. Afonso de Albuquerque did not normally destroy Hindu temples in order to have churches built (most of the temples in Ilhas were destroyed after his death between 1540 and 1541). This
temple, however, was possibly the only exception since documents record the
presence of the original Church of Our Lady on the hill which the ailing Albuquerque saw from his ship before he died in 1515.

This is where **Nossa Senhora de Piedade** (Our Lady of Piety), which
replaced the second church to Our Lady of Divar, now stands (the original
chapel had been rebuilt and renamed Our Lady of Piety in 1625). There are
wonderful panoramic views from this hilltop site. The present church dates
from 1699-1724 and is ascribed to Fr Frias, a writer and 'architect'. The church
with its 'groined' vault with plenty of stucco decoration, has a nave but lacks
aisles. There are six altars and a highly decorative monumental pulpit. At the
top of the main altar is a lovely granite Piet'a set in a niche. The fine interior has
been restored, its restrained Baroque plaster decoration being highlighted in
pastel colours.

The insignificant looking cemetery chapel to the south has an interesting
heavily carved stone ceiling and two perforated windows in stone which
almost certainly belonged to the Ganesh temple; if locked, ask the resident
priest to open it for you. The Ganesh image was initially taken to Khandepar
(Ponda taluka), then to Naroa (Bicholim taluka) and finally to its present location in **Candola** in Ponda (see page 92).

The other place of pilgrimage was the 12th-century **Saptakotesvar temple** to
Siva built by the Kadambas which stood in the northeastern corner of the island
at Old Naroa but was ransacked by Muslim invaders in the mid-14th century.
However, like the Ganesh image and many other Hindu deities within Goa, the
faceted *dharalinga* made out of five metals (*pancha dhatu*) – gold, silver, bronze,
copper and iron – was hidden in a field and reinstalled nearby by a Vijayanagar
king in 1391. Again, a wave of Portuguese temple destruction around 1540 saw
the end of the new temple. The remains of the temple tank can be seen near the
small Portuguese **Chapel of Our Lady of Candelaria** (1563) which originally
incorporated the ruins of the Siva temple in its unusual circular structure, which
was later extended on either side. The Siva linga was subsequently smuggled
across the river to Bicholim taluka to be placed in a rock-cut sanctuary in a village which adopted the old name Naroa (*Narve*). The popular pilgrimage was at
the same time transferred to the deity's new location. The Saptakotesvar temple,
which still attracts a large crowd of worshippers, was renovated in 1668 under
instruction from the Maratha leader Sivaji.

Divar was the scene of 'forced' mass baptisms of Hindu islanders to Christianity in 1560 by the Portuguese. Many of the 1,510 new converts continued
to make the pilgrimage to the rehoused deity in Naroa in spite of strong

Panaji & Central Goa

attempts by the Portuguese to stop the practice. The Archaeological Museum in Old Goa has some sections from the two Divar temples in its collection. Some temple parts found their way into Old Goa as in the New Pillory which was put up at the end of the 17th century at the foot of the hill of the Cross of Miracles on the Neura road. Inscriptions discovered by Dr PP Shirodkar in 1983 suggest that the parts probably came from the Saptakotesvar Siva Temple from Divar (1391). A part of the temple's *deepstambha* (which shows places for lighting oil lamps), is under the font in the Church of St Francis of Assisi. The lower section of the lamp tower is in the Archaeological Museum there.

Festivals August: *Bonderam Feast* is held to mark the harvest on the island at Goltim on the last Sat. Before the feast, the villagers process with colourful flags and then hold a mock battle with fatass which are imitation guns made out of bamboo sticks.

Jua Island Jua is immediately east of Divar and is approached by road from Banastari to *Colour map 1,* the south. **Santo Estevam** (St Steven's Church) was built in 1759. The rococo *grid B3&4* style church, again with a false dome and lantern central to its plain façade, is flanked by two smaller domes on the towers. The attractive interior shows a lightness of touch; note the fine pulpit and ceiling decorations. On top of the hill immediately above the village, in the fort, there are excellent views from the modern shrine to Christ the King.

Ponda and the Hindu heartland

Ponda is one of the smallest of Goa's talukas but also one of the richest in terms of its Hindu religious architecture. Within 5 km of Ponda town centre are some of Goa's most important temples, including the Shri Shantadurga Temple, Queula, and the Nagesh Temple near Bandora. But it is also home to spice gardens and wonderfully scenic views from the low hills over the sweeping rivers. The Bondla Sanctuary in the east of the taluka, small though it is (and disappointing in terms of its wildlife), is a reminder of the once forest-rich environment typical of the foothills of the Western Ghats.

Ponda

Colour map 2, grid B3 *Once a centre of culture, music, drama and poetry, the area around the town has*
Population: 14,700 *a group of important Hindu temples. Today Ponda town is an important trans-*
port intersection due to its convenient central location. Here the main road from
Margao via the Borim bridge meets the east-west NH4A.

Ins & outs **Getting there** Buses to Panaji and Bondla via Tisk run along the NH4A which passes through the centre of town. It is best to have your own transport to see the places nearby. **Getting around** Autorickshaws and taxis can be hired from near the bus stand.

The drive from Panaji via Old Goa to Ponda goes through a prosperous agricultural region with a mixture of beautiful rice paddies on the valley bottoms and a wide variety of tropical palms – coconut and areca being particularly striking. The Zuari Bridge at Cortalim in Mormugao has been restricted to light vehicles and a ferry service has been reintroduced at that point. If the bridge closes for repairs then passing through Ponda will become a necessary part of the road journey for all routes between north and south Goa.

The **Safa Mosque** (Shahouri Masjid), the largest of 26 mosques in Goa, was built by Ibrahim 'Ali' Adil Shah in 1560. It has a simple rectangular chamber on a low plinth, with a pointed pitched roof, very much in the local architectural style, but the arches are distinctly Bijapuri. Built of laterite, the lower tier has been quite badly eroded. On the south side is a tank for ritual cleansing which has *meherab* designs. The large gardens and fountains here were destroyed during Portuguese rule. Today the mosque is attractively set off by the low rising forest covered hills in the background.

Sights

D *Menino*, 100m east of Bus Stand junction, 1st floor, T313148. 20 rooms, some a/c, pleasant, comfortable, good restaurant, an impressive modern hotel, good value. **E** *President*, 1 km east of bus stand, T312287. 11 rooms (Rs 300), basic but clean and reasonable. **E** *Padmavi*, 100m north of bus stand on NH4A, T 312144. 20 large clean rooms, some with bath with TV (Rs 400). *Menino* has a good a/c restaurant on the 1st floor with pleasant décor, serves generous main courses (Rs 60). Popular, good service, clean toilet. *Kirti*, Nirankal Rd is 2 km east of centre. Simple but clean a/c room upstairs, cheap, reasonable food. *Café Bhonsle* serves good South Indian snacks. Very popular with locals.

Sleeping & eating

At Dhavli South of Ponda, *Hill Billies Restaurant and Bar*, T316317, stages an occasional evening of Indian classical dances from 1930-2130, followed by a buffet, US$22 (pick-up from Panaji 1500). Contact Passive Active Tourism, T422986, josephb@bom2.vsnl.net.in

Entertainment

Hospital *Community Health Centre*, T312115. **Forestry** *Deputy Conservator of Forests* (North) T312095.

Directory

Temples around Ponda

The Hindu temples around Ponda give a fascinating insight into the distinctive character of Goan Hindu architecture. Try to visit the Nagesh, Mahalsa and Mangesh temples which are good examples of this local style.

Farmagudi

North of Ponda as you approach Farmagudi off the NH4A, there is a new **Ganesh temple** on the left. The temple was built by late Shri D Bandodkar, the first Chief Minister of Goa, who had the idol consecrated on April 24, 1966. It is a good specimen of Indian temple architecture synthesizing both ancient and modern styles. Opposite is a **statue of Sivaji** which commemorates the Maratha leader's association with Ponda's fort. The stone image of Gopal Ganapati was discovered by herdsmen while grazing cattle near the hill and later installed in a small shrine with a thatched roof. **Ponda fort** was built by the Adil Shahi rulers and was destroyed by the Portuguese in 1549. It lay in ruins for over 100 years before Shivaji conquered the town in 1675 and rebuilt it. The Portuguese Viceroy attempted to re-take it in October 1683 but quickly withdrew, afraid to take on the Maratha King Sambhaji who suddenly appeared with his vast army. The episode is commemorated in Farmagudi by an equestrian statue.

Colour map 2, grid B3

C-D *Atish*, T313224, F313239. 40 comfortable rooms, some a/c (Rs 800), restaurant, pool, gym, good modern hotel, friendly staff. **E** *Farmagudi Tourist Cottages* (GTDC), 312922. 39 rooms, attractively located, though too close to NH4A (Rs 260), adequate restaurant with standard government fare (eat at *Atish*).

Sleeping & eating

Bandora

Colour map 2, grid B3 The **Shri Nagesh Temple** is 4 km northwest of Ponda. At Farmagudi junction on the NH4A, a fork is signposted to Bandora. A narrow winding lane dips down to the tiny hamlet of Bandora and its temple to Siva as Nagesh (God of Serpents).

The temple's origin can be established at 1413 by an inscribed tablet here though the building was renewed in the 18th century. The temple tank which is well-stocked with carp, is enclosed by white-outlined laterite block wall and surrounded by shady palms. The five-storey lamp tower near the temple has brightly coloured deities painted in niches just above the base.

The main *mandapa* (assembly hall) has interesting painted woodcarvings illustrating stories from the epics *Ramayana* and *Mahabharata* below the ceiling line, as well as the *Ashtadikpalas*, the eight directional guardians (Indra, Agni, Yama, Nirriti, Varuna, Vayu, Kubera, Ishana). The principal deity has the usual *nandi* and in addition there are shrines to Ganesh and Laxmi-Narayan and subsidiary shrines with lingas, in the courtyard. The *Nagesh Jatra* (November) is celebrated at full moon to commemorate Siva's victory.

South of the Nagesh Temple is the **Mahalakshmi Temple** which lies in a valley below the road and is thought to be the original form of the deity of the Shakti cult. Mahalakshmi was worshipped by the Silaharas (chieftains of the Rashtrakutas, 750-1030 AD) and the early Kadamba kings. The sanctuary has an octagonal tower and dome while the side entrances have shallow domes. The stone slab with the Marathi inscription dating from 1413 on the front of the Nagesh Temple refers to a temple to Mahalakshmi at Bandora. The *sabhamandap* has an impressive gallery of 18 wooden images of Vishnu. Mahalakshmi wears a linga in her head dress, and is considered a peaceful form of Devi.

Velinga

Colour map 2, grid A3 **Lakshmi-Narasimha Temple**, Goa's only temple to Vishnu's fourth *avatar*, the Lakshmi-Narasimha or Lakshmi-Narayana is just north of Farmagudi (see page 247). The small half man, half lion image was originally in a temple in Sancoale (Salcete) which was burnt down and destroyed by Diogo Rodrigues, the Captain of Rachol Fort in 1567 (who had by then destroyed temples in 58 villages and a mosque in Mormugao). The Shantadurga temple shared a similar fate.

This present temple dates from the 18th century and is fairly typical in style though the tower and dome over the sanctuary are somewhat Islamic. Inside there are well carved wooden pillars in the *mandapa* and elaborate silver work on the screen and shrine. The large spring-fed temple tank has steps down to the water on each side and is enclosed by a niched wall. A tall cosmic pillar with rings stands in the courtyard.

Mardol

Colour map 2, grid A3 The **Mahalsa Narayani Temple** is 2 km from Shri Mangesh. Here *Mahalsa* is a Goan form of Vishnu's consort Lakshmi or according to some, his female form *Mohini* (from the story of the battle between the *devas* and *asuras*). The deity, originally housed in a "fabulous" temple at Verna in Salcete taluka, was rescued and brought to Mardol around the same time as the Sivalinga of Shri Mangesh found a home nearby.

Shri Nagesh Temple lamp tower

You enter the temple complex through the arch under the *nagarkhana* (drum room). There is a seven-storeyed *deepstambha* which is lit up with lamps on special occasions, and a tall brass *Garuda* pillar which rests on the back of a turtle; the half human-half eagle *Garuda*, Vishnu's vehicle, sits on top. The pillar acts as a second lamp tower. The temple complex was renovated and extended in 1995.

The new *mandapa* (columned hall) is made of concrete, its severity hidden somewhat under the red tiling, finely carved columns and a series of brightly painted carvings of the 10 *avatars* (incarnations) of Vishnu (see page 247). The unusual dome above the sanctuary is particularly elegant.

The present *tulsi vrindavana* (basil enclosure), however, sadly replaces an earlier one of massive proportions. The original, which many would argue was worth restoring and preserving, was a fine example of its type, complete with arched niches, columns and balustrade, representing the influence of church architecture in the temple grounds. The large wooden *ratha* (temple car) for the deity can be seen in one corner.

A decorative arched gate at the back leads to the peace and cool of the palm-fringed temple tank. A palanquin procession with the deity marks the *Mardol Jatra* in February. *Mahasivaratri* is observed in February-March, while *Kojagiri Purnima* is celebrated at the August-September full moon.

Priol

The **Shri Mangesh Temple** is to the northwest of Ponda on the NH4A leading to Old Goa. The 18th-century temple to Siva as Mangesh, set on a wooded hill at Priol, is sometimes described as the most important Hindu temple in Goa. *Colour map 2, grid A3*

The *linga*, the representation of Mangesh, was originally in an ancient temple in Kushatali (Cortalim in Salcete taluka), across the river. However, after the Inquisition began in 1561, soldiers set out to destroy Hindu temples throughout Salcete and the deity was carried across the river to Priol. The devotee who saved the linga, named Mukto, has a shrine to his memory in the temple complex. The main linga was initially placed in a small shrine until in the mid-18th century an influential Hindu was able to acquire an estate for the present impressive temple complex. When the Portuguese regained control they exercised a far more liberal policy towards the Hindus and Muslims. Today the temple is supported by a large resident community who serve its various functions.

Ponda Taluka

Ponda Taluka, officially regarded as in North Goa, is actually right in the centre of the state.

The Zuari, for most of its short course a broad, languid and apparently tranquil river, was for 200 years a critically important barrier between the Christianized Old Conquests and the Hindu east. Forming Ponda's southwestern border with Salcete and Mormugao, Hindus fled the Inquisition to the comparative safety across the river, taking some of their most important idols with them. The river provided security.

Before the arrival of the Portuguese, Ponda had been regarded as an area of little use because it had none of the resources which made the coastal region of Tiswadi so well off, and its relative poverty had resulted in an almost total absence of stone built temples. The Zuari provided the defensive moat behind which the unique Hindu temples of contemporary Goa could be established.

Yet the resurgence of Hinduism is not without irony, for during the first two centuries of Portuguese rule in the Old Conquests, Ponda was ruled by the Muslim king of Bijapur. The district had come under Portuguese attack in the first wave of settlement led by Albuquerque. However, the family of Adil Shah, Sultan of Bijapur, fought back and quickly retook

the town and district. They built the Safa Mosque, which today is one of the relatively few significant Muslim buildings left in Goa. The Muslims were defeated by the Maratha Hindu leader Sivaji and Ponda was not re-incorporated into Portuguese Goa until it was ceded by the Hindu King of Sunda in 1763. By this time the Portuguese were less inclined to interfere with local custom and religious belief, and both Muslim and Hindu places of worship were respected.

If Ponda's history has been significantly shaped by the security afforded by the Zuari and the Cumbarjua Creek to its west, it is Goa's other major river, the Mandovi, which separates it from the rapidly industrializing northern district of Bicholim, with its massive opencast iron ores workings. Ponda too now has its share of iron ore and industrial development, as the environmentally controversial plants at Siroda in the south demonstrate.

Its own development has been increased by its newly strategic location on the national highway, the main route between Panaji and Belgaum. Yet despite the opening of a new bridge across the Zuari at Borim which now gives a direct road link to Margao and the south, many parts of the district are relatively isolated and Ponda also still has extensive areas of almost untouched forest.

The temple complex is architecturally typical of the highly distinctive Goan Hindu temple style. It has seen many additions and alterations through the years including pilgrims' rest rooms, but not always for the better. Sadly the *nagarkhana* (drum tower) over the arched gate which earlier had a pleasing red-tiled pitched roof is now a far poorer structure.

Although there is an arched entrance to the site near the main road, about 1 km from the temple itself, a lane by-passes this arch and leads up to the car park. Pilgrims walk up the path to the drum tower entrance. The farm land of the estate on which the temple depends provides a beautiful setting. Note the attractive temple tank on the left as you approach which is one of the oldest parts of the site. You can get a good view of the temple with its tank in the foreground by climbing the wall into the coconut grove. The tank is surrounded by striking, carefully pointed (mortared) laterite blocks, and on the higher ground behind it rises the lamp tower.

You enter the temple through an arch into the wide open courtyard. The seven-storeyed octagonal *deepmal* or *deepstambha* immediately in front of you, reputed to be the most famous lamp tower in Goa, is a typically stunning

Shri Mangesh – Siva in Goa

Panaji & Central Goa

The origin of the sanctity of all Hindu sacred sites is explained in mythical stories. Shri Mangesh is no exception. Hall recounts that in one of the stories explaining the origin of the Shri Mangesh temple, Siva had staked everything he possessed on a game of dice against Parvati and lost. He had to leave his home on Mount Kailasa and wandered south and chanced upon a spot in Goa, near Kushatali (present day Cortalim), where he remained to meditate. When Parvati came in search and was lost in a forest she was faced with a fierce tiger and called out for help to her husband. Crying out in her confusion to "Mam Girisha!" which gave rise to yet another name for Siva. The linga which was found in Kushatali was housed in a small temple to Shri Mangesh there.

white, but around its base are colourful little 'primitif' painted images, red and yellow on a blue background. Lamps are placed in the niches at festivals. The sacred *tulsi vrindavan* (basil enclosure) which is often seen in a modest scale in front of a Hindu home, stands nearby. The highest tower (two-storeyed) with an octagonal drum topped by a dome is over the sanctum. The octagonal entrance hall and the two side entrances also have domes above.

Shri Mangesh Temple

The *mandapa* (assembly hall), has the typical red-tiled, steeply pitched roof. At the entrance to the shrine, where you leave your shoes, is a beautifully carved wooden door. Nineteenth-century Belgian glass chandeliers hang from the ceiling of the main hall, usually crowded with pilgrims making offerings of flowers and coconuts bought at the entrance. The *nandi* (Siva's bull) is present, as are the silver *dwarpalas* (guardian deities) and the additional shrines to Parvati and Ganesh. The image of the deity is housed behind a highly decorated silver screen. Inside, it has eight white pillars, approximately 2½m high, supporting broad arches. The cusped arches above the windows illustrate a Muslim architectural influence.

As in nearly all major temples there are several subsidiary temples or "affiliated deities" (*parivar devtas*). On either side of the screen at the far end of the main temple are shrines to Ganesh on the right and Bhagavati (Parvati) on the left, while Devasharma is near the main temple in the courtyard. Nearby is a *nandi* which is particularly worshipped by the clan of Gaud Saraswat Brahmins who are the temple's *mahajans* (trustees). There are numerous other minor shrines. Behind the main temple are further shrines. Garlands of flowers for offering at entrances are Rs 5. Huge temple cars shelter to the northwest of the temple. During *Mangesh Jatra*, the *rath* (temple car) with Shri Mangesh is pulled by crowds of attendants.

The complex, with its *agrashalas* (pilgrims' hostel), administrative offices and other rooms set aside for religious ceremonies, is representative of Goan Hindu temple worship.

Oracles of Shri Mangesh

The Shri Mangesh temple was famous as a centre for various oracles (fortune tellers). Gomes Pereira records that one such oracle specialised in interpeting cases of crime. He would sit quietly shuffling grains of rice, which he would continue to do when any client came to seek his help in solving a crime. Without asking any questions or being told anything about the case he would simply describe the nature of the crime and then outline the chief characteristics of the perpetrator. Unlike other clairvoyants he never went into a trance but remained conscious and quiet throughout.

Other oracles in the temple practised a form of self-hypnosis called "bhar", and clairvoyancy, when dampened petals or leaves were attached to the statue of the village deity, leaves being fixed at 49 predetermined points. As they dried some fell off, and the question asked by the enquirer is answered by the pattern of the remaining leaves. These practices are still carried out.

Queula

Colour map 2, grid B3

One of the largest and most famous of Goa's temples dedicated to **Shri Shantadurga** (1738), the wife of Siva as the Goddess of Peace, lies just 3 km southwest of Ponda's town centre bus stand. The form of Durga was so named because at the request of Brahma she mediated in a great quarrel between Siva (her husband) and Vishnu, and brought back peace (Sanskrit – *shanti*) in the Universe. Hence, in the sanctuary she stands between the two other deities.

The temple is set in a picturesque forest clearing on a hillside at Queula (Kavale) and was erected around 1738 by Shahu, a grandson of Sivaji, the great Maratha ruler of the West Deccan. The deity, originally from Quelossim (also called Queula) had been taken to Ponda 200 years earlier.

Steps lead up to the temple complex which has a very large tank cut into the hillside and a spacious courtyard surrounded by the usual pilgrim hostels and administration offices. There is a six-storey *deepstambha* (lamp tower) and subsidiary shrines while the part-gilded *rath* (car) is also housed in the compound. The temple, neo-classical in design, has a tall tower over the sanctum. Its two-storey octagonal drum, topped by a dome which has a lantern on top, is an example of the strong influence of church architecture on Goan temple design. The interior of polished marble is lit by several chandeliers. Beyond the hall is the sanctum where the principal deity of Shantadurga, flanked by Siva and Vishnu, is housed behind a silver screen.

In December, there is a *Sangeet Sanmelan* (festival of classical singing) which honours the memory of Dinanath Mangeshkar, and in late January, a special ceremony is held to honour the *Mhars* or *Harijans* ("outcastes") who are not otherwise expected to enter temple precincts. The following day the temple goes through a "purification ceremony". *Kavale Jatra* (February) is marked by a procession of devotees accompanying the deity in a palanquin.

Shri Sausthan Goud Padacharya Kavale Math, named after the historic seer and exponent of the Advaita system of Vedanta, was established in Salcete between Cortalim and Quelossim (now in Mormugao). The Math was destroyed in the 1560s during the inquisition and transferred to Golvan and Chinar outside Goa. After 77 years, in the early 17th century, the Math was re-established here in Queula, the village where the Shantadurga deity (which had also originated in Quelossim), had been reinstalled. There is a temple to Vittala at the Math. There is another Math of the same foundation in Sanquelim.

Durbhat

Southwest from Queula, the road towards the river ends at Durbhat which was *Colour map 2, grid B3* once an important port on the Zuari. Although river transport remains important, the Zuari and the Mandovi both being vital arteries for the transport of iron ore, the port here has lost its significance as road transport has improved.

Close by, at **Agapur**, an old Madhavdeo complex of three small shrines found on a low hill. The three cell structural complex built out of laterite with a typical water tank is dated to the 11th century. The period of temple building when carpenters-turned-stone-masons continued to imitate wooden constructions is well illustrated here, especially since the mortarless masonry structures have not been covered by later plaster work. The stylized lotus-bud domes of the temples are well preserved and are particularly interesting since inside they are in fact *sikhara* style (as found in towers above sanctuaries of northern temples). Unlike later Goan temple domes which appear to have been influenced by Islamic or Christian architecture, here the corbelled dome is a pure Hindu feature. The condition of the shrines suggest that they had been protected from heavy rain by secondary roofing, possibly supported originally on attractively carved wooden columns. The present tiled roof over the ancient structure is, of course, a more recent addition.

Siroda

The **Kamakshi Temple** to the south of Ponda taluka is dedicated to a form of *Colour map 2, grid B3* Shantadurga (see Queula above). The image, together with the affiliate deities Raieshwar Siva and Lakshmi Narayana, had been rescued from Raia across the Zuari around 1564, when the original temples were destroyed by the Portuguese. The temple with an unusual sanctuary tower with a tiled roof has four kneeling elephants at its base. The red pyramidal tiled roofs on the *mandapas* and atop the *nagarkhana* over the arched entrance gate are also attractive.

The 16th century **Sivnatha Temple** was founded by a holy man 'Sidha'. The deity is taken out in a palanquin for *Siroda Jatra*.

Excursions around Ponda

The forest-rich environment of the foothills with scenic views over rivers, nurtures the Bondla Sanctuary and spice plantations. A visit to Savoi Verem plantation north of Ponda can be enjoyable and surprisingly informative, while Khandepar, northeast of Ponda has 10th-11th century cave sanctuaries.

Here is the site of Albuquerque's hard fought battle of 1512. Banastari lies 5 km **Banastari** east of Old Goa on the national highway. It is remembered for its clandestine *Colour map 2, grid A2* "Night bazaar" which would start trading at midnight on Fridays and continue until midday on Saturday, where stolen Portuguese goods as well as fruit and vegetables were bought and sold. Banastari still holds a traditional local bazar.

Marcela, north of Banastari, has a number of Hindu temples where most of the **Marcela** deities come from *Ilhas* in the Old Conquest territory, in particular from *Colour map 2, grid A2* Chorao. The village has several 'wedding halls' so is often busy, especially on auspicious dates of the Hindu calendar. **Shri Ravalnatha-Devki Krishna** has the most important deity in the village, which originally came from Chorao Island (Ilhas, now Tiswadi). The *festival* at full moon in January is celebrated with palanquin processions.

Candola
Colour map 2, grid A2

Candola has one of two Ganesh temples in the state. The ancient Ganapati image in the **Ganesh Temple** was originally installed in the Kadamba Temple at Navelim (Divar Island) and was moved to a place of safety when Albuquerque ordered a new church to Our Lady of Divar to be built on the site of the Hindu temple. It appears to have been first taken to Khandepar (Ponda), then to Naroa (Bicholim) and finally brought to Candola. Sections of the ancient temple can still be seen in the centre of Divar Island. See page 83.

Today the old Ganesh image which occupies a subsidiary position in the sanctuary has been replaced by a new one. The black Kalbhairav image of Siva which is also here was found in a house in the village where it had been used as a weight for weighing rice on scales; since the block was a little too heavy a corner was knocked out to make it equal to a *maund*! Other temples in Candola also house deities which had ancient origins, including Shri Bhagvati from Aldona (Bardez).

Around Ponda

Savoi Verem
Colour map 2, grid A3

Southeast of Candola, outside the village of Savoi, the **Ananta temple** dedicated to Vishnu as *Sheshashahi Ananta*, stands peacefully in a rural setting. The plain white exterior with pitched tiled roofs contrasts with the brightly coloured carvings on the wooden pillars and supporting beams of the *mandapa*. Visitors are allowed to view the principal deity which is carved on a black stone. The reclining Vishnu with the distinctive conical headdress, rests on the coils of the serpent *Ananta* (or *Shesha*) protected by his hood. He is shown in the period intervening between the creation of one world and the next, when a lotus emerges from his navel supporting Brahma the Creator.

The village's ancient Hindu roots are borne out by the 10th-century medieval basalt image of Vishnu showing his 10 incarnations (*avatars*) which was found here and is displayed in Old Goa's Archaeological Museum (No 320).

Savoi Spice Plantation

Colour map 2, grid A3

The plantation, now over 200 years old, covers 40ha focused around a large irrigation tank. Half the area is wetland and the other half on a hillside, making it possible for a large variety of plants and trees to be grown here.

Ins & outs

The plantation is 6 km from Savoi. Buses go from Ponda (towards Volvoi), and also from Banastari; it is best to ask for "plantation". Taxis ply from the coastal resorts (eg Rs 700 return from Candolim) but it is better value to ask a travel agent as many offer competitive rates which include the entrance fee (eg *Day Tripper Tours*, near Kamat Complex, Calangute, Rs 770). Some also throw in a visit to a local cashew nut processing plant.

The plantation was founded by Mr Shetye whose portrait hangs in the reception area/restaurant. It is still being run by the family (fourth generation) who donate funds to local community projects such as the school and temple. The families employed on the site are housed on the estate and men, women and the older children can be seen working at different seasonal tasks. Retired employees are encouraged to remain active by producing handicrafts for sale to visitors.

A large banyan tree stands here like a benevolent spirit; locals offer prayers along with feni, bread & bananas

The guided tour along shady paths, takes about an hour and includes soft drinks and snacks on arrival, and concludes with a chance to buy packets of spices which make ideal gifts to take home and a tot of feni to "give strength" for the return journey to your resort. You will even be offered several cheap, natural alternatives to Viagra, whether you need them or not! The tour is excellent, with detailed descriptions of the various plants including their medicinal and food uses. If you are able to spend just one day away from the beach, then a visit to Savoi is highly recommended.

On your walk, you will pass grapefruit, areca palms (some over 150 years old), and coconuts with pepper vines growing up their trunks, bay, cloves, *papaya*, bread fruit and *cocum*. The last has a scarlet flesh and once eaten the skin is cut into strips and sun-dried to turn into black *sola* used for flavouring curries. *Bimla*, akin to star fruit, hang like bunches of large green grapes and are especially good for prawn curries and pickles. You will be shown soft and hard skin jackfruit, which can grow to giants weighing over 20 kilograms, and banana plants which can produce 250 bananas from a single flower; one flower is cut off each plant to be eaten as a vegetable delicacy. The unripe jackfruit when used in curry has a strong resemblance to meat so in parts of the country it is called the 'tree goat'. The large banyan tree here stands majestically and is visited on Wednesdays and Sundays by local people with offerings who seek its blessing.

On the hillside grow pineapples, bamboo, basil, cardamom, cocoa, wood-apple, mangoes, and the surprising nutmeg (male and female) which you might mistake for lemons. No space is wasted on this densely cultivated plantation. Even the staple tuber (*suarn*), is grown under the surface, some of which can weigh up to two kilograms. The ubiquitous coconut is not only prized for its fruit which is cut off every three months but also the leaves used for thatching and the trunks for building. One of the experts will demonstrate the art of coconut picking by shinning up a tall palm with his feet tied together in a circle of rope, cutting fresh green coconuts which produce a most welcome instant cool drink and a soft succulent kernel. An areca nut picker uses a similar technique, and having climbed up one palm, gracefully sways at the crown in order to transfer to the top of a neighbouring tree without having to waste any energy climbing down and up again! Goa Tourism's discontinued "Village Tour" which included Savoi Verem, may be reinstated. ■ *Guided tours cost Rs 300. For information T340243/340272 (see Ins & outs above).*

200,000 pineapples are cut between Jun & Sep

An alternative spice plantation can be found between Ponda (8 km) and Tisk (2 km), near Khandepar (well signposted, 1½km off the NH4A). The plantation grows a wide variety of spices and exotic fruit and is pleasantly located by a river. A guided tour takes you through a beautiful and fascinating setting but sadly it is not yet geared up to receiving casual visitors. Spices are available for sale and there is the *Glade Bar and Restaurant* (1130-1800) which is good but a bit pricey. ■ *0800-1800. Guided tours Rs 225.*

Pascoal Spice Plantation
Colour map 2, grid B3

Panaji & Central Goa

Khandepar

Colour map 2, grid B3

Here is the latest and best preserved **cave site**, possibly of Buddhist occupation. It can be found 4 km northeast of Ponda close to Khandepar (Candepar), just off the NH4A. Ask for directions to the site which is hidden beyond a wooded area near a tributary of the Mandovi. Carry a torch and beware of snakes.

These are the best preserved caves in Goa dating back to the 10th or 11th century

As described by Hutt, the first three of the four laterite caves have an outer and an inner cell which were possibly used as monks' living quarters. Much more refined than others discovered in Goa, they show clear evidence of schist frames for doors to the inner cells, sockets on which wooden doors would have been hung, pegs carved out of the walls for hanging clothing and niches for storage. The first cave, which Hutt surmises was probably intended for the senior monk, has deep (though rather crude) lotus carvings on the ceiling of the outer cell. The much simpler fourth cave, which is a short distance away and faces the first cave, is only single-celled and was probably used as a prayer room.

The interesting feature in Khandepar is the evidence of a surmounting pyramidal structure in the form of horizontal laterite slabs, placed on top of the cell roofs to give the impression of a Hindu temple *sikhara* (tower). This feature and the carved ceiling (in the style of a *mandapa*) help to date the caves to 10th or 11th century, when the Kadambas allowed Buddhism to continue to be practised. Some scholars suggest that the caves were originally carved out of a rocky hillside. They may have had the soil and growth removed and been made freestanding at a later stage (around the 10th-11th centuries) and converted to Hindu temples with the addition of the pyramidal roof slabs and carving on the ceiling.

The State Archaeological Museum in Panaji has a Krishna image, a Nandi bull, and a 15th-century Hanuman image in its collection which were found in Khandepar.

Bondla Wildlife Sanctuary

Colour map 2, grid A4

The area harbours sambar, wild boar, gaur (Indian bison), monkeys and a few migratory elephants which wander in from Karnataka during the summer. Bondla is the most popular of Goa's three sanctuaries because it is relatively easily accessible. The small, 80sq km sanctuary is situated in the foothills of the Western Ghats.

The mini-zoo here guarantees sightings of "Goa's wildlife in natural surroundings", although whether the porcupine and African lion are examples of indigenous species is another matter. Thankfully, the number of animals in the zoo has decreased in recent years and those that remain seem to have adequate space compared to other zoos in India. Additions are generally rescued 'pets' or animals that have inadvertently fallen down wells! The small and basic Nature Education Centre has the facility to show wildlife videos, but is rarely used.

Short five-minute **elephant rides** are offered between 1100-1200 and between 1600-1700. A **deer safari** (minimum eight people) between 1600-1730, costs Rs 10. The park also has an attractive picnic area in a **botanical garden** setting and a 2.4 km **nature trail** with water holes, a lake and a tree-top observation tower (about one hour on foot, so take plenty of water). A single metalled road goes some distance into the sanctuary but the chances of seeing many animals is remote. You are most likely to see monkeys and attractive birds, and some deer and Gaur if you are lucky. ■ *Rs 5, still camera Rs 25, video camera Rs 100, two-wheelers Rs 10, cars Rs 50. Mid-Sep to mid-Jun, 0900-1730; closed Thu.*

F *Eco-Cottages*. 8 basic rooms with attached bath, newer ones better. Also 1 km inside park entrance (which may be better for seeing wildlife at night) are two 12-bed dorms (Rs 30). Reserve ahead at Deputy Conservator of Forests, Wildlife Division, 4th Floor, Junta House, 18th June Road, Panaji, T229701, although a room or bed is often available to anyone turning up. The *Den Bar and Restaurant* near the entrance, serves chicken, vegetables or fish with rice. Cheap. A small *Cafeteria*, inside the park near the mini-zoo, has snacks and cold drinks. **Sleeping & eating**

Buses from Ponda (via Tisk and Usgaon) stop near the sanctuary where taxis and motorcycle taxis are available. *KTC* buses may run at weekends from Panaji. During the season the Forest Department **minibus** is supposed to do 2 daily trips (except Thu) between Bondla and Tisk: from Bondla, 0815, 1745; from Tisk, 1100 (Sunday 1030) and 1900. Check at the tourist office first. **Motorbikes** can be hired from one of the central beaches for a pleasant ride out but ensure you have enough petrol since the nearest petrol stations are at Ponda and Tisk (and be prepared to give park officials a lift!). Bondla is well signposted from the NH4A east of Ponda (5 km beyond Usgaon, a fork to the right leads to the park up a winding steep road). **Transport**

Vasco da Gama

Vasco da Gama (Vasco, in short), situated 30 km south of Panaji, has grown to become the industrial heart of modern Goa and is the terminus of the Central Goa Branch Line. Its bleak industrial surroundings have little to attract the visitor; its only convenience being its proximity to the airport but few travellers need to stop overnight here. Hansa Beach is just 4 km away, in the naval area, and is safe for swimming (motorcycle taxis charge Rs 15). *Colour map 2, grid B1* *Population: 91,300*

Getting there The naval airport at Dabolim, 4 km away, is used by domestic airlines and international charter flights from Europe. Taxis meet arrivals while local buses pass along the main road outside. Trains from the north (eg Delhi, Agra) or the south (Hospet, Bangalore), and from towns within Goa terminate in Vasco, though few visitors choose to travel this far. Buses arrive at the stand 3 km northeast of town. **Getting around** Minibuses run between the Kadamba bus stand and the City bus stand in the town square. Autorickshaws and motorcycle taxis are easy to find. **Ins & outs**

C *La Paz Gardens*, Swatantra Path, T512121, F513302, lapaz.hotel@sma.sprint.rpg. ems.vsnl.net.in 68 rooms (Rs 1,000), need redecorating, some around internal 'atrium' or courtyard. Good a/c restaurants (Indian, Chinese, fast food), pleasant bar, free transport to airport and beach. Recommended. **C** *Bismarck*, behind Auto Service, T512277, F518524. 22 clean a/c rooms on 3 floors, some with bath tubs or balcony (Rs 1,000), small pool and terrace at back with an open-air restaurant. Recommended. **C-D** *Citadel*, near Tourist Hotel, Jose Vaz Rd, T512222, F513036, epson@bom2.vsnl.net.in 42 comfortable rooms, half a/c (Rs 850), restaurant, bar. **C-D** *Karma Plaza*, T518928, F513776, karmahotel@yahoo.com 20 a/c rooms (Rs 600-900) in a new shopping complex near the railway station but prone to damp and already looking tired. **D** *Maharaja*, FL Gomes Rd, T514075, F512559, mahahotl@ goa1.dot.net.in 40 smallish rooms, 18 a/c, Gujarati *thalis*, bar, not ideally placed. **E** *Annapurna*, D Deshpande Rd, T513735. 33 clean rooms with bath, good vegetarian food. **E** *Gladstone*, FL Gomes Rd, near railway station, T510005. Clean functional rooms, some a/c (Rs 350), restaurant, bar. **E** *Nagina*, D Deshpande Rd, T511670. 21 fair sized rooms, some a/c (Rs 395), restaurant serves Goan specialities. **E** *Tourist Hotel* (GTDC), off Swatantra Path, T510829. 64 rooms (up to 6 beds), some a/c, a bit dirty, limited canteen, can be noisy, tourist office. **E-F** *Westend*, D Deshpande Rd, T511575. 22 fair sized rooms, some a/c (Rs 350), restaurant, bar. **Sleeping**

Eating **Mid-range** *Goodyland* near La Paz. Western fast food joint. **Cheap** *Adarsh*, Swatantra Path, 100m south of railway station. Excellent *masala dosa*, Rs 8. *Ananta* near the Citadel Hotel. Recommended for Indian. *Leads* 300m from station. Indian, Goan, Chinese (no bar) good value. *Nanking* off Swatantra Path. Good value, authentic Chinese.

Entertainment **Festivals** *Vasco Saptaha* in **July/August** (5 August 2000) is marked by non-stop singing of hymns. Floats showing scenes from legends process down the streets. **Shopping** Swatantra Path is the main shopping street. Shops selling handicrafts and local wood carvings are to the north. The *Government Emporium* is at the Tourist Hotel.

Transport **Local** trains stop at **Dabolim** (for the airport and Bogmalo), **Cansaulim**, **Seraulim**, **Majorda** (for the beach), **Madgaon** (Margao) for Colva, Benaulim and the southern beaches, **Chandorgoa**, **Sanvordem**, **Calem**, **Colem (Kolamb)**, **Dudhsagar** (for the waterfalls when the station reopens), **Sonauli** and **Caranzol**.

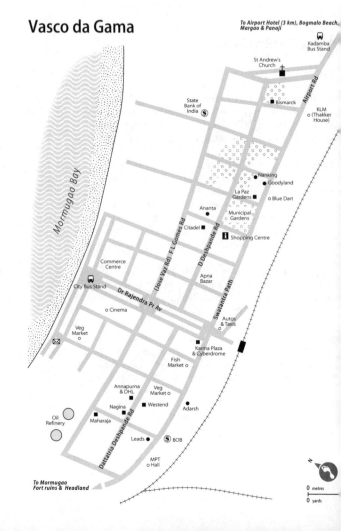

Vasco da Gama

Train Reservations, T512833. To **Londa**: by *Goa Exp 2779*, dep 1330, arr 1740; by *Vasco Bangalore Exp 7310*, dep 2110, arr 0120; both 4¼ hrs. To **Bangalore**: by *Vasco Bangalore Exp 7310*, dep 2110, arr 1240, 15 hrs. To **Delhi (via Agra) (Nizamuddin)**: *Goa Exp 2779*, dep 1330,

Warning

Part of Baina Beach, 2km from Vasco, is the red light district. It is notified as a high risk area for AIDS.

arr 0645 (after 2 nights), 41 hrs. To **Hospet (for Hampi)**: *Amravati Exp 7226*, dep 0505 arr 1525, 10 hrs. To **Pune** *Goa Exp 2779*, dep 1330, arr 0400, 15 hrs.

Road Buses from City bus stand near market, frequent, non-stop service to **Panaji**, and **Margao**, Rs 15, via **Airport**. Kadamba bus stand, northeast of town, with a very helpful information booth, has services to major towns in Goa (not non-stop), and to **Bangalore** via Hubli: 1500, 1645 (15 hrs), Rs 240; **Belgaum**, many, Rs 57; **Hospet**: 1130 (10 hrs) Rs 100; **Hubli** many (6 hrs) Rs 65; **Mangalore**: 1700 (10 hrs) Rs 156; **Mumbai**: 1330 (16 hrs), Rs 325. **Taxi** to and from Londa, about Rs 1,500.

Check timetable in advance

Banks *State Bank of India*, FL Gomes Rd; *Standard Chartered Bank*, Swatantra Path. **Communications** Courier: *Blue Dart*, T512748. *DHL*, Room 101, *Hotel Annapurna*, T513529. *Cyberdome*, Karma Plaza, T518687, 0930-2200 Mon-Sat (cheapest 1200-1600, Rs 70 per hr), 0930-1200 Sun, 8 terminals. **Medical facilities** *Salgaocar Medical Research Centre*, T512524, *Cottage Hospital*, Chicalim (2 km east of Vasco), T513864. **Tourist offices** At *Tourist Hotel*, T512673. **Useful services** Ambulance T512768. Fire T513840. Police T512304.

Directory

Around Vasco

Goa's airport is south of Panaji, across the Mormugao Bay. There are counters at the airport for car hire, foreign exchange and tourist information, all of which are normally open to meet flights, usually 1230-1530. For details of transport from the airport and international flights see page 20 and for details of internal flights see page 67.

Dabolim
Colour map 2, grid B1

The natural harbour by the rocky headland jutting into the Arabian Sea 4 km northwest of Vasco, is one of the busiest ports on India's west coast, mainly handling iron ore exports from the interior of the region.

When chosen as the ideal defensible point to become the capital to succeed Old Goa, a fort was built on the south headland of Mormugao Bay in 1685, and tentative building of a town started. In 1703 the Viceroy actually moved there but subsequently the plan to shift the capital was abandoned. Today, virtually nothing remains of **Mormugao Fort**, and what does is hidden by the industrial development that has taken its place.

A kilometre away, **Pilot Point**, at the base of the fort ruin, offers excellent views over the harbour, the sea, the Zuari River and Dona Paula beach. The passenger ferry to Dona Paula remained suspended in early 2000.

Mormugao (Marmagoa)
Colour map 2, grid B1

Panaji & Central Goa

Mormugao Taluka

Mormugao Taluka, a barren looking laterite projection into the Arabian Sea, is the industrial heart of modern Goa. The passenger terminus of Goa's oldest railway line, the metre gauge line opened in 1888 which connected the state with the interior and the south. The line has now been converted to broad gauge.

Although the agricultural potential of the district has always been limited, its coastal position and good natural harbour periodically tempted the Portuguese to move their capital there. According to Richards, at the end of the 17th century the authorities in Lisbon repeatedly told their Goa based representatives to destroy the buildings in Old Goa and to use the stone for building a new capital in Mormugao then a part of Salcete. The attacks of the Marathas made Old Goa increasingly insecure and steps were taken to shift the capital to the more remote and more readily defensible site of Mormugao along with Aguada, Mormugao was the 'throat' through which Goa breathed.

The rocky headland and the plateau inland saw little subsequent development until after Independence. The harbour became an important port for the Indian Navy who then developed Dabolim airport on the upland immediately above it.

Today, Vasco da Gama has become Goa's largest town with a population growth of up to 10 percent a year. Industrial estates have developed rapidly on the plateau above the town. The once barren peninsula is rapidly being converted into the commercial core of the state where over 80 percent of the population lives in its towns rather than depending on agriculture.

Bogmalo

Colour map 1, grid B1

Bogmalo, the nearest beach to the airport, is small, palm fringed and attractive, but is seldom visited. It can be a good beach base for those spending only a short time in Goa, though it can get overrun by sailors when foreign ships are berthed at Mormugao but this is relatively rare.

Hollant Beach is a small rocky cove fringed with coconut palms with a small section of sandy beach beyond the two bar/ restaurants here. From here, on a clear day, you can view the whole of the beach coastline from Arrosim to Mobor, with Cabo de Rama and the first foothills of the Western Ghats forming an impressive backdrop. About 2.5 km before reaching Bogmalo, the approach road forks. The right fork continues to Bogmalo whilst the left takes you to this beach (2 km) via Issorcim.

Santra Beach, further south, can be reached by going through the village behind the *Bogmalo Beach* resort. Local fishermen are at hand to ferry passengers to two small islands for about Rs 300 per boat, which can be shared by a group.

Essentials

Sleeping & eating
The hotels listed are booked up by package groups in season

AL-A *Bogmalo Beach Park Plaza* (was Sarovar), T513311, F512510, bbppr@ goa1.dot.net.in 121 rooms with sea view (US$95), Goa's only multi-storey beach hotel (built before planning regulations), palm-shaded poolside, some watersports, ayurvedic centre. **A** *Coconut Creek* (new sister hotel of *Joet's*). 20 rooms (10 a/c) set in 2-storey cottages (US$55), light and airy, pool, mainly packages. **C-D** *Saritas*, T555965, on the beach. 13 clean rooms with bath, some a/c (Rs 880), popular restaurant. **D** *El Mar*, T555329. Set back from the beach. 5 clean, large, basic rooms with shower (Rs 500), seafood available. **D** *Joet's Guest House*, right on the beach, T555036,

JOETS@goa1.dot.net.in. 12 small airy rooms with shower, good restaurant. Cheaper family guest houses in the village are set back from the beach. The beach cafés near *Bogmalo Beach Park Plaza* are dearer but do excellent seafood. *Joet's*. Good seafood and very friendly; sun beds on the beach and hammocks among the palms.

Watersports *Splash Watersports* have a shack on the beach, providing parasailing (Rs 850), windsurfing (Rs 400 per hour), water skiing (Rs 500 for 15 mins), trips to nearby island (Rs 1,500) etc; during the high season only. *Bogmalo Beach Park Plaza*, T513291, and *Joet's*, T555036, also offer these; diving is possible through the latter. **Museum** *Naval Aviation Museum*. 1 km from beach, on approach road. 1000-1700, closed Mon and public holidays, free. A few rusting examples of old planes.

Entertainment

Ritika Bookshop and Boutique, *Bogmalo Beach Park Plaza*'s verandah, a/c, good books and stationery, high quality gifts, good value. **Tailoring**: some beach gift shops offer good quality, made-to-measure cotton and silk jackets and shirts at reasonable prices.

Shopping

Taxis to Dabolim airport, 4 km (10 mins' drive), Rs80; **Vasco**, 8 km, around Rs 100; half-day hire to visit, say Panaji or Mapusa market, Rs 60. **Bus** erratic service to Vasco passes close to the airport.

Transport

Useful numbers Police: T512304.

Directory

Verna (the 'Place of fresh air') is actually in Salcete, to the east of the Mormugao taluka. It is surrounded by seven springs with special healing properties. Travelling south from Cortalim, immediately north of Verna and just off the NH17, are the Kesarval springs.

Verna
Colour map 2, grid B2

Named from Quensra-vodd, the **Kesarval Springs** have medicinal properties and are no longer a 'natural' remote watering place but are very popular with Goans as a picnic spot. From the large car park, paths lead past several enclosures through the gently sloping wooded hillside. The covered resting areas for picnics are near the entrance. The path to the springs leads down a short but steep slope into a vertical walled grotto where bathers can stand under the trickling spring water. There is an extraordinary change in the atmosphere from the hot open plateau to the moist, cooler but lush semi-enclosed area surrounding the springs themselves. There is a small hotel and restaurant where you turn off the NH17.

Panaji & Central Goa

North Goa

4

North Goa

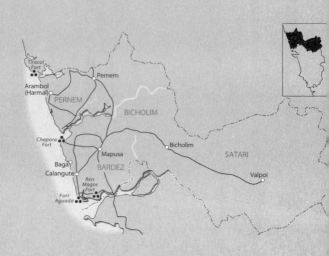

North Goa packs an astonishing range of scenery and landscapes, each area with a distinctive history which has helped to shape sharp contrasts between the four talukas which make it up. The coastline is dotted with historic sites interspersed with some of Goa's most beautiful beaches. The road east to the Western Ghats runs through a region of modern and rapid mineral development and industrialization, then goes back in time to the Bicholim taluka, where ancient Buddhist caves and Hindu temples are tucked away deep in the denseley forested slopes.

Bardez and Pernem talukas

The long coastline of Bardez and Pernem talukas has wonderful coconut fringed sandy beaches backed by dunes and only occasionally interrupted by rocky head-lands and coves. A string of fishing villages runs along the coast while further inland, there are rolling laterite hills covered in open forest.

It is possible to walk virtually uninterrupted along the waterline all the way from Aguada to Vagator since there are no private beaches and public access is guar-anteed everywhere. The NH17 provides the main north-south artery which gives access to Goa's coastal resorts. From Panaji, the highway crosses the Mandovi bridge, taking you to Alto Porvorim. Buses along the highway run fre-quently to Calangute, the central point and busiest town on this coast, but if you have your own transport you can turn left at the north end of the Mandovi Bridge and hug the coast through Reis Magos, then cross over to Aguada and travel up the coast road. Alternatively, if you go through Porvorim to Mapusa, you can head for Anjuna or Vagator, or continue northwards to Pernem.

Betim
Colour map 1, grid C2

Immediately to the north of the Mandovi Bridge, on the river bank facing Panaji, is the small fishing village of Betim. The attractive country road runs between tightly packed houses and then skirts the bay. The **F** *Tourist Complex*, T227362 has very basic facilities, some beds (Rs 10-30), mattresses (Rs 5) or floor space for students (Rs 3).

Alto Porvorim

The new development across the Mandovi River was chosen to be Goa's administrative capital. There are a few eateries here. *Don Pedro*, on the Panaji-Mapusa road, serves Mexican (and some Goan). Rustic setting, try *tostadas*, *fajitas*, *tortilla* and *chilli*, washed down with cocktails for Rs 45. *O Coqueiro*, near the water tank, serves excellent Goan (but pork best avoided when it gets hot), pleasant ambience, bar, choice of tables in or out. *Village Nook*, Church St, east off NH17 beyond the water tank there is a garden pub which serves home-cooked meals. For car hire see page 66.

Reis Magos

Colour map 1, grid C2
Population: 7,500

Reis Magos stands appropriately like a watchman facing Panaji across the Mandovi estuary. The small town of some charm (originally called Verem), is most noted for its 'Royal Fort' which was built by Don Alfonso de Noronha between 1551 and 1554. In fact, recognizing the site's great strategic impor-tance, Albuquerque stationed troops on the headland from the outset of Por-tuguese control. It was intended as a second line of defence should an enemy, notably the Dutch, manage to sail past Aguada and 'Cabo'. The first fortifica-tion was extended and repaired a few times during the next 50 years. Several underground rooms were excavated which were accessed by going down over 100 steps.

Reis Magos, though fairly small, played a vital role in defending the mouth of the Mandovi together with Gaspar Dias but after a new fort was built at Aguada in 1612 its importance waned and it was neglected. In 1703, it was re-erected; 35 years later it had to face the Maratha onslaught on Bardez, and alone with Fort Aguada remained in Portuguese hands.

The **Reis Magos Church** (1555), named after the 'Magi Kings', stands alongside and is one of the early Goan churches which, some believe, was built on the site of a Hindu temple. A Franciscan friar is believed to have crossed the

Bardez and Pernem talukas

Bardez may have derived its name from bara desh (12 'divisions of land') that comprised the district referring to the 12 Brahmin villages that once dominated the region. There are other possible explanations for the name. One popular one is that it refers to 12 zagors which were celebrated by the people to ward off evil. Yet another suggests that it is derived from Bahir des, meaning 'outside land' – the land beyond the Mandovi River. Whatever the origins of its name Bardez taluka, occupied by the Portuguese as part of their original conquest, bears the greatest direct imprint of their Christianizing influence.

Pernem (Pednem) taluka, sandwiched between the Tiracol and Chapora Rivers and their estuaries, was incorporated into Goa in 1788 as the final part of the New Conquests. Formerly it had been alternately under Hindu and Muslim rule. The Bhonsles of Sawantwadi in modern Maharashtra had been the latest rulers of the hilly district on the northern fringes of Goa before the Portuguese ousted them, and Maratha Hindu influences remain strong throughout the district.

Both the talukas have retained a strong sense of their distinctive identities. Bardez has its own characteristic ecosystem. The beach between Candolim and Baga is backed by a series of sand dunes, stabilized by grasses and casuarina, which form a shelter belt for the flat river-plains inland. The road and settlements all lie to the landward side of this strip. Inland again the short rivers meander across the flood plain between Mapusa and the sea. The Mapusa River itself was once an important transport artery, its banks offering rich and fertile soils for producing vegetables which were then moved to market in Mapusa or down to the Mandovi. Today its banks have been reclaimed for building, its waters abused by urban refuse and sewage, its importance dwindled and its attractiveness largely destroyed.

Interior Bardez and most of Pernem are formed of the rolling laterite hills which extend northwards into southern Maharashtra. More sparsely populated than the coastal fringe, the hills are now covered in open forest.

Southern Bardez has some of Goa's khazan lands. These saline flood plains, lying below the high tide sea level have been developed and maintained over centuries by an intricate system of sluice gates, keeping saline water out at high tide, allowing surplus fresh water out as the tide recedes. From this complex system has emerged an intricately managed land use, with salt-tolerant varieties of rice co-existing with aquaculture. Fish, Curry and Rice (third edition, Ecoforum, 1995) has pointed to the threats which have been posed to the khazans by a variety of current practices, including deliberate breaking of the river embankments to allow more intensive aquaculture, and the inadvertent destruction of embankments by the wash of ever larger iron ore carrying barges.

Mandovi in 1550 arriving in Verem where he put up a temporary altar and celebrated Mass for the first time on Goan territory. Viceroy Noronha had allotted Bardez to the Franciscans and the church was in a sense a launching pad for the conversion of the district. Dedicated to the three Magi, Gaspar, Melchior and Balthazar, the reredos illustrates the story of the Three Kings with a painted wooden panel showing frankincense, myrrh and gold being offered to the baby Jesus.

The church and the fort stand quite high above water level. The church façade has a most unusual protruding crown with the Portuguese crest on the gable. It is approached by a flight of steep laterite steps; the granite tiger is thought to have come from a Hindu temple.

Schools and a seminary were attached to the church. The St Jerome Seminary where Konkani was taught alongside philosophy and theology became a

Salt of the earth

The central and northern coastal districts of Goa have been renowned for salt production. Although this has decreased in importance recently, Tiswadi still has over 40 working salt pans, Bardez and Salcete have around 30 each, and Pernem nine.

Salt is produced traditionally in areas reclaimed from mangroves, the period of production being between February and May. Along the raised rural roads close to the sea you may notice a series of shallow rectangular enclosures where salt water is allowed to enter and stand. The water eventually evaporates to leave crystallized white salt which is piled up in heaps before being transported.

prestigious institution. Between 1597 and 1793 many Portuguese dignitaries, including viceroys and governors, *en route* to or from Old Goa, stayed here as guests of the friars.

It is a picturesque drive to the end of the peninsula beyond Reis Magos, although the road is a dead end and becomes the narrowest of country lanes, winding between palm trees growing in the middle of the road.

The Festival of Three Kings accompanied by a big fair is celebrated here on 6 January each year, as at Chandor (see page 164). There is accommodation at the **D** *Bamboo Motels Noah's Ark*, Verem, Reis Magos, T517321. There are 30 rooms facing the pool and a restaurant. The fort is expected to house an upmarket *Heritage Hotel*.

Nerul

Colour map 1, grid C2 The present temple in Nerul dates from 1910 when special permission was given to return the deity of Shri Shantadurga, which had been removed to Mandrem in Pernem taluka (see page 127). Gomes Pereira records that the present village church of **Our Lady of Remedies** was built in 1569 in place of the destroyed Shantadurga Temple. Workers restoring the parish house in 1893 found a 1m statue of the Hindu deity Betall in the holy well. He suggests that an underground passage which exists in the present church was probably part of the former temple, and that the stone tigers now found decorating the entrance to the church originally also came from it. The big tank in the parish church-house orchard (now in ruins) may have once been the temple tank.

The northern beaches

Sinquerim Beach

Colour map 1, grid C1 Sinquerim, 13 km north of Panaji, is where the Taj Hotel group set up its fabulous *Hermitage Hotel Complex* which dominates the headland around the historic Fort Aguada (which it partly occupies). The road from Aguada runs about 1 km inland behind the main line of sand dunes, with narrow lanes running down to the sea.

If you want a long beach walk, the firm sand is uninterrupted all the way north to Baga. Although there are many beach shacks open during the season, it is a good idea to take some water as well as a shirt and a hat.

Fort Aguada

On the northern tip of the Mandovi estuary with the Nerul River to the east, *Colour map 1,* Fort Aguada, felt as essential to keep the Dutch Navy at bay, was completed in *grid C1&2* 1612 through one percent of the revenue raised. It was the strongest of the Portuguese coastal forts and was paired with the 'Cabo' fort, on the opposite side of the estuary. A channel was excavated to make the headland an island and a platform built to help ships disembark. A large well and a number of springs provided the fort and ships at harbour with drinking water and gave it its name *'aguada'* or watering place; one of the sources of clean mineral water is still there. Two hundred guns were placed to give the fort all round defensive fire power as well as two magazines, four barracks, two prisons and several residential buildings for the officers. It saw repeated action against the Marathas, was used as a refuge by Goans who fled from Bardez during these attacks and was also used to detain prisoners during various revolts. The main fortifications with laterite walls, nearly 5m high and 1.3m thick, are still intact; the buildings lower down form the central jail.

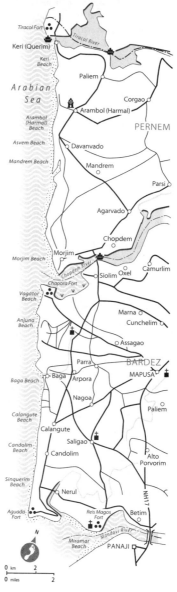

Northern beaches

The motorable road up to the plateau passes the small **Church of St Lawrence** (or Linhares Church, 1630-1643). It has an unusual porch with a terrace and balustrades on the towers and parapets. The *Feast of St Lawrence* (10 August), the patron saint of sailors, celebrated the natural annual clearing of the sand bars at the mouth of the Mandovi River after the monsoon, which once again allowed ships passage.

A 13m high **Old lighthouse** using an oil lamp was added at the top of the fort (84m above sea level), sometime in the 18th century, but records of 1817 report its poor condition. In 1864, a new mechanism allowed a rotating beam to be emitted every 30 seconds (one of the first of its kind in Asia), which was upgraded in 1906. The lighthouse ceased to function in 1976. ■ *Rs 2. It is supposed to be open from 1030-1730; there are good views from the top.* Next to the fort is the 21m high **New lighthouse** (1975). ■ *Re 1 (no photography). 1600-1700.*

North Goa

North Goa

Spoilt for sand

Despite the unending stretch of sand that Goa has as its gift, each section has its own distinctive character. The difference reflects, in part, the nature of the settlements dotted at intervals behind it. In the south there is far less beach shade and the dunes of loose sand are higher and wider.

Just north of Panaji is the exclusive resort near Fort Aguada on **Sinquerim** *Beach. Further along is a relatively quiet strip in* **Candolim** *and then from* **Calangute** *to* **Baga** *the coconut palms come closer to the beach with fishing villages nestled among them. There are clusters of fishing boats at various points along some beaches while others seem deserted. This section has close to 200 beach restaurants open during the season.*

Continuing north across the narrow inlet of the Baga River, **Anjuna** *still draws hundreds to the weekly Flea Market and to its thumping raves and all night 'parties' even though the beach is too rocky for comfortable swimming. The series of secluded beaches quickly empties towards* **Vagator** *and* **Chapora***, where some of the smaller coves have become home to long-stay westerners. In the far north low rocky headlands create a series of small, enclosed bays which are not as easily accessible. Some, like* **Arambol***, which allure day trippers, have limited facilities; for much of the time the beautiful 2km of sand at* **Keri***, Goa's northernmost beach just south of Tiracol, is almost entirely deserted.*

Further down the coast the smaller circular white Aguada Beacon (1890) emitted a red light

The government plans to allow a private sector development by a leading hotel group to restore the old fort and set up a Disneyland type theme park to attract tourists to the Aguada plateau. Rumour has it that the central jail at the end of the bottom road will be replaced by one being built in Vasco.

At the bottom of the hill, where sections of the fortification jut out to the sea, the Taj group has three superb hotels. Although the beach is supposed to be public, private security guards patrol this section to put off undesirables from entering the area.

Sleeping

Prices vary greatly depending on period; peak 21 Dec-10 Jan, lowest mid Jun-end Sep

Taj Complex: **LL** *Aguada Hermitage*, T276201, F276044 (for all 3). Exclusive and extremely luxurious, 20 fully serviced 1 or 2-room villas (US$600 peak season drops to US$180 in low), few some distance away from main building, each with its own spacious tropical garden, nightclub, former guests include Indira Gandhi and Margaret Thatcher! **L-AL** *Fort Aguada Beach Resort*, exceptional hotel, superb setting, built into the fort. 120 rooms in 2 wings and some villas with excellent views (US$230 down to US$85 in low season). Separate, similarly priced, **L-AL** *Holiday Village*, 300m away. 144 (most a/c), some well-designed single 'houses'. Some in less attractive 2-storey blocks further from the sea, imaginative planning, beautiful gardens of bougainvillea and palms, good restaurants (on beach and on dunes), excellent pool with a 'water bar' and hammocks between palms (better than at the *Resort*), informal, helpful efficient staff. Highly recommended. **B-C** *Marbella*, lane left off road to *Aguada Beach Resort*, T275551, F276509. 6 very clean, well-decorated rooms (Rs 950-1,850, depending on size), in large Portuguese villa, very imaginatively designed with mosaic tiles in bathrooms ("the bath tub in the Rajasthani suite must be the best in all India!"). Highly recommended. **D** *Village Belle*, near the main road by *Taj Holiday Village*, T/F276153, vbelle@vsnl.com 8 rooms (Rs 450-Rs 600 a/c), good, cheap restaurant, among palms, 500m from the beach, friendly owners, good value for the area. Recommended.

Travel tip

From any point on the northern coast between Fort Aguada and Tiracol it is easy to take day trips inland to enjoy something of this area's diversity. There is plenty in inland Bardez alone to repay a visit; Mapusa, with its market and the Church of Our Lady of Miracles, or the neo-Gothic church of Saligao just inland of Calangute, the southern coastal villages around Reis Magos, or the banks of the Chapora from Siolim to Colvale. Inland Pernem has the magnificent Deshprabhu Mansion or the Shri Shantadurga Temple of Dargalim.

Eating For something special, try the **Banyan Tree** at *Taj Holiday Village* entrance, for excellent Thai food in style. Encircled by a wide verandah, it is in an exotic setting surrounded by a water garden with a great banyan tree; expensive (about Rs 500 for a meal) though not overpriced by Western standards. The **Beach House** for the "most lavish and complete dinner, served attentively" is highly recommended. **Bon Appetit** and **Palm Shade** nearby, are also recommended.

Sports Taj Sports Complex with excellent facilities (open to non-residents) at the *Taj Holiday Village*, with a separate access between *Aguada Beach Resort* and the *Holiday Village*. Rs 440 per day for the complex, Rs 330 for the pool. **Tennis** with good markers (Rs 400 per hour); **squash** and **badminton** (Rs 100 for 30 mins); **golf** (Rs 150). A fine **health centre** offers massage, gym, steam, sauna, all recommended; hairdressers are at hand. **Watersports** Scuba diving: **sailing** and **water skiing** (Rs 450 per hour); **windsurfing** and (rod) **fishing** (Rs 400 per hour); **parasailing** (Rs 850); **jet ski** (Rs 900).

North Goa

Sinquerim Beach & Fort Aguada

N

Not to scale

■ **Sleeping**	4 Taj Holiday Village	2 Beach House
1 Aguada Hermitage	5 Village Belle	3 Bon Appetit
2 Fort Aguada Beach		& Palm Shade
Resort (Taj)	● **Eating**	
3 Marbella	1 Banyan Tree	

Fort Aguada

North of Aguada

The section of beach from Aguada to Chapora has close to 200 shacks open during the season. If you wish to be away from the crowds but within reach of good food, try the beach near *D'Mello's*, between Candolim and Calangute. Many shacks hire out sun-beds, which are quite unsightly and add to the feeling of overcrowding which is particularly bad at the Baga end.

Candolim

Colour map 1, grid C1
Population: 7,100

Candolim, which runs into Calangute, has more spacious and quiet resort hotels interspersed with modest guest houses and access to a beach which, by European standards at least, is empty.

The wide stretch of beach has firm, 'squeaky' sand, backed by scrub-covered dunes. There is little shelter but the shacks hire out sun-beds with umbrellas for Rs 50 per day. It is relatively quiet and relaxed compared to the beaches immediately to the north, although small, but regular deposits of oil and dead fish lining the shoreline mar the beauty somewhat. Rubbish is minimal but noticeable. As the season progresses, Union Jacks, Scottish, English and Welsh flags may catch the eye as you listen to endless Bob Marley. Sadly, the colourful fruit sellers are rarely seen now.

Sleeping **A** *Whispering Palms*, 300m from beach (looks a bit like a fortress), T276140, F276142, whispering.palms@gnpun.globalnet.ems.vsnl.net.in   www.whisperingpalms.com 66 well-equipped rooms, best in 2-storey villas, good restaurant overlooking excellent pool (non residents Rs 150), pleasant garden, mainly packages, good but pricey. **B** *Highland Beach Resort*, T276405, F277881. 205 a/c rooms (Rs 2,000 including breakfast), in a rather ugly, sprawling 4-storey complex (completed early 2000), 2 restaurants, package choice, health/sports club, pool (non residents Rs 100 per hour). **C** *Aguada Holiday Resort*, Bamon–vaddo, T422266, F229966. 11 a/c rooms, 17 non a/c with kitchenette (Rs 1,000) bit cramped, expensive restaurant and bar, uncrowded site with some palms (plenty of squirrels), pool, 10 mins from beach. **C** *Aldeia Santa Rita*, towards Aguada, T276868, F276684. 32 rooms with balcony (better upstairs) in colourful 'street' of villas in attractive setting, some a/c (Rs 1,100), good restaurant, bar, very small pool, friendly management. **C** *Costa Nicola*, near the Health Centre (500m from beach), T276343, F277343. 26 clean rooms in very pleasant Goan house, old wing with more character (Rs 1,000), new wing (Rs 1,200) some with kitchenette, restaurant, bar, gentle atmosphere, verandah, pretty garden, pool. **D** *Holiday Beach Resort*, short walk to beach, T276088, F276235. 20 clean rooms, some with balcony, in a rather faded guesthouse, covered terrace restaurant, small pool. **D** *Kamal*, towards Aguada, T276320. 6 large rooms in a fairly new, attractive building, *Fiesta* restaurant (some Italian dishes), pleasant garden, charming owner. Recommended. **D** *Per Avel*, 100m from beach, T277074. 13 simple rooms (Rs 600, a/c Rs 200 extra), courtyard garden for breakfast, among local family houses, friendly. **D** *Sea Shell Inn*, opposite

Canara Bank, Candolim-Aguada Rd, T276131. 8 spotless (Rs 450), comfortable rooms in 2 blocks (1 grafted onto an old colonial house with chapel), disappointing restaurant, residents may use pool at *Casa Sea Shell*. **D** *Summerville*, T277075. 15 well kept rooms, breakfast on rooftop, sunbathing terrace. **D** *Xavier*, down a lane and round the corner from the State Bank. T/F 276911, xavieran@goa1.dot.net.in 10 spacious, well furnished rooms (Rs 500), excellent restaurant (see below), close to beach, friendly. Recommended. **D-E** *Alexandra Tourist Centre*, Morodvaddo, in lane opposite the Canara Bank, T276097. 12 clean, comfortable rooms, better upstairs, restaurant. On a very quiet part of the beach, towards Calangute: **E** *D'Mello's Sea View*, turn at Monteiro Rd, T277395. 7 rooms (Rs 350), good food (tandoori specials), pleasant area. Recommended. Another nearby.

Candolim & Sinquerim

North Goa

Not to scale

■ Sleeping
1 Aguada Holiday Resort

2 Aldeia Santa Rita
3 Alexandra Tourist Centre
4 Casa Sea Shell
5 Costa Nicola
6 D'Mello's Sea View
7 Highland Beach Resort
8 Holiday Beach Resort

9 Kamal & Octopus Garden Restaurant
10 Per Avel
11 Sea Shell Inn
12 Summerville
13 Whispering Palms
14 Xavier, Restaurant & Bar

● Eating
1 Club 21
2 Coconut Inn
3 Palms 'n Sand
4 Stone House & Foto Finish
5 Titus Roma Pisa

Fishing craft

Fishing boats varying from under 6m to 9m in length, appear in clusters along Calangute and Baga beaches. They are worth a closer look. Their bases are carved out of solid wood while the sides are made of planks slashed on to the base with ropes, all made waterproof by a dark oil, traditionally using a by-product of cashew roasting! Many boats are fitted with outboard motors though they still have the old oars. Of particular interest are the distinctive outriggers on one side. During the day you may find the fishermen repairing their nets or engaged in fish-drying, while a growing number are turning to taking out tourists for fishing trips and dolphin watching.

Eating **Mid-range** *Coconut Inn*, a typical Goan house with indoor and open-air seating (closed May-Sep). *Club 21* on the beach, now crowded in with other shacks, does good breakfasts for about Rs 75, snacks (seafood, pancakes) and drinks. *Octopus Garden*, on the main road towards Aguada. Wide choice (1000-1500, 1800-2300) but some dishes lack subtlety. *Palms 'n' Sand* near the beach. Speciality roast piglet (order the day before). *Stone House*, opposite Octopus Garden. Excellent food, wide choice, good service from friendly young waiters, pleasant music (Blues lapsing into Bob Marley!), boat trips. *Titus Roma Pisa*, Candolim Beach Road. Not just pizzas. Well prepared food, very friendly staff (good place to ask about fishing trips, flea market etc), Soccer Bar for live football, but not rowdy at all, so not just for the younger crowd. Also internet, Rs 90 per hour. Highly recommended. *Xavier*. Western. Excellent meals (owner/chef spent 30 years in England), very attentive service (and highly efficient hotel cat!), roast dinner on Sun. Cocktail bar with a happy hour, 1800-1900. Recommended.

Entertainment **Dolphin watching** *John's Boats*, T277780, promises 'guaranteed' dolphin watch-
& sport ing, morning trips start around 0900, Rs 500 (includes meal); see page 41 for details. **Parasailing** Occasionally offered independently on Candolim beach, Rs 600-850 for a 5-min flight.

Directory **Medical services** *Primary Health Centre*. **Photography** Many outlets do quick processing of holiday snaps; fairly good quality, usually same day (processed at Calangute). *Foto Finish*, next to *Stone House*, stocks slides, black/white films and camera accessories. **Travel agent** *Davidair*, Old Post House, Escrivao, Main Rd, T277000, F276308, davidgoa@goa1.dot.net.in 0900-1800. Recommended. *Traveland*, Laxmi Apartments, T276773, F276124.

Calangute

Colour map 2, grid C1 Calangute, once the remote hippy retreat of the 1960s which attracted the disen-
Population: 11,800 chanted from across the world, is now a busy, rather dirty, commercialized small town. The centre can be crowded and pitifully congested with traffic, especially during the high season as it has become one of the main centres for package tours. It feels as if the whole settlement has been taken over by tourism.

Ins & outs **Getting there** There are regular buses to Calangute from Mapusa (Rs 4, 20 mins) and Panaji (Rs 5, 35 mins) which arrive at the bus stand near the market towards the beach steps; a few continue to Baga to the north, from the crossroads. **Getting around** Taxis and motor-cycle taxis wait near the bus stand. Alternatively, there are plenty of cycles and bikes for hire. On market days there are boats from Baga to Anjuna (see under Baga).

There is little of architectural merit in the town, though there is an interesting hexagonal "Barbeiria" (barber's shop) near the bus stand at the 'T junction' with the rather unsavoury market. The new fish market next door, however, is quite tidy and pleasant. The streets of Calangute (and Baga) are lined with shops offering a wide range of goods, mainly souvenirs, metal and leather items, clothes and jewellery from Kashmir and Karnataka.

The Baga road has several streets off it, giving access to the sea. The beach is reasonable – no rocks and good swimming (but beware of the seaward pulling current) and you won't need to go far to see a number of fishing boats, tackle and fishermen's huts. Hawkers selling sarongs, offering massages or wishing to tell your fortune can be a constant distraction while licensed shacks line the beach, some offering excellent food and a very pleasant evening atmosphere. Behind the busy beach front, coconut trees still give shade to village houses; some offer private rooms to let, while open space is rapidly being covered by new hotels.

The affluence of this coastal strip also attracts its fair share of out-of-state beggars. At weekends the beach near the *Tourist Resort* gets particularly crowded with domestic day trippers (some come in the hope of catching a glimpse of scantily clad foreigners).

Away from the town centre, the striking **Church of St Alex** gives one of the best illustrations of Rococo decoration in Goa, while the false dome of the central façade is an excellent example of 18th-century architectural development. Note the gold and white scheme and the delicate and restrained handling of the decoration as seen in the remarkable pulpit and the fine reredos.

North Goa

Sleeping
First 3 are full
with charters

B *Falcon*, Calangute-Baga Rd, 1 km from beach, T277327, F277330, falcores@bom2.vsnl.net.in Popular, but with possibly the noisiest generator in Goa which is frequently resorted to, pool (pleasantly shaded). **B** *Goan Heritage*, Gauravaddo, towards Candolim, T276253, F276120. 70 large, pleasant rooms but can get stiflingly hot, a/c and fridge (Rs 400 extra when used), some have sea view, expensive restaurant (others nearby), good pool, beautiful garden, close to beach. **B** *Paradise Village*, South Calangute, near the beach, T276351, F276155. 83 comfortable rooms in 2-storey chalets, pleasant restaurant, large pool, excellent service and management. **B** *Villa Goesa*, Cobravaddo, off Baga Rd, T277535, T/F276182, T/F276182. 57 clean rooms, some a/c, some very shaded, excellent restaurant, lovely gardens, pool, quiet, relaxing, very friendly owners, long walk from beach. Recommended.

C *Concha Beach Resort*, Umtavaddo, T/F276056. 13 good sized, clean, comfortable rooms, nets, best at front with large verandahs, close to beach. **C** *Estrela do Mar*, Calangute-Baga Rd, T276014. 12 clean, well kept rooms with nets (rare in these parts), size varies (Rs 900-1,200), restaurant, pool, pleasant garden, quiet, peaceful, close to beach. Recommended.**C** *Varma's Beach Resort*, Meddovaddo, T276077, F276022, varmabeach@hotmail.com 15 clean, comfortable a/c rooms, breakfast only, in busy area, nothing special.

D *Arabian Retreat*, Gauravaddo (near *Goan Heritage*), T279053, F271467. 11 rooms, some a/c, 1st floor better, includes breakfast, 250m from the beach. **D** *Coco Banana*, 5/139A Umtavaddo, back from Calangute beach, T276478, F279068. 6 spotless rooms with nets, airy, light and comfortable, excellent Goan/Swiss owners, very caring and helpful (when full, Walter will try to find a suitable alternative). Highly recommended. **D** *Golden Eye*, T277308. F276187. 26 clean, comfortable rooms (Rs 650), half price singles, right on the beach (built before restrictions) with genuine sea views! **D** *Martin's Guest Rooms*, T277306, martins@goa1.dot.net.in 5 rooms in family house (Rs 450), clean, attractive verandahs, use of kitchen but on busy noisy road. **D** *Mira*,

Umtavaddo, near the Chapel, 10 mins walk from beach, T277342. 17 rooms, restaurant, 24-hr coffee shop, pool, email facilities. **D** *Tourist Resort* (GTDC), on the beach, near the steps, T276024. 76 basic rooms, some a/c, cheap terrace restaurant, bar, can be noisy. **D** *White House*, Gauravaddo (near *Goan Heritage*), T277938, F276308. 8 rooms with seaview (Rs 500), very pleasant. Recommended.

Umtavaddo has a **E** *Calangute Beach Resort*, T276063. 16 reasonable rooms, some with bath (Rs 350),
variety of cheap guest restaurant, bar, beach on the doorstep. **E** *Dona Cristalina*, T279012. 8 clean, simple
houses rooms, some with balcony and sight of the sea, discounts for long-term stay.

Eating Near the *Tourist Resort*: *Angelina*, near the beach steps. Popular, varied menu (Goan, Tandoori, Italian) and *Cater's*, opposite, raised above the beach, with a large breezy, terrace, are recommended. *Souza Lobo* in a large shack on the beach, is still popular for seafood. *Lobster Pot* upstairs in a circular building set back from the beach. Has imaginative palm tree décor, good food (Rs 70 main course), some Goan specialities, friendly, unpushy hosts. *Delhi Darbar*, near the beach, towards Baga, candlelit dinner,

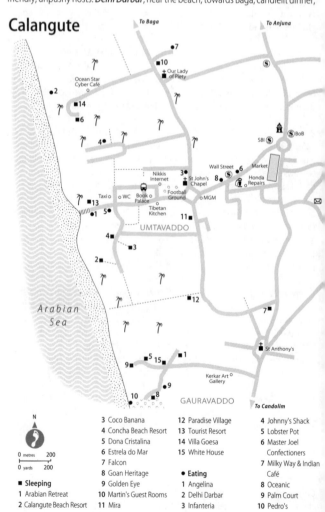

Calangute

Arabian Sea

To Baga
To Anjuna
Ocean Star Cyber Café
Our Lady of Piety
SBI
BoB
Wall Street
Market
Nikkis Internet
St John's Chapel
Honda Repairs
Taxi
WC
Book Palace
Football Ground
MGM
Tibetan Kitchen
UMTAVADDO
GAURAVADDO
Kerkar Art Gallery
St Anthony's
To Candolim

N
0 metres 200
0 yards 200

■ Sleeping
1 Arabian Retreat
2 Calangute Beach Resort
3 Coco Banana
4 Concha Beach Resort
5 Dona Cristalina
6 Estrela do Mar
7 Falcon
8 Goan Heritage
9 Golden Eye
10 Martin's Guest Rooms
11 Mira
12 Paradise Village
13 Tourist Resort
14 Villa Goesa
15 White House

● Eating
1 Angelina
2 Delhi Darbar
3 Infanteria
4 Johnny's Shack
5 Lobster Pot
6 Master Joel Confectioners
7 Milky Way & Indian Café
8 Oceanic
9 Palm Court
10 Pedro's

North Goa

Impact of tourism

It is not difficult to see why Calangute is at the centre of the controversy over 'the impact of tourism'. Despite the welcomed growth in income that tourism has brought to Calangute and Baga, it has not been an unmixed blessing. For those with memories stretching back 30 years, it is almost unrecognizable. The huge surge in land values, fuelled by a flow of money from Goans abroad eager to capitalize on the development opportunity, has seen plots covered in concrete flouting all attempts to control or direct, let alone halt, the building boom. Money has been there to be made, and Calangute is the place to make it.

Yet the area most affected by this transformation of a hippy hideout to a global tourist village is small. Calangute shades rapidly into its neighbouring, and still very different, villages.

Competition for limited ground water has affected some of the villages just inland, and some see its increasing use as threatening to let sea water into the underground supply, putting local people at risk. Others fear even more the cultural change which mass tourism has brought to this spot. It is here that Goa's nightlife is at its most audible, a transformation that some local people still find hard to accept, and the widespread availability of drugs is both feared and resented by many, just as nude or topless bathing are seen as deeply offensive. Calangute and Baga have become the area of Goa where the tensions between mass tourism and local needs are most exposed. Visitors can help greatly by being aware of the issues and behaving sensitively.

North Goa

excellent North Indian and fish dishes, dancing. It's up-market and expensive. *Johnny's Shack* does excellent pomfret (Rs 70). *Oceanic*, Beach Road, near the market. Spicy, succulent fish grills but quite pricey. *Palm Court*, near *Goan Heritage* gates. Recommended. *Pedro's* on the beach behind has authentic, interesting Tibetan dishes to compliment a very smartly printed menu. *Chinese House* is on Baga Rd. *Infanteria*, near the main crossroads, recommended for breakfast, baked goodies and snacks all day. *Master Joel Confectioners*, 9 Romano Chambers, opposite the petrol pump, makes good Goan specialities. *Milky Way*, inland off Baga Rd, good for health foods, ices during the day, French food (1900-2330), closed off-season. *Indian Café*, behind, serves snacks on a few tables on the verandah of a village home (no fans), pleasant, cheap, also changes money.

Entertainment *Kerkar Art Gallery*, Gauravaddo, T276017, sells paintings, sculpture and crafts; also holds open-air cultural shows on Tue and Sat from 1830, Rs 150.

Festivals **May** (second week): the *Youth Fête* attracts Goa's leading musicians and dancers.

Shopping It is best to look around first before buying. The asking price in most shops aimed at tourists are highly inflated so be prepared to bargain. *Book Palace*, Beach Rd, near the bus stand.

Transport **Bicycles** and **motorbikes** are widely available for hire, about Rs 200 and Rs 40 per day. There is a Kinetic Honda repair shop behind *Samir Electricals*, near the petrol station. **Taxis** to Mapusa, Rs 50 after hard bargaining. **Motorcycle taxis** are a bit cheaper.

Directory **Banks** *State Bank of India* changes some TCs but does not accept Visa. *Bank of Baroda* accepts some credit cards, but get there around 1030 and be prepared to spend at least an hour. Also many private dealers offer a convenient and speedy service but offer a poorer rate; *Wall Street*, opposite petrol pump, recommended for quick, efficient and polite foreign exchange. **Communications** Internet: *Nikki's Internet Café*, T275794, nikkis@goa1.dot.net.in, has 6 terminals, 0900 to midnight, Rs 80 per hr. **Travel agents** Several including *MGM Travels*, Umtavaddo, T/F276073. **Useful services** Police T278284.

Baga

Colour map 1, grid B1

Sandwiched between Calangute and Anjuna, Baga (really the north end of Calangute beach), has more character. Reached either directly along the beach or by the coconut-shaded road slightly inland, parts of Baga still retain something of its more 'distanced' feel, though even here development has been rapid. It has left behind almost completely the hippy past which brought it to prominence. That is not to say that it is entirely quiet as there are several late night hot spots.

The beach still has plenty of activity where traders compete with existing shops, and restaurant/beach shack clones pump out music to attract the hoards of over-indulgent, sunburnt package tourists. Although the beach is relatively clean, at high tide the strip is narrow after accounting for the rows of shacks, fishing boats and sun beds. It is congested here and if you have come to Goa for open, deserted beaches and peaceful relaxation, avoid Baga at all costs! There is also a high con-centration of trinket sellers, masseurs and ear cleaners (not hygienic) who will hassle you for custom at regular intervals. Sun beds are on hire for Rs 50, rising to Rs 100 during the peak season when they are all guaranteed to be occupied.

The northern end of Baga is quieter and you can wade across the attractive estuary at low tide (with care) for a pleasant 30-minute walk round the head-land leading to Anjuna beach. The enclosed concrete bridge (possibly one of the ugliest ever built), across the Baga River adds about 1 km to this walk. Take care when using this bridge at night as there are no lights and not even the full moon can penetrate the excess of concrete. Early risers may see fishermen returning with their catch, while at dusk you may spot individual fishermen casting their nets at the mouth of the estuary.

An Anjuna style 'Hippie Market', has become a regular feature here on Sat-urday evenings. Westerners and local vendors congregate near the headland from around 1700, north of the Baga river, to trade shabby 'ethnic' goods and comfort themselves on familiar snacks. Things hot up with nightfall though the frantic pace of the more famous Wednesday market is thankfully missing.

Sleeping
Many hotels offer big off-season discounts May-Sep; some attract package holidays

LL *Nilaya Hermitage*, near Arpora, 3 km inland, T276793, F276792, nilaya@ goa1.dot.net 11 superbly and uniquely designed, colourful rooms, excellent pool, secluded, peaceful woodland location overlooking Baga headland, health centre, res-ident French chef during season, very highly exclusive. Possibly the best hotel in Goa. If you can afford it, this is where you should stay (US$235).

B *Resorte Marinha Dourada*, towards Arpora, T276780, F276785, mdourada@goa1. dot.net.in 106 decent size a/c rooms in resort hotel, quiet location overlooking small lake, 1.5km from beach (hourly shuttle), restaurant, pool, health centre. **B** *Ronil Beach Resort*, T276099, F276068. 88 a/c rooms, good restaurant, in a cramped site. **B-C** *Capt Lobo's Beach Hideaway*, Cobravaddo, T276103, F276917, michx@hotmail.com 21 small apartments in 'street' of 2-storey flats, nothing special, very poor pool. Arranges breaks in sister hotels by the river at Verem and in the 'Forest' (at Dodo Marg, Maharashtra) which may prove more interesting.

C *CSM* Leisure Resort (Colonia Santa Maria), Cobravaddo, 15 minute walk to centre, T277447, F277423. 46 rooms in 10 colonial style villas among palms and bougainvillea, *Banana Grove* tandoori restaurant, bar, pool, beach across the dunes. **C** *Baia Do Sol*, Baga Sq, north end, T276084, F731415. 23 very clean rooms, a/c cottages, good restaurant with views (excellent seafood), watersports, entertainment, attractive garden setting. **C** *Sunshine Beach Resort*, Calangute-Baga Rd, T276003, F277474, sbr@goa1.dot.net.in 21 rooms, now upgraded to a resort hotel, pool, shops, beauty parlour and full with package tourists. **C-D** *Cavala*, Sauntavaddo, Baga-Calangute Rd, away from the beach, T276090, F277340, cavala@goa1.dot.net.in 22 clean rooms with bath, best at rear, overlooking fields ("you can almost imagine yourself away from the mess of the beachside!"), pool across road, non a/c better value (Rs 550 including taxes and breakfast), pay double for a/c.

Baga

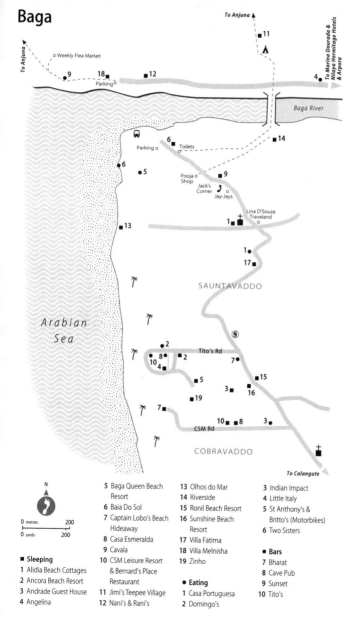

North Goa

D *Alidia Beach Cottages*, T276835, F279014. Behind the church, Sauntavaddo, 16 good clean rooms with attached bath, restaurant, friendly owner, beach 2 minute walk, excellent value off-season. Highly recommended. **D** *Jimi's Teepee Village*, Baga Hill, just north of bridge. 5 American-Indian style teepees with electricity, running water and secure storage, healing massage. Recommended for imagination and uniqueness (tents to reappear after Jimi's holiday). **D** *Resort Olhos Do Mar*, T275612, adi@goa1.dot.net.in 10 rooms (Rs 550 including.breakfast), new, comfortable rooms with sitting room and kitchenette (wasted space), limited menu restaurant, as close as you can get to the sea! **D** *Riverside*, near the bridge, 5 minute walk from beach, T277337. 22 rooms, restaurant, garden setting, pool, nothing special. **D-E** *Villa Fatima*, T277418, villa.fatima@sympatico.ca Calangute-Baga Rd, Sauntavaddo. 35 rooms (Rs 200-800) set round central courtyard, resort style, good for meeting people, ISD, internet facilities, motorbike hire, perfect for back packers. Recommended.

E *Ancora Beach Resort*, Sauntavaddo, T276096. 10 rooms (Rs 300), Tibetan restaurant. **E** *Baga Queen Beach Resort*, T276880. 15 good sized, clean rooms with bath (Rs 350), close to beach, better value than others nearby. **E** *Casa Esmeralda*, CSM Rd, T277194. Seven, new clean, reasonable rooms (Rs 350), good restaurant (Indian Impact).

F *Andrade Guest House*, Cobravaddo, behind Linda Goa, rooms are really basic but have mosquito nets, Mrs Andrade is very friendly and amusing, the cheapest option near the beach (Rs 100). **F** *Venar*, Cobravadd, T276867. 4 basic but clean rooms with shared bath (Rs 150).

Family guest houses on the northern side of Baga Creek, up towards Arpora, those to the left of the bridge are quieter. **E** *Villa Melnisha*, T277805. 4 simple, clean rooms with bath, kitchenette, good cheap thalis. **E-F** *Nani's & Rani's*, T276313, T9823088329 (mobile), few simple rooms (shared or own bath), quiet, relaxed, STD/ISD. **Rooms in houses/cottages** are available for about Rs 300 but good discounts are possible for weekly or monthly rental. Standards vary so check room and security first. Try Wilson Fernandes at *Nani's & Rani's* or ask at *Four Seasons Restaurant* at Jack's Corner. *Lourde's*, T279652, is round Jack's Corner, near the car park.Towards the bottom of Tito's Rd: **E** *Angelina*, T279145. Good rooms upstairs with balconies. **E** *Zinho*, T277383. **E** *Joaquim*.

Eating

There are plenty of good restaurants & small beach cafés

Expensive *Baia del Sol*, Casa Portuguesa, Calangute-Baga Rd, in an old villa with antiques, some tables on verandah, quite exclusive, plenty of atmosphere. Good food but reports of small portions and stomach upsets. Little Italy, right after crossing the river bridge. Excellent and authentic pastas and pizzas in the open. **Mid-range** *Bernard's Place* near CSM, for Sunday roasts. *Domingo's*, Tito's Rd. International. Well cooked and tasty, also one of the few (if not only) restaurants here to freeze perishables in portions rather than refreezing wholesale. *Indian Impact*, CSM Rd. Indian. Curries – "as good as Bradford!", tandoori, friendly. North, near the river there is *Nani's & Rani's*. Friendly, pleasant, good breakfasts. *Sunset* is further along the path, pleasant for watching the goings-on of Baga Beach and at the river mouth. *St Anthony's*, Goan and seafood. Wide choice, one of the most established. *Two Sisters*. Good muesli, curd and fruit salad.

Bars *Bharat* is friendly and a good place for an evening drink. *Tito's* is 'the place' for late night drinking (known for Domingo's Pina Colada) and dancing, generally packed from 2300 to 0300, though the entertainment on offer is variable, the a/c dance floor has been replaced by a cybercafé/games room. Scuffles are not uncommon and one in late 1999 resulted in an unfortunate death. *The Cave Pub*, Tito's Rd, is a new rival where the bar staff are mostly westerners. A 2-storey European-style pub which is a good meeting place, especially for information of parties. However, beware of short measures and sudden price increases!

The Sap Tappers

The Portuguese introduced the Western art of distilling when they settled in the palm fringed shores of Goa in 1510. The habit of drinking the spirit of the palm sap, the palm feni (and also the caju feni derived from the cashew apple), has become an indispensable part of Goan life.

The task of extracting the sap from the crown of the tall palm trees is left in the hands of some 6,000 toddy-tappers who, usually helped by their wives, also process the juice and distil it.

The sap flows when the apex of an unopened flower bunch is 'tapped', by slicing it off and tapping it with a stick to make the cells burst. The juice starts to flow about three weeks after the first cut. From then on, successive flower buds are tapped so that the sap can be collected for half a year. Fruit production, of course, stops during this period, but the tapping appears to result in an improved crop of nuts where the yield had been previously poor.

The skillful tapper ties a circle of rope around his ankles and with a cutter in hand, shins up the tall smooth trunk of the palm two or three times a day, to empty the pot of sap.

Traditionally tappers lived as tenants on a landowner's property exchanging the privilege of tapping the palm sap (toddy) with performing certain services in the landlord's fields and home. The tapper also enjoyed certain hereditary rights so the livelihood and skill was passed on from generation to generation. However, the government's attempts to remove their status as virtual bonded labour has resulted in unforeseen difficulties faced by those whose landlords are refusing to recognize their hereditary rights and privileges. Some tappers have been facing eviction, and with it, their means of earning a living. See also 'Coconut Palms' on page 230.

Shopping Countless shops sell souvenirs of all descriptions so shop around and don't be talked into buying something you don't want. **Books** *Jay-Jays*. Mostly second hand novels; 50% back if you return the book.

Transport **Bicycles** and **motorbikes** to hire, ask outside *Britto's* at the north end, for motorbikes. *Jay-Jays* is also recommended. **Buses** Several to Mapusa, Rs 5. **Boats** From the beach to Anjuna Flea Market, Rs 50 (one way); avoid in rough weather. You won't escape being approached by fishermen on Wed, around the bus stand. **Taxis** Baga to Mapusa or Anjuna; bargain down from Rs 100 to Rs 45; to Panaji down from Rs 150 to about Rs 60. **Autos** Bit cheaper than taxis. **Motorbike taxis** Not worth risking.

Directory **Banks** *Exchange*: just north of Tito's, T276492, oceanstar@india.com, has 5 terminals. Recommended. **Travel agents** *Lina D'Souza Traveland*, Villa Nova, Sauntavaddo, T276196, F276308, efficient ticketing.

Anjuna

Anjuna (pronounced Anzuna*) is now one of Goa's most 'popular' coastal villages, though the headland is rather too rocky for comfortable swimming. It took over from Calangute as the centre for hippies but they are long gone leaving '90s 'ravers' and pill-poppers and the season's 'in' crowd, who often stay here on a long-term basis.*

Colour map 1, grid C1

Ins & outs **Getting there** There are frequent buses from Mapusa and a daily bus from Panaji which stop along the main Mapusa road. Turn at the Starco's crossroads for hotels and guesthouses. Local boats ferry passengers from Baga and Arambol for the Wednesday market. **Getting around** Motorcycles are easy to hire.

North Goa

North Goa

A visitor writes: "If you want to fill your body with stimulants, party all night to Goa trance, risk harrassment and extortion from the local police with the added attraction of warm weather and a tropical setting, then Anjuna is the place for you". The aim, it seems, is to "get off your face, dance until dawn and amuse/bore your friends silly about the previous night's high points (those that can be remembered) over breakfast the next morning." During the season, all night beach 'parties' continue to attract crowds and even during the day there is a constant roar of motor bikes and scooters along the roads. The easy availability of drugs also attracts local police during the high season. They carry out raids on travellers' houses and harass partygoers and sometimes innocent motorcyclists, often demanding large bribes. Not all international peddlers get away; note that there are several foreigners serving long sentences.

Close to Our Lady of Piety Church on the way into Vagator from Mapusa, the splendid **Albuquerque Mansion** was built in the 1920s by an expatriate Goan who had worked as a doctor in Zanzibar, Dr Manuel F Albuquerque. Honoured by the Sultan of Zanzibar on his retirement he returned home to build what is now affectionately referred to by Teresa Albuquerque as 'the pride of Anjuna'. The house is in fact an exact replica of the Royal Palace of Zanzibar, so if you never have the chance to visit that African tropical island this is an opportunity to see what the king's home looks like – from the outside. The building was constructed by workers brought specially from Zanzibar.

Anjuna

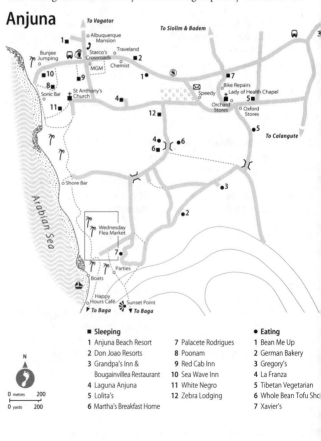

N

| 0 metres | 200 |
| 0 yards | 200 |

■ **Sleeping**
1 Anjuna Beach Resort
2 Don Joao Resorts
3 Grandpa's Inn &
  Bougainvillea Restaurant
4 Laguna Anjuna
5 Lolita's
6 Martha's Breakfast Home
7 Palacete Rodrigues
8 Poonam
9 Red Cab Inn
10 Sea Wave Inn
11 White Negro
12 Zebra Lodging

● **Eating**
1 Bean Me Up
2 German Bakery
3 Gregory's
4 La Franza
5 Tibetan Vegetarian
6 Whole Bean Tofu Sho
7 Xavier's

Anjuna's proud past

Few of Anjuna's visitors know anything of its pre-hippy past, yet as Teresa Albuquerque's fascinating profile of the village (available in local bookshops) shows, it has a history of which the local population is very proud. The name gives away part of the secret of its origins. Derived from Hanjuman, a word applying to the Arabs 'Chamber of Commerce', Anjuna was an important Arab trading post from the 10th-12th centuries. But, as was common with many such ports on the west coast of India, Arab Muslim traders often formed only a small minority of the population, and Hindu influences were also important, as both the lineage of some of the important Hindu castes and the existence of ancient temples illustrates.

Most traces of such temples have now been obliterated by years of Christianization, for Anjuna, along with the rest of Bardez, was deeply affected by Portuguese determination to convert everyone who lived in its Old Conquest territories. Ceded to the Portuguese by the Bijapur Sultans in 1543, it was allocated to the Franciscans as their sphere of missionary activity. Five years after the Franciscans began working in Bardez they established the parish of Nagoa, which included modern Anjuna. Local people still talk of the ghosts of this era inhabiting particular groves. According to Teresa Albuquerque, between 1546 and 1567 300 temples were destroyed in Bardez and the income which had previously gone from temple lands to the temples was transferred to Christian education. The Anjuna shrine of Bhumika Devi was moved across into Pernem. The rectorate of Anjuna was established in 1603 when the Church of St Michael was dedicated. It was subsequently re-built on a much grander scale in 1613.

A well attested story tells how in 1628 a Portuguese Vicar who had told a Hindu woman to have her child baptised was severely attacked by furious villagers. They were found guity of assault and executed. Their houses were confiscated and salt was mixed with the soil on their lands, and as a warning an account was carved in stone on a padrao (monument), and set up in the village. Gomes Pereira recounts that many years later the stone fell and broke in two, and that Hindu villagers often light candles on the stone in memory of the victims.

In the course of the next three centuries Anjuna produced a series of notable figures in Goa's history, both in Church and in secular life. The best known cleric was Fr Agnelo Gustav de Souza (1869-1927). Born and brought up in the village, Fr de Souza trained for the priesthood in Mapusa and Rachol before joining the Missionary Society of Pilar. He developed an extraordinary reputation both for his preaching and for his pastoral work. Twelve years after his death his body was moved to Pilar and became a place of pilgrimage. In 1986 he was raised by the Pope to the rank of venerable, the final stage towards canonization.

Little of this personal history is evident to casual visitors. However, both from the churches and from some of the splendid houses, something of the 400 years of cultural history can be inferred.

Warning Tourism has changed some features of the social face of Anjuna. The church remains strong and community life a powerful force, but the dramatic inflow of money and the wholly different life style of many of the visitors have produced tensions and conflict. The effects of easily available drugs are particularly resented by many in the villages. Incidents of break-ins and muggings have been reported, especially on the beach at night.

North Goa

AL-B *Laguna Anjuna*, T231999, F420213, anjungoa@goa1.dot.net.in, www.anjuna -goa.com 22 spacious, attractive apartments in individually designed cottages with 'Swiss interiors' (US$70 for 1-bedroom suite), exclusive hotel conceived by the same architect as *Nilaya Hermitage*, Arpora, new for the millenium. **C** *Grandpa's Inn*, Gaunwadi, Mapusa Rd, T273271, F274370. 10 comfortable rooms with bath in old

Sleeping
Prices rise in mid-Nov and over the Christmas period

North Goa

Flea Market

The Wednesday Flea Market is huge and very popular – some find it colourful and worthwhile for jewellery, souvenirs and ethnic clothes. From its origins as an opportunity for foreign travellers to sell personal possessions in order to get on – or get home – the Flea market has become an all-India market. Kashmiris and Rajasthanis set up stall alongside stallholders from much closer to home. Everything is geared gaudily and unashamedly at the tourist. Haircuts and henna 'tattoos' are on offer, alongside juggling equipment and chocolate cakes. Prices are extortionate compared to other shops. The best time to visit is the early morning (0800) or just before sunset to avoid the midday crowds who jam the approach roads. In the high season the afternoon can get oppressive and it can be difficult to move around but at least the beach provides a handy escape valve. Many Westerners end up at the Shore Bar for the Wednesday night rave.

Goan house (Rs 800), good restaurant and a pool. **D** *Don Joao Resorts*, Sorranto, T274325, F273447, Luzco@bom2.vsnl.net.in 48 large rooms with balcony and fridge (most with kitchenettes), some a/c, restaurant, exchange, small pool, friendly, good value off-season, away from beach but recommended.

D *Palacete Rodrigues*, Mazalvaddo, east of centre, T273358. 15 high-ceilinged rooms in old Potuguese villa (Rs 600), bit gloomy. **D** *Sea Wave Inn*, T274455. 5 clean rooms (Rs 500), close to beach, multicuisine restaurant. **D** *White Negro*, near the church, T273326. 10 rooms with nets (Rs 400-500), good restaurant and bar, very clean. **D-E** *Lolita's*, behind Oxford Stores (ask at nearest phone booth), T273289. 5 spacious, clean rooms with fridge and music system (to play your own tapes), some with TV and air cooler (Rs 350-450) good off-season discounts, friendly, secure. Recommended. **D-E** *Martha's Breakfast Home*, between bus stand and market, T273365. 10 clean, spacious rooms, some new with verandah (Rs 400), good breakfasts, garden, quiet, peaceful, friendly. Recommended. **D-E** *Poonam*, near the bus stand, T273247. 23 good size simple, clean rooms with bath (Rs 400-500), some larger for sharing, restaurant. **D-E** *Red Cab Inn*, T274427, F273312. 6 well designed comfortable, good-value rooms, restaurant ('local entertainment', Mon, 1900). Recommended.

Most beachside rooms are occupied by long-stay visitors who pay about Rs 2,000 per month for the most basic. **NB** Some travellers were robbed when staying in family houses which were not secure; it is safer to choose an approved hotel or guest house. Good padlocks are sold in the small shop next to the *White Negro Bar* for Rs 150. **E** *Anjuna Beach Resort*, DeMello Vaddo, opposite Albuquerque Mansion, T274433. 14 rooms with bath, balcony, restaurant (breakfast, snacks), bike hire, friendly, secure, quiet, good value. Recommended. **F** *Manali*, near the bus stand,

T274421. 7 basic rooms, shared bath (Rs 125), restaurant, bookshop, exchange, internet, but not the friendliest in town. **F** *Zebra Lodging*, inland from St Anthony's. Run-down but **camping** possible.

Eating

Anjuna is a vegetarian's paradise with plenty of Western and exotic options

Expensive: *Bougainvillea*, at *Grandpa's Inn*. Excellent food, bar (wines, imported beer), in a very pretty garden. Recommended. **Mid-range**: *German Bakery*, inland from the Flea Market. Outdoors with soft lighting, excellent espresso, capuccino, juice and snacks, 2/3 main courses each night (eg lasagna, tofu-burger). Recommended. *Gregory's*, next to a tennis court. Excellent continental, especially pizzas (try one with prawns); also tennis! *La Franza* with bar. Good continental. Pleasant, large verandah overlooking attractive tropical garden. Recommended. *Sea Breeze*, Market area, is busy on Wed. *Xavier's*, St Michaelvaddo, along a windy path, east from the market. **Cheap**: *Bean Me Up*, Soya Station and Salad Bar. Good vegetarian and vegan breakfasts, sandwiches, soups and cakes. All-day vegetarian English, American or continental breakfasts Rs 80. Open 0830-1700 (maybe later when busy) Closed Wed. Recommended. *Tibetan Vegetarian*, for momos etc ("Reflexology, massage offered is not recommended for women"). *Whole Bean Tofu Shop* offers tofu, tempeh and vegetarian snacks.

Sonic, is pleasant for a chilled beer at sunset.   **Bars**

Beach parties   Locations change every year so if you want to party, you'll soon find   **Entertainment** out where and when they are. Ask around locally and look out for flyers. Venues are often recognizable by illuminated trees and luminous wall hangings. **NB** It is best to walk there and back in a large group. *Shore Bar*, north of the Flea market, for the après-market hoedown. The good sound system complements the fire jugglers' playground; several elderly women set up *chai* stalls with cakes and king-size *rizlas* on sale, making a good profit.

Oxford Stores, for groceries, foreign exchange and photo processing. *Orchard Stores*,   **Shopping** groceries, toiletries (western brands). And of course the **Flea Market** which attracts hordes of tourists from all over Goa.

Bunjee jumping is an established business here with a permanent structure set up   **Sport** by a Mumbai based firm, should you wish to fling yourself off towards oblivion at Rs 500 per go. Safety is a priority with harnesses, carabinas and air bags employed. Staff are US trained and regular safety checks are carried out. There are pool tables, a bar, an auditorium for slide/film shows and also beach volleyball. Open 1000-1230 and 1730 until late. **Paragliding** Enterprising foreign long-stayers organize this from season to season with no guarantee of continuity. Try *Happy Hours Café*, south Anjuna beach, from 1230-1400; Rs 500 (children welcome), or at the hilltop between Anjuna and Baga. **Windsurfing** boards are sometimes available for hire at the south end of the beach for about Rs 100 per hour, Rs 800 per week.

Motorcycle hire: *Classic Bike Adventure* Indo-German company at Casa Tres   **Transport** Amigos, Socol Vado 425, Parra, Assagao, about 5 km east (off the Mapusa Rd), T0832-273351, F262076, recommended for reliable bike hire and tours. **Petrol** is sold near *Dinesh Hotel*, at the crossroads towards Siolim.

Banks *Bank of Baroda*, Mon-Wed, Fri 0930-1330, Sat 0930-1130, accepts most TCs,   **Directory** Visa/Mastercard, 1% (min Rs 50); better than private dealers closer to town. They also provide 'Safe Custody Packets'. **Communications** *Poste Restante* at Anjuna Post Office, open 1000-1600, Mon-Sat; efficient, parcels are also accepted without a fuss. **Internet** Several guest house and private booths charge about Rs 2 per min; *St Anthony's Store*, next to Post Office, Rs 100 per hour; 0900-2200. **Medical services** *Chemists* opposite Don Joao Resorts. *Health Centre*, T272250. **Travel agents** *MGM*, T274317; *Speedy*, T273266; *Traveland*, near the bus stand, T273207, F217535. **Useful services** Police: T273233.

North Goa

Chapora and Vagator

Colour map 1, grid B1
Sterling Vagator Resort signs direct you to Vagator and the Chapora Fort

At the north end of Anjuna village Chapora is an attractive little hamlet with its small bays between rocky headlands shaded by palms. It is quiet and laid back, though it can sometimes get crowded with day-trippers. The beach is particularly pleasant in the early morning, but the sea is not always safe for swimming. Cheaper than Anjuna for rooms and houses, it attracts long term travellers. Chapora is quite a dirty village compared to others in Goa so it is not surprising that there is very high density of laundries!

Chapora Fort

Despite the fact that none of the original buildings have survived the fort remains superbly atmospheric

The fort commands the hill top at the north end of the bay, only a short but steep walk away, immediately above *Sterling Resorts*. Now in ruins, it stands on the south bank of the Chapora River and dominates the estuary. It was originally built by Adil Shah, hence its original name *Shahpura* or Chapora. Aurangzeb's son Akbar (not Akbar the Great) used it as his headquarters when plotting against his father in a pact with the Mughal's greatest enemies, the Marathas. The Portuguese built it in its present form in 1717 as a secure refuge for the people of Bardez in face of the Maratha attacks as well as a defence of the river mouth. The fort with its irregular walls, one major gateway on its eastern side and a series of octagonal battlements, was once served by a series of underground tunnels which provided supplies to the beseiged. Old muslim tombs, huge ramparts and two tunnel entrances can still be seen. Views from the sea-facing walls are spectacular. To the north, across the ruffled waters of the Chapora estuary, the stunning blue of the sea meets the fine sand of Morjim beach, curving gracefully northwards towards Mandrem, Arambol and finally Tiracol. To the west a low circular knoll abuts into the sea in front of the fort, while to the south the small coves of Vagator give way to Anjuna beach. The fort is well worth a visit, but it is quite a climb. Soft fruit drinks are sold at highly inflated prices, so it is worth carrying your own.

Further along from the fort **traditional boat building** is carried out on the riverside. Further still, on the Siolim Road, Badem Church can be found. It overlooks the estuary and is one of the nicest **sunset spots**.

Just south of Vagator Beach which attracts day-trippers, there are two other **small beaches** which are more popular with younger travellers who fancy a change from Anjuna. **Little Vagator** is past the Disco Valley Party spot while a little further along the very attractive **Ozran** beach nestles at the bottom of a palm covered cliff. A steep path leads down to the sands where there is a face sculpture left by one of the original hippies in the 1970s – it is a frisbee hangout. ■ *Getting there: From Anjuna, to reach Ozran and Little Vagator Beaches, first take the road towards Siolim and follow it around the hill until you see the sign for the Alcove Restaurant and Pub. Turn left here and the rest is obvious. Ozran Beach is recognizable by a small shack on top of the cliff which usually has motorbikes parked outside. Little Vagator is a short distance further.*

Visitors may wish to donate shoes, clothes, spectacles, books and so on at the end of their stay to an **orphanage** run by an Englishwoman, Anita Edgar Victory House, 549 Coutinho Vaddo, T273564 (UK T01803-859094).

Sleeping

B *Sterling Vagator* (partly time-share), T273315, F273314. Attractive setting at the foot of the fort, 30 well-maintained cottages (Rs 2,500), some poolside (uphill) or in peaceful garden setting with shady *jambul* trees near the beach, restaurants (others 10 mins walk away), quiet, exchange for residents, but not the most efficient reception desk. **B** *Leoney Resort*, T273634, F274343, romio@goa1.dot.net.in 13 rooms, 3 cottages, a/c extra Rs 200. Clean, modern, family run, low-key, quiet location, pool, 10 mins walk from beach. **B-C** *Royal Resort*, T274365. 28 renovated rooms, 10 a/c (overpriced at Rs 1,400), new management, restaurant, jazz bar, pool, 500m from beach, camping proposed (Rs 500).

Chapora Village has a number of very cheap rooms and houses for long term rent; ask locally. Several budget places can be found along the streets leading to the beach from the bus stops. **E** *Abu John's*, 6 small rooms with bath (Rs 300), good restaurant, garden, pleasant, quiet. **E** *Dolrina*, T273382. 13 rooms, most baths shared between 2 rooms (Rs 300), safe, secure, friendly. Recommended. **E** *Garden Villa*, T273571. 8 clean rooms (Rs 150-250), some with bath, good value for the area, although away from the beach, restaurant with a decent choice. **E** *Hilltop Motel*, away from the beach, T273665. 14 small rooms, those with bath reasonable (Rs 300), genuine Italian baker. **E** *Reshma*, 12 reasonable rooms (Rs 250). **F** *Noble Nest*, opposite the Holy Cross Chapel, T274335. 21 rooms, 2 with bath but ample facilities for sharing (Rs 150), basic, but popular, exchange and internet. **F** *Ram Das Swami* restaurant on Little Vagator Beach, allows **camping** but provides no toilets.

Mid-price: *Alcove* on the cliff above Little Vagator. Smartish, ideal position, good fish dishes plus drinks to spend a whole evening. *Mango Tree*, in the village, offers a wide choice continental favourites. **Cheap:** In **Vagator**: several restaurants line the streets to the beach. Some serve good fresh fish including *Mahalaxmi*. *Milky Place* is good for lassi, yoghurt etc. *Primrose Café* serves tasty health foods and also has news of "spontaneous" parties. In **Chapora** the fly-ridden *Scarlet* does good muesli, ice creams and chilled fruity shakes.

Eating

Hoards of day-trippers congregate around the beach cafés

Chapora & Vagator

North Goa

Entertainment *Disco Valley* between Vagator and Little Vagator beaches is a party venue.

Shopping **Books** *Narayan*, a small bookstall has a selection of books and local newspapers.

Transport **Road** Daily bus from Panaji, 1hr; frequent from Mapusa to Chapora via Anjuna and Vagator.

Directory **Banks** No exchange facilities here except at *Sterling Vagator* (for residents only); nearest is at the *Bank of Baroda*, Anjuna. **Communications** *Mira Cyber Café*, Little Vagator, Rs 2 per min, 4 terminals, 0900-2230, also does pizzas, snacks and ice creams. **Hospital** Health centre T262211.

Siolim

Colour map 1, grid B1
Population: 9,700

The **Church of St Anthony** dominates the square in Siolim (pronounced *Show-lem*). Built in 1606, it replaced an earlier Franciscan church (1568). St Anthony, the patron saint of Portugal, is widely venerated throughout the villages of Goa. The high flat-ceilinged church has a narrow balustraded gallery and Belgian glass chandeliers. The attractive and typically gabled west end has statues of Jesus and St Anthony. Siolim is less than 1 km from the ferry crossing.

Transport Ferries are half-hourly, but will be made redundant by the new bridge when it opens. The direct route to Arambol and Tiracol passes through Mandrem (see below).

Morjim

Colour map 1, grid B1

Morjim lies on the north side of the Chapora River estuary right at its mouth. The area is popular for bird watching as a large number of land and sea birds can be spotted. The beach is still clean and idyllic with no more than 50 to 60 day-trippers visiting at the peak of the high season.

After crossing the estuary by ferry to Chopdem the coast road runs as a narrow village lane winding along the edge of the estuary giving beautiful views across to Chapora Fort until it reaches the point where the river meets the sea and the coast turns sharply north. Here the road ends behind the sand dunes.

The beach has been found to be a turtle nesting site

One or two beach shacks rent out sun beds and deckchairs for Rs 50 while palm umbrellas provide the only shade on this long and wide stretch of firm sand. Plans for a 5-star hotel complex here with a "private" beach, which would deny local people free access to that section of the waterfront, have been dropped so this fine stretch of beach should be safe for some time to come.

The **Shri Morja Devi Temple** complex in the village is of special interest because one affiliated shrine is dedicated to a Jain guru. This suggests an ancient heritage to the temple, since Jainism was sponsored by both the Chalukyas and the Rashtrakuta dynasties who ruled over the region from the sixth-10th centuries AD. The principal festival, the month-long *Kalas Utsav* takes place at intervals of three, five and seven years and closes with a large cultural fair. The six or so beach shacks provide simple food and drinks.

Asvem

Colour map 1, grid B1

The road from Morjim cuts inland over the low wooded hills to Mandrem village, which lies a few kilometres south of Arambol. Just before you get to the village, a road leads down to a deserted but attractive palm-fringed beach which has some cheap beach huts on the water's edge. If you don't want

---

Safe passage for turtles

Adult turtles come ashore on Morjim beach in Pernem between October and December, to lay their eggs which hatch after 54 days, usually on the night of the full moon. As soon as a nest is discovered, the Forest Department put a net over the site and mark it with a flag. When the eggs hatch, the forest officials escort the hatchlings to the sea to allow them a safe run into the unknowns of the ocean. The nesting sites are patrolled day and night to protect them from the worst of humanity.

---

company, fancy drifting off to sleep with the roar of the sea in your ears and awaken to the shrill call of sea gulls, Asvem may be for you.

D *Palm Grove* , towards Morjim, 4 tree houses built amongst the coconut palms, simple rooms with bed and fan, very close to the shoreline, bath facilities shared with **F** rooms, occasionally used by package tourists on "go native" trips, restaurant offers a limited menu. **F** *Beach huts* made of woven palm leaves on concrete bases are put up close to the shore line. They don't contravene building restrictions as they are not "permanent" structures, 1 or 2 rooms, shared facilities within a nearby *café*.

Sleeping & eating
Don't leave valuables in rooms

North Goa

Mandrem

Along the road, the fishing and toddy tapping village occupies a beautifully shaded setting. The beach, which is usually deserted, has little shade, but a little to the north is a beautiful little 'island' of sand with coconut palms between the sea and the river. Mandrem village has the **Shri Bhumika temple** housing an ancient image. In the **Shri Purchevo Ravalnatha Temple** there is a particularly striking medieval image of the half eagle-half human Garuda, who acts as the *vahana* (carrier) of Vishnu. It is unusual in that the crouching Garuda is dressed as a soldier with wings protruding from his back.

Colour map 1, grid B1

Five or six **F** *Beach shacks* have appeared on the quiet beach. **F** *Village rooms*, usually indicated by signs, are rented out to foreigners for up to 6 months through the winter. Simply ask around.

Sleeping

Banks *Canara Bank*, on the main road accepts travellers' cheques but has no facilities for card cash. **Hospital** T230081.

Directory

Arambol

Arambol (Harmal) is a large, strung out village by the seashore approached by a road which winds across the plateau and down through cashew trees. The main beach is a stunning stretch of curving sand but it is no longer an idyllic peaceful spot. The once precious quiet of this hidden corner is now broken by the mini building boom that has hit and the accompanying noise vies with the hum of traffic bringing a growing number of day-trippers, including motorcyclists from Anjuna.

Colour map 1, grid B1

Many visit Arambol by motorbike from other beaches. There are regular buses to the village from Mapusa and from Chopdem, the attractive coastal detour via Morjim being slightly longer. Coming from Vagator you must combine walking with a ferry trip or for the less energetic by bus or taxi and ferry.

Ins & outs
See transport section for further details

If you spend some time in the village you may discover the main village temple, dedicated to the deity **Shri Ravalnath**, which also has eight affiliated deities. Despite the fact that it is in the New Conquests, Arambol also has a Christian community and a church.

A sign at the crossroads in the village centre near the bus stop points down to the sea. The road passes a school and village houses sheltering under coconut palms before reaching the main southern beach where a large number of motorbikes and scooters line up in an unruly parking lot. Shops along the road sell cheap clothes, bags and trinkets but few of these seem to be of Goan origin.

To the north, a well-made track runs round the headland past a series of tiny bays to the second quieter beach which is relatively free of beach shacks. There is little shade save for the few sun umbrellas and is largely used for sunbathing by western visitors. Here you can walk for miles with starfish being washed up by your feet. Unlike the headlands around Anjuna, the rocks which run into the sea here are basalt, the hexagonal columns tilted almost horizontal but eroded into jagged shapes clearly visible for miles along the coast. There are sulphur pits and a freshwater lake which some visitors use for swimming.

Sleeping Touts meet newcomers at the bus stand, offering rooms close to the main beach for Rs 80-150 (bargaining expected); others are in a cluster on a parallel road, among trees (so more mosquitoes). Some don't provide bedding. Many rooms are exposed and lack the security of a hotel compound. Guest houses higher up on the rocky hills charge more but they are poorly maintained and there is a distinct smell of sewage. **E** *Ludo*, more like a country club, rooms. Typical family home with 3 **F** basic rooms with bed, fan (set back behind *Cottage* offering massage on the beach road) with cold shower (hot bucket Rs 5), quiet. **E-F** *Ganesh Rest House*, above Ganesh Stores on the first headland north, 250m from beach. Few rooms (Rs 250), shared smelly toilet, cold shower, balcony upstairs, restaurant. The tiny **F** *Lakes Paradise* also serves Goan curry and rice.

There is very spartan accommodation in Waddo, the small village near Arambol

Eating There are beach **cafés** all along the main beach and around the headland to the north. Italian food is in vogue. **Mid-range**: *Pirates Cabin*. Indian, succulent *tandoori* grills. **Cheap**: *Double Dutch*, from the beach turn left off the main beach road before *Ganesh Stores* (look for *I* for Information). Excellent tea, coffee, imported journals. Closer to the main beach: *Loecke*. Ideal for tea. *Seahorse*, says one, has the "best waiter in India!". *Welcome*, at the end of the road on the sea front. Best muesli. Basic eateries in the village do 'rice plate meals'.

Sports For **dolphin trips** or boats to Anjuna, contact *21 Coconuts Inn* , second restaurant on the left after stepping onto the beach; Rs 150 for each. **Paragliding** is also arranged from beach shacks.

Transport **Local Bike** and **taxi hire** from *Welcome Restaurant*. **Bus** and **ferry** There are regular buses to the village from Mapusa and a frequent service from Chopdem which is 12 km away along the main road (about 40 mins, Rs 6); the attractive coastal detour via Morjim being slightly longer. Coming from Vagator walk to Chapora village to find a local ferry across the estuary (Rs 20 each, Rs 40 for a boat), then a 2-hr walk north through Morjim and Mandrem along the coast. Or get a bus to Siolim, cross the river by ferry to Chopdem (Rs 3) and then pick up a bus or taxi. The bridge being built across the Chopden estuary was half-completed in early 2000 but progress is very slow.

Directory **Communications** The small village *Post Office* is at the 'T junction', 1,500m from the beach. **Emergency** Police, T297614. **Medical services** *Chemists*, on the main road; *Health centre*, T291249. **Travel agents**: *Delight* and *Tara*, in the village, exchange cash and TCs, good for train tickets (Rs 100 service charge); also buys bus tickets.

Keri

Keri beach, north of Arambol beach, is a completely unspoilt and rarely visited stretch of sand backed by casuarina trees all the way down to the Arambol highland. It can be reached from the north on foot from the ferry terminal, or from the south by walking round the headland from Arambol. There are dangerous currents near the mouth of the Tiracol estuary so it is best to avoid swimming there; a five-minute walk south along the beach will get you to safe waters. The beach is protected by CRZ regulations from being developed with permanant buildings near the high water mark.

Colour map 1, grid A1

Forest Department's simple **F** *Keri Forest Rest House*, can be booked through the DCF, North Ponda, T0834-312095. A solitary restaurant (limited menu), has 4 very basic **F** rooms with common bath (Rs 70).

Sleeping & eating

The tiny hamlet of Paliem lies on the edge of the plateau about 5 km north of Arambol just before the road drops down through dense wooded slopes to Keri and the Tiracol ferry. Its **Vetal** (Betall) **Temple** has charmingly painted designs of the tree of life on its blue walled exterior.

Paliem Village
Colour map 2, grid B1

North Goa

Tiracol

Tiracol (Terekhol) is the northernmost tip of Goa, an enclave on the Maharashtra border. The village probably derives its name from tir-khol (steep river bank).

Colour map 2, grid A1

The small but strategic **fort** stands above the village on the north side of the Tiracol River estuary on a rugged promontory which gives good views across the water. Its high battlemented walls are clearly visible from the Arambol headland. Built by the Maharaja Khem Sawant Bhonsle in the 17th century, it is protected from attacks from the sea, while the walls on the land side rise from a dry moat. It was captured by the Portuguese Viceroy Dom Pedro Miguel de Almeida (Marques de Alorna) in 1746 who renamed it Holy Trinity and had a chapel built inside (now St Anthony's). Tiracol was only fully and legally incorporated into Goa in 1788. The fort was armed with 22 cannons but saw a bloody massacre in 1835. During a military revolt, a ruthless Commandant, 'Tiger Killer' de Cunha, entered the fort and ordered the beheading of the garrison and civilians who were sheltering there, and went on to exhibit the heads on stakes. Far removed from the centre of administration in Panaji, Tiracol gained a reputation as a spot chosen by Goan freedom fighters to demonstrate their demands from time to time. A group entered the fort on 15 August (Independence Day) 1954 and succeeded in flying the Indian flag there for a day, before being captured and jailed.

St Anthony's church inside the tiny fort was built in the early 1750s soon after the Portuguese takeover. It has a classic Goan façade and is just large enough to have catered for the small village. In the small courtyard, paved with laterite blocks, stands a modern statue of Christ. Inside, the church has several charming features. The small gallery at the west end provides space for a harmonium and the choir, while in the body of the church are two old confessional chairs. Too small a church for full scale confessional boxes, two small hinged wooden flaps are pulled out to separate the priest from the penitent, and tucked back against the wall when not in use. There is a typically decorated altar reredos with St Anthony above. Some of the framed paintings on the walls have deteriorated with time. The *Festival of St Anthony* here is held in May (usually on the second Tuesday) to enable the villagers to attend who would otherwise be away on the conventional festival day of 13 June.

You can explore the fort's battlements and tiny circular turrets which scarcely seem to have been intended for the real business of shooting the enemy. The views from the fort are magnificently atmospheric, looking south to Arambol, Chapora and Fort Aguada. Steps lead down to a terrace on the south side while the north has an open plateau.

Sleeping **B-C** *Tiracol Fort Heritage*, T0831-782240, F782326, tiracol@usa.net 1 rooms in old fort conversion (Rs 800-1,750), sympathetically furnished, best are the spacious suites at either end on the 1st floor (number 1 is particularly good with own little tiny terrace with flag pole and resident *langur* monkeys), wonderful views, one of Goa's most peaceful and romantic places to stay. Power cuts can be a problem, especially at mealtimes, limited but very tasty menu in the restaurant in the unique setting of a reclaimed dry moat lined with laterite slabs, birdwatchers' haven, boat trips (dolphins, Redi Beach etc), scooter hire, discounts from 4 May-3 Sep. Non-residents may visit (0900-1800). Recommended. **E** *Hill Rock*, 1 km from the ferry, T02366-68264. Modern, 4 rooms (Rs 210-320) in a family hotel, restaurant, good location overlooking fort and Keri beach but neglected.

Transport From **Panaji** there is a bus around 1130. From **Mapusa**, take a share taxi to Siolim (Rs 8) where you cross the river Chapora by ferry; continue to Keri by share taxi, then cross Tiracol River by ferry and walk the remaining 2 km! The Tiracol half-hourly ferry runs between 0600-2130 and takes 15 min. Both the Tiracol and Siolim ferries take cars. From **Dabolim Airport**, pre-paid taxi to Tiracol Fort, Rs 700.

Shiroda

The short drive from Tiracol to the Maharashtrian town of Shiroda shows a wholly different face of India, with a landscape wearing the marks of industrialization and heavy lorries filling the roads. Yet the plant has done little to spoil the rural peace of the fort itself and this atmospheric coastal hotel.

Inland from the north coast

There are several fascinating one or two-day excursions from the northern beaches. It is possible to see not only the churches or forts built during the Portuguese period or remarkable Hindu temples in the interior, but also something of town and rural life in a state undergoing rapid change.

Saligao

Colour map 1, grid B2 Saligao, just east of Calangute, becomes a familiar crossroads for those who choose to spend some time on one of the beaches nearby. Occupied by Saraswat Brahmins many centuries before the arrival of the Portuguese, Saligao is believed by some to have taken its name from the *sal* trees, which were once abundant here. Others suggest it is derived from *sall*, a type of rice cultivated in the heart of this rich agricultural area. Today it is surrounded by coconut palms and the village has several good examples of attractive Goan houses standing in their shady gardens.

The **Our Lady Mother of God** (Mae de Deus) church in an imposing setting, which is clearly visible from the road, was built in 1873, replacing five earlier chapels. It is an unusual neo-Gothic structure but painted white like the traditional baroque churches in Goa. The prominent horizontal ribbed surface with crennalated parapets and stylized flying buttresses makes it quite unique. Inside, the attractive wooden ceiling with its pierced star design is most unusual. The miraculous statue of the Virgin, originally found in a ruined convent in Dauji Village, Old Goa, was enshrined here when the plague forced the population of Dauji to move out. Saligao also has a minor seminary which offers courses in philosophy and theology.

*Our Lady of God
church, Saligao*

Pomburpa

Colour map 1, grid B3

Renowned for its hot springs, Pomburpa, east of Porvorim, has one of Goa's more spectacular village churches. The magnificent painted and gilded wooden reredos in the Church of **Our Lady Mother of God** (Mae de Deus Church) bears the hallmarks of the style of the Church of St Catejan in Old Goa. The ornate decoration in stucco is particularly fine. The annual *Pomburpa Festival* on 4 February draws thousands of visitors and the village, and its church, are totally transformed.

The village also has ancient temples, among the most important being those to **Ravalnath** and **Santeri** (Shantadurga). Although nothing of the ancient buildings survives, the priestly community retains long-standing links with the past. Some of the main images of the deities were transferred to Mulgao, just north of Bicholim, to avoid Portuguese destruction.

West End is a popular night club, open 2300 onwards on Tue and Fri. (Rs 150). *FBI* and *VIP* also have regular parties for which flyers are distributed in advance. **Entertainment**

Mapusa

Mapusa is the administrative headquarters and main town of Bardez taluka. It suffers from almost permanent traffic chaos, especially near the market area, and it is hard to escape the resultant pollution from exhaust and the continuous hooting of horns. There is little reason to stay overnight with the northern beaches so close by. However, the market (daily except Sunday) is worth a visit for local colour and bargain hunting, especially on Fridays when village traders come from far and wide to sell their wares.

Colour map 1, grid B2
Population: 31,600

Getting there This is an important junction for interstate and local buses to the northern beaches. Buses arrive at the market square opposite the taxi stand, while the State Kadamba bus stand is a bit further south. **Getting around** You can walk around the small town and if you should need an auto, Rs 10 should be ample for short hops. **Ins & outs**

Mapusa (pronounced *Maapsa*), stands on a long ridge which runs east-west with fertile agricultural land occupying the flat valley floor right up to the edge of the town. The name may be derived from the extensive swamps which once covered the area; *maha apsa*' (great swamps).

Although there is little of architectural merit, **St Jerome's** Church, is interesting. Locally known as **Milagres Church**, Our Lady of Miracles, east of the market and originally built in 1594, was rebuilt in 1674 and in 1839 after it was destroyed by fire. The small church with its scrolled gable and balconied windows in the façade has a belfry at the rear. The main altar is to Our Lady, and those on the two sides to St John and St Jerome; the *retables* (shelves behind the

North Goa

altar) were brought here from Daugim, Old Goa. Note also the interesting slatted wood ceiling (similar to that found in some old Goan houses) and the ornate pulpit. The church stands near the site of the Shanteri Temple and so is sacred to Hindus as well. Besides, Our Lady of Miracles is believed to have been one of seven Hindu sisters converted to Christianity. Her lotus pattern gold necklace (now stored away) may have also been taken from a Hindu deity which preceded her.

The **Maruti temple** was built on the spot of a firecracker shop in the 1840s which had housed a picture and then the silver image of the Monkey God associated with the Rama (the son of Vayu, who represented Wind). Followers of Rama would gather in the shop since the Portuguese destroyed all Hindu temples and none was built for nearly three centuries. The temple faces south (which is normally avoided since evil spirits are thought to enter from that direction), but here the God protects from that danger; there is a northern entrance.

Sleeping
Most check out at 0900

C *Green Park*, Mapusa-Panaji Rd, bypass junction, T250667, F252698. 35 modern, comfortable, rooms, quiet (being 2 km from centre), good pool (the only one in town) and restaurants. **D-E** *Satyaheera*, near Maruti Temple, T262949. 34 reasonable rooms (Rs 300), a/c (Rs 600), enclosed rooftop restaurant (shared with mosquitoes and the odd mouse), bar. **Home stays** arranged by *Siddhartha*, Zed Point, Chandranath Apts, Phase II, BS7, opposite Police Station, T251153, F262076, info@siddharta.de **E** *Mandarin*, near Alankar Cinema T262579. 21 basic rooms with bath (a/c Rs 400), clean rooftop restaurant. **E** *Tourist Hotel* (GTDC), T262794, at the roundabout. 48 adequate rooms for 2-6, some a/c (Rs 300), reasonable restaurant, beers. **E** *Vilena*, opposite the Municipality, T263115. 14 neat, clean, rooms, some a/c, good restaurants, bar, very friendly. Recommended. **F** *Sirsat Lodge*, 2nd floor, Ramchandra Building, opposite taxi stand, T262419. 43 basic rooms, some a/c (Rs 100-200), some with shared facilities, full, busy, noisy.

Eating
Cuisine is not the highlight of a trip to Mapusa

Mid-range: *Hotel Vilena* has 2 restaurants, 1 on the rooftop and an a/c indoors. They serve the best food in town though the music will appeal only to the young! *Bawarchi* northwest of Hanuman Temple, behind the police station. Part a/c. *Mahalaxmi* Anjuna Rd. A/c, South Indian vegetarian. *Casa Bela*, near Coscar Corner, specializes in

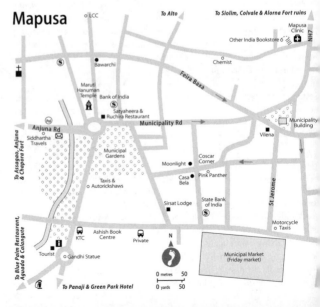

Mapusa

Mapusa's Market

Mapusa's busy and colourful **Municipal Market** is well planned and operates all week except Sundays. The colourful and vibrant 'Friday Market' is a must since vendors come from far and wide and there is a lot of activity right into the evening. There is rarely any backpacker here to be seen selling "ethnic" goods (as you might see in Anjuna). Open from 0800 to 1800 (though some stalls close much earlier). 0730 to 0800 is best for photography when the light is good and you can capture the local stalls being set up. **Warning** Beware of pickpockets.

Goan food. Opposite, *Moonlight*, Shalini Building, 1st floor. Good North Indian at lunchtime, rather dark in the evening, used more for drinking than eating. **Cafés** *Royal-T*, Shop 96, near the Shakuntala Fountain, Municipal Market, Goan snacks, sweets and spices. *Xavier's*, Municipal Market. Other cheap stalls and cafés in the market. From 1630 until late, carts and stalls near the Alankar Cinema sell popular meat and seafood dishes.

Feast of our Lady of Miracles On the Mon of the third week after Easter (6 May 2000), **Festivals** the Nossa Senhora de Milagres image is venerated by Christians as well as Hindus who join together to celebrate the feast day of the Saibin. A huge fair and market is held.

Books *Ashish Book Centre*, near the KTC bus stand. *Other India Bookstore*, 1st floor, St **Shopping** Britto's apartment, above Mapusa clinic, T263306, oibs@bom2.vsnl.net.in is different and excellent. **Photography** *Remy Studios*, Coscar Corner and Shop 8, KTC bus stand.

Local Bus: To Calangute (every 20-30 mins, Rs 5), some continue onto Aguada and **Transport** Baga, some go towards Candolim; check before boarding or change at Calangute. Non-stop mini buses to **Panaji**; buy tickets from booth at market entrance. Rs 6. Buses also go to Vagator and Chapora via Anjuna and towns nearby. **Car hire**: *Pink Panther*, T263180. **Motorcycle hire**: *Classic Bike Adventure* (Indo-German company at Casa Tres Amigos, Socol Vado 425, Parra, Assagao, 4 km west (off the Anjuna Rd), T0832-273351, F276124. Recommended for reliable bikes and tours. **Taxis** (often shared by up to 5); to Panaji Rs 70; Calangute/ Baga, Rs 60; Chapora/Siolim, Rs 80. **Auto**: Calangute, Rs 50; **Motorcycle taxi**: to Anjuna or Calangute, about Rs 40, but open to bargaining. **Long-distance buses** Private operators, lined up opposite the taxi stand, offer near identical routes and rates. To **Bangalore**: 1830, 12 hrs, Rs 250 (Luxury), 450 (Sleeper). **Hampi**: 1800, 11 hrs, Rs 450 (Sleeper). **Mumbai**, 1600, 14 hrs, Rs 250 (Luxury), Rs 450 (Sleeper).

Banks *Bank of India* opposite Municipal Gardens, changes TCs, cash Visa and Mastercard. **Directory** 1000-1400 Mon–Fri, 1000-1200 Sat. *State Bank of India* exchanges cash and TCs, 15-20 mins. Foreign exchange on 1st floor, 1000-1600 Mon-Fri, 1000-1200 Sat. *Pink Panther Agency* changes Visa and Mastercard Mon-Fri 0900-1700, Sat 0900-1300. **Communications** The Sub-Post Office is opposite the police station. **Couriers**: *Blue Dart*, T263208. **Internet**: Several across town, well signed. Most charge Rs 90 per hr. Best at *LCC* 3rd Floor, Bhavani Apartments, Rs 15 per 15 mins; 6 terminals, 0700-2130, 7 days a week. **Hospitals & medical services** *Asilo Hospital*, T262211. Pharmacies: including *Drogaria*, near the Swiss Chapel, open 24 hrs; *Mapusa Clinic*, T262350; *Bardez Bazzar*. **Travel agent** *Siddhartha*, Zed Point, Chandranath Apts, Phase II, BS7, opposite police station, T251153, F262076, info@siddharta.de, arrange special tours, including some for handicapped travellers. **Useful numbers** Ambulance: T262372. Fire: T262900. Police: T262231. Tourist Information: T262390.

North Goa

Moira

Colour map 1, grid B2 Moira is at the heart of a rich agricultural district despite being barely 5 km east of Mapusa. The town is certainly ancient though it is impossible to be certain exactly how old. Some claim it goes back to the sixth or seventh century AD. Until the arrival of the Portuguese it seems to have been a Brahmin village, with seven important temples. These were destroyed by the Portuguese during the Inquisition, the idols moved to Bicholim. Moira was one of the villages where mass baptisms were carried out.

Today it is dominated by the **Church of Our Lady of the Immaculate Conception** which has some unusual features to its impressive façade. The square towers are very close to the central feature, a false dome. The balustrades at the top of the first and second floors run right across the building and the central doorways of the ground and first floors have an Islamic appearance given by trefoil arches, in contrast to the Romanesque of the flanking arches. Inside, the crucified Christ image is unusual in having the feet nailed separately instead of together using a single nail.

Colvale

Colour map 1, grid B2 The bridge at Colvale (Kolvale) remains the lowest crossing point of the Chapora River. The first written record of the village goes back to an inscription datd 1011 AD, and the name itself (*Kol*, from Koli, the Konkani name of the local fishing community, and *vale*, meaning 'creek') still describes one of the villages main activities. The area is believed to have come under the influence of Buddhism since a second century (Gautama) Buddha image was found at Mushir near here in the 19th century by a historian, Fr Heras. It is interesting to note that one of the ancient deities of the village is "Gauthama".

Colvale has the attractive **Church of St Francis of Assissi** (originally 1591, the present building dates from 1713). The façade has a rather splendid plaster image of St Francis between two angels, looking down from above, his hands raised in the gesture of blessing. The principal altar inside is dedicated to the Wounds of St Francis. The feast day is 19 September.

Dargalim

Colour map 1, grid B2 Dargalim (Dhargal) is 2 km north of Colvale, along the NH17. The **Shri Shantadurga Temple** is invisible from the national highway itself but the road leading 500m to it is marked by a large yellow and white gateway and is a bare 200m from the Konkan railway line.

The temple's main entrance at the east end leads through a Romanesque arch into a large rectangular, walled and cloistered enclosure. A typical hexagonal lamp tower, *deepstambha*, is near the entrance. The central mandapam and tiled roof are supported by broad, squat round pillars. The *mandapa* (central hall) has a red tiled floor, pink painted pillars and a tiled roof interior.

As you approach the shrine two small tomb-like enclosures house two linga, opening towards the main shrine. The inner sanctum, which is open to all, has pale wooden doors, and a white ceramic tiled wall, interspersed with blue tiles. The entrance steps are black marble, leading into the immaculate white marble flooring of the shrine room. The image is almost invisible in its ornately worked silver fronted *garbagriha*. As with the typical inner shrines of Hindu temples it is cool, pleasant and airy. Worshippers ring one of the bells hanging at the entrance to the shrine to announce their presence to the deity. The annual festival is in December.

Moira's Magic Carpet

Legend has it that the villagers of Moira decided that there was too much space in front of the church and too little behind it. The Moira villagers decided that the answer lay in pushing the church forward. Humouring them, the Sacristan from the neighbouring village of Aldona suggested that they lay out blankets in front of the church to cover the area where they wanted the church to go, and then pushed it from behind until it covered the blankets. This they duly did, but while they were pushing the Sacristan quietly removed the blankets from the front. After a suitable interval he suggested that the villagers come round to the front to view the results of their efforts, as the blankets were now completely covered. They were delighted with the effect!

Parsi

The small hamlet of Parsi (Parchem, Parshem), 4 km from Chopdem, lies on the road between Agarvaddo and Pernem (6 km away), an attractive route which climbs steadily up onto the barren laterite plateau. The remarkable **Shri Bhagvati Senayan Temple** (rebuilt in the 19th century) has twin *deepstambhas* (lamp towers) in front and five romanesque arches. *Colour map 1, grid B2*

In addition to the shrine to Bhagvati, Siva's wife, also known as Parvati, there is a rare minor shrine to Brahma. The very elongated headdresses and the impassively smiling faces carved in the black stone are a remarkable testament to the art of the seventh century. This image, discovered in the undergrowth near the temple, is worshipped today in one of the subsidiary shrines.

Malpem

Just south of Pernem is the small Hindu temple of **Mulvir**. Set in a heavily shaded compound, the low, tile-roofed temple is protected by a large banyan tree at its entrance. The chief feature is the wall paintings illustrating scenes from the Mahabharata. The main story panel in rather faded, but still clear, colours is the churning of the ocean of milk, the simple figures of people, animals and gods charmingly represented. Sadly the pictures have suffered extensive weathering damage. *Colour map 1, grid A2*

North Goa

Bhagwati Temple, Parsi

Pernem and the national highway

Most guide books and maps show the NH17 running through Pernem and crossing the Tiracol River just to the northwest of the town. This is incorrect. The NH17 bypasses Pernem to its east and then runs northeast along the south bank of the Tiracol River through Torxem

(Torchem) and past the Patradevi Martyr's memorial into Maharashtra.

Just to the northeast of Pernem a new road bridge crosses the river to the Usha-ISPAT integrated steel plant, but is only open to company traffic. Immediately to its east is the Konkan Railway Bridge.

Pernem

Colour map 1, grid A2

Pernem (pronounced *Pedne*) ceded to the Portuguese in 1788, was among the last territories to be added to the area under Portuguese control. Today it is a small market town, just south of the Maharashtra border, with three major points of interest.

St Joseph's Church is in the heart of the town. This brightly painted white church on a hill has a statue of Christ in its forecourt and a Latin inscription which reads "Christ reigns over all". The date, 1864, is written on the central gable and there are two towers, one the belfry. The interior is plain and largely undecorated.

Shri Bhagvati Temple below the church immediately to its north is entered through an ornamental gateway flanked by large dark stone statues of trumpeting elephants. This temple is 500 years old and has a dark *ashtabhuja* (eight-armed) image of Bhagvati. Dasara celebrations here attract around 25,000 devotees.

Deshprabhu House is situated about 1 km from the bazaar on the road which runs north from Pernem to join the NH17. The great rambling 19th-century house belonging to the Deshprabhu family has 16 courtyards. Despite remaining Hindu the family was honoured by the Portuguese. The temple and museum which have been created in the courtyard can be visited by arrangement with the tourist office in Panaji.

Torxem (Torchem)
Colour map 1, grid A2

The northernmost village of Goa is noted for a 15th-century sculpture of Mahishasuramardini (Durga slaying the Buffalo Demon), which is now on display at the Panaji Museum.

Alorna
Colour map 1, grid A3

The Portuguese captured this important fort in the northeast corner of the state at Alorna from the Bhonsla in 1746. On the north bank of the Chapora River, it is now in ruins.

Bicholim and Satari talukas

A journey through the two talukas offers very attractive scenery. It is possible to make a full day round trip from the coast to Satari via Bicholim and to see a good deal of several sites.

Bicholim

Colour map 1, grid B3
Population: 13,700

The taluka headquarters, Bicholim town has little of interest in itself but is the crossroads on the main route between Mapusa and Valpoi and for the road from the south via Divar Island.

Naroa (Narve)

The **Shri Saptakoteshwar Temple**, across the river from Divar Island, is one
of Bicholim's main attractions. Like many in North Goa, the small temple nestles among trees and is shielded from view, almost a miniature. Here again like
so many of Goa's temples and small settlements, the deity originated some distance away and was re-established as a result of an enforced move. The faceted
dharalinga, which is the chief image, was moved when the original temple on
Divar island was destroyed in order to build a church. The marks on the stone
suggest that at one stage it was used as a pulley, probably for drawing water, but
was rescued and placed in its present setting as a result of Sivaji's visit in 1668.
There is nothing ornate about either the design or the decoration of the temple.
The simple and typical red-tiled roof and painted exterior walls house a simple
five-pillared *sabhamandapa* where a black stone *nandi* faces the linga in the
small square sanctuary. The *deepstambha* outside with 10 rings is typical of the
area. Near it the shrine to Kalabhairav has two rock carvings of sandals.
Mahasivratri (February/March) is the special festival here.

*Colour map 1, grid B3
The original site on
Divar Island is now
occupied by the Church
of Nossa Senhora de
Piedade*

North Goa

Mayem Lake

Mayem Lake is the last oasis before the heavy mining area around Sanquelim,
visible from the western shore but fortunately not from the lake itself. It is a
peaceful and picturesque spot, rich in birdlife, especially at the quieter, southern end of the lake away from the road. If you look closely, you may be able to
spot monkeys in the surrounding forest. It isn't heavily visited or commercialized with just a few souvenir stalls and bar/restaurants lining the short stretch
of road along the north bank.

Colour map 1, grid B3

Pedal boats may not be for everyone but it is worth stopping at the southern
end of the lake to enjoy birdwatching at close range (carry binoculars). Bring
some oil too to fix the irritating sqeaking which many of the boats are prone to.

D-E *Prabhu Smaran*, 100m north of lake, T361222. 6 rooms, some a/c (Rs 475) in a
friendly, family run guest house, clean and comfortable, well kept. Recommended.
E *Mayem Lake Resort* (GTDC), on the west bank, T600238.17 good-sized but shabby
rooms (Rs 220), wildlife includes frogs in the bathroom, good restaurant although
lunch-time is often reminiscent of Hitchcock's "The Birds" with crows lining up for
scraps. The *Government Restaurant* on the south side of the lake serves good food,
though the buildings are rather run-down. There are clean *sulabh* toilets in the
compound.

**Sleeping
& eating**

Rowing/pedal boats: Rs 80 per hour, Rs 60 for 30 mins. **Polycat** (a lightweight pedal
catamaran): Rs 60 per hour, Rs 40 for 30 mins.

Entertainment

From Panaji or Ponda, travel via Banastari, although the most direct route is via the
Ribandar- Chorao ferry from Panaji. There are direct buses from Charao to Mayem
Lake but they are few and far between so you may be forced to choose between a 2hr
wait or taking a motorbike taxi (Rs 100). From Mapusa there is a regular bus service via
Bicholim (Rs 8).

Transport

Sirigao (Shirgao)

The **Lairaya Temple**, northwest of Bicholim, is well-known for the **firewalking** which accompanies the Padvo festivities.

The Hindu *Lairaya Jatra* described by Gomes Pereira coincides with "New Year" celebrations in April/May (8 May 2000). Local villagers gather firewood to build a pyre, about 10m square at the base, and 6m high. Hundreds of *dhonds* (the name given to a special group of worshippers who participate in the ceremony) enter the village, recognizable by the piece of coloured cloth they carry on their back and the entwined cane in their hands. During the day, the goddess Lairaya gives *darshan* and is worshipped. Excitement mounts as midnight approaches and a noisy crowd of devotees accompanied by loud musicians, join the temple priest and the *dhonds* in a procession towards the pyre. They first call at a mango tree, which is believed to contain an evil spirit that has to be appeased by an offering of red flowers. The pyre is lit by the priest and the *dhonds* continue with their rituals and reach a state of frenzy before preparing to walk on the red hot ashes which the pyre presents. Then at a specified moment, early in the morning, they all step onto the ashes while some dare to run through the tongues of flame. Excitement reaches fever pitch until the last completes the act.

If a dhond is injured by the flames, he is considered impure – he had either not prepared himself properly for the ceremony or hides a guilty conscience!

Kansarpal

At the northern end of the taluka, the **Shri Kalikadevi Temple** is about 100 years old. An unusual feature of the structure is that it has two *sabhamandapas* preceding the sanctuary with seven rows of four pillars. One has a sunken section where dance and theatre performances are held during festivals; the *nagarkhana* to seat the musicians is above. The three silver-covered temple doors and the sanctuary door are ornately decorated. The inner sanctuary has an image of Devi, the fierce form of Goddess Kali. The goldsmiths, the temple trustees, traditionally set aside the gold dust collected when they make jewellery, to act as the reserve fund.

Sanquelim

Southeast of Bicholim, the town is the 'home' of the Rajput **Ranes tribe** who migrated south from Rajasthan in the late 18th century and spent the next century fighting for the Portuguese as mercenaries, then against them for arrears of pay! In 1895 one of their revolts necessitated the despatch of troops from Portugal.

The **Datta Mandir** (1882) north of the bazaar, backed by a hillock covered with dense groves of areca palms, has the *trimurthi* (three-headed) image of Dattaraia which is believed to cure insanity. The temple, with an interior of white marble, celebrates *Datta Jayanti* in December (10 December 2000). It is one of two temples in Goa where *Devadasis* (see page 241) play no part and are not permitted to enter (the other is the Ananta Temple in Savoi Verem).

The 14th-century **Temple of Vitthala** to Vishnu, built in the North Indian style, has been renovated but still retains some of the original carved wooden columns. The annual festival is in April when the temple 'car' is used to transport a Hanuman image. Shri Vitthala is the ancestral deity of the Ranes who still live in the old family house next to the temple.

....

🖐 **Travel tip**

If you are visiting Satari from North Goa it is well worth visiting Tambdi Surla, the small but beautifully preserved temple in Sanguem taluka, south of Valpoi (see page 174).

....

Overburdening – Goa's other environmental problem

The south central landscapes of Bicholim (or Dicholi) have been transformed by open-cast iron ore mining. Since the early 1980s Goa has accounted for over 40 percent of India's iron ore export, mainly to Japan, and Bicholim about 70 percent of that. The effects are not just the removal of iron ore but the dumping of the waste excavated to get at the ore, known technically as the 'overburden'. In Goa, on average, for every ton of ore mined six tons of waste rock are dumped. This has created huge steep-sided hills dominating some of the views and creating major environmental problems. Given the wide availability of restoration techniques in common use in other parts of the world, environmental lobbies are pushing Indian companies hard to take measures to reduce the damage that is being done to the environment.

Sesa Goa, one of the mining companies, has been experimenting since the early 1960s in using cashew plantations to restore mined land, a pathbreaking development now being followed by others, but it will be years before the dust and mud which characterize some of the most intensively mined districts are under control. Meanwhile the water table is also dropping and pollution of the ground water is held to be increasing.

Transport One road goes south to Tisk (25 km) at the intersection with the NH4A near a spice plantation. A longer circuit takes in Arvalem and the Tambdi Surla Temple, joining the NH4A at Molem which gives access to the Bhagwan Mahaveer Sanctuary. Buses between Mapusa and Valpoi pass through Bicholim and Sanquelim.

Arvalem

Colour map 1, grid B4

Two kilometres east of Sanguelim a turn goes south to this small settlement noted now for its waterfalls and small **Buddhist cave temples**. The latter were subsequently converted for Siva worship, the altars which probably originally supported Buddha images now having Siva lingas set into them. The caves are believed to date from the third-sixth centuries AD, though a Brahmi inscription found was dated to the first century. The two groups of caves were cut out of laterite outcrops, the cells opening out into two pillared porches. No architectural detail survives. Hutt suggests that they were too small ever to be used as living quarters for monks.

In a pleasant shaded site with a temple near their foot, the **waterfalls** are formed at the end of a small gorge and are impressive during the monsoon when the river is in spate. They are concealed from view until the last moment. Steps lead down from the parking place to the foot of the falls, then a track goes along the river and crosses it by a footbridge, leading a short distance to an open cast mine less than 1 km away.

Next to the falls is the **Shri Rudreshwar Temple** which is important for funeral rites. Although the present building is comparatively modern the temple itself is ancient, although no one knows exactly when it was founded. The *Mahasivaratri festival* (February/March), when devotees honour Siva through the night, is celebrated with processions, singing and theatre performances.

Travel tip

If you are visiting Naroa and the Shri Saptakoteshwar Temple from the coast, or travelling further east to Arvalem, Mayem Lake is a convenient midday rest stop. GTDC has a good restaurant.

Bicholim and Satari talukas

Bicholim, which shares its northern border with the central Indian state of Maharashtra, and Satari which borders both Maharashtra and the south Indian state of Karnataka, are in many senses two of the three most marginal talukas in Goa. Located on the edge of the Western Ghats where the hills rise up sharply to the interior of the Indian Peninsula, they have always been on the margins of political developments elsewhere. Only brought into Goa as part of the New Conquests, they were previously a battleground in the constantly shifting margins of Hindu and Muslim power for three centuries before.

Difficult terrain, dense forest cover and the lack of any widespread agricultural land meant that population density remained relatively sparse and towns very few. It was to these talukas that Hindus from the Old Conquests often escaped, taking with them the most sacred images and artefacts from the temples of Old Goa and the talukas of the Old Conquests. Even though the distances were short the remoteness of the forested hills of Bicholim and Satari was virtually absolute, protected not only by their own inhospitable character but by the Mandovi River to the south and the Mapusa River to the west.

That pattern of inaccessibility is being changed, and the balance of resources is now fundamentally altered by the discovery of massive iron ore deposits which are being extensively worked in Bicholim. Roads now connect Bicholim with the headquarters of Satari taluka, Valpoi. In turn roads now run south through the dense forest reserves of the Bondla Sanctuary to Tisk or southeast via Tambdi Surla to Molem in Sanguem taluka.

For hundreds of years before the Portuguese arrived however, it seems that these forested hills were also home to Buddhist and Jain communities. Buddhism, which had become possibly India's main religion in the early centuries before Christ, gradually went onto the defensive in following centuries. A resurgent Hinduism, followed by the invasions of Islam, restricted Buddhism to increasingly remote territories and it remained in these forested hills for some centuries after its elimination from most other parts of India.

Satari taluka

The second largest and the second least densely populated taluka in Goa has always been a largely forested district. The steep hills of the Western Ghats rise to the east and the forests of the Bhagwan Mahaveer Sanctuary are to the south. A government report noted in 1869 that Satari had few properly built temples the majority "being built of light materials with clay walls and roofs of palm leaves, straw or areca tree leaves." This was put down to the poverty of the district and the fact that the majority of the people lived in scattered settlements, grazing cattle or practising subsistence farming. Part of their poverty was the result of their being effectively bonded labourers for the neighbouring landlords who creamed off any surplus produce.

Valpoi
Colour map 1, grid B6
Population: 6,800

Valpoi, Satari's administrative headquarters, is only a small town, which has simple accommodation. The forest department's simple **F** *Valpoi Forest Rest House*, can be booked through the Wildlife Office, 3rd floor, Junta House, 18th June Rd, Panaji, T0832-224747/225926.

Carambolim
Colour map 3, grid A2

The town, also known as Brahma Carambolim or Karmali because of its unusual Brahma temple, is 9 km northeast of Valpoi. The original temple in Carambolim village in the Tiswadi taluka was destroyed during the first Portuguese conquest but the Brahma image (believed to date from the fifth century) was re-installed here in 1541.

North Goa

South Goa

5

South Goa

The difference between South and North Goa is more than just a convenient geographical division. The talukas of Salcete, Quepem and Canacona have a wholly different atmosphere from those of the north. The Zuari River acted not only as a great political and cultural divide between Christian Salcete and Hindu Ponda but also as a much wider economic and cultural marker. Some of Goa's finest churches and most magnificent country estates are in the interior of Salcete. Heavily influenced by Portuguese culture, southern Goa has also been drawn towards the state of Karnataka. The rising prosperity of Salcete has not created the packaged pop culture of the northern coast. Here the pace is gentler. While Colva acts as the chief beach resort for the nearby population of Margao, long stretches of sand are completely deserted. Inland there is a wide variety of places to explore. Virtually anywhere in the three talukas is within reach of a day trip from the coast.

Salcete's beaches

The southern beaches are less distinctive than those of the north. Government regulations have kept all the hotels back from the sea, but the character of the unbroken wide sand nonetheless varies. The road runs slightly inland with spurs leading down to the main sections of beach. Some, like Varca and Cavelossim, are little more than deserted stretches of dune-backed sand with isolated fishing hamlets. In contrast Colva's tall coconut palms come down to the beach edge, shading restaurants and a cluster of hotels and shops. At intervals are some luxurious beach resorts.

Arossim, Utorda, Majorda

Colour map 2, grid B2   These three beaches, rarely visited, are broad, flat and open with occasional fishing villages scattered under the coconut palms. Looking northwards up the beach the Mormugao headland is clearly viewed when not concealed by haze.

One of the distinctive features of this section of coast is the strip of land used for intensive rice cultivation that lies between the main series of villages and the dunes which front the sea. The road, set back between 1 and 2 km from the sea, runs through these villages. Old mansions of wealthy families still standing in the villages include **Utorda House** which is known for its well kept gardens. The villages from here southwards to Benaulim and beyond are noted for the high level of emigration to the Gulf. Some have become relatively affluent and have returned to invest money in new hotels.

Sleeping & eating   **Arossim Beach**   At the north end of a largely deserted beach: **A** *Heritage Village Club* (was *Sita*), T754311, F754324, sitashrl.del@sita.sprintrpg.ems.vsnl.net.in, www.sitaresorts.com 2-storey blocks, 100 rooms (Rs 3,835 includes meals and house drinks), in large gardens set around pool (sells itself as India's first fully all-inclusive boutique resort!). Besides this, a beach shack offers food and drinks.

Utorda Beach   On a quiet stretch of white-sand beach with just a few shacks, 10 mins' walk north of Majorda: **LL** *Kenilworth Beach Resort* (was *Golden Tulip*), T754180, F754183, kbrgoa@satyam.net.in, www.kenilworth.allindia.com 92 rooms, 5 suites, central a/c, being completely refurbished over 2 years and aiming very high, focused on the pool(s) with plenty of watersports, underwater games, sunken bar, loads to amuse the children, while adults amuse themselves at the casino with live entertainment, and keep 1 eye on their offspring through 1-way mirrors, managed by enthusiastic New Zealander.

Majorda Beach   On a slightly busier section of the beach (though still quiet compared to Colva): **A** *Majorda Beach Resort*, 2 mins walk from the beach, T754871, F755382, mbr.goa@rma.sprintrpg.ems.vsnl.net.in 108 'rustically' furnished a/c rooms and 10 more expensive individual 'village' suites (Rs 3,995), 3 restaurants, pools, designed on a grand scale but with a barn-like public area, covered 'Mediterranean village' street, lush gardens behind, all very well maintained. **D** *Shangrila*, 600m from sea, T755133, F754264. 12 reasonable rooms, some a/c (Rs 695), but overpriced. **D** *Shalom Guest House*, T754240, shalome81@satyam.net.in 1 large family room (more planned), with cooking facilities (Rs 300), excellent value.

Spoilt for sand

The southern coast comprises two contrasting sections. The whole coastline of Salcete is one unbroken stretch of sand from **Velsao** to **Mabor** whereas from Quepem southwards the coastline changes dramatically. **Betul** has a rocky headland and a small but inaccessible sandy cove, encapsulated by the laterite cliffs of the **Cabo da Rama** headland, already in Canacona taluka. The coastline then sweeps southeast with the beaches of **Saleri** and **Agonda** providing a prelude to the magnificent and beautifully protected beach of **Palolem**, the southernmost of the beaches increasingly visited by tourists.

Each section of beach has its own character, depending partly on the villages behind the beach. Unlike the northern beaches, in Salcete virtually the whole coast is lined with village houses scattered beneath the coconut palms, with rice fields immediately behind. The southernmost of the Old Conquests, many of the coastal villages have spectacularly attractive whitewashed village churches.

Salcete has no rocky headlands and the beach at low tide is a wide stretch of firm sand, backed in places by quite high dunes. Only occasionally does settlement come down to the beach itself, as at **Colva**. The largest beach resorts, some of which have been controversial in Goa, serve largely package tours in the winter and Indian tourists during the monsoon season. Several have excellent facilities and are largely self-contained, although the south is nowhere near as commercialized as the north.

Betalbatim

The beach south of Majorda was named after the main temple to Betall which once stood here; the deity was moved to Queula (Ponda) for safety. This is a pleasant stretch with some coconut palms and a few casuarinas on the low dunes that separate the seaside from the resort development. A few beach shacks tend to the needs of visitors, including hiring out sunbeds. Unfortunately, the peace is disturbed by the constant drone of generators and Bob Marley!

Colour map 2, grid B2

In **Betalim** are **B** *Nanu Resorts*, near the beach and open paddy fields, T734950, F734428. 72 comfortable and spacious a/c rooms (Rs 2,000 including breakfast, dinner), 2-storey "chalet" complex. Imaginatively planned and well managed with efficient service, 1st floor restaurant with verandah facing pool serves good food (occasionally slow service), good pool, garden, beach beyond a narrow stream, secluded and peaceful (though time-share blocks are alongside). Very good value from 1 May-30 Sep. Recommended. **D** *Alagoa*, 1 km from beach along track, simple, clean rooms, pleasant location, quiet. Situated on the **beach** are **E** *Baptista*, T720273. 3 simple clean rooms with kitchen facilities (Rs 250). **E** *Manuela Tourist House*, 1 km from beach. 5 good clean rooms with bath, TV lounge, some food available, secure, quiet. Recommended. **E** *Ray's Rest Rooms*, T738676. 3 good-sized, clean rooms, some a/c (Rs 300-400), use of kitchen.

Sleeping & eating

Rail Majorda station is on the Vasco-Margao line. **Road** Regular buses from Margao (12 km); motorcycle taxis charge about Rs 30. Taxis take 20 mins from the airport, under 15 mins from Margao.

Transport

Useful services Health Centre T754036. **Police** T782325.

Directory

South Goa

Colva

Colour map 2, grid B2

Colva (pronounced Koll-wa) is one of the most popular beaches in southern Goa. Compared to some of the northern resorts, it is less developed and consequently less busy, but has plenty of good accommodation, as well as some excellent restaurants.

Ins & outs
See transport section for further details
From the airport, taxis charge about Rs 250. Those arriving by train at Margao, 6 km away, can choose between auto-rickshaws, taxis and buses for transfer. Guest house owners with vacancies (not touts) meet new arrivals at the bus stand.

Colva beach was used as a summer retreat before the monsoon by Margao's élite who would rent fishermen's houses, who in turn would move into shacks. The beachfront of Colva town itself, which is rather dirty, has nothing special to recommend it. Today, it is popular with domestic tourists and day-trippers (especially at weekends) although they tend to leave litter in large quantities, especially at the main entrance to the beach.

Three rather ugly little concrete bridges cross a muddy stream to the beach, where the original dunes have all been removed to give direct access to the sea. During the season the area is lined with trinket stalls and a constant succession of beach vendors. However, the beach sand itself is lovely with coconut palms and blue waters (though this can sometimes turn rough and grey-green).

On the road into Colva from Margao you pass the large **Church of Our Lady of Mercy** (Nossa Senhora das Merces, 1630, re-built in the 18th century). The church has a relatively simple façade. Its single tower on the south side of the façade is so short as scarcely to be noticeable, and the strong horizontal lines normally given to Goan churches by three of four full storeys is broken by a narrow band of shallow semi-circular arches above the second floor. However, the church is much less famous for its building than for its association with the miraculous **Menino Jesus**. The Jesuit, Father Bento Ferreira, found the original image in the River Sena, Mozambique, *en route* to Goa, and brought it to Colva where he took up

Southern beaches

South Goa

is position as rector in 1648. The image was found to have miraculous healing powers and became an object of special veneration. However, when in 1834 religious orders were banned, it was removed to the Rachol Seminary for safe-keeping although a diamond ring given as an offering to it was left behind. The church in Colva failed in its attempts to have the statue returned and so installed another figure in 1836 (which is still here today) and put on it the special ring. It was soon found to work miracles, whereas the original statue taken to Rachol ceased to have special powers. The story is celebrated today in the special annual festival, the *Fama of Menino Jesus* (16 October 2000), when thousands of pilgrims flock to see the statue in the hope of witnessing a miracle. Near the church, specially blessed lengths of string are sold, as well as replicas of limbs which are offered to the image in thanks for cures effected.

Teams of fishermen operate all along the coast from here down to Benaulim further south. Their pitch-boarded catamarans are drawn up on the beach, while motorized craft are anchored offshore. They provide added interest and colour and it is worth waking early to watch them haul in their nets. If you are really early you may even be invited out on a boat.

The hamlets between Colva and Benaulim retain their rural charm and many families run cheap guest houses which are often much better value than in the northern resorts.

B-C *Sea Coin*, T720892, F710312, seacoin@bom8.vsnl.net.in 32 large comfortable rooms, some a/c (Rs 1,450), restaurant, but unappealing views. **B** *Sea Queen Beach Resort*, close to beach, north of Colva, T720499, F734257. 44 rooms (Rs 2,000 including breakfast and tax) in 2-storey blocks, mainly for package tourists, restaurant, pool. **B** *Vista De Colva*, 4th Ward, T704845, F704983, colmar@ satyam.net.in 25 large a/c, studio rooms (Rs 2,000 including breakfast), restaurant/bar with several Goan specialities, small fish-shaped pool, live entertainment, very comfortable new resort. **B-C** *Longuinhos Beach Resort*, on the beach, 1 km from resort centre, T731645, F737588, lbresort@goa1.dot.net.in 50 clean rooms with balcony, 6 a/c (no TV), good restaurant, boutique, near fishermen's huts. **B-C** *Star Beach Resort*, just off Colva Beach Rd, T/F734921. 41 rooms, some a/c (Rs 1,200), new resort hotel in a barren site. **B-C** *William's Resort*, 500m from beach, T721077, F732852. 36 spotless rooms, some a/c (Rs 1,200), restaurant, large pool (non-residents pay Rs 40), tennis, friendly, good value.

C-E *Skylark*, T723669, skylark@goa1.dot.net.in 21 rooms (Rs 350), 2 a/c (Rs 900), restaurant, cycle hire. **D** *Colva Beach Cottages* (GTDC), near the sea, T721206, F737753. 47 pleasant, clean rooms, few a/c (Rs 560), in 2-storeyed building or cottages (need redecorating), good restaurant, bar, garden, friendly, secure, popular with Indian tourists. **D-E** *Sukhsagar Beach Resort*, close to beach, T702888, F731666. 20 fair sized rooms, some a/c (Rs 480), minor maintenance needed, "ideal for honeymooners, high and middle income group families"!

E *Colmar*, on the beach (just beyond *Colva Beach Cottages*), T721253. 85 rooms (Rs 350), dearer than similar in area but popular, restaurant (see below), travel desk, motorbike hire, bus to Anjuna flea market (Rs 85), exchange. **E** *Garden Cottages*, behind *Johnny Cool's* restaurant, 10 mins from beach. 6 basic rooms with bath (Rs 210), private balcony. Pleasant surroundings, quiet, clean, friendly, helpful owner, good value. **E** *Graciano Beach Resort*, T730019. 13 small rooms with bath (Rs 210). **E** *Tourist Nest*, 2 km from the sea, T723944. Old Portuguese house, 12 rooms, some with bath (Rs 250), good restaurant, run by 2 Norwegian women, popular with backpackers. **E** *Vailankanni*, H No 414/2, 4th Ward, near the crossroads, 500m from beach, T737747. 10 basic, clean rooms (Rs 200) although a bit musty, 5 new flats (Rs 300-400) friendly, family run, good value restaurant. **F** *Maria Guest House*, 4th Ward, near

Sleeping
Prices rise on 1 Dec. Discounts are possible for stays of a week or more

beach cafés. 7 rooms, some with bath, very friendly, interesting owners, helpful car-hire, popular with backpackers, good value. Recommended. **F** *Romeo's Tourist Cottages*, H No 9, Novo Vaddo, T730942. 2 clean rooms with bath (Rs 160) in family guest house in quiet location, 5 mins' walk from beach. **F** *Sam's Beach Resort*, 3rd Ward, T735304. 16 good sized clean rooms (Rs 200) set around quiet garden court yard, good value. **F** *White Sands*, H No 470, 4th Ward, T720364. 8 clean comfortable rooms (Rs 200) in new, family run guest house.

Eating **Mid-range** *Sea Pearl*, 476 4th Ward. Chef/owner cooked for the Queen Mother on an overnight train in Africa! Produces excellent western dishes especially roast beef, good desserts, fish pie. Recommended. Arrive early in season (about 1930). Also has simple **E** rooms with bath. **Cheap** Many offer Western food and chilled beer. *Chine Dragon*, on beach. Mainly Chinese, good food and friendly service. *Joe Con's*, 4th Ward. Excellent fresh fish and Goan dishes, good value. Colmar's *Pasta Hut*. Good Italian with bar showing live European football. Recommended. *Sucorina*, 1 km north and *Zappia's*, on the beach. Recommended for seafood.

Bars Several hotels on the beach have bars. *Splash* is 'the' main place for music, dancing and late drinking, open all night, trendy, very busy on Sat; during the season it gets full after 2300 on weekdays; serves good cocktails but poor bar snacks – may not appeal to all.

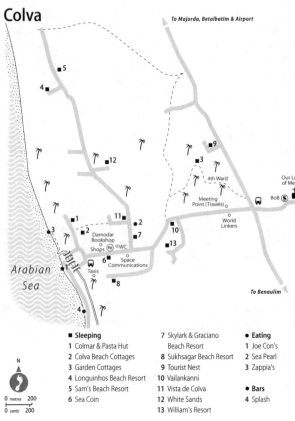

Colva

To Majorda, Betalbatim & Airport

4th Ward

Meeting Point (Travels)

World Linkers

Our Lady of Mercy

BoB

Damodar Bookshop Shops WC

Space Communications

Taxis

Arabian Sea

To Benaulim

N

0 metres 200
0 yards 200

■ Sleeping		7 Skylark & Graciano	● Eating
1	Colmar & Pasta Hut	Beach Resort	1 Joe Con's
2	Colva Beach Cottages	8 Sukhsagar Beach Resort	2 Sea Pearl
3	Garden Cottages	9 Tourist Nest	3 Zappia's
4	Longuinhos Beach Resort	10 Vailankanni	
5	Sam's Beach Resort	11 Vista de Colva	● Bars
6	Sea Coin	12 White Sands	4 Splash
		13 William's Resort	

South Goa

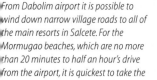

Down from Dabolim

From Dabolim airport it is possible to wind down narrow village roads to all of the main resorts in Salcete. For the Mormugao beaches, which are no more than 20 minutes to half an hour's drive from the airport, it is quickest to take the shortest route down off the plateau to Velsao and Cansaulim. For Colva and the resort hotels further south, it can be quicker to join the national highway and go to Margao before heading for the coast road.

Shopping

Small square with usual craft shops – Kashmiri papier mâché and Karnataka mirror-work are good value. *Damodar* bookshop, near the car park and beach, has a good selection of used and new books.

Transport

Local Bicycle hire: mostly through hotels, Rs 20-25 per day. **Motorbikes**: for hire through most hotels (see also Panaji), Rs 150-200 per day (less for long term); more for Enfields. Bargain hard. **Long distance** To **Margao** half-hourly buses, take 30 mins, Rs 3 (last bus 1915, last return, 2000); motorcycle taxi, Rs 20-25 (bargain hard); auto-rickshaw, Rs 30-40. To **Anjuna** on Wed for the flea market, bus (through travel agents), dep 0930, return 1730, Rs 90-100.

Directory

Communications *WorldLinkers* has 24-hr ISD/fax. **Internet**: difficult to work offline in Colva itself as most terminals are used primarily for email. *Cyberide*, 1 km north of crossroads, T735706, single terminal but good for offline work at reasonable rates. *Space Communications*, Beach Rd. 2 terminals, 0900–2100, Rs 100 per hr. Avoid *Trans Global Communications*, expensive and unfriendly. **Hospital** T722164. **Travel companies** *Meeting Point*, opposite, T723338, F732004, is recommended for very efficient, reliable travel service, Mon-Sat, 0830-1900 (sometimes even later, if busy). **Useful services** Police, T721254.

Benaulim

Benaulim, also called Banaley, is more tranquil, pleasant and relatively cleaner than Colva beach. However, during the season it is a popular destination for budget travellers so the approach road to the beach can get very busy. To escape the crowds, walk, or cycle some distance south along the beach. The 4 km walk or cycle ride between Colva and Benaulim, through idyllic countryside is also recommended.

Colour map 2, grid C2
Population: 9,900

The road to the beach is poorly lit after dark - it is best to walk accompanied

Benaulim is 'the place where the arrow fell', referring to the myth of Parashurama and the creation of Goa (see page 213). It is also famous throughout Goa as the birthplace of the Venerable Joseph Vaz, who is commemorated in the Church of the Holy Spirit in Margao. The village was noted for producing carved wooden furniture.

Benaulim Church

This small church, re-built in 1596, is on a hill beyond the village. It is a superb example of Goan Christian architecture. The twin towers are

Church of St John the Baptist

South Goa

surmounted by shallow domes while the typical scrolls are flanked by crosses. Although the gable façade is striking, the chief beauties of the church are inside. The magnificent altar reredos is uniquely decorated, and there is a wonderful Rococo pulpit which is surmounted by a representation of the Lamb of the Apocalypse from the Book of Revelation. Fr Joseph Vaz, who ultimately died as a missionary to Ceylon (Sri Lanka), was baptised in the font here in 1651. Note also the very charming St Christopher carrying a child across a river, painted in the nave opposite the baptistry. See also 'Festival' below.

Sleeping **LL** *Taj Exotica*, Calvaddo, towards, Varca, T705666, F738916. Large luxurious hotel deluxe rooms (US$165) to presidential suites (US$450), all facing 800m sea frontage, excellent pool, 9-hole golf, lovely gardens, health club with latest equipment, sumptuously designed by Hawaiian architect.

B *Royal Palms*, Vasvaddo, T732391, F710617. 50 apartments (Rs 1,500), some expensive villas (Rs 3,500) in new resort hotel within time-share development, restaurant, pool, exchange, travel counter. **C-D** *Carina Beach Resort*, Tambdi-Mati, T734166, F711400. 35 rooms, new wing better with solar powered showers (Rs 700), some a/c (extra Rs 150), light and airy with balcony, restaurant, pool. **C-E** *Camilson's Beach Resort*, Sernabatim, T732781. 15 simple rooms with attached bath (Rs 250-Rs 300) better in new 2-storey building (Rs 800), restaurant, close to the beach. **D** *Failaka*, Adsulim Nagar, near Maria Hall crossing, T734416. 16 clean comfortable rooms with shower (Rs 420), quieter at rear, excellent restaurant, friendly. Recommended. **D-E** *Palm Grove Cottages*, H No 149, Vasvaddo, T722533, palmgrovecottages@yahoo.com 14 rooms (Rs 250-600), new rooms better with shower and balcony, pleasant palm-shaded garden, good food (but slow service). Recommended.

Budget hotels can be found along Benaulim Beach Rd, and in the coconut groves on either side, there are numerous rooms available in private houses and "garden cottages", from Rs 50-150; south along the beach from *Johncey's* rooms with bath, just off the beach, are Rs 80-100. **E** *Caphina*, Beach Rd, past crossroads, away from road), 8 spotless rooms (Rs 250) on 2 floors, friendly and helpful owners (if not in, ask at *Tansy*) good value. Recommended. **E** *D'Souza Guest House*, T734364. 5 very clean rooms (Rs 250), good food (see below), exchange, beauty salon, garden, friendly family. Recommended. **E** *O'Palmer Beach Cottages*, T733278. 20 rooms (Rs 350), very close to the beach, has had a recent facelift, internet. **E** *Oshin*, near *Palm Grove*, down a path. Good

Benaulim

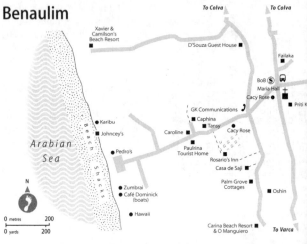

South Goa

large rooms with bath, breakfast, friendly manager. **E** *Paul Rina Tourist Home*, Beach Rd, T738250. 6 large, airy rooms with balcony (Rs 200), good value. **E** *Rosario's Inn*, Beach Rd, T734167. 28 rooms with bath (Rs 200) in a peaceful setting, popular, restaurant, cycle/motorbike hire. Recommended. **E** *Tansy*, Beach Rd, T734595. Large, very clean rooms with bath (Rs 200), some in cottages, good restaurant (super breakfast), friendly, good value. Recommended. **E** *Xavier*, Sernabatim, T730780. 8 reasonable rooms with bath (Rs 250), restaurant, close to the beach. **E-F** *O Mangueiro*, next to *Carina*, 10 min walk to beach, T734164. 15 rooms (Rs 150-400), including 10 new with bath, very clean, peaceful, safe and friendly. **F** *Caroline*, Beach Rd, T739649. 6 clean, light rooms with bath (Rs 150) in family run guest house. **F** *Casa de Saji*, 5 mins' walk from beach, T722937. 5 clean rooms (Rs 150-175), common bath, better with balcony overlooking fields, very quiet. **F** *Priti Kunj*, south of Maria Hall crossing, 15m off the main road, behind church. 4 clean, pleasant rooms, 3 with bath, also large 6-bed rooms in family house, meals to order, helpful owners.

Cheap *Cacy Rose*, is just off the main road near the bus. *D'Souza's*. Good juices, lassis and fast food. *Johncey's*, the most popular (not necessarily the best). Varied menu, good seafood, generous portions, *tandoori* recommended (after 1830) but service can be erratic, pleasant atmosphere though (backgammon, scrabble). **Mid-range** *Palm Grove*, offers high quality Chinese in its garden setting. *Pedro's*, on the beach. Good seafood and tandoori. Imaginative menu, friendly, the 'in' place so go early to get a table. *Karibu* to the north, and *Hawaii* and *Zumbrai* south along the beach. Recommended for fresh fish, prawn and lobster.

Eating
Over a dozen places on the beach. Service can be tediously slow during the season. Most close in the monsoons

Dolphin watching trips are scenic and chances of seeing dolphin are high, but it gets very hot (take hat, water and something comfy to sit on). Groups of dolphins here are usually seen swimming near the surface and don't oblige by performing tricks. Boats from *Café Dominick* (signs on the beach) and several others ask for about Rs 250.

Entertainment
Competition in season is intense, so bargain

Feast of St John the Baptist (*Sao Joao*) (24 Jun 2000) is a thanksgiving for the arrival of the monsoon. Young men wearing crowns of leaves and fruits tour the area singing for gifts. They also jump into wells to commemorate the movement of St John in his mother's womb when she was visited by Mary, the mother of Jesus!

Festivals

Local **Bicycles** and **scooters** for hire in village, Rs 25 and Rs 150 per day. **Taxis** and **auto-rickshaws** are available from the beach esplanade near *Pedro's* and at Maria Hall crossing. **Long distance** To/from **Margao**: bus Rs 3; taxi Rs 70; rickshaws, Rs 50. Anjuna flea market (Wed): bus 0930, return 1530, about Rs 90, 2 hrs. Buses to Benaulim stop near Maria Hall, Dangvaddo, 1 km walk from the beach.

Transport

Bank *Bank of Baroda*, near Maria Hall, best rates (better than at travel agents and STD booths). **Communications** *GK Communications*, Beach Rd. 24hr phone, money exchange and internet with 4 terminals, very busy at times so may have to book ahead, Rs 100 per hr. **Medical services** Late night *Chemists* near the main crossroads.

Directory

Varca, Cavelossim and Mobor

The narrow and attractive road south from Benaulim runs about 1 km inland from the sea through small villages, some with superb white painted churches. Paddy fields and palm groves alternate, and periodically roads run down to the sea, sometimes to small settlements, sometimes to deserted beaches. Benaulim beach runs into Varca, and then Cavelossim which has some up-market resorts. The beaches here are quieter and cleaner than Colva. Mobor (or Mabor), further south, about 8 km from Varca, lies on the narrow peninsula

Colour map 2, grid C2

where the river Sal joins the sea. Some exclusive hotel resorts have been developed, but visually, they are quite unobtrusive. The Sal is a busy river and harbour for fishing boats, but it is also very pleasant for boat rides.

The **Nossa Senhora da Gloria Church** at Varca (1700), a short way north of the village, has a particularly striking façade, making use of a fan-like central feature based on the conch shell to give an effect of radiating light. Its twin towers are topped by semi-domes, but doors on the ground floor and the windows on its two upper storeys are Romanesque. Cavelossim's small and relatively simple **Santa Cruz Church** (1763) has a highly decorated altar piece, the gold leaf being set against a turquoise painted Romanesque arch.

Sleeping **LL-AL** *Leela Palace* (Kempinski), Mobor, T746363, F746352, leela.goa@ leela.sprintrpg.ems.vsnl.net.in Almost 200 rooms, superb villas and pavilions blending Eastern and Western architecture, spacious site, good watersports, 9-hole golf, very plush. **AL** *Goa Renaissance Resort*, Fatrade Beach, Varca, T745208, F245225. Interesting design, comprises 202 rooms, spacious impressive entrance with beams and arches, watersports and 9-hole golf, miles of white sand beach with no rocks, no mosquitoes or flies, high standards but expensive meals and drinks (little else in vicinity), casino open to non-residents. **AL-A** *Holiday Inn*, Mobor, T746303, F746333, hi.goa@sma.sprintrpg. ems.vsnl.net.in Over 100 luxurious rooms (prices vary) with shady balconies around pool and pleasant, part-shaded gardens, all facilities, health club, tennis, very close to beach, good views of hills. **A-B** *Dona Sylvia Resort*, Tamborim, south of Cavelossim, T746321, F748320, Dona_samaria@mailcity.com Comfortable rooms (176), some a/c, low-rise complex with a spacious feel, mainly packages and buffet meals, some watersports (1,500m from beach).

B *Luisa by the Sea*, T/F as *Dona Sylvia*. Mainly timeshare but 20 rooms (Rs1,200) and 8 studios with kitchenette (Rs1,500), non a/c, breakfast at *Dona Sylvia*, clean, comfortable, attentive staff. **B** *Resorte de Goa*, Fatrade Beach, Varca, T745066, F745310. 56 rooms and suites in main building and smaller rooms in colourful cottages, remote, idyllic, pleasant pool in large gardens, tennis (good discounts in Jun-Sep) palm-dotted dunes on either side, clean deserted beach with some shade. **C-D** *Dona Sa Maria*, Tamborim, T745672, F745673, Dona_samaria@ mailcity.com 16 good sized clean rooms in modern colonial style villa, 1 km from deserted beach, good food, pool, family run, very friendly, isolated, recommended (closed Jun-Sep). **D** *Gaffino's*, opposite Dona Sylvia, Mobor, 5 mins' walk from beach, T746385. 16 clean, simple rooms with bath on 4 floors, 2 a/c, balconies overlook river or sea (far away), bed and

Varca to Betul

To Taj Exotica Hotel & Benaulim
Varca Beach
Fishing Village
Nossa Senhora da Gloria
Varca
Chinchi…
8
4
Carmona
Fatrade Beach
1
Santa Cruz
Cavelossim
6
Cavelossim Beach
2
Ass…
2
3
9
Arabian Sea
5
4
Sal River
Velim
Mobor Beach
5
Betty's Place
Fishermen's Boats
N
Mobor
3
Betul
Betul Beach
0 km   2
0 miles   2
To Cabo de Rama

■ **Sleeping**
1 Dona Sa Maria
2 Dona Sylvia Resort
3 Gaffino's & Hippo Cool
4 Goa Renaissance Resort
5 José
6 Leela Palace
7 Leela Palace
8 Resorte de Goa

9 Sao Domingos & Go
  Village Restaurant

● **Eating**
1 Fish Thalis
2 Jazz Inn
3 River Sal
4 River View
5 Shallop

breakfast, personal service, becoming package oriented. **D** *Hippo Cool*, next to *Gaffino's*, T746201. 6 clean, very comfortable rooms with fan (a/c on request) and shower, restaurant (heavily used by local people), 5 mins' walk from beach, the Almeidas are very helpful. Highly recommended. **D** *Sao Domingos* (was *Edwin's*), opposite Dona Sylvia, T746649. 15 comfortable rooms with fans or a/c and bath (Rs 600-700), rooftop breakfast area, same owner as *Goan Village* restaurant. **E** *José Holiday Home*, T746127. 10 good clean rooms (Rs 300) with attached bath, some a/c, friendly. Recommended.

Varca Church

South Goa

Mid-range *River View* in an excellent location next to the river. Wide choice, international menu, good ambience. Recommended. At Dona Sa Maria's, *La Afra* does excellent steaks. Boatmen ferry holidaymakers to *River Sal* at Betul. **Cheap** Beach shacks offer Goan dishes and seafood at reasonable prices. Around *Dona Sylvia*, several come alive in the evening *Goan Village*, lane opposite Dona Sylvia. The best here for all cuisines. Also recommended for good food, drink and service in a pleasant atmosphere are *Get Down*, *Mike's Place*, *Shallop* and *Walk In* (limited menu). *Jazz Inn* is 500m towards Cavelossim. For authentic Goan fish *thalis* (Rs 20), try the first house on the left past the church in Cavelossim if heading north. **Eating**

Betty's Place, in a road opposite the *Holiday Inn*, arranges boat trips for **fishing, dolphin viewing** as well as trips up river Sal from 1030-1630 (food included) which is recommended. **Entertainment**

Local **Bike hire** from *Rocks* outside Dona Sylvia, **cycles** Rs 10 per hr, Rs 150 a day; **scooters** Rs 300 a day without petrol, Rs 500 with 7 litres of fuel. **Autos** wait at the bus stand to transfer to the resorts. **Long distance** **Buses** from Margao to Cavelossim, are uncomfortably slow (18 km); taxis charge Rs 150.**Taxis** from Margao charge around Rs 180 and from Dabolim airport (41-48 km), to the resorts take under an hour. **Ferry** Crosses the River Sal (east of Cavelossim); the road goes through Assolna and joins the main road, NH17. **Transport**

Banks *Bank of Baroda* near the church in Cavelossim accepts Visa, Mastercard and TCs, helpful staff, open 0930-1330, Mon-Wed, Fri, Sat. **Medical facilities** Health centre T735421. **Useful services** Police T745100. **Directory**

Exploring inland Salcete

The beaches in Salcete are within easy reach of enjoyable day trips which give a glimpse of both historic Goa and of modern day village and town life. Goa's second largest town, Margao, is 10 km from Colva and connected directly with all the resorts. It is a bustling town with a market that serves the whole of Salcete and beyond. The Konkan railway offers a relatively fast way for visiting the neighbouring states of Karnataka or Maharashtra using India's legendary rail network.

Verna

Colour map 2, grid B2 The church here was initially built on the site of the Mahalsa Temple before being transferred. The Jesuits were permitted to work exclusively in Salcete and claimed to have celebrated the first Mass in the territory at **Cortalim** nearby in 1560. However, the Franciscans had reached Verem (Reis Magos) 10 years earlier.

The original Mahalsa Temple which housed the deity now in Mardol (see page 86), which according to old Portuguese records had some exquisite carvings, was destroyed and marked by the cross to prevent it being re-used for Hindu worship. It had been a sanctuary for widows who did not commit *sati*, and so became known as the 'Temple of Nuns'.

Verna is also the place chosen in 1988 for re-siting the ancient Mother Goddess figure (fifth century BC) from Curdi (Kurdi) in Sanguem, which was threatened by the Selaulim Dam project. Two megalithic sites were found in the area.

Margao (Madgaon)

Colour map 2, grid B2
Population: 72,100 *Margao is the largest commercial centre after Panaji and the capital of the state's richest and most fertile taluka, Salcete. It is at the heart of its district and wider region. Tourism has had little impact on Margao so it has more of an authentic air of an Indian town going about its business.*

Ins & outs   **Getting there** The Konkan Railway connects Margao directly with Mumbai, Mangalore and Kerala. The new railway station is 1,500m southeast from the town bus stands in the Municipal Gardens and the market area (where most of the hotels and restaurants are located). Rickshaws charge around Rs 15 from the station's pre-paid counter, while local travellers walk the 800m along the rail line! Buses from other states and from north Goa first arrive at the New Kadamba (state) bus stand, 2 km north of town. City buses take you to the town bus stands for destinations south of Margao. Colva and Benaulim buses leave from the local stand, east of the gardens.
Getting around There are plenty of auto-rickshaws and 8-seater van taxis for hire in addition to city buses. **Tours** *North Goa* – dep 0930, Rs 110; *Traditional Goa* – dep 0930, Rs 110; *Santa Monica Cruises* (from Panaji) – dep 1800 and 1915, Rs 80. Tickets from the GTDC *Tourist Hotel* reception desk, not from the tourist information office.

Sights

Feast Day is in June Once a pleasant provincial town it was given the status of a 'vila' by Royal decree in 1778. Today, modern characterless buildings have cropped up and slow-moving traffic chokes the streets around the busy business centre near the Municipal Gardens and the bazaar. Even crossing the road can be quite hazardous here but away from the untidy hub you can walk down quiet side streets and see old Portuguese town houses or climb Monte Hill for a breath of fresh air and good views.

Salcete taluka

Salcete was named after the 66 (saashesht) places that made up the taluka. Unlike Bardez, where the area round Calangute has developed into an almost continuously built-up town, Salcete has no coastal town.

The chief focus of economic and cultural life is the taluka headquarters of Margao, but there is a series of large villages and small towns which form a network across the flat plain of the Sal River and its estuary as it drains south, parallel with the coast, from Cansaulim to Mobor. The Konkan Railway offers a relatively fast way of travelling north-south along the coast while the upgraded line from Vasco east through the ghats has brought the interior within range of exciting short excursions using India's legendary railway network.

Church of the Holy Spirit

This impressive Baroque church with its classic Goan façade dominates the Old Market square, the Largo de Igreja, surrounded by a number of fine town houses. Originally built in 1564 over the ruins of a Hindu temple, it was sacked by Muslims in 1589 and rebuilt in 1675. While the west end is covered typically with white painted plaster, the south wall has extensive exposed laterite. A remarkable pulpit on the north wall has carvings of the Apostles. The carved reredos is flanked by gold pillars, and there are three Baroque style central pictures. The window arches are in the shape of sea shells while a moulded peacock appears on the north transept wall. There are statues of St Anthony and of the Blessed Joseph Vaz, kept in glass cabinets in the north aisle near the north transept. In the square is a monumental cross with a mango tree beside it.

Abade Faria Street

Many 18th-century houses, though dilapidated, can be seen, especially in and around Abade Faria Street. The **de Joao Figueiredo House** has a splendid collection of Goan furniture. The **da Silva House** is a fine example of an impressive town house built around 1790 when Inacio da Silva became the Secretary to the Viceroy. No simple pied-à-terre, it was an impressive mansion; it had a long façade with the roof divided into seven separate cropped 'towers' hence its other name, **Seven Shoulders House**. Today, however, only three of these 'towers' remain. The house retains an air of grandeur in its lavishly carved dark rosewood furniture, its gilded mirrors and fine chandeliers. The first floor reception rooms which face the street are lit by large wood and oyster shell windows which are protected by wrought iron balconies. (Unfortunately, the wide 'awning' of corrugated iron which has been added here, as in other fine buildings elsewhere to shield the rooms from monsoon downpours and strong sunlight, is far from attractive.) The chapel screened by wrought iron-work on the first landing is ornately decorated around the altar, quite

Margao Cross

South Goa

strikingly set off by a background of blue and gold. The descendants continue to live in a small wing of the diminished house which has the traditional flower-filled courtyard garden at the back. Intending visitors should contact the local tourist office at the GTDC Tourist Hotel.

Markets The covered market is interesting to walk around. The Old Market was rehoused in the 'New' (Municipal) Market in town. The covered market is not at all touristy although holiday-makers come here from the beaches for their 'shopping trip' to avoid paying inflated prices in the resorts. ■ *Mon-Sat, 0800-1300, 1600-2000*. To catch a glimpse of the early morning arrivals at the fish market head south from the municipal building.

Other attractions The pleasant municipal and children's **parks** are near the city bus stand. **Monte Hill**, a hillock, has good views over the town and surroundings up to the coastal palms beyond paddy fields ('motorcycle taxis' charge Rs 7 for return trip, from centre). The **Damodar Temple**, 2 km from Kadamba Bus Terminal hosts the winter *Dindi festival* when there is a palanquin procession along with singing of devotional hymns. The town also boasts Goa's largest **football stadium** of international standard which can seat 40,000.

Excursions A fascinating trip can take in two of the most important Christian sites in Salcete giving a glimpse of both past and present village life. **Loutolim** and **Rachol** can both be reached by taking the main Ponda road out of Margao, Loutolim being just to the north of the road. Rachol is 6 km to the south, and is also signposted off to the left, 5 km east of Margao, for those combining this trip with a visit to **Chandor**. See page 160 for further details. ■ *Getting there: Buses from Margao will get you to within walking distance of all the sights but it is worth considering a taxi.*

Essentials

Sleeping
Some budget hotels like Gold Star and Green View don't accept foreign visitors

Holiday-makers usually head for the beaches, using Margao for an overnight stop for making travel connections. It is the main point of access to Goa for travellers on the Konkan railway. **NB** Station Rd is still universally called by that name, though the road signs give it its official name of Francisco Luis Gomes Rd.

C *Nanutel* (was *Metropole*), Padre Miranda Rd, T733176. F733175, nanutelmrg@nanuindia.com 55 smart rooms, comfortable business hotel, good food, nice pool but unattractive poolside area, bookshop. **D-E** *Goa Woodlands*, ML Furtado Rd, opposite city bus stand, T712838, F738732, woodland@goa1. dot.net.in 46 rooms (Rs 270), 18 a/c (Rs 500), clean and spacious with bath, restaurant, bar, popular with businessmen, good value. **D-E** *Tourist Hotel* (GTDC), Luis Miranda Rd, T731996. 69 acceptable rooms in 6-storey building so some have good view over the city, a/c (Rs 500) better, others are cramped, simple restaurant (good vegetable vindaloo), tourist information, travel desk. **E** *Apsara*. 22 basic rooms (a/c Rs 350), run-down but bearable for a night. **E** *La Flor*, E Carvalho St, T731402. 35 rooms with bath, half a/c (Rs 300), restaurant, clean and good value. **E** *Mabai*, Praca Dr George Barreto, T721658. 20 rooms, 9 a/c (Rs 270), poorly maintained, literally crumbling. **E** *Milan*, off Station Rd, T722715. Useful if arriving late by train, good Indian vegetarian restaurant. **E** *Poonam*, T732945. 12 good-sized, clean rooms (Rs 190), best of the budget hotels but often full. **E** *Rukrish*, Station Rd, opposite Bank of India, T721709. 17 basic but clean rooms, some with balconies (Rs 209), some toilet seats missing (check first).

Expensive *Banjara*, T722088. North Indian. Plush but not flashy, a/c, good service, pricey but "food not all that special". **Mid-range** *Casa Menino*, LIC Building, Luis Miranda Rd. Goan. Part a/c, with bar. *Chinese Pavilion*, M Menezes Rd (400m west of municipal gardens). Chinese. Smart, a/c, good choice (Rs 80). *Food Affair*. North Indian. Basement café, main course Rs 75, open all day. *Gaylin*, 1 V Valaulikar Rd. Chinese. Tasty hot Schezuan, comfortable a/c. *Longuinhos* near the Municipality. Goan, North Indian. Open all day for meals and snacks, also bar drinks and baked goodies.

Eating
Pork is not usually available

Margao

South Goa

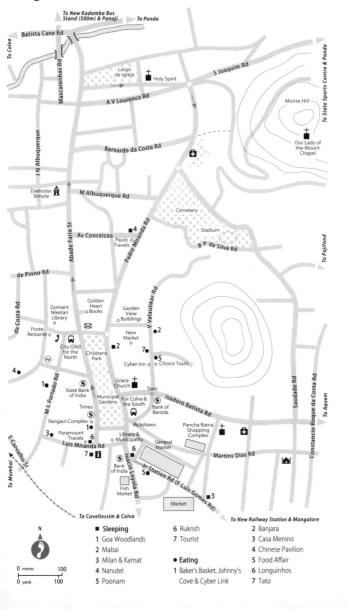

■ Sleeping	6 Rukrish	2 Banjara
1 Goa Woodlands	7 Tourist	3 Casa Menino
2 Mabai		4 Chinese Pavilion
3 Milan & Kamat	● Eating	5 Food Affair
4 Nanutel	1 Baker's Basket, Johnny's	6 Longuinhos
5 Poonam	Cove & Cyber Link	7 Tato

The burning of a virtuous woman

According to a myth, Sati (Parvati) had been forbidden by her father Daksha to marry Siva but she disobeyed him. Daksha slighted Siva by not inviting him to the special yagnya (horse sacrifice) to which everyone in the kingdom was to be present. Sati attended the ceremony, against her husband's wishes, but on hearing her father grossly abusing Siva she threw herself into the sacrificial fire. The act gave rise to the term **sati** *(or suttee) meaning simply a good or virtuous woman. In another story, Krishna's eight wives too are remembered for having followed their husband to be burnt on his funeral pyre.*

Recorded in the Vedas, the self immolation of a 'virtuous woman', often out of a sense of duty, probably became accepted practice until the early centuries BC and even then it was mainly restricted to the Kshatriya caste. There are references to the mimed ceremony in which the widow symbolically joined her dead husband on the pyre but was led away before the pyre was set alight. The burning of widows was resumed by around the sixth century AD, mainly along the River Ganga, and in Bengal and Rajasthan. If a woman refused she would have been considered to have brought dishonour to her husband's family. She would then be deprived of all means of support and was sometimes forced into prostitution.

In Goa, Afonso de Albuquerque forbade the practice of widow burning which was prevalent among the Hindus when the Portuguese arrived. In 1550, a further order meant that anyone reported to have "assisted" a widow to commit sati would be taken into custody and his property divided between the person who denounced him and the work of the Church of St Thomas. The pressure to abandon the customary sati led to widows being prevented from remarriage by insisting that they shave their heads and stop wearing jewellery (thus removing the means of making herself attractive) and also adopt a restricted diet. These observances also were attacked by the colonial rulers during the 16th and early 17th centuries. There are some sati stones (and hero stones) in the the Old Goa Archaeological Museum.

The Bengali religious leader and social reformer Raja Rammohan Roy made great efforts to abolish sati and allow widow remarriage in the early 19th century and the act was made illegal in 1829. The practice however, continued and even today, cases are reported where family pressure has a led a woman to her husband's funeral pyre.

Tato, G-5 Apna Bazaar, Complex, V Valaulikar Rd. Excellent vegetarian including *thalis*, a/c upstairs, immaculate. *Utsav*, Nanutel Hotel. Pleasant, serving a large range of Goan dishes. **Cheap** *Café Margao* is good for South Indian snacks. 4 *Kamats*. Indian vegetarian. Clean and good value *thalis* and snacks, including a/c *Milan Kamat*, Station Rd. **Bakery** *Maria Luiza Bakers* near the Municipal Garden and *Souza Bakery*, towards Kadamba bus terminal, do reasonable cakes and breads. *Baker's Basket* and *Johnny's Cove* at Rangavi Complex, west of Municipal Gardens, have Goan sweets including bebincas.

Shopping See 'markets' under sights. **Books**: *Golden Heart*, Confident Building, off Abbé Faria Rd, behind the GPO, T726339, (closed 1300-1500), is the biggest bookshop in Goa, wide collection, a bit like a warehouse but very helpful staff. Small shop at *Nanutel* hotel. **Handicrafts**: *Tourist Hotel* shop. *AJ Mavany*, Grace Estate. **Photography**: *Lorenz*, opposite the Municipality. *Wonder Colour Lab*, Garden View Building. **Textiles**: *MS Caro*, Caro Corner, has been in business since 1860, and has an extensive range including 'suiting', and will advise on tailors who can make up garments to order, in a few days; some will make near perfect copies of a sample. **Tailor**: *J Vaz*, Martires Dias Rd, near Hari Mandir, T720086. Good quality reliable men's tailor.

Choice Tours, V Valaulikar, Grace Church, T731332; *Paramount Travels*, Luis Miranda Rd (opposite *Tourist Hostel*), T722150, also exchange. **Tour operators**

Local Buses: The local bus stand is by the Municipal Gardens. You can usually board buses near the *Kamat Hotel*, southeast of the gardens. **Car hire**: Rs 650-900 per day or Rs 5,500 per week with driver from *Sai Service*, T735772, recommended. **Motorcycle taxis** also battle for road space. **Transport**

Long distance Train: enquiries, T732255. The new station on the broad gauge network is 500m south of the old station. Most *Express* trains on the Konkan Railway stop at Margao (Madgaon) and a few at Chaudi (Canacona), but they are still very slow. The reservation office on the first floor of the new station is usually quick and efficient, with short queues. Open 0800-1400, 1415-2000, Mon-Sat, 0800-1400, Sun. Tickets for Mumbai and Delhi should be booked well ahead. The **pre-paid taxi stand** is to the right of the exit; to Margao centre Rs 50, Panaji Rs 422, Colva Rs 115, Palolem Rs 422. **Autos** are to the left; to Margao, Rs 40; to Colva Rs 70, to Panaji Rs 275, although bargaining may produce better rates. **Train details** for the major routes are as follows: To **Mumbai (CST)**: *Madgaon Mumbai Exp 0104*, 1230, 10hrs; *0112*, 1815, 12hrs. To **Mumbai Kurla (Tilak)**: *Netravati Exp, 6636*, 2020, 10hrs. From **Mumbai (CST)**: *Madgaon Exp 0103* 0515, 11hrs; *Konkan Kanya Exp 0111*, 2230, 12hrs (often fully booked a week ahead). To **Ernakulam (Jn)**: *Lakshadweep Exp 2618*, 2115, 14 hrs. From **Ernakulam (Town)** for Kochi: *Rajdhani Exp 2431*, 2325, 12hrs. To **Thiruvananthapuram (Trivandrum)**: *Rajdhani Exp 2432* (Thur, Fri), 1305, 16hrs (originates in Delhi **(HN)** on Wed, Thur, 1100). From **Trivandrum**: *Rajdhani Exp 2431* (Fri, Sat), 1915, 17hrs (continues to **Delhi (HN)**, 1215, arrive 1350 next day). The broad gauge line between **Vasco** and **Londa** in Karnataka, runs through Margao and **Dudhsagar Falls**, connects stations on the line with **Belgaum**. There are services to **Bangalore**, **Delhi** (via Agra), and **Hospet (Hampi)** among others. See page 97.

Road Bus: the Kadamba (New) bus stand is 2 km north of town (city buses to the centre, Re 1 or motorcycle taxi Rs 8); buses arriving before 1000 and after 1900, proceed to the centre. To **Benaulim**, Rs 3; **Cabo da Rama**: 0730 (2 hrs) Rs 15; **Canacona** and **Palolem**, several; **Colva**: hourly, Rs 4; **Gokarna**, 1300 daily, Rs 50. **Non-stop** KTC buses to **Panaji**: 1 hr, Rs 15; **Vasco**: Rs 14. Buy tickets from booth at stand number 1. **Private buses** (eg *Paulo*, Metropole Hotel, T721516), Padre Miranda Rd: to **Bangalore**, 1700 (15 hrs), Rs 275; to **Mangalore**, 1800, 2130 (8-10 hrs), Rs 140; to **Mumbai (Dadar/VT)** 1400, 1700 (16 hrs), Rs 600 (sleeper), 400; to **Pune**: 1700 (13 hrs), Rs 450 (sleeper). **Auto-rickshaw**: to Colva, Rs 30; beach, Rs 50. **Taxi**: to Panaji, about Rs 300; to **Colva**, Rs 80 (after bargaining).

Avoid tourist taxis, they can be 5 times the price

Banks *Bank of Baroda*, behind Grace Church; also in market, Station Rd. *Bank of India*, exchanges cash, TCs, Visa and Mastercard, 0930-1400, 1500-1900, Mon-Fri; 0930-1400 Sat. *State Bank of India*, west of the municipal gardens. *Times Bank* (now merged with HDFC), 24hr ATM for Mastercard, minimum withdrawal Rs 100, maximum, Rs 10,000 per day. **Communications** *GPO*, north of Children's Park. *Poste Restante*, near the Telegraph Office, down lane west of Park, 0830-1030 and 1500-1700 Mon-Sat. **Couriers**: *Skypak*, T724777 and *Rau Raje Desprabhu*, near Hotel Mayur, Old Market. **Telephones**: STD (and sometimes fax) at several places in town, including the New Market near the post office and taxi stand. **Internet**: *Cyber Link*, Shop 9, Rangavi Complex, inefficient staff. *Cyber Inn*, 105 Karnika Chambers, V Valauliker Rd, T733232, cyberinn@bom2.vsnl.net.in, 2 terminals, Rs 3 per min, internet, Rs 60 per hr offline. **Medical facilities** *JJ Costa Hospital*, Fatorda, T722586. *Hospicio*, T722164. *Holy Spirit Pharmacy*, open 24 hrs. **Tourist offices** GTDC, Tourist Hotel, T722513, 0800-1800 (lunch 1300-1400), claims to be open 365 days a year. **Useful addresses** Ambulance:T722722. Fire:T720168. Police:T722175. *Frank Shipping* for catamaran to Mumbai, if and when it resumes, at GTDC Tourist Hotel, T731966.

Directory
Get cash before visiting beaches to the south where it is more difficult

South Goa

Excursions around Margao

By the late 18th century, as Hall points out, a middle class was developing in the villages of the Old Conquest. With newly established rights to property, well to do Goans began to invest in large homes. The village of Loutolim is one of a number which saw the distinct development of estates and their houses built on a grand scale.

Ins & outs Buses from Margao will get you to within walking distance of all the sights but it is worth considering a taxi.

Loutolim

Colour map 2, grid B2 This small village (Lutolim) has several interesting **Goan country houses** around it, all of which are open to the public by prior arrangement.

Miranda House Miranda house, near the church, one of the earliest, is a fine country house built around 1700. The Mirandas became wealthy as owners of areca plantations and the garden here still has specimen palms as reminders. It is situated at the end of a rough track, which starts near the church square leading west, and is approached through impressive iron gates. The main door is to one side, instead of being central, to the front of the house. The house, now owned by the Goan cartoonist Mario Miranda, though, is typical in having a garden courtyard at the back around which run the family rooms and bedrooms (note the attractive panelled wood ceilings), protected by shady verandahs. There is also the family chapel with the kitchen and servants' quarters at the far end. The formal reception rooms are to the front, lit by equally formal dark wood windows. The grand dining hall upstairs, accessed from the front hall, in turn leads to the large library. The bedroom suite on the other side once offered sanctuary to the Ranes in the 19th century (see page 138), and a defensive gun hole in the wall by a door still serves as a reminder of those uncertain years. The house retains little of the original furniture but more recently acquired pieces of period artefacts are now set off by imaginative furnishings in some of the rooms.

Salvador Costa House Another fine late 18th-century house, in its private compound, is the Salvador Costa House now shared by two descendants. It is a little further west from the square . Here too, the household revolved around a central courtyard at the back, but unlike the Miranda House, a wide welcoming verandah greeted the visitor. The impressively gilded family chapel is still used for daily prayers.

A typical Goan rural house

South Goa

Some fine features of its grand past are still evident in the original beautifully carved furniture, grand chandeliers and mirrors in one part of the house.

Finally Casa Araujo Alvares, the 19th-century Roque Caetan Miranda House, a short distance south of the square, has been renovated (somewhat unsympathetically) to attract visitors to its grand salon upstairs with chandeliers and fine carved wood furniture. Considering there is little inside it is pricey.There is a large chapel downstairs. ■ *Rs 100. 1000-1230 and 1500-1800.* **Casa Araujo Alvares**

Ancestral Goa

The village on the Ponda road has started attracting visitors to Ancestral Goa, a privately developed open-air site, designed to illustrate Goa's traditional past. Conceived by Maendra Alvares an artist/sculptor who has devoted considerable time and energy (and finance) to create a unique centre, a visit is recommended.

The '**model village**' built on a slope behind his own home has examples of old town and village houses and artisans' huts and traces the evolution of buildings. Great care and research have gone into constructing authentic replicas with an eye to detail when fitting them out with appropriate tools, utensils and artefacts, and providing a sympathetic setting.

Set on a hillside in very attractive surroundings, visitors are given a **guided tour** by well-informed guides who lead you through a socio-historical journey. Parts of the trail now have protection from the sun while a cooling mist of water provides a welcome escape from the midday heat during the hotter months. Take a hat, nevertheless. ■ *Rs 20. 0830-1830 daily.*

The tour takes you through the changing styles of structures from the humblest to the most comfortable, and at the same time illustrates interesting details of day-to-day life: the **fisherman's** shack, a simple shelter made out of palm fronds and bamboo with sand and shells on the ground; the **farmer's** home comprising one room built of mud and laterite blocks, with distinctive small clay tiles on the verandah roof. There is a stone fireplace and clay benches; the **taverna** progresses to being partly white-washed, with larger terracotta "Mangalore tiles" on the roof, a layer of cowdung covers the mud floor and it has a long verandah with benches made of wood and clay; and the **landowner's** impressive house which shows Portuguese influence in its raised balcao (verandah), plastered walls built of laterite and mortar, clay floor tiles, red cement seats, the family altar, and the use of decorative ceramic wall tiles, slatted wood ceilings and oyster-shell windows. See page 234.

Various interesting village activities are illustrated, from the distillation of the feni liquor from cashew apples in a *bhati*, to the potter and the village violin master. Of particular interest are structures like the *Boca da Vaca* (the 'Cow's Mouth') spring, which supplied a community with water, *Sant Kuris* (the wayside Holy Cross), where an annual feast is celebrated, *dhone* (pairs of pillars) which were found on roadsides (which the owner interprets as rests for heavy loads carried long distances), and the travellers' "safe passage" *racondar* lamps found under trees at significant points on a route. Brightly painted models of human figures may appear a little strange in the rustic surroundings but it is hoped that they will be supplemented by real artisans since live demonstrations of some crafts may be possible in the peak season.

South Goa

An added attraction is a chance to see a range of Goa's spices and fruit trees recently planted here which will become more productive as they mature. At the top of the site is "Natural Harmony", a sculpture of Sant Mirabai singing a devotional song accompanied by her one-string instrument *ektara*, carved out of a single horizontal block of laterite (15m x 5m) by Maendra Alvares. A little further up is the *Big Foot*, designed as a dance floor for wedding parties and other functions; each toe forms a platform for the band!

At the end of the tour, visitors are invited to have a glass of "fresh lime" (not bottled water but safe to drink) and visit a small gift shop with local handmade crafts, pottery, ceramics and paintings. A bakery about 500m away in a private house sells exceedingly mouth watering '*melting moments*' macaroons made with ground cashew nuts. Ask for directions.

Transport Regular buses to Loutilim from Margao stop at the church square, Rs 5.

Rachol

Colour map 2 grid B3 *Rachol (pronounced* Rashol*) is set in a fertile valley, vivid green during the wet season and into the New Year, but burnt brown in the summer heat. A stone archway crosses the road marking the entrance to the settlement, the road coming to an abrupt end in a hamlet by the river bank. The seminary is well worth a visit. Its white painted buildings are scattered on the left around a garden court.*

The fort There is little evidence of one of Goa's early important forts save a gateway and parts of some walls. Originally Muslim, it was captured by the forces of the Hindu Vijayanagar King in 1520 who then handed it over to the Portuguese who, they hoped, would in turn keep the Muslims at bay. During the Maratha Wars of 1737-9, and the siege that followed, the fort was badly damaged. Having lost the northern provinces the Portuguese paid a huge indemnity to keep the southern forts. The one in Rachol was repaired by the Marquis of Alorna in 1745. With the threat of aggression removed, the 100 cannons here were dispersed and most of the buildings gradually disintegrated over the ensuing years.

Seminary The seminary was established here in 1580 (after the earlier one at Margao was destroyed by Muslims the previous year), since the site had the protection of the fort. Originally known as the College of All Saints, it was rededicated to **Ignatius Loyola** in 1622. The Rachol complex, principally an ecclesiastical college, also includes a hospital, a primary school, an early printing press

Rachol seminary

which printed the Bible in Konkani, and is nearly a self-sufficient community. The seminary was under the Jesuits from 1610 until 1759 when they were expelled and the 'Oratorians' installed in their place. However, in 1835, when all religious orders lost favour in Portugal they too were removed and the seminary became the responsibility of the Diocesan Clergy of Goa.

For successive generations the seminary has been the most prestigious centre of education in Goa, producing some of Goa's secular as well as religious leaders and now is a forward-looking institution which trains clergy so as to be able to meet the challenges of society today. The vast stone structure of the seminary is built round a large courtyard. There is an underground cistern which some suggest belonged to an ancient Siva temple, now destroyed, and an underground passage from the courtyard conjuring images of an escape route through the fort in the precarious years of the 17th and 18th centuries. The seminary also contains large galleries and a famous library on the first floor containing rare books.

Churches

The church, dating from 1609, was rebuilt in 1622. The impressive interior, beautifully restored and rich with gilding, has nine altars including one to St Constantine containing his relics, and one with the celebrated Menino Jesus statue (which was considered miraculous when it had been installed in Colva, see page 146). There are many murals in the seminary and church including several portraits of saints. There is a daily service at 0700 to which visitors are welcome. ■ *Free. An attendant will show you round the church and the seminary between 0900-1300, 1430-1700; open to visitors even during term time, though quiet is requested.* The **Church of Our Lady of the Snows** (Nossa Senhora das Neves), now the parish church, is a short distance away on the riverside.

Museum of Christian Art

The small, well-kept museum is attached to the seminary but run independently by the Department of Archaeology. It was opened in January 1994 with funding from the Fundaçao Calouste Gulbenkian, Lisbon and Indian institutions. Exhibits include Indo-Portuguese sacred art mainly from Goa's churches, convents and Christian homes. The 155 precious items reflect a wealth of workmanship in wood, ivory, silver and gold. ■ *Rs 5. 0930-1300, 1400-1700, closed Mon.*

Transport Hourly buses from Margao run along the road below the Seminary.

Curtorim

Curtorim (Kurhtori) is a straddling village on the left (south) bank of the Zuari, 9 km from Margao and southeast of Rachol. The **Church of St Alex** (1597) possibly on the site of a Hindu temple, was rebuilt 50 years later and further renovated 200 years ago. Its siting, away from the village centre, is unusual. Here it stands in an attractive open setting, with its huge square facing a tranquil tank edged by shady palms. The large ornamental piazza cross resembles the monumental cross in front of Margao's Church of the Holy Spirit. The church towers illustrate the influence of Hindu design in 18th-century Goan churches. The octagonal drums topped by domes and lanterns recall the principal tower over the *garbagriha* of the Shri Mangesh Temple at Mardol. The interior with its five altars is profusely and elaborately decorated with some very fine detail. Nearby, at Maina-Curtorim village **C Naari**, a guesthouse for women among cashew groves, not far from the river, bed and breakfast ($160 pw double/$85 single), spacious living space, rooms with bath (hot water), home cooking, garden/terrace, book and pay at least a month ahead, DA/8B Phase 2, DDA Flats, Munrika, New Delhi 110067, T11-6138316, F6187401, naari@del3.vsnl.net.in.

Colour map 2, grid B3

South Goa

Chandor

This interesting village lies about 13 km east of Margao on the site of the 11th-century Kadamba capital of Chandrapur. The once navigable tributaries of the Zuari river allowed trade to flourish with distant Arab ports as early as the seventh century. Even earlier, a fourth-century Bhoja king's copper-plate inscription dates the existence of an ancient fort which once stood at Chandrapur nearby, taking advantage of the natural defensive moat the two rivers provided. In addition to the fort walls, brick foundations of a seventh-century Siva temple were found in 1929, near the sign on the roadside which marks the site of the old capital. The massive body of a *nandi* bull too was discovered, which must have come from the Siva temple. Today, Chandor is very much a backwater. Succeeding Muslim and Christian rulers destroyed much of Chandor's Hindu past. The **Church of Our Lady of Bethlehem**, built in 1645, replaced the principal *Sapta Matrika* (Seven Mothers) temple which was demolished in the previous century.

Three Kings Festival Crowds gather on 6 January each year, for the Three Kings Festival at Epiphany, which is similarly celebrated at Reis Magos, where there is a big fair, and at Cansaulim (Quelim) in southern Goa. The three villages of Chandor (Cavorim, Guirdolim and Chandor), come together to put on a grand show. Boys chosen from the the villages dress up as the Three Kings and appear on horse back carrying gifts of gold, frankincense and myrrh. They process through the village before arriving at the church where a large congregation gathers.

Menezes Braganza House Chandor also retains several fine Portuguese mansions, among them the enormous Braganza family house which faces one side of the large Church square, about 400m from the railway station, and receives visitors right through the year. Luis de Menezes Braganza was an influential journalist and politician (1878-1938) who not only campaigned for freedom from colonial rule but also became a champion of the less privileged sections of Goan society. The late 16th-century mansion he inherited (extended in the 18th and 19th centuries), shows the opulent lifestyle of the old Portuguese families who established great plantation estates, still complete with much of the family furniture and effects. The two wings are occupied separately by members of the Braganza family who have inherited the property. The central staircase, which divides the house into two halves, leads upstairs to the public reception rooms in the front and the private rooms at the back. The kitchen and servants quarters were downstairs at the back around the courtyard. Typically, the reception rooms at the front are lit by large glazed windows.

The west wing, which is better maintained, is owned by Aida de Menezes Bragança. The guided tour by this elderly member of the family who resides here, is fascinating. She has managed to completely restore the teak ceiling of the 250 year-old library gallery to return it to its original state; the old *mareta* wood floor survives since this native Goan timber can withstand water. In the dining room, the original polished *argamassa* floor has been replaced by new mosaic though a small section of old tiles has been retained near a window, as an example. The original ceiling of the grand salon (ball room) has been cleverly refurbished with patterned fibreglass to imitate the original American zinc panels. There is much carved and inlaid antique furniture and very fine imported china and porcelain, some specially ordered, and bearing the family crest. ■ *Donations of Rs 50 per visitor are appreciated. The house is usually open 0900-1800 everyday but it is best to confirm by phone, T784201. You will find the front door open; go up the stairs and knock on the door to the left.*

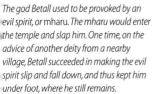

The banquet of the Mharus

The god Betall used to be provoked by an evil spirit, or mharu. The mharu would enter the temple and slap him. One time, on the advice of another deity from a nearby village, Betall succeeded in making the evil spirit slip and fall down, and thus kept him under foot, where he still remains.

This event is celebrated in the sacrifice of animals in his honour. Pereira goes on to say: "When the date has been fixed one man from the class of devdasis (literally, temple servants) goes on its eve, at night, to convoke the spirits (mharus and bhuts), in the boundaries of the village, in the streets and around the trees where they dwell.

On the following night the Mhars, carpenters, ironsmiths, washermen and other low-caste artisans gather in the temple. They take inside two buffaloes (which they overwork on purpose) and

three goats. The doors are then closed and there remain only twelve persons and the caller who sits down and embraces Betall, blindfolded.

At midnight, when all of them are in a rave, amidst cries which express the joy of the spirits and at the sound of drums, they cut the heads off the buffaloes and the goats and sprinkle their blood on a heap of boiled rice at the feet of Betall.

This is the banquet of the Mharus. The caller then leaves hold of Betall who would have fallen if he had not been caught and who is seen rocking at the time when the Mharu comes out from below his feet and goes with others to take part in the banquet.

The Mhars of the village then take the animals to an isolated palm grove and eat them there."

The east wing, occupied by Sr Alvaro de Perreira-Braganza, partly mirrors the west wing. It also has some fine carved furniture and a large salon where it requires some imagination to conjure up the grand occasions it witnessed in the past. The family chapel at the back now has a prized relic added to its collection, the decorated nail of St Francis Xavier, which had until recently, been kept guarded away from public view.

Paroda

Paroda, 15 km southeast of Margao (and about 4 km northwest of Quepem), is the start of the climb up the 350m-high Chandranath Hill (only signposted in Hindi), which has the **Chandresvar Bhutnath Temple** at the top. The temple was referred to in copper plate inscriptions as early as the fifth or sixth century AD. The final climb on foot is up rough steps to bring you to a superb open site for the brilliant white temple dedicated to Siva as the Lord of the Moon. Water is believed to ooze from the rock linga, which has a face carved on it, when it is touched by moonlight at each full moon; the temple was reputedly designed to make this possible. The moon was worshipped by Bhoja kings who ruled South Goa from the pre-Christian era up to the mid-eighth century. There is a separate shrine to Siva Bhutnath, an unadorned tall linga. An enclosure houses two wooden temple chariots; the older one has some good carvings. There are distant views from the hilltop, particularly at sunset, across to the sea. It is also believed that the hill is one of the 180 holy ancient pilgrimage centres for Hindus.

Colour map 2, grid C3

A second temple in the village, dedicated to Raibondkaranchem Deul, which has ancient sculpted images, is visited regularly by pilgrims from Ribandar in Tiswadi.

Cuncolim

Colour map 2, grid C3
Population: 15,000

Cuncolim is one of the
few places in the area to
have a petrol station

Cuncolim saw the destruction of its three principal Hindu temples (including the Shantadurga), when the Jesuits were Christianizing the area and later built churches and chapels on their sites. The annual Shantadurga *jatra* takes place in December-January when thousands accompany the image, in procession from Fatorpa to Cuncolim.

According to Souza's account, Cuncolim was also the scene of the massacre of five Jesuits and several converts by local Hindu 'rebels' who had been incensed by the repeated destruction of temples and defilement of temple tanks. Most of them were subsequently captured by the captain of Rachol fort and 15 were killed by his soldiers. The Christian 'martyrs of Cuncolim' were initially buried in Rachol but were transferred to Old Goa where their relics are lodged in the Se Cathedral. The golden bell, the largest in Goa, which hangs in the remaining single tower of the same cathedral, was cast here in 1652.

The far south

Quepem and Canacona are the two southernmost talukas. Towards the south of Goa the Western Ghats get closer to the sea, rising as a clearly visible range of hills from the coastal road. They are the only talukas that have both hill ranges and a coastline, but they share some of the geographical features of the talukas to the north. Low laterite plateaus and wooded valleys, but the forest comes closer to the sea here in the south than anywhere else in Goa. Hence Canacona's small Cotigao Sanctuary is a bare 15 km from the sea. The chief attractions in Canacona taluka are on the coast, Cabo de Rama and Palolem, but each has its share of Hindu temples inland and some very attractive scenery.

Cacora

Colour map 2, grid C4

This tiny hamlet in north Quepem, on the road between Sanvordem and Chandor, is noted for its **Shri Mahadeva Temple**. Although the temple is unremarkable in appearance it has some very unusual features. One is that among its affiliated deities is a shrine in the precincts to a Muslim *Pir* (saint) which Gomes Pereira notes is served by a Muslim who is permanently employed by the temple. Even more remarkable is the annual ritual during which a buffalo is sacrificed in a ceremony known as '*Reddebhogvoll*', not uncommon in Maratha and Sudra villages.

Quepem

Colour map 2, grid C4
Population: 12,000

Quepem is 15 km southeast of Margao. The forest department's simple **F** *Quepem Forest Rest House*, can be booked through the Wildlife Office, third floor, Junta House, 18th June Rd, Panaji, T224747. To go to **Cabo de Rama**, from Margao or Quepem, travel via **Bali** on the NH17, through Fatorpa.

Fatorpa

Colour map 8, grid B1

Fatorpa is no more than a tiny hamlet on the road from Bali to Cabo de Rama. Leaving the NH17 in Bali the road runs to a junction at Fatorpa, dropping down to the **Shri Shantadurga Temple** partially concealed in its shallow valley. There are 14 affiliated deities. The image of Shantadurga, originally from **Cuncolim** in Salcete, was brought to Fatorpa (with several others) in 1583. The modern concrete temple has no trace of the original structure, although the deity is still lodged in her sanctuary behind a silver screen.

The annual *jatra* (once held on 20th day of *Phalgun*), now takes place in December-January, when the deity is taken in procession by a large number of pilgrims. They travel from Fatorpa to the site of the original temple in Cuncolim, where the Chapel of the Sacred Heart stands. The *Fatorpa Gulal* (March/April) is similar to *Holi* when people throw coloured powder and water on each other.

Old Shantadurga Temple

Betul

Betul, in Quepem taluka, is an important fishing village in an idyllic setting. *Colour map 3, grid A2* Just after the bridge, which crosses the mouth of the river, a narrow road zigzags through the village along the south side of the Sal estuary. The village, depending on fishing and coir production, is delightfully shaded by coconut palms, jackfruit, papaya and banana. A sand bar traps the estuary into a wide and protected lagoon. Cool breezes from the sea moderate the temperatures of the plateau above so that even in the hottest season it is perfectly bearable. A walk along the 'jetty' past dozens of colourful fishing boats will reveal busy fisherfolk loading fish into baskets or their catch of tiny silvery fish glistening in the sun trapped under nets spread out on the bank.

E *River Sal*, Zuem Velim, on the waterside, T760276. 12 rooms, offers wide choice of menu including fresh river fish, excellent location, good ambience. Boatmen bring holidaymakers from Mobor to eat here in the evening. **Sleeping & eating**

From Cavelossim the shortest route to Betul is by taking the **ferry** across the Sal (signposted, just southeast) to Assolna where after a left turn into the village you turn right to join the main road towards Betul. From Margao, the NH17 forks right towards Assolna at Chinchinim. **Buses** from Margao to Betul can be very slow. **Transport**

Route

To Bali The road to the south from Betul village climbs steeply from the lush tropical valley to the searing heat of the bare plateau. It passes a new development by IPSEN for the Oil and Natural Gas Commission of India, after 2.6 km reaching a crossroads. From the crossing a road goes to northeast to Bali, passing Shakti Bauxite mines on the plateau's stark landscape.

To Cabo de Rama The road southwestwards from the crossroads towards Cabo de Rama first has coconuts growing in the valleys with breadfruit trees, then it traverses a really bleak landscape, dominated in the dry season by almost black laterite which is enlivened during the rains by patches of green cultivation. People here have meticulously reclaimed land where tiny rectangles of levelled plots have laterite block bunds to trap the rain. After winding down into another valley for 1 km, a minor road forks off to the right to Cabo de Rama (the sign may be almost invisible), going through beautiful lightly wooded countryside, dominated by cashew trees, while the fork left leads to the southernmost beaches of Goa.

South Goa

Cabo de Rama

Colour map 3, grid B2 Cape Rama is named after the hero of the Hindu epic the *Ramayana*, who is said to have lived there with his wife Sita during their period of exile. The cape was an obvious site for a fort to any power whose interests might be threatened from the sea. Its origins pre-date the arrival of the Portuguese who captured it in 1763 and used it as a prison too.

The fort
Untroubled by more than a handful of visitors, the atmosphere creates a sense of history & drama - only the most unimaginative could fail to respond

The gatehouse, which has been restored, looks rather quaint, with narrow firing slits irregularly spaced like a miniature design by Le Corbusier. The main entrance seems far from impregnable, considering the scale of the fortifications, but note the strategically positioned hole in the wall, pointing straight at the door, behind which a cannon could be stationed.

The outer ramparts are excellently preserved, with several cannons still scattered along their length. Despite the absence of buildings, other than the church, the magnificence of the site gives it an extraordinary atmosphere. There are stunning views from several of its major bastions, and you can walk virtually the entire outer length of the fort. From two of the gates it is possible to scramble down to the sea, but great care is needed on the crumbly laterite paths. The most dramatic of the walls is on the landward side, where it rises 10-15m above the floor of the moat which was dug both to provide laterite blocks from which the fort is constructed and to create the moat itself.

The gatehouse is at the lowest point of the whole fort, the ground rising to its highest in the southwest. The view is particularly good to the south in the evening light, across bays stretching down past Palolem to Karnataka easily visible on a clear day. From the highest point and observation post (where a modern but disused and run-down building has been built), there is a 360° view, and the wall then drops down to the north. At its lowest it is only 20m or so above the sea. At this point of the compound, deeply wooded now, is the source of the Fort's water supply. A huge tank was excavated to a depth of about 10m, and even today it has water right through the dry season. There are two springs, one of which gives out water through two spouts at different temperatures.

Sleeping & eating Near the fort entrance, these offer meals, drinks and some very basic rooms: *Pinto's Bar* and *Zina Bar*, and 200m beyond, the brightly painted *Fernandes Corner Restaurant* .

Transport From Margao, buses leave at 0730 from the southeast corner of the Municipal Gardens (Rs 10, 2 hrs), return at 1200 or later. From Betul or Palolem, hire a motorbike.

Route After retracing your steps along the road from Cabo de Rama to the junction you can either return along the Betul/Bali road or take the road south, the coast road to Agonda and Palolem (there are no signs to tell you this). It is a attractive alternative to the national highway. **Agonda** has few facilities for the visitor but the beach is a long stretch of sand though the sea can be very rough.

Palolem

Colour map 3, grid B3 *South of Agonda the remarkably beautiful curve of palm-fringed golden sand is one of Goa's best beaches. The search for this last unspoilt idyll has led to an almost exponential increase in the number of visitors. It is no longer a deserted bay since day packages from other resorts to this Paradise Beach (cynics refer to it as 'Paradise Lost'), has firmly fixed it on the tourist map. However it still retains an air of peace and calm though more shacks line the shore, behind which are countless bamboo huts offering simple and cheap accommodation.*

The fruit and nut case of cashew

The cashew or (kazu) tree which you will see in many parts of Goa, particularly in Bardez, Bicholim and Satari talukas, produces the 'apple' which turns yellow or red when ripe and is then harvested between March and June (see page 229). The tree, which is one of the principal and dependable 'plantation crops', is often not formally planted in separate orchards, but grows productively without much attention of fertilizers or irrigation. Cashew was introduced by the Portuguese in the early days of colonization, principally to conserve soil, but later better varieties were introduced (including those from South America), which would yield high quality nuts.

The cashew nut, which is enjoyed all around the world, is obtained from roasting the lower part of the fruit in large wood-fired kilns until charred, and then painstakingly cracked open (often by village women) to reveal the pale nut. The dried nut is sometimes roasted and salted before packing. The charred nut-case produces a valued waterproof 'paint' which is used to seal wooden boats.

The 'apple' takes a different route. Traditionally, the juice was squeezed out by crushing the fruit under foot in the village bhati (distillery) in the same way as grapes are treated in traditional wineries, but now there are modern distilleries. The juice is then strained to produce a delicious sweet drink niro, which needs to be kept cool to avoid fermenting. However, most of the juice extracted is allowed to ferment for 15 days; this is then boiled in large earthen pots and distilled to first yield the low alcohol urak. Further distillates produce the stronger cashew feni.

Getting there Palolem is 3 km from Canacona Junction station, which is on the Konkan Railway (*Netravati Express*); from there taxis and auto-rickshaws charge around Rs 25-30 to Palolem beach. There are also several direct buses from Margao which take an hour to Chaudi village (see below). You can get off the bus at Canacona Junction (before the village) and walk the 2 km to the beach. **Getting around** You can hire a bicycle from the village for Rs 3 per hour or Rs 25 per day.

Ins & outs

The fairly narrow strip of beach has rather strange rocky outcrops at each end which are locally referred to as 'Pandava's drums' and 'footprints'. An added attraction here is the fresh water stream to the north, as well as the small Canacona Island which can be reached by a short swim or by wading across at low tide. Nudism is not welcomed by the local people.

The main beach is to the north with the bulk of the beach shacks, while the relatively smaller southern section has fishermen's huts and some novel accommodation options. The shaded palm tree area is unfortunately becoming increasingly littered. This is worse at weekends when an influx of local trippers bring their picnics, fill the air with loud music and leave behind a pile of garbage and dead whisky bottles.

D *Bhakti Kutir*, over the hill at the southern end, T643472, F643469. 11 cabanas of varying sizes (Rs 400-600) more being added, one imaginatively and sympathetically built with local materials, all with mosquito nets, common bath and organic toilets (neutralizing compound used instead of water for flushing), away from the beach and very quiet, emphasizing peace and meditation. Highly recommended.

Sleeping
Prices tend to rise on 1 Dec. There may be a shortage of electricity

E *Cocohuts*, towards the southern end (as lease on original site expired, landlord has set up his own Cocohuts clone!), T643296, F233298, ppv@goa1.dot.net.in 15 breezy, shaded huts (Rs 300-400) built among palm trees, raised on bamboo stilts about 3m above the ground, each divided into 2 rooms with 2 beds, electricity and fan, separate shared toilets on the ground, on the beach (dismantled during monsoon, so 200m building regulations don't apply), restaurant, original imaginative development by local doctor now overtaken by imitations. **E** *Ciaran's Camp*, T643477, johnciaran@hotmail.com Based on *Cocohut* model, 20 good huts on the beach front with restaurant. **E** *Cozy Nook*, at the northern end, T643550. 9 plastered bamboo huts (Rs 250), in a good location sandwiched between the sea and freshwater river, ayurvedic centre, art and crafts encouraged ("occupational therapy for beach bums!"), friendly, one of the best. Recommended. **E** *La Allegro*, T643498. 4 small rooms (Rs 300), basic and fairly bleak but right on the beach, often full. **E** *Palolem Beach Resort*, T/F643054. 9 rooms with bath (Rs 300-400), 9 tents and 10 basic cottages with shared facilities, shower blocks (Rs 200-300), ISD phones, reliable travel service and

Palolem

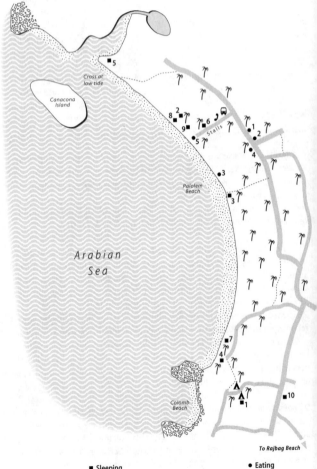

0 metres 300
0 yards 300

■ **Sleeping**
1 Bhakti Kutir
2 Camp Palo
3 Ciaran's Camp
4 Cocohuts
5 Cozy Nook
6 Cupid Castle
7 Hi-Tide Beach Huts
8 La Allegro
9 Palolem Beach Resort
10 Unic Resort &
  Oceanic Restaurant

● **Eating**
1 Nature
2 Rosy Bar
3 Silver Star
4 Sun & Moon
5 Sunset

exchange. Friendly, clean, quiet shaded site, popular with package groups and families so book at least a week ahead. Recommended. **E** *Hi-Tide Beach Huts*, on site formally occupied by Cocohuts towards the southern end, T643104. 11 huts (Rs250 – Rs400), possibly the largest of them all, best one on stilts at the beach front. **E** *Unic Resort*, away from the sea (about 1 km to Colomb Beach), T643059, F739688. 9 clean but uninspiring rooms (Rs 300-350), friendly, good restaurant specializing in seafood, excellent cocktails.

F *Camp Palo*, behind La Allegro, T643173 (ask for Irshad). 13 well built huts (Rs 200) set in a pleasant compound. **F** *Cupid Castle*, Beach Rd, T643326. 8 clean, reasonable huts (Rs 200), some with attached bath, short walk to the beach, restaurant. **F** *Rooms* in village houses, very basic facilities ('pig' toilets, unconnected to sewers, are raised on a platform where pigs do the necessary 'cleaning out' below). **F** *Camping*: Parking for campers and travellers (Rs 15-20 per day) at *Palolem Beach Resort* and south of *Cocohuts*. Public toilets are at the end of the road to the south.

Mid-price *Bhakti Kutir*. Tasty western dishes, home-grown produce, very pleasant though away from the water's edge. **Cheap** *Nature*, bar and restaurant, away from the beach. Also runs a travel and money exchange service. *Silver Star*, with hammocks in the shade. *Sun & Moon* T643314. Relocated, now set back from the south end of the beach, under palms. A friendly, popular 'hang-out' with great atmosphere, large helpings of well-cooked Goan food. *Sunset* on the beach and *Rosy Bar*, near the main road, are recommended.

    Eating

Dolphin watching and **fishing** trips are best in the morning, between 0830-1230. Arrange through Palolem Beach Resort, travel agents or a fisherman (eg Dattu Pagi, Boat No 520); 4 people for about Rs 600 for 1 hr. **NB** Take sun-block, shirt, hat and drinking water. You may be able to see some dolphins from the headland to the south of Palolem, just before sunset.

    Entertainment

A good **clothes** shop near Palolem Beach Resort has a friendly owner, not pushy.

    Shopping

6 daily direct buses run between Margao and Chaudi (Canacona, 40 km via Cuncolim), Rs 9. From Chaudi, taxis and auto-rickshaws charge Rs 25 to Palolem beach. From Palolem, buses for Margao leave at around 0645, 0730, 0930, 1415, 1515, 1630 and take 1 hr.

    Transport

Banks No bank here, so arrive with enough funds. *Palolem Beach Resort* and *Nature Bar* change foreign currency. **Communications** Post Office: Nearest is at Chaudi. **Internet** at *Nature Bar* and *Sun & Moon*, Rs 2 per min. **Medical facilities** T643339. **Useful services** Police: T643357.

    Directory

Colomb and Rajbag beaches

South of Palolem, a walk along the shore over rocky outcrops gives access to attractive sandy coves of Colomb Beach with huts of the fishing community nearby; some take in paying guests and allow parking for campers and travellers (Rs 15-20 per day). Further south, by wading across a stream (which is possible before the monsoon), you reach the unspoilt Rajbag Beach backed by dunes and casuarinas. It remains virtually unvisited and provides excellent swimming. The opening of an upmarket *Bharat-Hilton Resort* with 280 rooms and all the usual facilities, however, will change this.

At **Kindlebaga**, east of Rajbag, 2 km from Chaudi, is the isolated and somewhat surprising **C** *Molyma*, off NH17, west from the crossroads, T643028,

South Goa

F643081, 43 modern, large rooms, airy restaurant with limited menu, bar, friendly service, good value though rather deserted, set among trees within 15 minutes' walk to a good beach beyond dunes.

Galgibaga
Colour map 3, grid B3

South of the Talpona River, which has a ferry crossing, a short strip of land juts out to sea. Galgibaga is a change from the fishing villages across the river as it has well-built houses belonging to the townspeople. There are lucrative casuarina plantations in addition to the ubiquitous palms.

Chaudi (Canacona)

Colour map 3, grid B3
Population: 10,400
There is not much in the way of facilities at the moment

Chaudi (Chauri), also called Canacona (locally pronounced *Kannkonn*), is a crossroads settlement on the NH17 between Panaji and Karwar in Karnataka. 'Chaudi' refers to the town's main square, where the bus and auto stands are. The large church and high school of **St Tereza of Jesus** (1962) are on the northern edge of town. The rail link on the Konkan line has brought the idyllic beaches nearby to the attention of developers.

Shri Malikarjuna Temple, 6 km northeast of town, with 60 auxiliary deities is believed to date from the mid-16th century and was renovated in the year 1778. The *mandapa* has substantial carved wooden pillars. The temple 'car' festival *Rathasaptami* in February and *Shigmo* in April attract large crowds.

Sleeping & eating

The forest department's simple **F** *Canacona Forest Rest House*, nearby, can be booked through DCF, South Margao, T0834-735361. *Canacona Palace*, 50m east of the crossroads, serves good Udupi vegetarian food.

Transport

Trains from Canacona Junction station, 2 km away: to **Ernakulam**, *Netravati Exp 6635*, 0348, 17hrs; to **Mumbai (T)** (Kurla), *6636*, *1936*, 11hrs; and to **Margao (Madgaon)** *1936*, 30 mins. **Buses** run to Palolem and Margao as well as south into Karnataka.

Directory

Banks *State Bank of India*, next to Canacona Palace, has no foreign exchange facility. **Communications** *Post Office* is 200m down the highway towards Karnataka. *Internet Café* at Dias Apartment, Nagorcem, at the Agonda Crossing, 1 terminal, Rs 3.50 per min. **Medical services** *Pai Chemists*, is 100m east of the crossroads. **Useful services** *Petrol* from the small house opposite the big tree about 1 km north of the village.

Partagali

Colour map 3, grid B4

Close to the Cotigao Wildlife Sanctuary and just east of the NH17, the **Shri Sausthan Gokarn Partagali Jeevotam Math** at Partagali Village is on the banks of the river Kushavati. The followers, who were originally Saivites, were converted and became a Vaishnav sect and a *math* (religious establishment) was set up in 1475 AD at Margao. However, during the period of Portuguese Christianization (1560-68), the foundation was moved to Bhatkal (northern Karnataka). After a time, the sixth Swami (who was also responsible for the temple to Rama, Lakshman, Sita and Hanuman here), re-established it at Partagali where it has continued uninterrupted. The symbol representing the spiritual movement which is over 500 years old, is an ancient *Vatavriksha* (Banyan tree) which spreads over an area of about 65m x 70m. Known as '*Bramhasthan*' it has been a place for meditation, and the sacred tree with the Ishwarlinga in front of it is believed to have drawn worshippers from the surrounding area for over 1,000 years. Partagali has been developed into a centre of culture and learning, while continuing with its ancient traditions. The temple, which also has a typical tall Garuda pillar, celebrates its festival in March/April.

South Goa

Cotigao Wildlife Sanctuary

The second largest of Goa's wildlife sanctuaries, Cotigao, 60 km south of *Colour map 3, grid B4* Panaji, was established in 1969. One of the most densely forested areas of the state, the 105 sq km sanctuary is in part hilly to the south and east and has the Talpona River flowing through it. The vegetation is mostly moist deciduous with some semi-evergreen and evergreen forest cover. There are several small settlements of *Velip* and *Kunbis* who are forest-dwelling groups existing on subsistence farming, so it offers a good opportunity to observe traditional rural life. Some regret that their hunting and wood-gathering activities have been curbed with the establishment of the sanctuary. The villagers grow chillies and harvest cashew from the forest to take to the market in Cotigao. There have been attempts to introduce sugarcane, rubber and eucalyptus by some agencies but environmentalists argue that this would lead to clearing of trees and change the nature of the forest.

The sanctuary is 7 km south of Chaudi (Canacona); a 2 km road along a left **Access** turn (east) off the NH17 between Chaudi and Poinguinim leads to the sanctuary. ■ *Rs 5, 2-wheelers Rs 10, cars Rs 50. Still camera Rs 25; Video Rs 100. 0730-1730 throughout the year (but may not be worthwhile during the monsoon). There is a Nature Interpretation Centre with a small reference library at the entrance.*

The sanctuary claims to have a wide range of mammals including panther, **Wildlife** sloth bear and hyena, and several reptiles, but you are really only likely to see wild boar, the odd deer and gaur and many monkeys on a visit, although bird spotting is more rewarding. Birds not easily seen elsewhere in Goa include rufous woodpecker, Malabar crested lark and white-eyed eagle.

You need your own vehicle to reach the tree-top watch towers and water holes **Viewing** which are now signposted, 3 km and 7 km off the main metalled road on a very rough track. There are no guides but the Forest Office by the Interpretation Centre at the entrance may draw you a map and give his opinion on what is worth seeing (for example the rubber plantation) and steer you away from a village. The forest paths are easy to follow but make sure you have enough drinking water and petrol. The chances of seeing much wildlife however are slim, since by the opening time of 0730 it can be warm enough to reduce animal activity to a minimum, but it can be rewarding to take a short walk through the forest and immerse yourself in the sounds of the jungle.

Visitors usually come for a day trip. Those wishing to stay close by, choose to stay in **Sleeping** Palolem or at **Molyma** at Kindlebaga. In theory an overnight stay in the forest is possible *No food is available* with permission. 3 **tents**, with concrete floors are available. Free, but only the hardiest of *near the entrance or* campers could endure a night here, made even more difficult by the prolific insect life. A *inside the sanctuary* room may be available at the simple **F** *Forest Rest House*, **Poinguinim**. Contact the Conservator's Office, 3rd floor, Junta House, 18th June Rd, Panaji, T224747.

Buses run from Chaudi (Canacona), or hire a motorbike from one of the southern **Transport** beaches.

South Goa

To Karnataka

The NH17 continues south to the Karnataka border through some beautiful countryside and unspoilt villages. There is a border checkpost, just under an hour's bus ride from Chaudi, with a barrier across the border to stop vehicles. Motorcyclists must carry all documentation. See page 33. Across the border there is a marked improvement in the road surface. It no longer winds through the forest but is relatively wide and straight as it runs along the Karnataka coast towards Karwar.

The interior hills

Sanguem covers Goa's eastern hill borderland with the South Indian state of Karnataka. The still forested hills, populated until recently by tribal peoples practising shifting cultivation, rise to Goa's highest points. Just on the Goan side of the border with Karnataka are the Dudhsagar Falls, some of India's highest waterfalls, where the river, which ultimately flows into the Mandovi, cascades dramatically down the hillside. Much of the southeastern part of the taluka is inaccessible. The north of Sanguem taluka is more accessible, traversed by the NH4A which runs from Ponda to Molem before passing into Karnataka. Both the Bhagwan Mahaveer Sanctuary and the beautiful small Tambdi Surla temple can be reached in a day from the coast (about two hours from Panaji).

Tambdi Surla

Colour map 2, grid B5 The Mahadeva Temple is a beautifully preserved miniature example of early Hindu temple architecture from the Kadamba-Yadava period. Tucked into the forested foothills, the place is often deserted, though the compound is well maintained by the Archaeology Department. The entrance to the temple is a short walk from the car park.

Getting there From the crossroads at Molem on the NH4A, the road north goes through dense forest to Tambdi Surla. 4 km from the crossroads you reach a fork, take the right fork and after a further 3 km take a right turn at Barabhumi village (there is a sign). The temple is a further 8 km, just after *Shanti Nature Resort*. Make sure you have enough petrol before leaving Molem! It is also possible to reach the site along minor roads from Valpoi.

The only major remaining example of pre-Portuguese Hindu architecture in Goa may well have been saved from destruction by its very remoteness The 12th to 13th-century black basalt temple stands on a platform with three plain mouldings. The stone used must have been transported some distance as basalt is not available locally. The exterior walls have little decoration save for the breaks provided by the vertical pilasters. However, there are good miniature reliefs and sculptures on the shikara above the *garbagriha*, showing deities including Brahma with Swarasvati above, Siva with Uma-Mahesh above, and Vishnu with Kumarashakti above. The low wall near the open-sided entrance hall has finely carved lozenge-with-rosette motifs which still appear crisp.

Aligned east-west, the entrance/main hall (*sabhmandapa*), middle hall (*antaralaya*) and sanctuary (*garbagriha*) are on the same east-west axis. The 10 pillars, each different, are relatively plain, but four monolithic pillars which support the stone ceiling with a very fine example of the conventional floral design, are deeply incised. Hutt suggests that the carving showing an elephant trampling a horse (on the lower section of the first pillar on the right), may have political significance, since horses were the favoured animals of war of the Muslim invaders, in contrast to the elephants used by Hindu kings.

Tambdi Surla Temple

The *shikharas* of the four niches in the *mandapa* which contain images including *Nagas*, throw light on how the original temple must have looked with its tower over the *garbagriha* complete. A *Naga* with two hoods appears on a separate slab.

E *Shanti Nature Resort*, 500m from the temple. 9 large mud huts with palm-thatched roofs, electricity and running water in natural forest setting, emphasis on rest, ayurvedic treatment and meditation. Restaurant for all tastes, visits to spice gardens, bird watching, hikes, Dudhsagar etc arranged (2 nights, US$120). Highly recommended for location and eco-friendly approach. Contact ahead Passive Active Tourism, *Hotel Four Pillars*, Panaji, T/F0832-422986, josephb@bom2.vsnl.net.in (offered usually as a 'Jungle Book' package). **Sleeping & eating**

There is no public transport to Tambi Surla. It is possible to hike from Molem. **Transport**

Molem

Molem, south of Tambdi Surla, is the start of hikes and treks in December and January. Popular routes lead to Dudhsagar (17 km), the sanctuary and Atoll Gad (12 km), Matkonda Hill (10 km) and Tambdi Surla (12 km). Contact the Hiking Association, 6 Anand Niwas, Swami Vivekananda Road, Panaji. Molem is also a stop on the bus route between Panaji and Belgaum and the truck stop atmosphere is redeemed by the presence of a section of the national park which is easily accessible (see below). As visitors soon discover, it is "very pleasant, though you are unlikely to see any wildlife other than monkeys". *Colour map 2, grid B5*

E *Tourist Resort* (GTDC), 300m east of police check post, about 500m from the temple, T0834-600238. 23 simple but well maintained, clean rooms, some a/c, dorm (Rs 50), checkout 1200, giving time for a morning visit to Tambdi Surla, uninspired restaurant with limited menu serving North Indian food and beer. The forest department's simple **F** *Molem Forest Rest House* , can be booked through the Conservator's Office, 3rd floor, Junta House, 18th June Rd, Panaji, T224747. **Cheap**: truckers' *dhabas* serve snacks and breakfast omelettes **Sleeping & eating**

Buses between Panaji, Ponda or Margao, and Belgaum/Bangalore, stop at Molem for visiting the Bhagwan Mahaveer Sanctuary and Dudhsagar Falls. **Transport**

From **Molem**, a road to the south off the NH4A leads through the forested hills of Sanguem taluka to Colem and **Calem** railway stations and then south to **Sanguem**. From there, a minor road northwest goes to **San Vordem** and then turns west to **Chandor**. **Routes**

Bhagwan Mahaveer Sanctuary

Goa's largest wildlife sanctuary covers 240 square kilometres comprising lush moist deciduous to evergreen forest types. The Molem National Park in the central section of the sanctuary occupies about half the area with the Dudhsagar Falls in the southeast corner while the remote Tambdi Surla temple is hidden in the dense forest at the northern end of the sanctuary.

Access
Colour map 2, grid B6

The entrance to the Molem National Park about 150 metres east of Molem crossroads is clearly signed but the 14 km of tracks within the park are not mapped. The Tourist Complex is a little further east along the NH4A. Tickets are available at the Nature Interpretation Centre. ■ *Rs 5, 2-wheelers Rs 10, cars Rs 500, 0830-1730 (except for national public holidays).There is no accommodation inside the sanctuary; carry provisions. The nearest GTDC accommodation is the Tourist Complex.*

Wildlife

The 240 sq km sanctuary contains a herd of gaur (*Bos gaurus* – often called Indian Bison), deer, monkeys and rich birdlife. Occasionally elephants and tigers wander in from neighbouring Karnataka during the summer months, the tigers remaining on higher ground favoured by the few black panthers in the sanctuary, but these are rarely spotted.

Viewing

Within the sanctuary, forest department jeeps are available; contact the Range Forest Officer (Wildlife), Molem. Motorbikes can manage the rough track, outside the monsoon period, but not a scooter. In theory it is possible to reach Devil's Canyon and Dudhsagar Falls via the road next to the Nature Interpretation Centre (from where entrance tickets are sold), although the road is very rough and it may require a guide. Make sure you have a full tank of petrol if attempting a long journey into the forest!

Devil's Canyon

This canyon is an impressive gorge, through which the Dudhsagar River flows, which can be visited after getting permission from the Nature Interpretation Centre where you can get directions. The river is believed to have crocodiles.

Dudhsagar Falls
Colour map 2, grid B6

The spectacular falls on the border between Goa and Karnataka, which are the highest in India, measure a total drop of about 600m. The name, 'the sea of milk', is derived from the white foam that the force of the water creates as it drops in stages, forming pools along the way. They are best seen just after the monsoon, between October and December, but right up to April there is enough water to make a visit worthwhile.

Arriving by rail To experience the delights of a beautiful part of the forested Western Ghats, people visit Dudhsagar by rail; the line runs across about the mid-point of the vertical drop of the cascades. The small Dudhsagar railway station (when open) allows you to step down and then walk back to the opening between the two train tunnels. A rough, steep path takes you down to a viewing area which allows you a better appreciation of the falls' grandeur, and to a beautifully fresh pool which is lovely for a swim (take your costume and towel). There are further pools below but you need to be sure-footed. **NB** The final section of the journey is a scramble on foot across stream beds with boulders; it is a difficult task for anyone but the most athletic. The really fit and adventerous may wish to make the arduous climb up to the head of the falls with a guide, which is well worth the effort. Allow three hours, plus some time to rest at the top, and make sure of returning before the train you will need to catch.

Dudhsagar Falls

Arriving by road For those on a motorbike (but not a scooter), for the start of the trail to the falls, from Molem crossroads take the road south towards Colem. From there it is 17 km of rough track with at least two river crossings, so is not recommended after a long period of heavy rain. The ride through the forest is very attractive and leads to the spectacular reward at the end, even in the dry season. A swim in the pool at the falls is particularly refreshing after a hot and dusty ride. Guides are available but the track is easy to follow even without one.

Transport

Train When Dudhsagar station reopens, from the southern beaches, you can get the *Vasco-Colem Passenger* from Vasco at 0710, or more conveniently at Margao (Madgaon) at 0800 arriving at Colem (Kulem) at 0930. Return trains at 1640, arriving Madgaon at 1810, which leaves plenty of time to enjoy the falls. Hire a jeep from Colem Station. **Road** If coming from the south, travel via Sanguem. The road from Sanvordem to the NH17 passes through mining country and is therefore badly pot-holed and has heavy lorry traffic. From Colem, **jeeps** do the rough trip to Dudhsagar (Rs 300 per head, Rs 1800 per jeep). **Buses** between Panaji, Ponda or Margao, and Belgaum/Bangalore, stop at Molem.

Sanguem

Sanguem is the headquarters of the largest taluka in Goa and lies 20 km from Molem. Although inland it has the 'backwaters' feel. The 19th-century Jama Masjid was renovated in 1959. The forest department's simple **F** *Sanguem Forest Rest House*, can be booked through the Conservator's Office, third floor, Junta House, 18th June Rd, Panaji, T224747.

Colour map 3, grid A4
Population: 6,200

Colem (Kulem)

A busy small town which is the best point to connect with the Dudhsagar train (when the station to the falls opens) for those touring Goa by car. Colem is not to be confused with Kalem station, further west. Jeeps are, at present, available for the trip to the falls (see transport above).

Colourmap 3, grid A4

Zambaulim

Zambaulim, 22 km southeast of Margao, has the **Damodar Temple** which is attractively set along the banks of the Kushavati (Panti) River. According to Hall, the deity – originally from Margao – was transferred here in 1567 but the temple structure is fairly modern, dating mainly from the 1950s to the 1970s. The water of the river here is believed to be especially blessed and have medicinal properties, so attracts pilgrims from both the Hindu and Christian communities. *Zambaulim Gulal* is celebrated like *Holi* in March/April. Festivities continue for a week with much feasting, cultural shows and a big fair.

Colour map 3, grid A4

South Goa

The area around also came under the influence of Buddhism. Punna, a monk, is believed to have lived in the village and preached the doctrine of Buddhism. A statue of the Buddha was found in Rivona nearby (see below).

Curdi

Colour map 3, grid A4

Curdi (Kurdi), 8 km south of Sanguem, is known as a megalithic site where a 2½m laterite Mother Goddess statue (fifth century BC) was excavated. The statue was taken to Verna (also a megalithic site) by the Directorate of Archaeology and re-sited on the spot where an old Mahalsa temple stood until 1560. This is also where sections of a Kadamba Temple to Siva (11th century), described by R Gomes Pereira as built of laterite and granite and consisting of a *garbagriha* and a pyramidal *shikhara,* were discovered. The Mahadeva Temple was threatened by the Salauli Irrigation Project and was re-sited in the new settlement. A short distance away rock-cut steps led down to a stream where a small rock shelter was also found with two statues of Siva. The shelter is now under water.

Colomba
Colour map 3, grid A4

The road to Rivona to the west, first passes through Colomba which has the Shantadurga Temple, one of the few places in India where Brahma is worshipped; here as an affiliate deity.

Rivona

Colour map 3, grid A4

Ask for directions in the village and carry a torch; beware of snakes

Hall suggests that the name is derived from *Rishi-vana* (Forest of Saints), recalling a period around the seventh century when groups of Buddhist monks are believed to have established cave retreats in this part of Goa.

The rock-cut **cave sites**, where a statue of the Buddha was found, are referred to as the Pandava Caves locally. The headless stone statue, described by R Gomes Periera as belonging to the seventh century and missing the left arm, was found seated on a throne with three lions in front; it is now in the Archaeological Museum, Panaji. The caves were later taken over by Hindus who left carvings on stones, including a stylized long-tailed Hanuman holding a tree in one hand.

Just south of the bazaar along the main road through the village, a dirt path opposite the water pump leads to the first cave site after about 100m. The small set of excavated cells, which Hutt suggests were used as a monastery, is approached by steps that lead down to a vestibule with a well which has a funnel-shaped hole channelled through to the surface to provide light and air. Another entrance porch, facing a pool, also gave access to the cells within through the vestibule. Natural springs supplied water which was stored in tanks. While most of the caves were excavated, Hutt suggests that part is structural, being built out of stone blocks.

To find the second cave site return to the main road, and follow a path for about 400m down to the river and along it. The cave shelter near the valley bottom, which is more open, has a platform at the back. Here too, there was no shortage of water. The hole to the right of the cave entrance is believed to have been the start of a tunnel to Curdi, some 8 km. It is best not to attempt to enter either cave. Carry a torch and keep a safe distance away as they are likely to harbour snakes.

Usgalimal

South of Colomba, this is where the latest dicoveries of prehistoric rock carvings were made in the 1990s. Some of the finds are displayed in the Panaji Archaeological Museum.

Excursions

6

Excursions

Within easy reach of the coast and just beyond Goa's borders are fascinating glimpses of the India beyond the old Portuguese enclave. Both the physical and the cultural contrasts are immediate, and two or three day excursions from the beaches of Goa allow you to see at least something of peninsula India beyond the steamy coastal fringes of the Western Ghats. Hampi, on the banks of the Tungabhadra River in the heart of the boulder strewn peninsula, retains the still remarkable ruins of the once glorious capital of the Vijayanagar Empire. Travelling north from Panaji (or south from Mumbai) there are yet more deserted beaches and ruined Maratha forts along a still little-visited but often beautiful coastline. To the south in coastal Karnataka, the ancient pilgrimage site of Gokarna is rapidly gaining a reputation as the most recent of India's 'dropping out' beaches, becoming the third point of the Goa-Gokarna-Hampi triangle.

Excursions

Excursions south of Goa

Just across the southern border of Goa, the national highway enters the coastal lands of northern Karnataka. Broad estuaries and long stretches of golden sand mark the coastline, while inland, low wooded hills rise rapidly into the Western Ghats. The Konkan railway now cuts through this landscape to the port of Mangalore.

Gokarna

Phone code: 08386

The narrow streets, traditional houses and temples together with its long wide expanse of beach, lure growing numbers of backpackers moving on from Goa who search for an alternative hideaway on the unspoilt beaches, to Gokarna. There is a somewhat curious mix of Hindu pilgrims and castaways from the hippy era here. You will also notice tribal women wearing their colourful traditional costume – a cloth held at the neck by bead necklaces, their only pieces of jewellery.

Today Gokarna is a centre of Sanskrit learning

The specially sanctified **Mahabalesvara temple** is famous for its Atmalinga. **Ganesh** is believed to have tricked **Ravana** into putting it down on this spot. As Ravana was unable to lift the linga up again, it is called *Mahabala* (the strong one). The **Tambraparni Teertha** stream is particularly sacred for casting the ashes of the dead.

The walk down to Gokarna beach is flanked by pilgrims and *sadhus* begging for alms so come prepared with small change. Walk northwards if you are searching for a quiet stretch. Most travellers head for the beaches to the south. The superb **Om Beach** shaped like the sacred Hindu symbol, about 3 km south, can be reached by a path from the town temple or by walking over the cliffs and passing the **Kudle** (pronounced *Koodlee*) **Beach** which was the first to be 'discovered' by beach campers. Popular with younger travellers, the beach has picturesque views of paddy fields and the Western Ghats. Om Beach can now also be reached by a motorable track which can be accessed from near Mayura Samudra hotel. It is no longer quite the secluded paradise that people came searching for years ago when looking for an alternative Goa. As with Kudle, in season it can get extremely busy and the combination of too many people, shortage of fresh water and the apparant lapse in the standards of hygiene, results in the beaches getting rather dirty. **Half Moon** and **Paradise Beaches** can be reached by continuing to walk over the headlands and are another 2 km or so apart. Here, too long-timers congregate and are catered for in a similar fashion to the other beaches.

Sleeping **Town D-E** *International Gokarna*, T56622. 43 modern rooms (some a/c) with bath (Rs 200-600), back quieter and have balconies, restaurant (some food akin to "liquid salt"), bar, and the first lift in Gokarna when it is inaugurated! **E** *Green's 'Om'*, 6-minute walk from bus stand, T56445. 16 rooms with bath, 2 a/c (overpriced), restaurant, chilled beer, not very friendly. **E** *New Prasad Nilaya*, near the bus stand, T57135. Spacious rooms with bath (hot water), some colourful balconies, upstairs rooms better, friendly staff. **F** *Mayura Samudra* (KSTDC), 2 km north on hilltop facing the sea, T56236. 3 rooms (Rs 135 double), dining room, garden, helpful staff but quite a trek. **F** *Nimmu Guest House*, near temple, T56730. 15 clean rooms with shared Indian WC, 5 newest are better value as they are big, bright and catch the breeze, limited roof space for overspill, garden, laid and friendly. Recommended. **F** *Ramdev Lodge*, 4 simple rooms with bath, cheap. **F** *Shastri's Guest House*, Dasanamath, T56220. 24 rooms with bath, some 3/4, set back from road, quiet, short walk uphill behind gives superb views of town and sunset, good value. **F** *Vaibhav Nivas*, Ganjigadde off Main St (5 minutes walk from bazar), T56714. Family guest house, small rooms (Rs 60+), new annexe with 10 rooms, some with bath (Indian andwestern WC), meals (alas no "pain-cakes and forage" for breakfast!), taxi, full of travellers from nearby beaches.

Beaches The usual mud and palm leaf huts with shared facilites charge Rs 30-60 (extra for a mattress). The lack of security in beach huts has prompted the guest-houses in town to offer to store luggage for a small charge. The exceptions are: at the southern end of **Kudle**: **F** *Shiva Prasad*,with decent brick-built rooms with fan; on **Om**: **F** *Namaste* with acceptable rooms.

Eating

Cheap Cheap vegetarian thalis are available near the bus stand and along Main St while shacks at the entrance to the town beach serve up the usual disarray of travellers' favourites. *Pai*, near Vegetable Market does good masala dosa. *Vishwa*, on beach, Nepali run, varied menu including Tibetan, large helpings. Icecream parlours abound; try gudbad with nuts and fruit. *Prema*, opposite Mahabalesvar temple, now expanded with a large room upstairs, does great fruit salads, ices and gudbad and makes its own delicious soft garlic cheese, popular with westerners for its thalis. The southern beaches have their share of chai shops and shacks. The only one that stands out is the *Spanish Chai shop* on Kudle which has clean fresh food including humus and pitta.

Transport

Train Gokarna Road station is 10 km from the town, 2 km from the NH17; a few rick-shaws ferry passengers to and from town but you may have to walk 1 km from the sta-tion to the road linking Gokarna and NH17 to find transport. Daily service to Margao (Madgaon) via Chaudi, 1125; to Mangalore 1630. Road KSRTC buses provide a good service: **Chaudi** 2 hrs **Karwar** (via Ankola) frequent (1 hrs); **Hospet** 0700, 1425 (10 hrs); **Jog Falls** 0700, 1130 (6 hrs); **Mangalore** via Udipi 0645 (7 hrs); **Panaji** 0800 (5 hrs).

Directory

Exchange *Pai STD*, opposite Ramdev Lodge, changes money.

Excursions

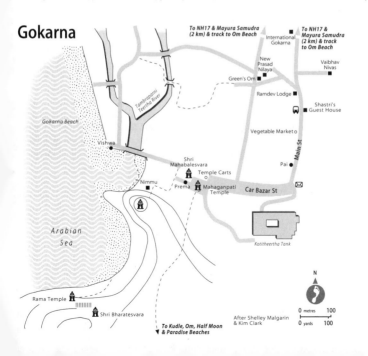

Following the Portuguese trail

On the coast itself is a string of small ports, once a part of the chain of Arab trading posts which linked Arabia with Southeast Asia. Many retain a significant Muslim population and cultural identity. This section of the coast is also linked with Vasco da Gama, the first European to find the sea passage around the Cape of Good Hope on his way to the emporia of the East. He had been sent to establish a foothold to gain access to the lucrative spice trade which then lay in the hands of the Arab seafarers. The small trading bases which resulted, however, didn't prove successful, so Albuquerque arrived with his fleet a decade later and established a Portuguese presence in Goa (see page 215). Travellers eager to piece together a bit of Portuguese history along the Malabar coast on their journey south may wish to check out some of these historical spots.

Karwar & On the banks of the Kalinadi River, 8 km south of the Goa border, Karwar has a
Anjedive deep-water naval port protected by five islands. One of these was '**Anjedive**', known to seafarers centuries before Vasco da Gama called at the island in 1498, and the Portuguese built a fort there. It was later used as a Goan penal colony. Since it is now under the control of the Navy it is off-limits to all foreigners.

Eating A roadside stall outside hotel *Bhadra* on NH17 (4 km north of Karwar), serves very good value vegetarian food. There is also an excellent bistro type *Fish Restaurant*, along the street.

Transport Frequent **buses** from Karwar to Palolem, Margao and Panaji, also direct buses to Colva (they often get full so you may have to fight to get on). Those on **motorbikes** risk being stopped and fined by police, often for no obvious offence.

St Mary's Isle There is another site associated with Vasco da Gama along the NH17 *en route*
near Malpe to Mangalore. Across the bay from Malpe near Udupi, is the island of Darya Bahadurgarh. Five kilometres to the southwest of this is **St Mary's Isle**, composed of dramatic hexagonal basalt, where Vasco da Gama landed in 1498 and set up a cross.

Kannur Further south, on the Kerala coast, Kannur stands on raised ground with cliffs
(Cannanore) at the sea face. The coconut-fringed coastline has some attractive beaches nearby. At the end of the northwest promontory, **Fort St Angelo** in the old cantonment area, is surrounded by the sea on three sides and a dry ditch on its landward side. Fort St Angelo was built out of laterite blocks by the Portuguese in 1505 and taken over by the British in 1790 as their most important military base in the south. The highly picturesque **Moplah town** is around the bay to the south of the fort.

Kappad near Kappad, 19 km north of Kozhikode (Calicut), is where Vasco da Gama first
Kozhikode came ashore on 27th May 1498 with 170 men and erected a stone pillar to mark a discovery and started a turbulent, often violent, contact with European powers. An old plaque by the approach road to the beach commemorates the event. The site is now occupied by a small, poor, mainly Muslim, fishing village. Calicut at that time was under the control of the Vijayanagar Empire based in Hampi, over 500 km to the northeast, but the town gradually became dominant under the Zamorin (literally *Lord of the Sea*). By some accounts he was the wealthiest ruler in contemporary India. After a decade of violent raids, the Zamorin made peace with the Portuguese and gave them the right to build a fort in Cochin (Kochi). However, during the 16th century there was fierce

Excursions

competition and sometimes open warfare between the Portuguese, bent on eliminating Arab trading competition, and the Zamorin, whose prosperity depended on that Arab trade. Today Calicut is a pleasant if rather anonymous town, no longer a port although there are still remnants of the trade in spices, copra and coconut oil in the Court Road/Big Bazar Road area.

A plaque in Vasco da Gama Square near the customs jetty in Fort Cochin commemorates the landing of **Vasco da Gama** in 1500. Next to it is one of the seven bastions of Fort Emanuel, named after the Portuguese King. Little remains of the old Portuguese fort (founded 1503), except parts of the wall. Originally dedicated to Santo Antonio, the patron saint of Portugal, St Francis Church nearby was built by the Portuguese. The original wooden structure (circa 1510) was replaced by the present stone building. Vasco da Gama died on the site in 1524 and was originally buried in the cemetery but 14 years later his body was taken home. On **Vypeen Island** across the bay, the Portuguese Azhikotta Fort (the plaque calls it Pallipuram), built around 1503, stands by the police station. You can see cannon holes on the walls of this octagonal fort which was garrisoned by 20 soldiers when it guarded the entrance to the backwaters.

Kochi (Fort Cochin)

Excursions north of Goa

Excursions

From North Goa, a visit to southern Maharashtra offers Maratha coastal forts, almost totally unvisited beaches, and even the minor 'hill station' of Amboli, all within easy reach by motorbike or car, and can be visited en route *to the important former Muslim capital of Belgaum.*

Crossing the Tiracol River by the Keri ferry the road crosses into Maharashtra. The route up through the southernmost corner of Maharashtra has a quite different feel to it from Goa. In the coastal belt there are many salt pans which provide an important source of income in the district.

Just 3 km north of the Goa border and Tiracol, a turn off from NH17 south of Shiroda, leads to Redi village and **beach** 4 km further on. Sivaji, the great 17th-century Maratha leader built the coastal fort here. Though in ruins, it is interesting to wander round. It dominates the view over a stunning deserted beach with a lagoon.

Redi
There are no facilities or shops here - carry water & food

Returning to the NH17 from Redi beach and continuing north, passing through the small market town of Shiroda. A left turn at the cross roads goes to Vengurla, the right turn going to Sawantwadi.

Routes

Sawantwadi was the capital of the Bhonsle kings of southern Maharashtra who were constantly trying to extend their territory into Goa. Today it is a large market town, centred on the big tank and palace buildings. It was once noted for the production of fine hand-painted *ganjifa* (playing cards) but this is a dying tradition. The Sawantwadi royal family is actively keeping this ancient art and other local crafts alive, allowing a few artists/craftsmen to work in the once impressive palace darbar hall. They also produce painted lacquered furniture, chessmen, board games and candlesticks. Intending visitors should contact Sawantwadi Lacquerware, Sawantwadi Palace, Maharashtra, or call T02363-72010, in advance.

Sawantwadi

The brightly coloured *gangifa* were originally produced by pasting layers of cloth together, using tamarind seed gum then coating the 'card' with chalk before polishing it with a stone to provide a smooth white base for decorating the face with natural pigments while the back was stiffened with lacquer. The packs of circular cards come in various sizes and suits. The ten suits of the *Dasavatara* (featuring Vishnu's 10 incarnations), for example, form a pack of 120 cards while the *Navagraha* (nine planets) has nine suits. The miniature paintings with patterns drawn from mythology, history and nature, often reflect the folk tradition. A few towns in Bengal and Orissa continue the tradition of producing *gangifa*. Prices range from Rs 800 to Rs 3,000.

Sleeping D *JRD International*, Vengurla-Belgaum Road, 1 km from bus stand. 30 pleasant clean rooms, a few 'cottages', and a reasonable Indian restaurant with a permit room. Alternatively the **E** *Resort* (MTDC), offers a reasonably comfortable base.

Transport Sawantwadi now has an out-of-town station on the Konkan railway and is connected by frequent buses to Panaji, about 30 mins away.

Amboli
Altitude: 690m

There are attractive walks and several waterfalls

The Western Ghats rise steeply inland of Sawantwadi as the road winds its way up the Sahyadri Ranges giving superb views over the coastal plains out towards the sea. Set on the flat topped heights of the Western Ghats overlooking the coastal plain below, Amboli is quiet and little visited. Amidst hilly wooded countryside the tiny holiday resort is usually visited by Indians during the monsoons when it is either shrouded in mist of experiencing torrential rain.

Transport Easiest by car. Local buses run from Kolhapur and Belgaum, which can be reached by train.

Belgaum

Phone code: 0831
Population: 420,000
Altitude: 770m

Today a large Indian city, Belgaum has none of the tourist influences which contribute to the character of modern coastal Goa, and it is a fascinating and relaxing contrast to the much more westernised coastal resorts. For a glimpse of a contemporary Indian town, rooted in tradition but still responding to rapid economic and social change, Belgaum is the nearest large centre to Goa's borders.

Easily accessible, the crowded market in the centre gives a glimpse of India beyond the influence of foreign travellers. With its strategic position in the Deccan plateau, the town had been ruled by many dynasties including the Chalukyas, Rattas, Vijaynagaras, Bahmanis and the Marathas. Most of the monuments date from the early 13th century. The **fort** (currently being renovated), though pre-Muslim, was rebuilt by Yusuf Adil Shah, the Sultan of Bijapur, in 1481. Inside is the **Masjid-i-Sata** (1519), the best of the numerous mosques in Belgaum, built by a captain in the Bijapur army, Azad Khan. Belgaum is also noted for its Jain architecture and sculpture. The late Chalukyan **Kamala Basti**, with typical beautifully lathe-turned pillars and a black stone Neminatha sculpture, stands within the fort walls. To the south of the fort and about 800m north of the *Hotel Sanman* on the Mumbai-Bangalore by-pass, is a beautifully sculpted Jain temple, which according to an inscription, was built by Malikaryuna. Along the entrance wall are well carved sculptures of musicians.

Burgess has described a further Jain temple which stands in the former government store yard. The temple has "massive square pillars ... but relieved by floral ornamentations". He comments on the care taken in carving the door leading from the central mandapam. "On the centre of the lintel is a Tirthankar, and above the cornice are four squat human figures". Outside, **Kapileswara**, the oldest Hindu temple, is worth visiting.

D *Adarsha Palace*, College Rd, T435777, F431022. Small, modern, 'personal' hotel and **Sleeping**
friendly management. Recommended. **D** *Milan*, Club Rd, 4 km to the railway station,
T425555, F423535. 45 rooms with bath (hot shower), some a/c, veg restaurant, good
value. **D** *Sanman*, College Rd, T430777. Bus stand and station, 2 km away.
E-F *Sheetal*, Khade Bazaar near bus station, T429222. Rooms with bath (prices vary),
veg restaurant, Indian style, noisy hotel in busy and quite entertaining bazaar street.
Recommended.   **F** *Mayura Malaprabha* (KSTDC), Ashok Nagar, HUDCO Complex,
T470781. 6 simple clean rooms in cottages, dorm (Rs 40), restaurant, bar, tourist office.

Train The railway station is about 4 km from the centre. **Bangalore**: *Miraj Bangalore*   **Transport**
Exp 6590, 1845, 13 hrs. **Mumbai (CST) via Miraj** and **Pune**: (change at Miraj) *Hubli*
Miraj Pass/Mahalaxmi Exp 305/1012, 1655, 15 hrs (50 mins wait at Miraj) and for Pune
10 hrs. **Goa**: broad gauge now connects Vasco in the west of Goa with **Belgaum**,
Bangalore, **Delhi via Agra**, and **Hampi** among others. **Road** There are frequent
buses through Belgaum, between Mumbai and Bangalore. Panaji is around 5 hrs by
bus. From Panaji, buses for **Belgaum** dep 0630-1300.

Excursion east of Goa

Hampi-Vijayanagar

The combination of an extraordinary boulder strewn landscape and the ruins
of the great Vijayanagar Empire make Hampi one of the most atmospheric his-
toric sites of the Deccan. Hospet is the nearest small market town, and a base for
seeing Hampi.

Hospet

Hospet can be used as a base by visitors to **Hampi** since it offers a variety of   *Phone code: 08394*
accommodation and has the nearest railway station. The remains at Hampi are   *Population: 135,000*
very scattered and need at least one whole day, and two to see more fully.   *Altitude: 480m*

Getting there The station, about 500m north of the town centre, has connections   **Ins & outs**
with Hyderabad and Bangalore, but buses offer a better alternative for many destinations, including Goa, 10 hrs away. The bus stand is right in the town centre and most
hotels are within easy walking distance. **Getting around** Though there are buses
and rickshaws to Hampi, hiring a cycle might be the best option as the site is spread
out though some paths are too rough to ride on. **Tours** From KSTDC, T21008, and
Malligi hotel, to Hampi, Rs 75 (lunch extra); 0930-1630. English speaking guide but
rather rushed. Hampi is also offered as a tour by travel companies from Goa.

The main bazaar in Hospet is interesting to walk around, with old houses and
character. There is a significant Muslim population and *Muharram* is celebrated with vigour with *firewalkers* walking across burning embers along with
noisy celebrations, a custom which may go back to long before Islam arrived.
Villagers still celebrate events such as the beginning or end of migrations to
seasonal feeding grounds of livestock, with huge bonfires. Cattle are driven
through such fires to protect them from disease. The archaeologists Allchin
and Allchin suggest that Neolithic ash mounds around Hospet could have
resulted from similar celebrations over 5,000 years ago.

The 2 km **Tungabhadra Dam**, 6 km away, is 49m high and offers panoramic   **Excursions**
views. One of the largest masonry dams in the country it was completed in

1953 to provide electricity for irrigation in the surrounding districts. Local buses from Hospet take 15 minutes to the dam.

Sleeping **C-F** *Malligi*, 6/143 Jambunatha (JN) Rd, T28101, F27038, mallingihome@hotmail.com Expanded to 150 rooms (Rs 140+). 65 a/c (newer **D** are large rooms with bath, 4 **B** suites are overpriced), a/c restaurant and bar by good covered pool (economy-room guests pay Rs 25 for pool), exchange, travel (bus/train tickets, Rs 10/25 commission; good Hampi tour Rs 75), local guide books, well-managed, friendly. **D-E** *Karthik*, Pampa Villa, IV Ward, 252/3 Sardar Patel Rd, T24938. Modern large rooms, some a/c, good a/c restaurant. **D-E** *Priyadarshini*, V/45 Station Rd, near bus station, T28838. Variety of rooms, some a/c, extra bed Rs 35, good restaurants. Recommended. **E** *Sandarshan*, MG Rd, T28574. Few a/c rooms with bath (limited hot water). **F** *Mayura Vijayanagara* (KSTDC), TB Dam Rd, 3 km west of centre on bus route, T39270. 21 basic rooms with fans, mosquito nets and bath (Rs 160), simple dining hall serves good *thalis*. **F** *Vishwa*, MG Rd, opposite bus station, away from the road, T27172. Clean rooms (some 4-bed) with bath, *Shanthi* restaurant.

Station Rd has been renamed Mahatma Gandhi Rd (MG Rd)

Eating **Mid-range** *Malligi's Waves* open-air by pool. Multi cuisine. Reasonable food, bar. *Priyadarshini's* vegetarian *thalis* are recommended; also good garden restaurant with bar. The hotels serve chilled beer. **Cheap** *Aparna* at *Malligi* serves vegetarian fast foods. South Indian meal options near the bus station.

Transport **Local** From Hospet to/from **Hampi**, travel via Kamalapuram, especially in the rainy season when the slower road to Hampi Bazaar, which winds through villages, is barely passable. **Bus**: frequent buses to Hampi's 2 entry points (via Kamalapuram and museum, Rs 4 and via Hampi Bazaar, 30 mins, Rs 3.50), from 0630; last return around 2000. **Auto-rickshaws**: to Hampi, demand Rs 150. **Cycle-rickshaw**: from railway station to bus stand about Rs 10. **Cycle hire**: from Hampi Bazaar or *Shanti*. **Taxi**: KSTDC, T21008 or from *Malligi Hotel*; about Rs 700 per day (possible to share).

Hospet

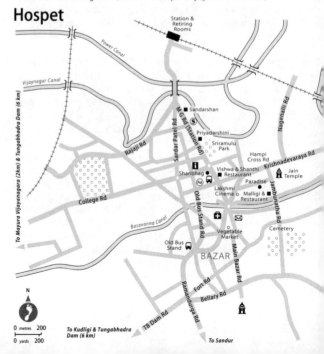

Long distance   Train: Bangalore, *Hampi Exp, 6591*, 2010 (via Guntakal, 2 hrs) 10 hrs.
Guntakal: *Vijaynagara Exp, 7310*, 1905, 2 hrs. **Secunderabad**: *Vijaynagara/Venkatadri
Exp*, *7310/7598/7604*, 1905, 14 hrs (2-hr wait in Guntakal). For **Belur/Halebid**: take
train to Hubli *Amaravati Exp, 7225*, 1040; then to Ariskere; walk 5-min to bus station
down the main road and get the bus to Halebid, 1 hr. To **Badami**: via Gadag, 4 hrs.
Road: *Express* bus to/from **Bangalore** (road upgraded), several from 0700, 6/7 hrs;
Mysore, 1830, 10 hrs (*Express* buses to Belur/Halebid from both). Services to other
sites, eg **Badami** (6 hrs) and **Bijapur** (6 hrs). Overnight Karnataka Tourism luxury
coaches to various towns. Direct buses to **Panaji** (Goa) – *Luxury*, 0630 (10 hrs), state
bus, 0830 (reserve a seat in advance); others involve a change in Hubli (4 hrs). *Sleeper*,
1900, Rs 350 (strangers may be expected to share a bunk). *Paulo Travels Luxury
Sleeper* coach from *Hotel Priyadarshini* at 1845, Rs 350, daily; *West Coast Sleeper* from
Hotel Shanthag, 1830, Rs 350, daily (Oct-Mar only).

Banks *State Bank of India*, next to tourist office, does not exchange TCs but will change cash   **Directory**
(US$ and £ sterling); *State Bank of Mysore* may oblige. *Monica Travel*, near bus station, changes
TCs (3% charge). **Communications** Post office: opposite vegetable market. **Telegraph office**:
in *Hotel Sandarshan*. **Fax and ISD**: *Essar Area Fax*, beside New Bus Stand, Station Rd. **Tourist
offices** *Karnataka*, MG Rd, Taluka offices, near bus stand, T28537. Free map and leaflets, and
sometimes guides for the sites.

Hampi (Vijayanagar)

Hampi-Vijayanagar is one of India's most remarkable former capital city sites.   *Phone code: 08394*
The rocky outcrops of the peninsula provided the 14th-century Vijayanagar   *Altitude: 467m*
kings with an apparently impregnable hill fortress in which they built a stupen-   *Best season: Oct-Mar*
dous range of palaces and temples. Although now largely in ruins the site is still
hugely impressive. Within range of a three to five day excursion from Goa, it
offers a chance to see something of the wealth of India's past.

Hampi was once the seat of the Vijayanagara Empire and a great centre of   *Known as the 'The*
Hindu rule for 200 years from its foundation in 1336, although there may have   *town of victory',*
been a settlement in the area as early as 1,000 years before then. The city was   *Vijayanagara, is*
enormously wealthy, 'greater than Rome', with a market full of jewels and pal-   *13 km northeast*
aces plated with gold, having held a monopoly of trade in spices and cotton. It   *of Hospet town*
was very well fortified and defended by a large army. With the defeat in 1565 at
Talikota at the hands of the Deccan Sultans, the city was largely destroyed.
Today the stark and barren area of 26 sq km on the right bank of the river
Tungabhadra has the ruins of the great empire strewn across it.

The site for the capital was chosen for strategic reasons but the craftsmen
adopted an ingenious style to blend in their architectural masterpieces with the
barren and rocky landscape. Most of the site is early 16th century, built during
the 20-year reign of Krishna Deva Raya (1509-1529) with the citadel standing
on the bank of the river. Excavations undertaken by the Archaeological Survey
of India are still in progress. You enter the area from the west at *Hampi Bazaar*
or from the south at *Kamalapuram*. The **tourist office** is located here on the
approach to Virupaksha Temple.

The road from the west comes over Hemakuta Hill, overlooking the sacred   **Sacred Centre**
centre of Vijayanagara, the Virupaksha Temple and the Tungabhadra River to   *Go in a group and don't*
its north. On the hill are two large Ganesh monolithic sculptures and some   *carry valuables as*
small temples. Good views at sunset. Climb Matanga Parvat, over the road,   *muggings have been*
early in the morning (around 0530) for a spectacular sunrise.   *reported*

The road runs down to the village, the once world-famous **market place**.
You can now only see the wide pathway running east from the towering

Virupaksha (*Pampapati*) **Temple** with its nine-storey *gopuram*, to where the bazaar hummed with activity. The temple is still in use; note the interesting paintings on the *mandapam* ceiling. The monkeys here can be aggressive. ■ *Rs 2. 0800-1230, 1500-1830. Before entering the precinct, foreigners are expected to register at the police office on the left.*

The Riverside You can walk along the river bank (1,500m) to the famous Vitthala Temple. The path is easy and passes several interesting ruins including small 'cave' temples (worthwhile with a guide).

Alternatively, a motorable road skirts the Royal Enclosure to the south, and goes all the way to the Vitthala Temple. On the way back you can visit the **Raghunatha Temple**, on a hill top, for its Dravidian style, quiet atmosphere and excellent view from the rocks above, especially at sunset.

Hampi - Vijayanagara

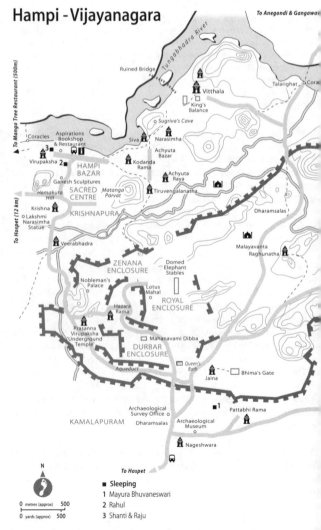

Tungabhadra River, Hampi

After passing **Achyuta Bazaar**, which leads to the Tiruvengalanatha Temple 400m to the south, the riverside path goes near **Sugriva's Cave**, where it is said that Sita's jewels, dropped as she was abducted by the demon Ravana, were hidden by Sugriva. There are good views of the ancient ruined bridge to the east, and nearby the path continues past the only early period Vaishnavite shrine, the 14th-century **Narasimha Temple**. The **King's balance** is at the end of the path as it approaches the Vitthala Temple. It is said that the rulers were weighed against gold, jewels and food, which were then distributed to Brahmins.

The **Vitthala Temple**, a World Heritage Monument, is dedicated to Vishnu. It stands in a rectangular courtyard, enclosed within high walls. Probably built in the mid-15th century, it is one of the oldest and most intricately carved, with its *gopurams* and *mandapas*. The *Dolotsava mandapa* has 56 superbly sculpted slender pillars which can be struck to produce different musical notes. It has elephants on the balustrades and horses at the entrance. The other two ceremonial *mandapas*, though less finely carved have some interesting carved pillars, eg Krishna hiding in a tree from the *gopis*, a woman using a serpent twisted around a stick to churn a pot of buttermilk. In the courtyard is a superb chariot carved out of granite, the wheels raised off the ground so that they could be revolved!

Krishnapura

On the road between the Virupaksha Bazaar and the Citadel, you pass Krishnapura, Hampi's earliest Vaishnava township with a Chariot Street 50m wide and 600m long, which is now a cultivated field. The **Krishna temple** has a very impressive gateway to the east. Just southwest of the Krishna temple is the colossal monolithic statue of Lakshmi Narasimha in the form of a four-armed man-lion with fearsome bulging eyes sheltered under a seven-headed serpent, *Ananta*. It is over 6m high but sadly damaged.

The road south, from the Sacred Centre towards the Royal Enclosure, passes the excavated **Prasanna Virupaksha** (misleadingly named 'underground') **Temple** and interesting watchtowers.

Royal Enclosure

At the heart of the Metropolis is the small **Hazara Rama Temple**, the Vaishanava 'chapel royal' (*hazara* meaning 1,000). The outer enclosure wall to the north has five rows of carved friezes while the outer walls of the *mandapa* has three. The episodes from the epic *Ramayana* are told in great detail, starting with the bottom row of the north end of the west *mandapa* wall. The two-storeyed **Lotus Mahal** is in the **Zenana** or ladies' quarter, screened off by its high walls. The watchtower is in ruins but you can see the domed **stables** for 10 elephants with a pavilion in the centre and the guardhouse. Each stable had

Trouble at the ruins

Over the last few years, there have been incidents of thefts and attacks on foreign visitors to Hampi, and growing concern over the emergence of the rave/party scene drawing large crowds of young travellers to Hampi especially over the Christmas and New Year period. UNESCO has intervened and warned that the World Heritage status of the site will be withdrawn unless the government takes steps to stop illegal activities.

Unauthorized guest houses and restaurants in the Hampi Bazaar area have been shut down and a state government Task Force has been formed in March 2000 to ensure the restoration of the earlier pleasant atmosphere at the ancient site.

a wooden beamed ceiling from which chains were attached to the elephants' backs and necks. In the **Durbar Enclosure** is the specially built decorated platform of the **Mahanavami Dibba**, from which the royal family watched the pageants and tournaments during the nine nights of *navaratri* festivities. The 8m-high square platform originally had a covering of bricks, timber and metal but what remains still shows superb carvings of hunting and battle scenes, as well as dancers and musicians.

The exceptional skill of water engineering is displayed in the excavated system of aqueducts, tanks, sluices and canals, which could function today. The 22m square **Pushkarini** is the attractive stepped tank at the centre of the enclosure. The road towards Kamalapuram passes the **Queen's Bath**, in the open air, surrounded by a narrow moat, which had scented water filling the bath from lotus shaped fountains. It measures about 15m x 2m and has interesting stucco work around it.

Further reading Longhurst's *Hampi Ruins* recommended; Settar's *Hampi* (both at *Aspirations Bookshop*, Hampi Bazaar, which has an interesting selection of books as well as postcards, crafts from Aurobindo Ashram, Pondicherry and soft drinks).

Sleeping Hampi Bazaar has plenty of character and several basic lodges with more being built. *Mosquitos can be a real problem, especially at dusk. The main bazaar is sprayed daily with insecticide* **F** *Mega Lodge*, has good simple rooms (Rs 70-130). **F** *Rahul*, south of the bus stand, T41648. Basic sleeping and washing, but clean. **F** *Raju* behind *Shanti*. Tiny rooms and shared facilities, fairly clean. **F** *Shanti Guest House*, down path to the right of the temple (signed) T41368. 13 rooms with fans around courtyard, common shower, roof for overspill, very clean and friendly, cycle hire, good cakes (see below). **Across the river** a few guesthouses take in foreign guests. **F** *Rasta Riverview* has rooms with fan, shared facilities. **Near the complex** may be preferable for travellers planning to spend more than a day. Kamalapura: **D-E** *Mayura Bhuvaneswari* (KSTDC), 2 km from site, T41374. Clean rooms (27), some a/c, reasonable restaurant, cycle hire.

Eating **Cheap** *Ganesh* in main street and *Raju* behind *Shanti* recommended for *parathas*. *Gopi* for good simple, cheap *thalis*. *Mango Tree* on the riverside half a kilometre west of the Vitupaksha Temple. Very pleasant Indian food. *Sambhu* opposite *Shanti*, for fresh pasta/noodles and espresso plus all the usual; also bus/train tickets for small commission (better than trying in Hospet). Recommended. *Suresh*, 30m from *Shanti*, down a small alley, very friendly family, made to order so takes a while, but well worth the wait. Simple places serving vegetarian meals near the bus stand including open-sided *Krishna* and *Trisul*. *Shanti* does good carrot/apple/banana/chocolate cakes to order. Kamalapuram: *Mayura Bhuvaneswari*, does cheap adequate meals Snacks are available near the bus stand.

Excursions

The **Archaeological Museum** at Kamalapuram has a collection of sculpture, paintings, copper plates and coins. Archaeological Survey booklet is on sale; a scale model of Hampi in the courtyard. 1000-1700, closed Friday.

Entertainment

January-February: *Virupaksha Temple Car festival*. November (3rd-5th): *Hampi Music festival* at Vitthala Temple when hotels get packed.

Festivals

Corneleo take passengers across the river from the jetty west of the Virupaksha Temple, Rs 3. Bicycle hire from the bazaar. See also Hospet above.

Transport

Mumbai (Bombay)

Excursions

Mumbai is one of India's most remarkable cities. The commercial hub of the Indian economy for over 150 years, it remains uniquely open to the rest of the world and is yet a city shaped by India's diverse cultures. There is plenty to see in a short visit, including good museums, galleries and the Elephanta caves, which, within an hour's boat ride across the harbour, illustrate the artistry of India's ancient craftsmen.

Phone code: 022
Population: 12,570,000
Languages: Marathi, Gujarati, Hindi, English & Tamil

Ins & outs

Sahar International air terminal is 30 km from Nariman Point, the business heart of the city. The domestic terminals at Santa Cruz, 5 km closer. Pre-paid taxis to the city centre are good value and take between 40 minutes and 1½ hrs, depending on traffic but there are also cheaper but slower buses. If you arrive late at night without a hotel booking it's best to stay at one of the hotels near the domestic terminal, Santa Cruz, before going into town early in the morning or continuing with your journey to Goa.

Getting there

Mumbai's sites are spread out and you need transport. Taxis (yellow-top and blue a/c) are metered and generally good value. Autos are only allowed in the suburbs. There are frequent buses on major routes, and the two suburban railway lines are useful out of peak hours on some routes, but get horrendously crowded.

Getting around

History

Hinduism had made its mark on Mumbai long before the British transformed it into one of India's great cities. The caves on the island of Elephanta were excavated under the Kalachauris (500-600 AD). From well before that until the arrival of the Portuguese, Arab *dhows* traded down the coast, but less than 350 years ago the area occupied by this great metropolis comprised seven islands inhabited by Koli fishermen (from whom we have the word 'coolie') and their families. The modern name of Mumbai is derived from the local Koli name for the goddess Parvati, Mumba devi.

Connecting Mumbai

Daily flights from many parts of the world make Mumbai an attractive alternative to the normal charters which carry most tourists into Goa. It gives you a chance to see something of India's largest city as well as some of India's countryside on the way to and from Goa. The opening of the Konkan railway has reduced a tortuous 18-hour train to about 11 hours. A motorbike or car allows you to explore something of the Konkan coastline or the peninsula on the way south.

The British acquired these marshy and malarial islands as part of the marriage dowry paid by the Portuguese when Catherine of Braganza married Charles II in 1661. Some suggest that Bombay took its English name from the Portuguese Bom Bahia, or 'good harbour'. Four years later, the British took possession of the remaining islands and neighbouring mainland and in 1668 the East India Company leased the whole area from the crown for £10 sterling per year, which was paid for nearly 50 years.

Today Mumbai has become the hub of India's commercial activity. It is the home of India's main stock exchange and headquarters for many national and international companies and it is also a major industrial centre. Mumbai is still growing fast. One third of the population live in its desperately squalid *chawl* of cramped, makeshift and miserable hovels. There are also many thousand of pavement dwellers, yet despite the extreme poverty Mumbai remains a city of hope for millions.

Sights

Apollo Bunder & The Gateway Of India
The area around the Gateway is popular with city dwellers for evening strolls & is a pleasant place to visit at sundown

The Indo-Saracenic style Gateway of India (1927), to commemorate the visit of George V and Queen Mary in 1911, is modelled in honey-coloured basalt on 16th-century Gujarati work. The great gateway comprises an archway with hall on each side capable of seating 600 at important receptions. The arch replaced an earlier, lighter building. It was the point from which the last British regiment serving in India signalled the end of the empire when it left on 28 February 1948.

The original red-domed *Taj Mahal*, one of the world's leading hotels, has been adjoined by a modern sister, the *Taj Mahal Inter-Continental*. **NB** Drug addicts, drunks and prostitutes frequent the area behind the hotel; be careful.

The **Bombay Natural History Society** (BNHS), Hornbill House on SB Singh Marg, founded over 100 years ago, is dedicated to the conservation of Indian's flora and fauna. It has a knowledgeable PR officer, a shop, wildlife collection and library.

Colaba

South of the Gateway of India is the crowded southern section of Shahid Bhagat Singh Marg (Marine Street) which leads to Colaba. The Afghan Memorial **Church of St John the Baptist** (1847-58) is at the northern edge of Colaba itself. Early English in style, with a 58m spire, it was built to commemorate the soldiers who died in the First Afghan War. Fishermen still unload their catch early in the morning at **Sassoon Dock**, the first wet dock in India; photography is prohibited. Beyond the church near the tip of the Colaba promontory lie the **Observatory** and **Old European cemetery** in the naval colony (permission needed to enter). Frequent buses ply this route.

Mumbai Central

The area stretching north from Colaba Causeway to Victoria (renamed Chhetrapati Sivaji) Terminus, the heart of British Mumbai, dates from after 1862, when Sir Bartle Frere became Governor. Under his enthusiastic guidance

Excursions

Mumbai

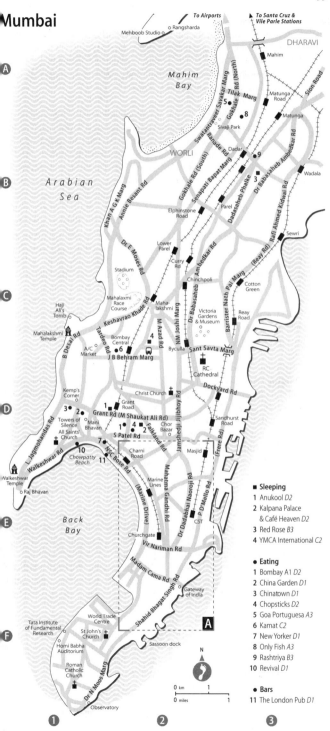

A **B** **C** **D** **E** **F**

To Airports
To Santa Cruz &
Vile Parle Stations

Mehboob Studio ○ Rangsharda

Mahim Bay

DHARAVI

Mahim

Arabian Sea

Matunga Road

Sion Road

Matunga

Sivaji Park

WORLI

Dadar

Wadala

Sewri

Elphinstone Road

Parel

Lower Parel

Curry Rd

Chinchpoli

Cotton Green

Reay Road

Stadium

Mahalaxmi Race Course

Mahalakshmi

Victoria Gardens & Museum

Haji Ali's Tomb

Mahalakshmi Temple

A/C Market

Bombay Central

Byculla

Sant Savta Marg

RC Cathedral

Kemp's Corner

Christ Church

Dockyard Rd

Grant Road

Towers of Silence

Mani Bhavan

All Saints' Church

Chor Bazar

Sandhurst Road

Walkeshwar Temple

Chowpatty Beach

Charni Road

Masjid

Raj Bhavan

Marine Lines

Back Bay

Churchgate

CST

Vir Nariman Rd

Tata Institute of Fundamental Research

World Trade Centre

St John's Church

Gateway of India

Homi Bhabha Auditorium

Roman Catholic Church

Sassoon dock

Observatory

0 km   1
0 miles   1

Excursions

A

■ Sleeping
1 Anukool *D2*
2 Kalpana Palace & Café Heaven *D2*
3 Red Rose *B3*
4 YMCA International *C2*

● Eating
1 Bombay *A1 D2*
2 China Garden *D1*
3 Chinatown *D1*
4 Chopsticks *D2*
5 Goa Portuguesa *A3*
6 Kamat *C2*
7 New Yorker *D1*
8 Only Fish *A3*
9 Rashtriya *B3*
10 Revival *D1*

● Bars
11 The London Pub *D1*

Mumbai became a great civic centre and an extravaganza of Victorian Gothic architecture, modified by the Indo-Saracenic influences. Just behind the Prince of Wales Museum in Shahid Bhagat Singh Marg is **St Andrew's Kirk** (1819), a simple neo-classical church. The steeple, irreparably damaged by lightning in 1826, was rebuilt a year later. At the south end of Mahatma Gandhi (MG) Road is the Renaissance style **Institute of Science** (1911).

The old buildings of the centre are floodlit after 1900

Pope Paul (Oval) Maidan On the east side of the Pope Paul (Oval) Maidan, is a series of striking buildings, bringing together a range of European styles from the early English Gothic to the Romanesque. From south to north they are the old Secretariat, the University Library and Rajabai Clocktower, the High Court and the Public Works Office. The Venetian Gothic style old **Secretariat** (1874) is 143m long, with a façade of arcaded verandahs and porticos faced in buff-coloured stone from Gujarat. Decorated with red and blue basalt, the carvings are in white stone. The University **Convocation Hall** (1874) to its north is in a 15th-century French decorated style. The **Rajabai Clocktower** (1870s) next door has sculpted figures in niches on the outer walls, which represent the castes of India. Originally the clock could chime 12 tunes including 'Rule Britannia'. The **High Court** (1871-9), in early English Gothic style, has a central tower flanked by lower octagonal towers topped by the figures of Justice and Mercy. The Venetian Gothic **Public Works Office** (1869-72) is to its north. Opposite, and with its main façade to Vir Nariman Road, is the former General Post Office (1869-72). Now called the **Telegraph Office**, it stands next to the original Telegraph Office adding Romanesque to the extraordinary mixture of European architectural styles.

Horniman Circle Turn right at the Flora Fountain (1869), now known as **Hutatma Chowk**, along Vir Nariman Road to the Old Custom House, Town Hall and Mint on the imposing Horniman (Elphinstone) Circle. The **Custom House** is believed to incorporate a Portuguese barrack block of 1665. Over the entrance is the crest of the East India Company. Parts of the old Portuguese fort walls can be seen. Many Malabar teak 'East Indiamen' ships were built here. **The Mint** (1824-9), built on the fort rubbish dump, has Ionic columns and a water tank in front of it. The **Town Hall** (1820-3) has been widely admired as one of the best neo-classical buildings in India. The Doric columns that give the Town Hall its grandeur were shipped from England. The Corinthian interior houses the Assembly Rooms and the Bombay Asiatic Society. Horniman Circle was laid out in 1860. On the west edge are the Venetian Gothic **Elphinstone Buildings** (1870) in brown sandstone. **St Thomas's Cathedral** was begun in 1672 and was subject to a number of later additions. Inside are a number of monuments forming a heroic 'who's who of India'. Going north to Victoria Terminus (CST) you pass the **Port Trust Office** on your right, while a little further on, to your right by the station is the **General Post Office** (1909), based on the architecture of Bijapur (Karnataka) in the Indo-Saracenic style.

Chhatrapati Sivaji Terminus (CST) Area

Over half a million commuters use the station every day

The railway terminus (formerly Victoria Terminus or VT) (1878-87), the most remarkable example of Victorian Gothic architecture in India, was opened during Queen Victoria's Golden Jubilee year. The first train in India left from this terminus for Thane in April 1853.

The large central dome flanked by two wings is capped by a 4m-high statue of 'Progress'. The booking hall with its arcades, stained glass and glazed tiles was inspired by London's St Pancras station. It was built at a time when fierce debate was taking place among British architects working in India as to the

Central Mumbai

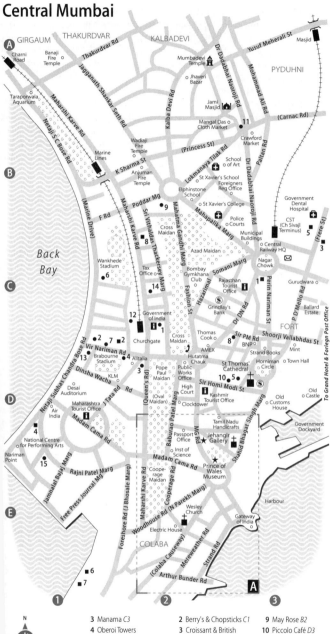

N

| 0 metres | 300 |
| 0 yards | 300 |

■ **Sleeping**
1 City Palace *C3*
2 Chateau Windsor Guest House *C2*
3 Manama *C3*
4 Oberoi Towers & Oberoi *D1*
5 Rupam *B3*
6 Santoor *E1*
7 Supreme *E1*
8 West End *C2*

● **Eating**
1 Balwas *C2*
2 Berry's & Chopsticks *C1*
3 Croissant & British Airways *D2*
4 Gaylord & Gazebo Open House *D2*
5 George *D3*
6 Jazz by the Bay *C1*
7 Kamling *D1*
8 Mahesh Lunch Home *C3*
9 May Rose *B2*
10 Piccolo Café *D3*
11 Rajdhani *B3*
12 Sapna *C2*
13 Talk of the Town *D1*
14 Thacker's *C2*
15 Woodlands & British Council *E1*

most appropriate style to develop to meet the demands of the late 19th-centur boom. One view favoured imitating the best in western tradition, as the Britis were to be seen as a 'civilizing force' in India. Others argued that architec should draw on Indian models. Tillotson argues that the introduction c Gothic allowed a blending of western traditions with Indian (often Islami Indian) motifs, which became known as the Indo-Saracenic style.

Crawford Market (1865-71), now Jyotiba Phule Market, is further nortl along Dr DN Road. It was designed by Emerson in the 12th-century Frenc Gothic style. Over the entrance is Lockwood Kipling's work; the paving stone are from Caithness! The market is divided into sections for fruit, vegetable fish, mutton and poultry. From Crawford Market you can return to the Gate way of India or take a taxi to either the Victoria and Albert Museum at Byculla or Malabar Hill.

Marine Drive & Malabar Hill

You can do an interesting half-day trip from Churchgate Station, along Marir Drive to the Taraporewala Aquarium, Mani Bhavan (Gandhi Museum), th Babulnath Temple, past the Parsi Towers of Silence to Kamla Nehru Park, th Hanging Gardens and the Jain Temple. If you wish you can go further towarc Malabar Point to get a glimpse of Raj Bhavan and the Walkeshwar Temple before returning via the Mahalaxmi Temple and Haji Ali's tomb.

The **Hanging Gardens** (Pherozeshah Mehta Gardens) immediately sout of the Towers of Silence, in the centre of a low hill, are so named since they ar located on top of a series of tanks that supply water to Mumbai. These form gardens have some interesting animal topiary and good views over the city.

Nearby is the Church of North India **All Saints' Church** (1882). Across th road from the Hanging Gardens is the **Kamla Nehru Park** (1952), named aft the wife of India's first Prime Minister. There are very good views over Bac Bay especially from the top terrace.

Museums

Mahatma Gandhi Museum (Mani Bhavan) This private house, at 19 Labur num Road, where Mahatma Gandhi used to stay on visits to Mumbai, is now memorial museum and research library with 20,000 volumes. Not easy to fin (taxi drivers often don't know it) but well worth a visit. Display include diorama depicting important scenes from Gandhi's life. ■ *Rs 3. Colour slide (Rs 100), cards, pamphlets at the door. Open 0930-1800. Allow one hour.*

Victoria and Albert Museum (Bhav Daji Lad Museum). Inspired by the Vic toria and Albert Museum in London and financed by public subscription, was built in 1872 in a Palladian style. The collection covers the history c Mumbai and contains prints, maps and models. ■ *North of Byculla statio Open 1030-1700 (Sunday 0830-1645, closed Wednesday).* In front of th museum is a **clocktower** (1865) with four faces (morning, noon, evening night), and a stone statue of an elephant found by the Portuguese in the har bour. Elephanta Island was named after it. The **Victoria Gardens** are ver attractive. A list at the entrance shows which trees are in blossom.

Prince of Wales Museum Designed by George Wittet to commemorate th visit of the Prince of Wales to India in 1905. The dome of glazed tiles has a Per sian and Central Asian flavour. The whole is Indo-Saracenic, in keeping wit the Gateway of India built at the same time. The archaeological section ha Brahminical, Buddhist and Jain, Prehistoric and Foreign. The Indus Valle section is well displayed. The art section includes an excellent collection c Indian miniatures and well displayed *tankhas*. There are also works b Gainsborough, Poussin and Titian as well as Indian silver, jade, tapestries an collection of arms. The natural history section is based on the collection of the Bombay Natural History Society founded in 1833 and includes dioramas. ■ *South end of MG Road. Rs 5. Closed Monday. 1015-1730 (October-February), 1015-1800 (July-September), 1015-1830 (March-June). Camera fee Rs 15 (no flash or tripods). Good guide books and reproductions on sale. Citywide bus connections; ask at Inspectors' booth outside.* **Jehangir Art Gallery** (in the Prince of Wales Museum complex). This is Mumbai's principal art gallery. The '*Samovar*' café is good for a snack and a drink including chilled beer; pleasant garden-side setting. Temporary members may use the library and attend lectures. **Gallery Chemould** on first floor. ■ *Open 1030-1900, closed Monday. Phones and toilets.* **National Gallery of Modern Art**, Sir Cowasji Jehangir Hall, opposite Prince of Wales Museum.

Elephanta Caves

More than 1,200 cave sites have been discovered across India. The vast majority of these were purpose-built as temples and monasteries and were excavated over the period from third century BC to the 10th century AD. Jain, Buddhist and Hindu caves often stand side by side in the same rock formation. The heavily forested Elephanta Island, often barely visible in the mist from Mumbai only 10 km away, rises out of the bay like a giant whale.

Maharashtra Tourism launches leave the Gateway of India every 30 mins from 0900 (last one leaves Elephanta at 1730), with good guides. The very pleasant journey takes 1 hr (Rs 70 return) except during the monsoon from Jun-Sept (though some small private boats continue); reservations, T2026384. From the landing place, a 300m unshaded path along the quayside and about 110 rough steps lead to the caves at a height of 75m. The climb can be trying for some, especially if it is hot, though *doolies* (chairs carried by porters) are available for around Rs 300 (unnecessary for the reasonably fit). At the start of the climb there are places selling refreshments, as well as lines of stalls with knick-knacks and curios along the way. Early morning is the best time for light and also for avoiding large groups with guides which arrive from around 1000. The caves are prone to damp, favoured by bats and tend to be quite dark so carry a powerful torch.

Ins & outs
Maharashtra Tourism normally organize a festival of classical music and dance on the island, third week of Feb

History

The temple cave on Elephanta island, dedicated to Siva, was probably excavated during the eighth century by the Rashtrakuta Dynasty which ruled the Deccan from 757 to 973 AD. The Portuguese stationed a batallion on Elephanta who reportedly used the main pillared cave as a shooting gallery. Muslim rulers and the British were not blameless either. Sadly a large proportion of the sculptures have been severely damaged, but enough remains to illustrate something of the sculptors' skill.

Entrance

Originally there were three entrances and 28 pillars, eight of which have been destroyed or have collapsed. The two side entrances on the east and west have subsidiary shrines which may have been used for different ceremonies. The main entrance now is from the north. At dawn the rising sun casts its rays on the approach to the *garbagriha* (main shrine), housed in a square structure at the west end of the main hall. On your right as you enter is a carving of Siva as Nataraj (see page 246). On the left is a badly damaged carving of Siva as Lakulisa. Seated on a lotus, the symbol of the unconscious mind and enlightenment, the figure has a Buddha-like feel. From the steps at the entrance you can see the *yoni-linga*, the symbol of the creative power of the deity.

Main hall The ribbed columns in the main hall are between 5 and 6m high and in a cruci form layout. At each corner of the pillars is a dwarf signifying the earth spiri (*gana*), and sometimes the figure of Ganesh (Ganapati). To the right, the mai Linga Shrine has four entrances, each corresponding to a cardinal poir guarded by a *dwarpala*. The sanctum is bare, drawing attention to the *yoni-lir gam* which the devotee must walk around clockwise.

Wall panels To the north of the *garbagriha* is Bhairava killing the demon Andhakasura This extraordinarily vivid carving shows Siva at his most fearsome, with necklace of skulls and a skull and cobra on his head, crushing the power Andhaka, the chief of darkness. It was held that if he was wounded each dro of his blood would create a new demon. So Siva impaled him and collected h blood with a cup which he then offered to his wife Shakti. In winter the be time to see this panel is in the early afternoon.

Opposite, on the south side of the *garbagriha* is the badly damaged panel the Marriage of Siva and Parvati. Siva stands with Parvati on his right, just befor their wedding (normally a Hindu wife stands on her husband's left). She look down shyly, but her body is drawn to him. Behind Parvati stands her fathe Himalaya and to his left is Chandramas, the god of the moon, carrying a pot *soma*, the food of the gods, as a gift. On Siva's left is Vishnu and below is Brahma

At the extreme west end of the temple are Siva as Nataraja (left) an Yogisvara (right). The former shows a beautiful figure of Ganesh above an Parvati on his left. All the other gods watch him. Above his right shoulder is th four-headed god of creation and intellect, Brahma. Below Brahma is the ele phant-headed god Ganesh.

On the south wall, opposite the entrance are three panels. Gangadhara is o the west. The holy Ganga (Bhagirathi) flowed only in heaven but was brough to earth by her father King Bhagiratha (kneeling at Siva's right foot). Here Ganga is shown in the centre with her two tributaries, Yamuna and Saraswa on either side. These three rivers are believed to meet at Allahabad.

To the left of the Gangadhara is the centrepiece of the whole temple, th remarkable Trimurti sculpture of the triple-headed Siva as Lord of the Uni verse (*Maheshwara*). Nearly 6m high, he unites all the functions of creatio preservation and destruction. Some have seen the head on the left (your right as representing Vishnu the Creator, while others suggest that it shows a mor feminine aspect of Siva and may be that of Uma. To his right is Rudra o Bhairava. He has snakes in his hair, a skull to represent ageing from which onl Siva is free, and appears angry. The central face is Siva as his true self, balancin out creation and destruction – Siva Swarupa. In this mode he is passive an serene radiating peace and wisdom. His right hand is held up in a calming ges ture and in his left hand is a lotus bud.

The panel to the left has the Ardhanarisvara. This depicts Siva as th embodiment of male and female, representing wholeness and the harmony opposites. In the rock sculpture the female half is relaxed and gentle, the mir ror in the hand symbolizing the woman reflecting the man. Siva has his vehicl Nandi on the right.

To the east, opposite the *garbagriha*, was probably the original entrance. O the south is Siva and Parvati on Mount Kailash. Siva is the faceless figure wit Parvati on his left. They are shown playing at dice. Parvati has lost and is sulk ing but her playful husband persuades her to return to the game. They are sur rounded by Nandi, Siva's bull, celestial figures above an attendant carrying child and an ascetic with his begging bowl.

On the north is Ravana Shaking Mount Kailash on which Siva is seated. Siv is calm and unperturbed by Ravana's show of brute strength and reassures th

ightened Parvati. With his toe, he pins down Ravana who fails to move the
mountain and begs Siva's forgiveness which is granted.

The larger shrine on the east side has a lingam. There are also damaged images
of Karttikeya, Ganesh and the Matrikas.

Essentials

Mumbai is usually **heavily booked** so whenever possible make reservations in
advance. If you have not, arrive as early in the day as possible. The following **street
names** have been abbreviated: Dr Annie Besant Rd is AB Rd; Bhulabhai Desai (War-
den) Rd is B Desai Rd; Dr Dadabhai Naoroji Rd is Dr DN Rd; Mahatma Gandhi Rd is MG
Rd; Sardar Vallabh Bhai Patel (Linking) Rd is VB Patel Rd.

*Hotlink, India's first
on-line reservation
system, links 300
medium to top class
hotels, T6152394*

The hotels are less than 10 km from the airport and about 20-25 km from the centre;
most are close to a suburban railway station. Many down to **D** category offer free coach
transfer to and from airport. The Tourist Information Counter will assist with bookings.

Airport

Sleeping and eating LL-L *Leela Kempinski*, Sahar (near International Terminal),
T6363636, F86360606. 460 rooms, first class restaurants, good sports facilities, pricey
but excellent. **L-AL** *Orchid*, 70C Nehru Rd, Vile Parle (east), T6183391, F6105974. 5
mins walk from domestic terminal. Totally refurbished, attractive rooms, 'eco-friendly'
(energy saving, recycling etc), *Boulevard* boasts a '15 minute lightening menu' and
good midnight buffet, handy coffee shop. Recommended. **B-C** *Airport International*,
/6, Nehru Rd, Vile Parle (E), T6122891, F6141773. Near domestic terminal, 27 rooms,
modern business hotel, clean, comfortable. **B-C** *Atithi*, 77A Nehru Rd, Vile Parle,
6116124, F6111998. 47 rooms, functional, clean, 7 mins walk from domestic terminal, good value, efficient. **B-C** *Host Inn*, opposite Marol Fire Brigade, Andheri-Kurla Rd,
Andheri (east), near International airport, T830105, F8391080. Decent, clean rooms,
friendly. **B-C** *Kumaria Presidency*, Andheri-Kurla Rd, facing International Airport,
Andheri (east), T6042025, F8373850. 32 a/c rooms, 24-hr exchange, pool. **B-C** *Transit*,
off Nehru Rd, Vile Parle (E), T6105812, F6105785. 54 rooms, modern, reasonable 'overnight halt' for airport.

Mumbai airport & Juhu Beach

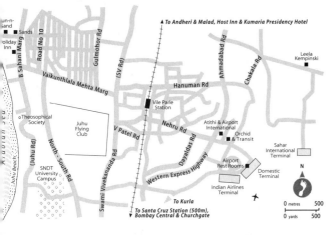

Excursions

Mumbai's accommodation

*Town hotels are clustered into four main areas, between 25-30 km from airport: around **Dadar and Mumbai Central Stations** (Mumbai map); near **Churchgate, Nariman Point and Marine** Drive (Mumbai Central map), near **Victoria (CS) Terminus** (Mumbai Central map), and around **Colaba** (Gateway of India and Colaba map).*

Juhu Beach Juhu Beach used to be quite attractive and relaxed, but the sea is now polluted. O Sunday evenings the beach takes on a fairground atmosphere.

Sleeping and eating L-AL *Holiday Inn*, Balraj Sahani Marg, T6204444, F6204452. 19 rooms, 2 pools, courtesy coach to town, reliable. **AL** *Sun-n-Sand*, 39 Juhu Beac T6201811, F6202170. 118 rooms, best refurbished, comfortable, though cramped poo side, good restaurant. **A** *Citizen*, 960 Juhu Tara Rd, T6117273, F6227270, ci zen@bom2.vsnl.net.in Despite unexciting appearance, 45 smallish but very we appointed rooms, suites, efficient airport transfer. **B** *Horizon*, 37 Juhu Beach, T611797 F6116715. 161 rooms, facilities including disco, good but no sea view. **B** *Juhu Hot* Juhu Tara Rd, T6146122. Spacious comfortable room, cottage-style, large sea-facir lawns, good restaurant (esp Mughlai and seafood), bar, soundproofed disco. **B** *Sanc* 39/2 Juhu Beach, T6204511, F6205268. 40 rooms, excellent restaurant. **D-E** *South En* 11 Juhu Tara Rd, T6125213. 38 rooms, some a/c, light refreshments.

Dadar, Mumbai Central & Grant Road area Dadar can be a good option to stay – plenty of restaurants and good trains Churchgate and VT. See the map on page 195.

Sleeping C-D *Red Rose*, Gokuldas Pasta Rd (behind Chitra Cinema) Dadar T4137843. 31 rooms, some a/c, mostly shared but clean baths, flexible checkou friendly – "welcoming at 0530 with no booking". **D** *Anukool*, 292-8 Maulana Sauk Ali Rd, T392401. 23 rooms, some a/c, good value. **D** *Kalpana Palace*, 181 P Bapura Marg, opposite Daulat Cinema, Grant Rd, T3000846. 30 decent rooms, some a/ **D-E** *YMCA International House and Programme Centre*, 18 YMCA Rd, near Mumb Central, T3091191. Decent rooms, shared bath, meals included, temp membership 60, deposit Rs 1,300, good value, book 3 months ahead with deposit.

Eating Expensive: *China Garden*, 123 August Kranti Marg (Kemps Corner), T363084 Chinese, some Thai, Vietnamese and Japanese. Interesting, imaginative menu but se vice can be slow, bar. *Goa Portuguesa*, THK Rd, Mahim. Goan. Authentic dishes, tavern style with guitarist, try *sungto* (prawn) served between *papads*, *kalwa* (oyster), *teesry* (shell) and clams, lobsters cooked with tomatoes, onions and spices and *bibinca* to er the meal. *Only Fish*, Lady Jamshedji Rd, Dadar, T4373821. Indian regional recip (including Bengali). Seafood too, small but stylish. *Revival*, Chowpatty Sea Face (ne footbridge). Classy, good Indian/continental buffets and desserts, ices. **Mid-rang** *Bombay A1*, 7 Vadilal A Patel Marg (Grant Rd Junc). Parsi. Cheerful, varied menu, t *Patrani machli*. *Chinatown*, 99 August Kranti Marg. Szechwan, Cantonese, Mandari Varied menu (27 soups), upstairs more comfortable. *Rajdhani*, Mangaldas Rd, opposi Crawford Market. Indian. An a/c oasis, excellent lunch *thali*, very friendly welcom *Rashtriya*, road leading to Dadar (East) stairway. South Indian vegetarian. Good foo and excellent coffee. *Viva Paschim*, City View, Dr AB Rd, Worli, T4983636. Superb foo from the Western region. **Cheap**: *Heaven*, corner of Grant Rd/P Bapurao Marg. Ve cheap, friendly (eg *aloo matar* Rs 10). *Kamat*, Navrose Mansion, Tardeo Rd. Indian. Ve inexpensive *thalis* and veg snacks. *St Mary Hotel*, 120 St Mary Rd, Mazgaon, T86847 Goan. Small upstairs restaurant, chutney fish fry and beef tongue specialities. **Fast foo**

Kobe, Hughes Rd, 12 Sukh Sagar. For Japanese sizzlers. *New Yorker*, 25 Chowpatty Sea Face. Pizzas, sandwiches and Mexican fast food, ice cream. *Swaati,* Tardeo Rd for clean *bhelpuri* and *chaats*. *Under the Over*, 36 Altamount Rd (by flyover). For Mexican, Creole dishes etc and rich desserts, reasonably priced, no alcohol.

Sleeping LL-AL *The Oberoi*, Nariman Pt, T2025757, F2041505. 350 large rooms, the newer Oberoi combining modern technology with period furniture, excellent restaurants. **LL-AL** *Oberoi Towers*, Nariman Pt, T2024343, F2043282. 643 rooms, superb views from higher floors, good buffets, garden pool, excellent shopping complex. **A-B** *West End*, 45 New Marine Lines, T2039121, F2057506. 80 small, pleasant suites but need refurbishing, good restaurant, excellent service, very efficient front desk, well located, good value. **C-D** *Chateau Windsor Guest House*, 86 Vir Nariman Rd, T2043376, F2851415. 36 rooms (some a/c) vary, some very small and dark, 24-hr coffee house, friendly, clean, good value, cash only. **D** *Supreme*, 4 Pandey Rd, T215623. Clean rooms with bath, good service but a little noisy.

Churchgate, Nariman Point & Marine Drive
See map on page 197

Eating Expensive: *Indian Summer*, 80 Vir Nariman Rd, T2835445. Indian. Excellent food, tasty *kebabs*, interesting modern glass décor, smart dress, reserve. *Gaylord*, Vir Nariman Rd. Indian. Good food (huge portions) and service, tables inside and out, barbecue, pleasant, good bar, tempting pastry counter. *Santoor*, Maker Arcade, Cuffe Parade, near *President Hotel*. North Indian. Small place, Mughlai and Kashmiri specialties: creamy chicken *malai* chop, *chana* Peshawari (*puri* with chickpeas), *Kashmiri soda* made with salt and pepper. **Mid-range**: *Berry's*, Vir Nariman Rd, near Churchgate Station. North Indian. Tandoori specialities, good *kulfi*, reasonable prices. *Chopsticks*, 90A Vir Nariman Rd, Churchgate. Chinese, good, hot and spicy Schezwan. Offering unusual dishes eg taro nest, date pancakes, toffee bananas. *Kamling*, 82 Vir Nariman Rd, T2042618. Genuine Cantonese. Simple surroundings, but excellent preparations, try seafood, often busy. *May Rose*, Cinema Rd (next to 'Metro'). Chinese. clean a/c, very good food. *Sapna*, Vir Nariman Rd. Indian, very traditional Mughlai delicacies, bar, some tables outside, attentive service, good value. **Cheap**: *Balwas*, Maker Bhavan, 3 Sir V Thackersey Marg. Inexpensive, well-prepared food. *Thacker's*, corner Maharshi Karve Rd and 1st Marine St. Indian. Good *thalis; Woodlands*, Mittal Chambers, Nariman Pt. South Indian. Excellent *idli* and *dosai*, busy at lunchtime, closed Sunday; *Piccolo Café*, 11A Sir Homi Mody St. Parsi. 0900-1800, closed Saturday afternoon and Sunday, profits to charity, homely, clean, good *dhansak; Purohit's*, Vir Nariman Rd. Indian. Excellent veg *thalis*, also Parsi. **Cafés & fast food**: *Croissants*, Vir Nariman Rd, opposite Eros Cinema. Burgers, sandwiches, hot croissants with fillings, ice cream, lively atmosphere. *Fountain*, MG Rd, T2875315. For sizzlers and apple pie in a café atmosphere. *Fountain Dry Fruit Stall*, Flora Fountain. *Badami* (rich almond collection), *pedah* (milk and sugar sweet) and nuts. *Gazebo Open House*, Vir Nariman Rd, opposite Churchgate station. Burgers, pizzas, confectionery and ice creams. *Jazz by the Bay*, 143 Marine Drive. All-you-can-eat soup and salad buffet, excellent value at around Rs 140. *Talk of the Town*, 143 Marine Dr. Mainly continental, some Indian. Pleasant outdoor café for coffee and snacks, band nightly for dancing except Monday, 1100-2400.

Sleeping C *Grand*, 17 Sprott Rd, Ballard Estate, T2618211, F2626581. 73 a/c rooms, exchange, bookshop, old fashioned, built around a central courtyard but relaxing. **C-D** *City Palace*, 121 City Terrace (Nagar Chowk), opposite VT Main Gate, T2615515, F2676897. Tiny though spotless, rooms (some without window), with bath (Indian WC), some a/c, modern, good value. **D-E** *Manama*, 221 P D'Mello Rd, T2613412. Reasonable rooms, few with bath and a/c, popular. **D-E** *Rupam*, 239 P D'Mello Rd, T2618298. 37 rooms, some a/c with phone, clean, friendly, comfortable beds.

CST (VT)
See map on page 197

Excursions

Eating *Bharat*, 317 SB Singh Marg, opposite Fort Market. Excellent seafood and cra
as well as *naans* and *rotis*. *George*, 20 Apollo St (near Horniman Circle). Pleasant quie
atmosphere, faded colonial feel, good service, lunchtime *biriyanis* and *thalis* goo
value. *Mahesh Lunch Home*, Sir PM Rd, Fort. Excellent for Mangalorean, Goan an
tandoori sea food, a/c, bar, inexpensive, very popular.

Gateway of India and Colaba

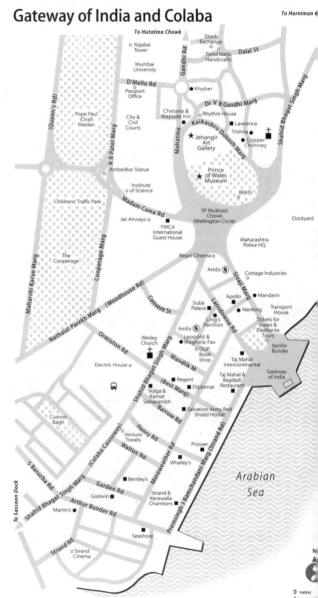

Sleeping AL *Taj Mahal*, the original, with great style and character, 294 rooms, and *Taj Mahal Intercontinental*, Apollo Bunder, T2023366, F2872711. 306 rooms, good shopping arcade and pastry shop, excellent restaurants (no shorts), very good Indian dance performance (evenings Rs 50, 1 hr). **B** *Apollo*, 22 Lansdowne Rd, Colaba, behind Taj, T2020223, F2871592. 39 rooms, some a/c, best with sea view, excellent, helpful, friendly. **B** *Diplomat*, 24-26 BK Bonam Behram Marg (behind *Taj*), T2021661, F2830000. 52 a/c rooms, restaurant, exchange, quiet and homely, good value. **B** *Regent*, 8 Ormiston Rd (Best Marg), T2871854. Well furnished a/c rooms, no restaurant. **B-C** *Godwin*, 41 Garden Rd, T2841226, F2871592. 48 large, clean a/c rooms (some on upper floors have better views), rooftop garden, helpful management. **B-C** *Suba Palace*, Apollo Bunder, T2020636, F2020812, just behind *Taj*. Clean, modern, well run.

C-D *Bentley's*, 17 Oliver Rd, off Garden Rd, T2841474, F2871846. 37 rooms, 4 a/c, breakfast included, good value. **C-D** *Whalley's*, 41 Mereweather Rd, T2834206. 25 rooms (inspect first), some good a/c with balcony and bath, including breakfast, accepts travellers' cheques, old-fashioned. **C-D** *YWCA International Guest House* (for men and women), 18 Madam Cama Rd (entrance on side), Fort, T2020445, F2822057. 34 clean, pleasant rooms with bath, breakfast included, temp membership – Rs 25-50, deposit with advance reservations in writing.

E *Lawrence*, Rope Walk Lane, behind Prince of Wales Museum, T2843618. 9 rooms, usually full, very good value. **E** *Seashore*, 4th Floor, 1/49 Kamal Mansion, Arthur Bunder Rd, T2874237. Has good rooms facing sea (avoid others), good value. Many **E-F** category are clustered around the *Taj Mahal Hotel*. **E-F** *Salvation Army Red Shield Hostel*, 30 Mereweather Rd, T2841824. Mostly dorm (Rs 150 with breakfast), some double rooms (Rs 480, all meals included), lockers 0800-2200, showers Rs 30, check out 0900, book in advance or arrive early, check in as others check out, convenient, friendly, good value. **E-F** *Volga*, above Citywalk Shoes, Colaba Causeway, simple but acceptable.

Eating Expensive: *Chetana*, 34 K Dubash Marg, opposite Jahangir Gallery, T2844968. Indian vegetarian. Excellent Gujarati *thalis* (also small religious bookshop), reserve. *Copper Chimney*, 18 K Dubash Marg, T2041661. Indian. Subdued lighting and quietly tasteful, excellent North Indian dishes, must reserve. *Excellent Sea*, Ballard Estate. Excellent crab, prawn and lobster. *Khyber*, 145 MG Rd, Kala Ghoda, Fort, T2143229. North Indian. For an enjoyable evening in beautiful surroundings (traditional carved furniture, paintings by Hussain, AE Menon), excellent food, especially lobster and *reshmi* chicken kebabs, try *paya* soup (goat's trotters!), outstanding restaurant, reserve. *Ling's Pavilion*, 19/21 KC College Hostel Building, off Colaba Causeway (behind *Taj* and Regal Cinema), T2850023. Stylish décor, good atmosphere and delightful service, colourful menu, seafood specials, generous helpings. *Nanking*, Apollo Bunder. Chinese. Good choice of very good Cantonese dishes, try fish ball soup, pomfret nanking, pickled fish, and beef with watercress. *Trishna*, 7 Rope Walk Lane, behind Kala Ghoda, by Old Synagogue, T2672176. Indian. Good coastline cuisine, seafood, excellent crab. "Swinging, crowded and fun".

Mid-range: *Bagdadi*, Tullock Rd (behind Taj Hotel). Mughlai. One of cheapest, first class food, fragrant biryani, delicious chicken (Rs 40), crowded but clean. *Mandarin*. Chinese. Excellent food and service (also cold beer). *Ming Palace*, Apsara Building, Colaba Causeway. Chinese. Try 'Shanghai potatoes'. *Pathuk's*, near Stock Exchange. Indian. Very good veg and non-veg, a/c, bar, friendly owner.

Cheap: *Kamat Samarambh*, opposite Electric House, SB Singh Marg. Indian vegetarian. Very good *thalis* and snacks, try *chola battura* (puri topped with spiced chickpeas). *Martin's*, near Strand Cinema. Goan. Simple, authentic Goan food, excellent seafood and

Colaba area
Few hotels charge less than Rs 400

Excursions

Getting to and from the airport

Buses Red BEST buses connect both terminals with the city (Rs 38-45 plus baggage). Drop-off and pick-up points in town are Air India and Indian Airlines offices, Taj Mahal Hotel and Prince of Wales Museum. From the airports every two hours (odd hours); **from the city**, the bus starts from Air India, Nariman Pt.

Pre-paid taxis From the counter at the International terminal, recommended.

Retain your receipt as the driver requires this at the end of the journey. Small additional charge for luggage. To Narima Pt or Gateway, about Rs 260, one hour. **NB** During the rush hour it can take two hours.

Train Outside the 'rush hour' and if travelling light, between Churchgate/ Dadar and Santa Cruz (Domestic)/Andher (International), the train is a good option.

pork *sorpotel*. *Mezeban*, Arthur Bunder Rd. Tasty Indian Muslim. *Paradise*, Sindh Cham bers, Colaba Causeway. Parsi, and others. Spotless, excellent *dhansak*, try *Sali boti* (mu ton and 'chips'), closed Mon (not a/c). **Cafés & fast food**: those serving chilled beer a the craze; prices have gone up and waiters care too much for large tips from touri groups: *Churchill*, Mereweather Rd, opposite Woodlands. Wide choice of Western an Indian, good ices, no alcohol. *Leopold's*, Colaba. Still full of young backpackers for goo Western food and drink, friendly but getting expensive. (Similar cafés nearby are f better value). *Wayside Inn*, 38 K Dubash Marg, T2844324. Olde English pub-style foo laid back and leisurely. *Food-Inn* 50m from Leopold's. Mainly Indian (some wester snacks. Pleasant (a/c upstairs), reasonably priced, friendly service.

Bars & pubs All major hotels and restaurants have bars, others may only serve beer. *Taj Mahal* on top floor of the newer building, has excellent all-round views. *Oberoi* too, but all a a price. Pubs charge around Rs 25 for draft beer, Rs 100 for a 'pitcher' (bottle); cocktail Rs 75-150. Flashy *Ecstasy*, B Desai Rd/Napean Sea Rd crossing. Interesting déco younger crowd. *The London Pub*, Chowpatty. Upmarket (couples only), with Rs 17 cover charge, good inexpensive snacks. *The Pub*, 50m from Churchgate station. Vide circuits, expensive cocktails, free entry.

Shopping
Mumbai prices are often higher than in Goa

Most shops are open 1000-1900 weekdays; the bazaars sometimes staying open a late as 2100. Best buys in Mumbai are textiles, particularly tie-and-dye from Gujara hand-block printed cottons, Aurangabad and 'Patola' silks, and gold bordered sar from Surat and Khambat. Wood carving, brass ware and handicrafts make good gift Jewellery and leather goods also attract the Western shopper. The top hotel arcad shops often stock a good selection of high quality goods but prices are usually highe than elsewhere in the city.

Bazaars: *Crawford Market*, MR Ambedkar Rd (fun for bargain hunting). For a differ ent experience try *Chor (Thieves) Bazaar*, on Maulana Shaukat Ali Rd in centr Mumbai. Full of finds – from Raj leftovers to precious jewellery. Some claim that th infamous name is unjustified since the original was 'Shor' (noisy) bazaar! On Friday 'junk' carts sell less expensive 'antiques' and fakes. Cheapest clothes at **Fashion S** opposite Mumbai Gymkhana, S Bhagat Singh Marg, but check quality (often expo surplus) and bargain vigorously.

Books: *Crossword*, 22 B Desai Rd (near Mahalakshmi Temple). Smart, spacious, goo selection. *Danai*, 14th Khar Danda Rd and *Centaur Hotels*, good for books and musi *Nalanda*, Taj Mahal Hotel, one of the best for art books. *Strand Books*, off Sir PM R near HMV. Excellent selection, arranges shipping (reliable).

Excursions

Handicrafts: Government emporia sell good handicrafts and textiles at fixed prices. *Bihar Emporium*, Dhun Nur, Sir PM R. *Black Partridge* (Haryana), Air India Bldg, Nariman Pt. *Central Cottage Industries Emporium*, Apollo Bunder, represents a nationwide selection, especially Kashmiri embroidery, South Indian handicrafts and Rajasthani textiles; most representative of the region is *Gurjari*, 27 Khaitan Bhavan, J Tata Rd, particularly good for textiles, furnishings, wood carving and brassware.

Jewellery: you can buy silver by weight at the *silver bazaar*, Mumbadevi, and gold jewellery at *Zaveri Bazaar*.

Government of India, 123 M Karve Rd, opposite Churchgate, T2033144, F2014496, **Tourist offices**
Monday-Saturday 0830-1730 (closed second Saturday of month from 1230). Counters open 24 hrs at airports. *Taj Mahal Hotel*, Monday-Saturday 0830-1530 (closed second Saturday of month from 1230). Helpful staff who can also issue Liquor Permits (essential for Gujarat). *Maharashtra*, CDO Hutments, opposite LIC Bldg, Madam Cama Rd, T2026713; Express Towers, 9th Floor, Nariman Pt, T2024482; Information counters at airport terminals. *Goa*, Mumbai Central Station, T3086288.

Local Auto-rickshaws: Metered; about Rs 6 for first 1,500m, revised tariff card held **Transport**
by the driver (x 5, in suburbs). **Victorias** (horse-drawn carriages), available at Mumbai Central, Chowpatty and Gateway of India. Rates negotiable. **Buses**: Red BEST (Bombay Electrical Supply Co) buses are available in most parts of Greater Mumbai, T4128725. Within the Central Business District, buses are marked 'CBD'. **Car**: with driver (including fuel) may be hired for varying numbers of hours with a specified km allowance, eg 4 hrs or 50 km, 8 hrs or 80 km, 12 hrs or 120 km.

Out-of-town Car hire: a 'kilometre rate' applies when a car is hired for out-of-town journeys. In addition there are driver and 'night halt' charges of about Rs 250. An Economy car taken out for one night and covering 200 km would cost Rs 1,920. Self-drive cars are also available but are not recommended for anyone who is unaccustomed to Indian road conditions. **Auto Hirers**, 7 Commerce Centre, Tardeo, T4942006; **Sai**, Phoenix Mill Compound, Senapati Bapat Marg, Lower Parel, T4942644, F4937524, recommended; **Wheels**, T4948168. **Taxis** (yellow top, blue a/c): easily available. Metered charge about Rs 10 for first 1,600m. Pay according to revised tariff card (meter x 11). **Train**: Suburban electric trains are economical. They start from Churchgate for the western suburbs an CST (VT) for the eastern suburbs but are often desperately crowded (Stay near the door or you may miss your stop!); there are 'Ladies' cars. **NB** Avoid the rush hour, and keep a tight hold on valuables.

Long distance Air: The **international** (Sahar) terminal is 30 km from Nariman Pt. *International Departure*
There can be long queues at immigration; 24-hr Thomas Cook exchange offers good *Tax, Rs 500*
rates. **Left luggage** counter, international airport, Rs 35 per item. The **domestic terminals** (Santa Cruz) are a little closer to the centre of town. The **new** domestic terminal, exclusively for Indian Airlines, is about 400m from the **old** domestic terminal used by all other domestic airlines. *Santa Cruz Airport*, T6144433. *Sahar Airport*, enquiries, T6329090, 8366700. **NB** It is often difficult to get reasonable **accommodation** in Mumbai, particularly late in the evening. Touts are very pushy at both the international and domestic terminals, but the hotels they recommend are often appalling. It is worth making your own telephone call to hotels of your choice from the airport. *Indian Airlines*: Air India Bldg, Nariman Pt, T2023031, Airport T142 and *Jet Airways* fly daily to *Goa* and many cities across India.

Excursions

To book trains at CST (VT) tourists must have either foreign currency or an encashment certificate

Train: **Enquiries**: Central Railway, T134/135. **Reservations**: CST, T2623535 0800-1230, 1300-1630 (Foreigners' Counter opens 0900); Western Railway Churchgate, and Mumbai Central, T2038016 (for foreigners, ext 4577); 0800-1345 1445-2000. All for first class bookings and Indrail Passes. **Foreign tourists**: tourist quota counter on mezzanine floor above tourist office opposite Churchgate Station. Otherwise, queue downstairs at reservations. **NB** For all trains, book as early as possible; sometimes sleeper reservations are possible for same-day travel. CST has TV screens showing availability of seats 3 days in advance.**Indrail Pass** holders: confirm return reservations in Mumbai. All leave from **CST (Victoria Terminus**, and still called 'VT') unless stated. It has TV screens showing availability of seats 3 days in advance. **NB** Some trains for Goa (**Konkan Railway**) leave from **Kurla**; to get there, suburban trains leave CST every few minutes from platforms 1and 2 and take 20-30 mins. The Kurla terminus is a 10 min walk from the suburban line station. For **Goa** (Margao), *Madgaon Exp, 0111*, from CST dep 2230, 11 hrs (avoid berths 5 and 6); dep from Dadar 2255, 10 hrs, 2 tier a/c Rs 950, 3 tier a/c Rs 512; *Netravati Exp* from **Kurla** (see note above), *6635*, 1640, 11 hrs, arr 0305. These are often late.

Good roads connect Mumbai with Panaji (Goa – 597 km)

Road Bus: Maharashtra RTC operates bus services to neighbouring states. Information on services from MRTC, Central Bus Stand, Mumbai Central, T3076622, or Parel Depot, T4229905. Private buses also travel long distance routes. Some leave from Dadar. Information and tickets from just outside the station, T4113398.

Sea To Goa: 'catamaran' services remained suspended in early 2000.

Directory **Airline offices** Domestic: *Indian Airlines*, Air India Bldg, Nariman Pt, T2023031, Airport T6114433. *Jet Airways*, B1 Amarchand Mans, Madam Cama Rd, T2855788, Airport, T6193333. *Sahara* T2832446. **Banks** Most are open 1000-1400, Mon-Fri, 1000-1200, Sat. Closed on Sun, holidays, 30 Jun, 31 Dec. Best to change money at the airport, at Bureau de Change (upstairs) in Air India Bldg, Nariman Pt or at *Thomas Cook*, Dr DN Rd, 64, Bajaj Bhavan, Nariman Pt, A/2 Silver Arch, JB Nagar, Andheri. **ATMs** for Visa card holders using their usual PIN have opened at a few points. **Communications** Usually open 1000-1700. Sahar Airport 24 hrs. Post offices all over the city. GPO, Nagar Chowk. Mon-Sat, 0900-2000 (*Poste Restante* 0900-1800) and Sun 1000-1730; parcels from 1st Floor, rear of building, 1000-1700 (Mon-Sat); cheap 'parcelling' service on pavement outside. **Credit cards** **American Express**, Majithia Chambers, 276 Dr DN Rd; **Mastercard**, Bank of America, Express Towers; **Visa**, ANZ Grindlays Bank, 90 MG Rd. **Emergency numbers** Police Emergency: T100. Fire T101. Ambulance: T102. **Medical facilities** Most hotels have a doctor on call. *Prince Aly Khan Hospital*, Nesbit Rd near the harbour, T3754343, is recommended. Chemists: in all localities especially near hospitals. *Kemps*, *Taj Mahal Hotel*, Apollo Bunder open until late.

The road journey to Goa

From Mumbai, travelling along the NH17 allows you to cool off at the hill station of Mahabaleshwar after visiting the Maratha Sivaji fort at Pratapgarh.

Pratapgarh The fort stands in a spectacular setting. From the summit (1,080m) on which it is sited there is a splendid view down the forested hillside. A road leads to the foot of the hill, then 500 steps run up to the top of the fort with its double wall with corner bastions. The gates are studded with iron spikes. Inside, the Bhavani temple in the lower fort has two *dipmal* (lantern towers); their exteriors are covered with regularly placed projections like giant coat hooks. Presumably lanterns were placed on these or hung from them, the towers then acting as beacons. The upper fort has a Siva temple. Its ramparts can be seen nearly all of the way down the very scenic (but slow) road to Poladpur where you turn off for Pratagarh.

Excursions

In one of the wettest parts of the Western Ghats during the monsoon, Mahabaleshwar is in a pleasantly wooded setting at the head of the Krishna River. It is the main hill station for Mumbai and Pune. Cool and relaxed with some good walking trails and excellent views from the ghats, it's a good place to have an overnight stop. It is, however, becoming increasingly touristy with crowds of Mumbai holiday makers.

'Discovered' by General Lodwick in 1824 (to whom there is still a monument on the Elephant's Head Point), Mahabaleshwar was declared an official British sanatorium in 1828 and was once the summer capital of the Bombay Presidency. The altitude makes the climate very pleasant during the dry season.

Mahabaleshwar
Phone code: 02168
Population:10,600
Altitude: 1370m
Best season: Nov-May

There is a Rs 5 tax to enter the town

Sights From **Mumbai Point** and the hills around the town you can see the sea on a clear day. There are pleasant walks and waterfalls to visit. **Arthur's Seat** (12 km) looks out over a 600m precipice to the Konkan. The nine-hole golf course is built on a cliff side. **Venna Lake** has boating and fishing. The bazaar sells local soft fruit, local honey and jams from fruit grown in the area. There are several typical 19th-century British hill station buildings.

The old town contains three temples which you can walk to from a turn off Elphinstone Road. **Krishnabai** or Panchganga with a self-formed linga resembling a piece of volcanic lava, is said to have five streams, including the **Krishna** flowing from it. The 13th-century Yadav King Singhan built a small tank at the Krishna's source which starts its 1,400 km journey across the Deccan to the sea. This part of the 'Deccan Trap' has underground caverns which hold water and give rise to springs.

Sleeping and eating **A** *Surya Resort*, 19/B Metgutad, Panchgani-Mahabaleshwar Rd, out of town, T60424, F60825. Modern resort facing wooded valley, rather shabby, pool. **A** *Valley View Resort*, Valley View Rd, off James Murray Peth Rd, T60066, F60070. 80 rooms. **C** *Brightland*, Nakhinda Village (4 km centre), Kates Pt Rd, T60707. 30 rooms, restaurants, bar, pool. **C** *Fountain*, opposite Koyna Valley, T60227, F60137. 98 rooms, veg restaurant with a good choice. **C** *Fredrick*, NH71 near Satara Rd junction, T60240. 32 rooms, restaurant, bungalow hotel. **C-D** *Dreamland*, off MG Rd, behind ST Stand, T60228. 80 rooms, older cottages and new a/c suites by the pool, restaurant (Indian veg) in large garden. **D-E** *Grand*, Woodlawn Rd, away from centre, T60322. Modest rooms with verandah, lovely gardens, quaint. **D-F** *Holiday Resort* (MTDC), 2 km from centre, T60318, F60300. Cottages, rooms and garden suites, dorm (no beds) Rs 75, restaurant, permit room, pleasant setting and atmosphere, tourist office.

Many hotels to choose from; several family run

Tours The main viewing points are very spread out so it is best to take a MTDC tour. Their deluxe buses for sightseeing, 1400, Pratapgarh, 0930, 1000, and Panchgani, 1100. Reservations at *Holiday Resort*, T60318, F60300.

Transport Road Bus station, T60254. MTDC several deluxe buses daily (except monsoons) to Mumbai 1500 (6 hrs) and from Mumbai (7 hrs), Rs 145.

Alternatively enjoy a night at Chiplun on your way south, stopping at Sivaji's coastal fort at Sindhudurg or the atmospheric ruins of Redi fort just before entering Goa.

Chiplun lies on the banks of the Vashishti River which is fed from the Koyna Lake, one of the largest artificial lakes in the Western Ghats. There are spectacular views across the flat valley bottom, criss-crossed by the several courses of the meandering river. After Khed and 10 km before Chiplun, near an attractive small village and temple is **A** *Riverview Lodge* (Taj), T2355-52853, F72059.

Chiplun

Thirty-seven comfortable rooms, most a/c, restaurant (meal times only), attractive garden setting, with superb views. There are several very cheap lodges around the town centre.

Sindhudurgh   Sivaji's coastal fort of Sindhudurg, just south of Malvan, now deserted, is on a low-lying island just off the coast. Rowing boats ferry passengers from the tiny port of Malvan. There are still several shrines – to Maruti, Bhavani, Mahadeo and uniquely, to Sivaji himself.

Redi Fort and the attractive beach below are described on page 185.

Background

7

Background

History

Early Goa

Some identify Goa named as Gomant in the great 4th century BC Hindu epic, the Mahabharata (see page 251). Here Vishnu, in his sixth reincarnation as **Parasurama**, shot an arrow from the range of mountains now known as the Western Ghats into the Arabian Sea and with the help of the god of the sea reclaimed the beautiful land of Gomant. **Siva** is also supposed to have stayed in Goa on a visit to bless seven great sages who had performed penance for seven million years. In the equally ancient texts, the Puranas, the small enclave of low-lying land enclosed by the Ghats is referred to as **Govapuri, Gove** and **Gomant**. The ancient Hindu city was built at the southernmost point of Ilhas. The jungle has taken over and virtually nothing survives.

Myth and legend gradually intertwine with evidence as to the origins of settlement of this part of the west coast of India known as the Konkan. On the interior plateaus just over the Western Ghats, India saw some of its earliest settlements, stone age cultures stretching back over 100,000 years being established on the upper reaches of great rivers like the Krishna and Tungabhadra, which rise just inland of Goa. It may be that some of the forest tribes are related to the aboriginal settlers who came in the first wave of homo sapiens settlement from Africa around 100,000 years ago. The modern population however is almost entirely descended from the **Indo-Aryans** who entered from the north west after 1500 BC. Between 1300 and 1000 BC the heartland of this new culture developed in the plains of North India, gradually stretching its influence southwards.

The great events of Indian history at this stage were taking place across the northern plains. Goa often found itself on the borders of developments taking place in both north and south. When the Mauryan emperor Asoka (272 BC) extended his administration from Patna on the banks of the Ganges southwards across the Deccan plateau, the area of modern Goa may have been incorporated into the great **Maurya** Empire of the third to second centuries BC. Well to the south other great kingdoms contested for power - the Cholas, Keralaputras and Pandiyas all pushing their influence northwards.

The **Bhojas** followed the Mauryas and based their kingdom in **Chandrapur** (modern Chandor). From the third to the eighth centuries AD the **Kadamba Dynasty** established itself on the western borderlands, though it was normally seeking alliances with powers such as the Guptas or the later Rashtrakutas to the north or the Chalukyas to the south. Indeed some Goans actually claim the **Rashtrakutas** as their own dynasty. Some of the Rashtrakuta kings are revered for their patronage of the arts, Krishna I (r756-773), for example, commissioning the great Kailasanath temple at Ellora. From the eighth century AD until the arrival of the Muslims from the north in 1312 AD the Kadambas' power was reduced to a narrow coastal and hill belt, and they were almost entirely subservient to the dominant **Chalukyas** who controlled most of central peninsular India. One of the most remarkable of the Chalukyan kings, Someshvara III (r1126-1138) was passionately devoted to the arts and made an outstanding collection of folksongs, including Konkani songs.

In 1052, the Kadambas established their capital in the port town on the north bank of the Zuari (near Goa Velha) which had been developed by the Chalukyas as the flourishing port of **Gopakapattana** or **Govapuri** (**Gove** as it came to be known by traders).

Contact with the Muslim world

Since before the birth of Christ, the Arabs traded along the west coast of India and Arab geographers knew Goa as Sindabur. As the Arab world converted to Islam, the traders spread their new religion and many settled in Goa. However, while the Muslim-based coastal trade was largely peaceful, the penetration of Islam into the Deccan was anything but. In 1312, Muslim invaders from the Delhi Sultanate took power, destroying much of Govapuri and forcing the **Kadambas** to return to **Chandrapur**. In 1327 the Muslims under Mohammad Tughluq carried out further incursions into the interior, going as far as Chandrapur. However, their power was challenged 20 years later by the Bahmanis.

In 1347 Muslims in the Deccan peninsula broke away from the Delhi Sultanate to the north and established the **Bahmani** Dynasty (1347-1527). While the Bahmanis were in control of Goa from approximately 1348-1369 (and again for 26 years from 1470) they entered a renewed period of temple destruction and terrorising the Hindu population. From then until well after the arrival of the Portuguese, Goa's territory was the subject of repeated contests between the Hindu and Muslim powers of the interior and the maritime Portuguese.

The Bahmanis were, however, defeated by the Hindu **Vijayanagars** in 1378 and there followed nearly a hundred years of relative peace and prosperity. Goa had already become an important centre for the inward trade in Arab horses with the Vijayanagar Empire, who began to export the much prized spices and cotton cloth. The port of Govapuri had been silting up and power and attention was shifted to **Ela** on the south bank of the Mandovi which began to flourish and function as an alternative port.

It was control of maritime trade that attracted the peninsular powers into repeated conflict rather than ideological or religious competition. However, brutal attacks on the Muslim population of Bhatkal to the south of Goa by the Vijayanagar king encouraged the Bahmanis to return with renewed force in 1470. They destroyed what was left of the old capital Govapuri (which became known as Goa Velha) and moved the administration to the port of Ela on the Mandovi, taking the name 'Govapuri' (later Velha Goa). The Bahmanis themselves split into five different states, the largest of which, the Adil Shahis of Bijapur (1490-1686) played a key role in Goa's political fortunes. They took control from 1498-1510. When the Portuguese arrived, Yusuf Adil Shah, the Muslim Sultan of Bijapur, was the ruler. At this time Goa was an important starting point for Mecca bound pilgrims, as well as continuing to import Arab horses and, after Cochin (Kochi), it was the major market on the west coast of India.

Under the Muslim Bahmanis, the new Govapuri (which was Ela and subsequently Velha Goa) developed into a significant town, prosperous as a result of the trade in horses and spices and of great geopolitical significance. Adil Shah, the Bijapuri Sultan himself had come from Iran, and links with the Middle East remained economically and politically important to the Deccan Sultanates. Ships from many lands laden with precious merchandise arrived in Velha Goa and traders came from Persia, Arabia, East Africa, Central Asia, Bengal, Deccan, the Malabar and China. The wide streets of the city were lined with shops and the Adil Shahs built mosques, mansions with gardens and an impressive palace facing the river (see page 76).

The Portuguese

For the first Portuguese, their encounter with Islam on the coast of India was an extension of the contest for power between Catholicism and Islam in the Iberian Peninsula. They had come, not only to rescue the early Syrian Christians who had been converted by the Nestorians in the fourth century from the threat of Muslim dominance, but also to bring them under the influence of Rome. The Portuguese were also intent on setting up a string of coastal stations on the way to the Far East in order to control the lucrative spice trade (see page 184)

Although Vasco da Gama landed in India in 1498, Goa, the first Portuguese possession in Asia, was only taken by **Afonso de Albuquerque** in 1510. For the intervening 12 years the Portuguese set up 'factories' along the Malabar coast (modern Kerala) and a fort in Cochin (Kochi). Originally intending to take his fleet up from Karwar, just south of Goa, to Egypt, to complete the previous year's destruction of the Egyptian fleet, Albuquerque changed his plans when he obtained vital information about Goa from his ally Timoja, an officer and spy of the Vijayanagar Empire. He discovered that the Muslims were building their ships in 'Goa', that the administration was fairly weak and that Bijapuri taxes were becoming increasingly unpopular among the local subjects.

Afonso de Albuquerque grasped the advantages of this island site, an excellent natural harbour, large enough to give a secure food-producing base but with a defensible moat, at the same time well placed with respect to the important northwest sector of the Arabian Sea. He found out details of the capital's defences and mounted an attack, successfully taking it on 1 March 1510. Yusuf Adil Shah died almost immediately after the defeat, but two months later his 13-year-old son and successor, **Ismail Adil Khan** (known to the Portuguese as the **'Idalcan'**), blockaded Goa with 60,000 men and recaptured it. Albuquerque and his men had to retreat to ships at sea. However, Adil Khan's victory was short-lived. Ismail found himself no match to defend the city against Albuquerque when he returned after the monsoon with reinforcements and recaptured the city on the 25 November (St Catherine's Day) in 1510, after a bloody struggle. He massacred all the Muslims and appointed a Hindu as Governor, thereby establishing his alliance with the Vijayanagar Empire which was more than happy to see the maritime power of its Muslim rivals curtailed.

The territory over which Albuquerque gained control was the roughly triangular shaped island with a rocky headland and two harbours which was given the name **Ilhas** ('island' in Portuguese), together with the islands of **Chudamani (Chorao), Dipavati (Divar), Vamsim** (the tiny island between the two) and **Jua**. In 1534 the adjoining lands of Bardez and Salcete which were dependencies of Govapuri came under Portuguese control. Although skirmishes continued with the Bijapuri Adil Shahs, the two territories were annexed by the Portuguese around 1543 to makeup the territory known as '**The Old Conquests**'.

Once Albuquerque established his own control, the Portuguese started replacing the main Muslim buildings in

Afonso de Albuquerque

Historical table

Dates	Events in Goa	Events in India and the world
Before 2000 BC	Earliest agriculture reaches the coast from the Peninsula	Indus Valley Civilization in North India
1200 BC		Earliest Vedas composed
600-500 BC		The Buddha born; Upanishads completed
250 BC	Mauryan Empire reaches Goa under Ashoka	
1st-3rd C AD	Trade with Arabia and Gulf begins	Discovery of monsoon winds
300-500		Gupta Empire in North India: the 'classical' period
6th-8th C	The Chalukyan kings dominate central peninsula and Goan coast	629 Death of Mohammad; 750 Rajputs become powerful in Northwest India
8th-11th C	Rashtrakutas dominate peninsula, followed by Kadamba control of Goan coast Cholas control South India	
1050	Kadamban kings trade with Zanzibar and with Sri Lanka. Build Gopakapattana as capital	
1192		Muslims defeat Rajputs nr Delhi. Angkor Wat built in Cambodia
14th C		Muslim Delhi Sultanate carries Islam south 1290 Marco Polo reaches China
1351-88	Bahmani dynasty established captures Goa	Incas centralise power in Peru
1367	Bahmanis defeated by Vijayanagar Empire	
1469	Bahmani Muhammad Shah II captures Goa	
1489	Yusuf Adil Shah establishes Bijapur Sultanate	
1498		Vasco da Gama lands in Kappd near Calicut
1510	Afonso de Albuquerque captures Old Goa looses it recaptures it	Vijayanagar Empire contest with sultanates for control of peninsula
1542	St Francis Xavier reaches Goa	Mughal Emperor Humayun re-conquers Delhi

Velha Goa with their own, took over the trading interests which had sustained the town, and started to develop it as a major Christian centre. To avoid conflict between missionaries in the Old Conquest territories, Bardez was offered to the **Franciscans** (Grey Friars because of the colour of their habit), while Salcete was under the **Jesuits** and Ilhas was principally allotted to the **Augustinians** and **Dominicans**.

From 1510, until the establishment of British rule over the rest of India, the fortunes of Goa depended on quickly changing patterns of alliances and on the fortunes of the principal parties which were often determined by events outside Goa itself. For the first century of their occupation of the Old Conquests the Portuguese took advantage of the animosity between the powers on the Peninsula inland. Although some Hindu practices like *sati* (the burning of widows on the funeral pyre of their husbands), were stamped out by Albuquerque, in other respects he did little to interfere with local

Dates	Events in Goa	Events in India and the world
1556		Akbar becomes Mughal Emperor
1560	The Inquisition starts	
1565		Vijayanagar Empire defeated
1571	Portuguese granted rights over 'Old Conquests' by Bahmanis	
1603	Dutch blockade Goa	
1605		East India Company base at Surat
1667-83	Marathas extend control over Peninsula; attack Goa	
1690		Calcutta founded
1695	Viceroy moves residence out of Old Goa	
1737-39	Maratha wars Portuguese victorious	Mughal Empire in decline
1774	Edict banning the Inquisition	1757 Clive wins battle of Plassey
1782-1791	"ew Conquests' incorporated into Goa	
1787	The Pinto Revolt in Candolim	
1797-1813	British occupy Goa during Napoleonic wars in Europe	
1812	Inquisition finally ended	
1821	Goa representatives in Lisbon Parliament	
1843	Panaji declared capital	
1851		First railway in India – Bombay
1857		Indian Mutiny in North India
1881	First railway links Mormugao with peninsula	
1905	First iron ore and manganese mines	
1928	Founding of Goa Congress Party	
1947		Indian Independence
1946-58	Independence demands leaders deported to Portugal	
19 Dec 1961	Indian Army enters Goa	
30 May 1987	Goa becomes full state of the Indian Union	

Background

custom. By 1570 the colony had become so wealthy that it had acquired the sobriquet "Golden Goa". Goa became the capital of the Portuguese Empire in the East and was granted the same civic privileges as Lisbon.

During the 16th century, the Portuguese established themselves as a superior maritime power along the western peninsular coast, building forts in small enclaves such as Daman, Diu and close to Bombay (as at Bassein) and further south, along the coast of Goa. They terrorized Indian ships and those of the other colonizing countries to protect their monopoly in spices and the trade of cotton goods from the sub-continent to Southeast Asia.

Goa's reputation as a centre of culture and learning was enhanced by its association with **St Francis Xavier**, who visited Goa for the first time in 1542. His first mission was directed at ending the degeneracy of the *fidalgos* ('gentlemen'). He also contributed to the establishment of Goa's reputation as a centre of learning, setting up its first printing press. In the Ilhas and Salcete the Jesuits became dominant, while Franciscans worked throughout Bardez.

Throughout the 100 years after their arrival the Portuguese were intent on trying to build an empire in Asia. In that effort Goa played a pivotal role, acting as both a military and trading staging post between Portugal and its territories to the East. It was their misfortune that in 1565 the Vijayanagar Empire was suddenly – and unexpectedly – routed. Five years earlier the Portuguese had embarked on the Inquisition, attacking Hindus and Muslims alike within the Old Conquest Territories. In 1570 Muslim rulers from Bijapur to Sumatra attempted a concerted attack on Portuguese interests, and Goa was subjected to a 10 month siege. The harassment from the Bijapur Sultanate was only finally ended by the overpowering dominance of the much greater Muslim power of the Mughals.

When the Dutch began to control trade in the Indian Ocean, Portuguese dominance of the sea declined. The fall of the Vijayanagar Empire in 1565 caused the lucrative trade between Goa and the Hindu state to dry up. Nonetheless, by 1600 the population of the city may have been as much as 225,000, equal to London or Antwerp, then the largest cities in Europe. However, according to Della Valle who visited Goa in 1623 most of the population comprised slaves. Though this might have been an exaggeration, the Portuguese certainly had no objections to mixed marriages or inter-racial liaisons, so there was a large population of *mestizos*.

The Dutch blockaded Goa in 1603 and 1639. They weakened but did not succeed in taking it, but it was ravaged by an epidemic in 1635, and manpower was so severely depleted that the Portuguese brought criminals from Lisbon's prisons to maintain their numbers.

By the early part of the 18th century Portuguese fortunes had already experienced wide fluctuations and the territorial base was still restricted to the Ilhas Salcete in the south and Bardez in the north. The greatest threat to security had come through the latter part of the 17th century from **Sivaji** (1627-80) and his Maratha confederacy (1674-1818). Sivaji and his son took the whole of the northern territories, only to be forced to withdraw in 1683 by the threat they faced from the Mughals on their own northern flank. Goa remained safe in its isolation, though it was threatened again briefly in 1739.

The risk of attack from both land and sea encouraged the Portuguese to establish a series of forts inland as well as on the coast. The forts are small compared with even the modest Indian forts, due to the small number of expatriate Portuguese who manned them. Even at the height of Portuguese domination Richards suggests that there were no more than 1,000 Portuguese based in Goa, and over 700 of these were members of the religious orders. Through the 19th century the Portuguese developed Panaji as their capital, and it became a centre of education and civil administration.

Despite extraordinary cultural achievements, notably in the church building of Old Goa itself, Portugal's political base in Goa remained weak. In the mid-18th century a series of reforms were introduced under pressure from the Portuguese Government in Lisbon. These included the ending of the Inquisition and the confiscation of Jesuit property. These moves were matched by a determination to abolish racial discrimination, especially in the church.

In 1741 King Joao V of Portugal (r1706-50) had decided to extend Portuguese control to the provinces which were to become '**The New Conquests**'. The implementation of this plan had to wait four decades, when a succession of military victories led to the integration of the New Conquests into Portuguese territory. **Bicholim** and **Satari** were conquered in 1781 and 1782, victories which were celebrated by the first public display of the body of St Francis Xavier in 1782. **Pernem** was ceded to Portugal in 1788, while **Ponda, Sanguem, Quepem** and

Canacona followed three years later, along with official acceptance by the Raja of Sunda of the capture in 1763 of the headland of Cabo de Rama. Portugal's hold on its Goan territory was complete.

While Portuguese Goa grew, Portugal's other Asian interests shrank. Struggles in continental Europe, notably between Britain and Napoleonic France, had an impact on alliances in India, and Goa itself was occupied by the British between 1799 and 1813.

It was during this period that Goa experienced its most important revolt against the Portuguese. In 1787 a group of priests met in the house of the Pinto family in Candolim and formed a plot to overthrow the government, a plot which became known as the **Pinto Revolt**. Fifteen of the 47 conspirators who were arrested and tortured were subsequently executed in Panaji. It was an event which left a deep feeling of unease, but may have speeded the process of reform and in particular the determination to end the racist policies by which Indians had been excluded from positions of authority both in the church and the state.

Independence

By the end of the Second World War when the rest of India was on the point of achieving Independence there were less than 30 Portuguese officials based in Goa. The Portuguese came under increasing pressure in 1948 and 1949 to cede Goa, Daman and Diu to India, and in response despatched over 4,000 troops to hold on to the territory. In 1955 *satyagrahis* (non-violent demonstrators) attempted to enter Goa. They were deported but later, when larger numbers tried, the Portuguese used force to repel them and some were killed. At a demonstration in Margao, Portuguese police fired on the unarmed mob, killing 32 and injuring 225. The problem festered until 19 December 1961 when the Indian Army, supported by a naval blockade, marched in and brought to an end 450 years of Portuguese rule. Originally Goa became a Union Territory together with the old Portuguese enclaves of Daman and Diu, but on 30 May 1987 it became a full state of the Indian Union.

Recent political history

The Goa Legislative Assembly has 40 elected members while the state elects three members to the Lok Sabha in the Central Government. Although the Congress has been the largest single party, political life is strongly influenced by the regional issue of the relationship with neighbouring Maharashtra, and the debate over the role of Marathi led to the creation of the Maharashtrawada Gomantak Party which was in power in the Union Territory of Goa from 1963 until 1979. Regional issues remain important, but there is now also a strong environmental lobby, in which the Catholic Church plays a prominent part. In the Lok Sabha elections of 1996 the Congress lost both its seats, one to the Third Front and one to an Independent. Goan politics remain sharply distinct from its neighbours.

Background

The Land

By Indian standards Goa is a tiny state. The coastline on which much of its fame depends is only 97 km long. The north and south of the state are separated by the two broad estuaries of the Zuari and Mandovi rivers. Joined at high tide to create an island on which Panaji stands, these short rivers emerge from the high ranges of the Western Ghats less than 50 km from the coast and then glide almost imperceptibly to the sea. On either side of the rivers are extensive tidal marshes, and to north and south a series of minor streams run through flat bottomed valleys into the sea. From Tiracol in the north to Betul in the south these estuaries provided an important though far from wholly effective defence against intruders. Often overlooked by steep sided hillocks rising to the flat tops of the laterite plateaus which make up much of the area between the marshes, some of the estuaries contain the last remains of mangrove swamp and its associated ecosystem in western India.

The long sandy beaches, which run for much of the length of both the north and the south coasts, are backed by parallel sets of dunes. Apparently barren and economically useless the dunes have provided an important part of the wider ecosystem, providing shelter for housing and transport just inland. The beaches themselves are interrupted at various points by seaward extensions of the laterite plateaus which sometimes form impressive headlands. These provided ideal sites for coastal forts, as at Chapora, Fort Aguada or Cabo de Rama.

Inland from the coast, Goa occupies a shallow indentation in the Sahyadri Ranges of the Western Ghats. Rising to around 1,000m along this section of their crest line, the Ghats were developed on the old fault which marked the separation of the Indian Peninsula from the ancient landmasses of Gondwanaland – which today have become South Africa, South America and Antarctica. Separated from that great continental land mass less than 100 million years ago, the Indian Peninsula has been pushing northwards ever since. At its northern margins as it thrust under the Tibetan Plateau it was responsible for the creation of the massive mountain wall of the Himalayas. That has caused huge instability along the northern margins of the peninsula, with earthquakes frequent in the foothills of the Himalaya themselves. In contrast, the land on which Goa stands is largely stable.

Despite its stability, geologically Goa represents a transition point in the Ghats. To the north the often precipitous ridge is formed by volcanic lavas which poured out over the Indian Peninsula over 60 million years ago, laying the foundation today for the rich black soils that cover so much of the Deccan plateau to the northeast of Goa. In contrast, from Goa southwards, the ridge of the Ghats is formed from the ancient and hard rocks of the Indian Peninsula, granites and gneisses. However, the ridge of the Ghats has been pushed back much further from the coast in Goa than anywhere else, because its short but powerful streams have eaten into the catchment areas of the great rivers of the peninsula. This process has given Goa the 'breathing space' which marks it out from the rest of the much narrower strip of lowlands between the Ghats and the sea to both north and south.

The slightly greater extent of its coastal lowlands has not given Goa much easier access to the interior. The hill ranges rise sharply from the coastal plains, creating a wholly distinct, remote and rugged environment and pierced only by narrow gorges which lead up onto the plateau. Minor seasonal streams cascade down the mountain sides in the monsoon, while at the 600m high Dudhsagar ('sea of milk')

Falls the River Candepar plunges in a series of dramatic leaps throughout the year. The forested slopes of the Ghats are relatively sparsely populated, forming a natural barrier between the coastal lowlands and the much more open landscape immediately across the ridge of the hills in neighbouring Karnataka.

Where the laterite plateaus reach the coast, as at Chapora in the north, Dabolim in the centre or Cabo da Rama in the south, they produce rocky headlands jutting out into the sea, ideal sites for the string of coastal forts with which both the Portuguese and the Marathas defended their maritime and landward interests. The estuaries formed near such headlands – at Tiracol or Fort Aguada, Chapora or Betul – all suggest that in recent times local sea level has risen slightly to flood the lower courses of the streams at high tide, pushing salt water several kilometres inland.

While the sandy beaches of the coast have provided the basis for Goa's rapidly expanding tourist industry, the land of the interior of Goa has also become a vital resource. Rich in iron ore and manganese, huge open cast mines have provided enormously important exports. While the income derived from this has helped to boost Goa's foreign exchange, it often scars the landscape of the interior and has had a much criticized effect on neighbouring agriculture.

Climate

At a latitude of 15° North Goa lies well within the tropics. Throughout the year therefore it is warm, but its position on the coast means that it never suffers the unbearable heat of India's northern plains. However, from mid-April until the beginning of the monsoon in mid-June both the temperature and the humidity rise sharply, making the middle of the day steamy hot and the sand of the beaches almost untouchable. But it is the monsoon itself which defines Goa's climate and its seasons, standing like a dividing wall between the heat of early summer and the beautiful warm clear and dry weather of its tropical winter, stretching from October to March.

Many myths surround the onset of the *monsoon*, derived from an Arabic word 'maunsam' which means simply 'season'. In fact its arrival is as variable as is the amount of rain which it brings. What makes the Indian monsoon quite exceptional is not its regularity but the depth of moist air which passes over the sub-continent. Over India, for example, the highly unstable moist airflow is over 6,000m thick compared with only 2,000m over Japan, giving rise to the bursts of torrential rain which mark out the wet season. Goa's location half way up India's west coast places it directly in line as the moisture laden winds sweep up from the southwest across the Arabian Sea. Forced to climb rapidly as it hits the Western Ghats the cooling air mass immediately releases its water, making June and July in Goa wet months. In an average year Panaji for example receives around 1,500mm in just six weeks. On the coast itself this rain often comes as torrential storms accompanied by lashing winds, while up in the cooler air of the Ghats if it is not raining you can usually rely on the hill tops being in swirling cloud and mist. It's a good time of year for the waterfalls!

While heavy showers persist into August and September and the high humidity can continue to make life unpleasant the rainfall drops sharply away and in October most of the state

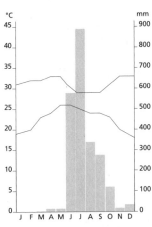

Climate: Panaji
The best time to
visit is between
Dec & Mar

receives less than 100mm. Life returns to normal as the cooler dry air of the northeast monsoon pushes southwards from the Tibetan plateau, bringing beautifully invigorating dry clear air to the rainwashed skies. It is the perfect season for visiting Goa, cool enough at night sometimes to need a pullover, but still hot in the open sun on the beach.

The climate of Goa itself is dominated by its position to the west of the Ghats, yet the land immediately across the ridge of the hills experiences quite a different climate. Almost straight away on crossing the Ghats you notice the effects of far lower total rainfall. Although the entire region of neighbouring Karnataka and Maharashtra experiences exactly the same seasonal pattern of change in the wind system which brings Goa its wet monsoon, once the winds have climbed the Ghats and start their descent over the plains they dry out rapidly.

Wildlife

Goa has a fascinating range of birds and animals. According to one authority, Blanford, there are 48 genera of mammals, 275 genera of birds and 60 genera of reptiles, seven of which are endemic to the Western Ghats. The wildlife sanctuaries are worth visiting for their scenery, vegetation and birdlife but can be disappointing if you are expecting to see a variety of exotic animals.

Mammals

Deer There are several species of deer, including the magnificent **sambar** (*Cervus unicolor*) which can be up to 150cm at the shoulder. Sambar live on wooded hillsides in groups of up to 10 or so, though solitary animals are also quite common. The much smaller **chital** or spotted deer (*Axis axis*), only about 90cm tall, are seen in herds of 20 or so, in grassy areas. The bright rufous coat spotted with white is unmistakable; the stags carry antlers with three tines.

Chital

Wild boar

Sambar

Oxen

By far the most visible member of the family is the domesticated **water buffalo** (*Bubalus bubalis*), widely seen in the coastal districts. The **Indian bison** or **gaur** (*Bos gaurus*) looks superficially like a large buffalo. The 'state animal' of Goa, this massive animal can be up to 200cm tall at the shoulder, with a heavy muscular ridge across it. It usually lives in forested uplands. There are large herds in the Bhagwan Mahaveer Sanctuary and as far south as Canacona.

Wild boar

Although declining in numbers, wild boar (*Sus scrofa*, known in Goa as *Ran Dukar*) are found in the foothills of the Ghats, and have a reputation for causing immense damage to paddy, banana and sugar cane crops.

Striped hyena

One of the most important scavengers of the open countryside, the striped hyena (*Hyena hyena*) usually comes out at night. It is about 90cm at the shoulder with a large head and a noticeable crest of hairs along its sloping back.

Sloth bear

The sloth bear (*Melursus ursinus*), about 75cm at the shoulder, lives in broken forest and has been seen in the Cotigao Sanctuary and Surla ghat. Unkempt and mangy looking, it has a distinctively long and pendulous lower lip.

Big cats

The Bhagwan Mahaveer Sanctuary, Goa's largest wildlife park, is reputed to have 18 **panthers** (*Panthera pardus*). A few **tigers** (*Panthera tigris*, or '*Vag*') are known to stray in occasionally from neighbouring Karnataka in the summer but are rarely seen. Despite their greater numbers panthers (locally '*Bibtto Vag*') have the reputation of being even more elusive. The smaller species include the **jungle cat** (*Felis chaus*), **leopard cat** (*Felis bengaliensis*), and **small Indian civet** (*Vivirrecula indica*).

Indian elephant

The Indian elephant (*Elephas maximus*) is not normally found in Goa, though a wild elephant is occasionally seen in the Bhagwan Mahaveer Sanctuary or the Bondla National Park when they wander in from neighbouring Karnataka during the summer months.

Background

Flying fox

Hyena

Common langur

Gaur

Squirrels   The **common giant flying squirrel** (*Petaurista petaurista*) which inhabits the Western Ghats, is found around Valpoi and the Bhagwan Mahaveer and Cotigao sanctuaries. The body can be as much as 45cm long and the tail another 50cm or so. They glide from tree to tree using a membrane stretching from front leg to back leg which acts like a parachute. This squirrel is also noticeable by its strange call. **Palm squirrels** are very common. The **five-striped** palm squirrel (*Funambulus pennanti*) and the **three-striped** palm squirrel (*Funambulus palmarum*), both about the same size (30cm in length, about half of which is tail), look very similar. The five-striped squirrel is the one usually seen in towns.

Monkeys   In addition to the animals that still live truly in the wild there are many species which have adapted to village and town life. India's various monkeys are rare on the coastal strip but inland they are far more common. The **common langur** (*Presbytis entellus*) is a long tailed monkey with a black face, hands and feet which lives largely in the forest. The **bonnet macaque** (*Macaca radiata*) is more solid looking with shorter limbs and a shorter tail, and has the distinctive whorl of longer hairs on the head. They are seen both in forests and near villages. All monkeys can be aggressively demanding and are carriers of rabies, so should be kept at a distance. Food, which invariably attracts them, should be kept concealed.

Bats   The two bats most commonly seen in towns differ enormously in size. The larger is the so-called **flying fox** (*Pteropus giganteus*) which has a wing span of 120cm. They roost in large noisy colonies, often in the middle of towns or villages, where they look like folded umbrellas hanging from the trees. In the evening they can be seen leaving the roost with slow measured wing beats. The much smaller **Indian pipistrelle** (*Pipistrellus coromandra*), with a wing span of about 15cm, is an insect eater. It comes into the house at dusk, roosting under eaves and has a fast, erratic flight.

Common mongoose   The common mongoose (*Herpestes edwardsi*) lives in scrub and open jungle as well as in gardens and fields. It kills snakes, but will also take rats, mice, chickens and birds' eggs. Tawny coloured with a grey grizzled tinge, it is about 90cm in length, of which half is pale-tipped tail.

Sea mammals   An increasingly popular activity from several points on the Goa coastline is dolphin spotting. Both the **long-beaked dolphin** (*Steno spa*) and the **finless black porpoise** (*Neomeris phocaenoides*) are common right along the coast ("Dolphin Watch" boat rides are becoming popular), and the endangered **dugong** or sea cow (*Dygong dugon*) rather like a large seal is also found.

Birds

Like other parts of the Western Ghats and the west coast, Goa has a very rich birdlife. Many species have adapted to man and live in towns and villages.

Town & village birds   Some of these perform a useful function scavenging and clearing refuse, one of the most widespread being the **pariah kite** (*Milvus migrans*, 65cm), an all brown bird with a longish tail. The much more handsome **brahminy kite** (*Haliastur indus*, 48cm) is also a familiar scavenger, but is largely confined to the waterside. Its chestnut and white plumage is unmistakable. The common **white-backed vulture** (*Gyps bengalensis*, 90cm) is a heavy looking, ungainly, brown bird with a bare and scrawny head and neck. In flight the white rump and broad white band on the leading edge of the under surface of the wing identify it. The **feral pigeon**, or **blue rock dove** (*Columba livia*, 32cm), is generally a slaty grey in colour and invariably has two dark bars on the wing and a white rump. The **little brown dove** (*Streptopelia senegalensis*, 25cm) is quite ame and shows little fear of man. It is bluey grey and brown above, with a pink head and underparts, and a speckled pattern on the neck. The **collared dove** (*Streptopelia decaocto*, 30cm) is common especially in the drier parts of Goa, in gardens and open spaces. It has a distinct half collar on the back of its neck. The **red-vented bulbul** (*Pycnonotus cafer*, 20cm), a mainly brown bird, can be identified by the slight crest and a bright red patch under the tail. The **common myna** (*Acridotheres tristis*, 22cm) feeds on lawns, especially after rain. Look for the white under the tail and the bare yellow skin around the eye, yellow bill and legs, and in flight the large white wing patch. A less common, but more striking bird also seen feeding on lawns and in open country is the **hoopoe** (*Upupa epops*, 30cm), easily identified by its sandy plumage with black and white stripes, and long thin curved bill. The marvellous fan-shaped crest is sometimes raised. Finally there is a member of the cuckoo family which is heard more often than seen. The **koel** (*Eudynamys scolopacea*, 42cm) is commonly heard in gardens and wooded areas, particularly during the hot weather. The call is a kuoo-kuoo-kuoo, a double note which starts off low and flute-like, but rises in pitch and intensity, then suddenly stops, only to start all over again. The male is all black with a greenish bill and a red eye; the female streaked and barred.

Goa's marshes form an enormously rich bird habitat. **Cormorants** abound, the commonest, the **little cormorant** (*Phalacrocorax niger*, 50cm) is an almost entirely black bird with just a little white on the throat. It has a long tail and hooked bill, and is seen both on the water and in colonies in waterside trees. The **coot** (*Fulica atra*, 40cm), another black bird which has a noticeable white shield on the forehead, is found on open water, especially in winter. The **openbill stork** (*Anastomus oscitans*, 80cm) and the **painted stork** (*Ibis leucocephalus*, 100cm) are two of the commonest storks of India. The openbill stork is a white bird with black wing feathers, and a curiously shaped bill. The painted stork is also mainly white, with a pinkish tinge on the back and greenish black marks on the wings and a broken black band on the lower chest. The bare yellow face and yellow down-curved bill

Water & waterside birds

Background

Brahminy kite

Little cormorant

Hoopoe

Pariah kite in flight

Common myna

Pariah kite

are conspicuous. By almost every swamp, ditch or rice paddy up to about 1,200m you will see the **paddy bird** (*Ardeola grayii*, 45cm). An inconspicuous buff-coloured bird, it is easily overlooked as it stands hunched up by the waterside but as soon as it takes off, its white wings and rump make it very noticeable. Goa is also home to wonderful **kingfishers**. The most widespread of the Indian kingfishers is the jewel-like **common kingfisher** (*Alcedo atthis*, 18cm). With its brilliant blue upperparts and orange breast it is usually seen perched on a twig or a reed beside the water, or just a flash of eye-catching blue in flight. The much larger black and white **pied kingfisher** (*ceryle rudis*) is adept at fishing from the air and can sometimes be spotted hovering over water.

Open grassland & cultivated land birds The **cattle egret** (*Bubulcus ibis*, 50cm), a small white heron, is usually seen in small flocks, frequently perched on the backs of cattle. Birds in breeding plumage have buff plumes on the head and shoulders, and a yellow bill. The all black **drongo** (*Dicrurus adsimilis*, 30cm) is almost invariably seen perched on telegraph wires or bare branches. Its distinctively forked tail makes it easy to identify. Weaver birds are a family of mainly yellow birds, all remarkable for the intricate nests they build. The most widespread is the **baya weaver** (*Ploceus philippinus*, 15cm). These birds nest in large colonies, often near villages. The male in the breeding season can be distinguished by the combination of black face and throat and contrasting yellow top of the head and the yellow breast band. In the non-breeding season the male and the female are both brownish sparrow-like birds.

Painted stork

Openbill stork

Paddy bird

Cattle egret

Reptiles and amphibians

India is famous for its reptiles, especially its snakes which feature in many stories and legends, and despite its small size Goa has its share. The dense flora and heavy rainfall of the interior provide a perfect environment for snakes. Although about 200 people a year report being bitten in Goa, snakes generally keep out of the way of people.

One of the most common in the well watered areas of the hills is the **Indian rock python** (*Python molurus*). About 4m in length (and sometimes longer). Pythons are 'constrictors' which kill their prey by suffocation. The *Dhaman* or *Sodne Nagin*, or **Indian rat snake** (*Pytas musosus*) is often seen in houses. The bright yellow snake grows to nearly 3m and has an unpleasant smell. A common harmless snake in the forests of the foothills is the *Kalinagan*, **golden tree snake** (*Chrysopelea ornata*), can be almost black with greenish cross bars. Living on small mammals, geckos, birds and insects, it can swing and 'jump' up to 6m from tree to tree. There are several species of the poisonous cobra all of which have a hood, which is spread when the snake draws itself up to strike. The best known is probably the *Nag*, **spectacled cobra** (*Naja naja*), which has a mark like a pair of spectacles on the back of its hood. The largest venomous snake in the world is the *Raj Nag*, **king cobra** (*Ophiophagus hannah*) which grows to 5m in length. It is usually brown, but can vary from cream to black. In their natural state, cobras generally inhabit forests. Equally venomous, but much smaller in size, the *Kaner* or *Maniar*, the **common krait** (*Bungarus caeruleus*) grows to just over 1m. This is a slender shiny, nocturnal, blue-black snake with thin yellowish bands across the body. The bands vary from very conspicuous, to almost indiscernible. The smaller and harmless *Pasko*, kukri snake (*Oligodon taeniolatus*), common on farmland, is very similar as its markings resemble the krait's bands. Another common non-poisonous snake mistaken for a krait is the *Kaydya* or **common wolf snake** (*Lycodon aulicus*) which can be found near houses and in gardens. The grey-brown body has 12-19 darker cowrie-shaped markings which resemble the krait's cross bars.

Snakes

Background

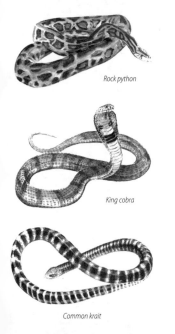

Rock python

King cobra

Common krait

Spectacled cobra

Lizards In houses everywhere you cannot fail to see the **gecko** (*Hemidactylus*) on the wall. There are several species of this small, totally harmless, primitive lizard which is active after dark getting rid of undesirable insects. One falling on your head is thought to bring luck! At the other end of the scale is the **monitor** (*Varanus*), which can be up to 2m in length. There are several species in India and they vary from a colourful black and yellow to plain or speckled brown. Sadly, they are being threatened with extinction in Goa as people are killing them to eat.

Crocodiles The most widespread crocodile in India is the **mugger** or **marsh crocodile** (*Crocodylus palustris*) which lives in fresh water and grows to 3-4m in length. The enormous **estuarine** or **saltwater crocodile** (*Crocodylus porosus*), as much as 7m long, is a much sleeker looking species than the mugger. It is found in brackish waters and unlike the rather docile mugger, has an aggressive temperament. Both are found in the wild in Goa, notably in the Cambarjua Canal which separates the island of Tiswadi from Ponda.

Turtles Although turtles are commonly found in ponds, ditches and wells, the **sea turtles** including the **olive ridley** (*Lepidochelys olivacea*) which visit certain Goan beaches (Morjim, Calangute and Cabo de Rama among them) between October and December for laying their eggs, are being severely affected. Few baby turtles return to the sea since the eggs are taken to end up as a culinary delicacy despite attempts by the Forest Department to prevent the nests being plundered by villagers (see page 127).

Gecko

Mugger (Marsh)

Estuarine or saltwater crocodile

Monitor

Vegetation

None of Goa's original vegetation remains untouched. The **mangrove** forests of the tidal marshes have been steadily eroded by the need to drain land for agriculture, while the estuarine waters have been increasingly polluted by mining activity. The most important mangroves are found today in the Mandovi-Zuari estuary, with minor forests remaining along the Chapora, Talpona, Galgibag and Tiracol estuaries.

Inland, the tropical rain forests which once covered both the Ghats and the lowland have been steadily reduced by clearance for farming and by cutting for timber. Two types of deciduous tree were once particularly common across peninsular India and even today they remain important. **Sal** (*Shorea robusta*), now found mainly in eastern India, and **teak** (*Tectona grandis*). Most teak has been planted. Both are resistant to burning, which helped to protect them where man used fire as a means of clearing the forest, common along the Western Ghat ranges from north to south.

The most striking vegetation contrasts are provided by the regular succession of laterite plateaus and riverine valleys. The valley sides are still densely covered in cultivated trees – the tall and usually gently curving coconut palms and the equally tall but slender and arrow-straight areca palms, interspersed by a dense and rich cover of valuable nut and fruit trees. The most widespread – and economically the most important – is the shiny-leaved cashew, introduced originally from South America, with its distinctive almost pear-shaped fruit and highly valued nut. These drought-tolerant trees sprawl across the thin soils of the laterite pavements and down into the richer more fertile soils of the valleys, giving Goa one of its most important sources of income.

Background

Trees

Cashew apple and nut

Tamarind flower and fruit

Goa's economy depends heavily on two crops, cashew and coconut, though other trees are also significant. The **cashew** tree (*Anacardium occidentale*) or *cazu* was introduced into India, but now grows wild as well as being cultivated. It is a medium sized tree with bright green, shiny, rounded leaves. The rather thick foliage casts a dense shadow. The nut grows on a fleshy bitter fruit called a cashew apple, although this looks more like a small squashed pear than an apple, and the nut hangs down below this. Both the fruit and nut are used in different ways and nothing is wasted (see box on 169). Despite its haphazard cultivation, it is Goa's most important economic crop and the nut is a good foreign exchange earner. The **coconut palm** (*Cocos nucifera*) grows best along the coast and river banks of Goa and is a familiar sight along the country roads of coastal districts. It has a tall (10-15m), slender, unbranched trunk, feathery leaves and large green or

Economically useful trees

The indispensable eco-friendly coconut

The coconut palm, so much a part of the coastal strip and the interior waterside scene, is a great gift of nature. Grown as the second most important crop, Goa is estimated to have over two and a half million trees producing on average 30 fruit each per year.

The green fruit yields an excellent refreshing 'milk' which is on tap whenever the top is cut off. The 'shell' is split open to expose the soft white kernel which is edible. The outer fibrous coir, just under the skin, is soaked in tanks before being woven into mats or twisted into rope. The dry, older nut with a white layer of 'flesh' or kernel (copra), which is grated or pounded for cooking curries and preparing sweets, is often seen being sold in market stalls. The Goans prize the sap which the toddy tapper collects from the base of a fresh leaf. The fresh sap can be drunk as a sweetish juice before it begins to ferment in the warmth, or it can be processed to produce vinegar or jaggery sugar. Most Goans, however, prefer it as the lightly alcoholic fermented urak or the intoxicating feni which is produced through distillation, a method learnt centuries ago from the Portuguese (see also 'Sap Tappers' on page 119).

Palm oil and cattle feed in the form of oil cakes are also products in demand. But, the trees' uses don't stop here since throughout the year the leaves are used for weaving baskets and providing thatch for shelter. Then, when the tree dies, its trunk comes in handy for cutting up for use in building.

It is not surprising therefore that every Goan family living anywhere near water will tend a coconut or two.

orange fruit (so different from the brown fibre-covered inner nut which makes its way to Europe). The **areca palm** (*Areca catechu*), also known as betel nut, which grows abundantly in the Ponda taluka in particular, is about the same height as the coconut palm, but prefers shade and needs more attention in the dry months. The leaves are similar, and fall cleanly off the trunk leaving decorative ring marks. Betel (areca) nuts, which grow in large hanging bunches, are smooth, round and only about 3cm across. The economically valuable **tamarind** (*Tamarindus indica*), which may have originated in Africa, is another handsome roadside tree with a straight trunk and a spreading crown. It is an evergreen with feathery leaves and small yellow and red flowers which grow in clusters. The valuable fruit pods are long and curved and swollen at intervals down their length. **Bamboo** (*Bambusa*) which is, strictly speaking, a grass is also an export crop. The larger varieties have stems strong and thick enough to be used for construction and as pipes in irrigation schemes in small holdings. Goa has a unique thornless type. The **silk cotton tree** (*Bombax ceiba*), also known as the kapok, can grow to 25m in height. The bark is light coloured, often grey and often has conical spines. In big trees there are noticeable buttresses at the bottom of the trunk. Its wide, almost horizontal branches, though deciduous, keep their leaves for most of the year. The dramatic

Coconut palm

Half a coconut

Papaya

flowers, which appear when the tree is leafless, are cup-shaped, with fleshy red petals up to 12cm long. It is the fruit which produces the fine silky cotton which gives it its name.

The **banana** plant (*Musa*) is actually a gigantic herb arising from an underground stem. The very large leaves grow directly off the trunk which is about 5m in height. The fruit grows in bunches of up to 100 fruit. **Bread fruit** trees are common, with large almost spiky leaves and fruit rather like giant knobbly acorns. The fruit (really a nut) is boiled and used in savoury dishes. The **jackfruit** (*Artocarpus heterophyllus*) is one of India's most remarkable fruit trees. A large evergreen with dark green leathery leaves, its huge fruit can be as much as 1m long and 40 cm thick. It grows from a short stem directly off the trunk and branches. The skin is thick and rough, almost prickly. The fruit of the main eating variety itself is quite sickly sweet. Each fruit has dozens of segments, each with a nut about the size of a brazil nut at its centre which are often roasted. The **kokum** (*bhirand*) is used in curries and is made into a syrup for making a refreshing cool drink in the summer. The peel is prepared into a magic cure (*sol coddi*) for hangovers! The **mango** (*Mangifera indica*) is widespread. It is a fairly large tree being 6-15m high, with spreading branches forming a rounded canopy. The distinctively shaped fruit is quite delicious and unlike any other in taste. A favourite variety is the Alphonso from Goa and Maharashtra. The **papaya** (*Carica papaya*) which often grows to only 4m has distinctive palm-like leaves. Only the female tree bears the shapely fruit, which hang down close to the trunk just below the leaves.

Fruit trees

Of all Indian trees the **banyan** (*Ficus benghalensis*) is probably the best known. Featured widely in Indian literature, it is planted by temples, in villages and along roads. In a wall, the growing roots will split the wall apart. If it grows in the bark of another tree, it sends down roots towards the ground. As it grows, more roots appear from the branches, until the original host tree is surrounded by a cage-like structure which eventually strangles it. The largest banyan in Goa is in a *math* (seminary) near the Cotigao Sanctuary. Related to the banyan, and growing in similar situations, is the **pipal** (*Ficus religiosa*), which also cracks open walls and strangles other trees with its roots. It has a smooth grey bark, and is commonly found near temples and shrines. It can easily be distinguished from the banyan by the absence of aerial roots, and by the leaves which are large, rather leathery and heart shaped, the point of the leaf tapering into a pronounced 'tail'. The **casuarina** (*Casuarina*) is a slender, rather wispy looking tree which grows in poor sandy soil, widely seen on Goa's coast and village waste land. It has the typical leaves of a pine tree and the cones are small and prickly to walk on. Despite their normally modest size, they are said to attract lightning during a thunder storm. The **ashok** or **mast** (*Polyalthia longifolia*) is a tall evergreen which can reach 15m or more in height. One variety, often seen in avenues, is trimmed and tapers towards the top. The leaves are long, slender and shiny and narrow to a long point.

Other trees

Background

Crops

Goa's main crops are typical of India's whole coastal belt. The single most important crop is **rice** (commonly *Orysa indica*). Soon after planting in the early monsoon the fields turn a beautiful light green as the young paddy shoots from the flooded fields. It takes between three and five months to mature, and some areas with irrigation manage to get two crops a year, so you can sometimes see rice ready for harvesting in November alongside newly planted seedlings. The tending of rice is very labour intensive, planting or harvesting often being done by hand. **Sugar cane** (*Saccharum*), a commercially important crop in some areas, looks like a large grass which grows up to 3m. The sweet juice is sometimes extracted for selling along the roadside. It produces crude brown sugar which is sold as jaggery. **Pineapples** (*Ananas comosus*) are often grown under trees, especially under coconut palms on the coast. The fruit grows out of the middle of a rosette of long, spiky leaves. Of the many **spices** grown in India, the two climbers **pepper** and vanilla and the grass-like **cardamom** are the ones most often seen. **Vanilla** (*Vanilla planifolium*), which belongs to the orchid family, also grows up trees for support and attaches itself to the bark by small roots. It is native to South America, but grows well in Goa as in other Indian regions which have high rainfall. It is a rather fleshy looking plant, with white flowers and the long slender pods can be seen hanging down.

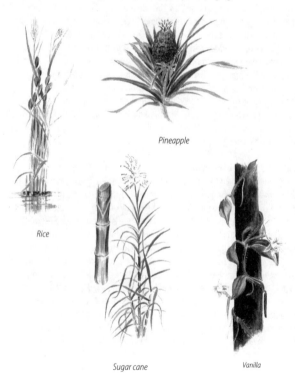

Pineapple

Rice

Sugar cane

Vanilla

Architecture

All Goan architecture is in some sense atypical. Even church architecture is not a simple transplant from Europe, though the influence of the Baroque on many of Goa's most famous churches is obvious. In their turn, Hindu and Muslim architecture in Goa are strongly influenced by the mixture of cultural traditions from which they grew. Yet the distinctiveness of both Christian and Hindu traditions remains clear, and the fundamental features of their design can be traced back to their wholly different roots.

Goan Christian architecture

Almost nothing remains of the first great development of Portuguese church building during the reign of the Portuguese King Manuel I (r1495-1521). The doorway to the church of St Francis of Assisi in Old Goa, and the Church of Our Lady of the Rosary, the oldest church standing in Goa (1543) illustrate the incorporation of Indian features in its predominantly European model.

Both the influence of the Italian late Renaissance as well as the early Baroque influence are evident. The Church of Il Gesu in Rome (completed in 1584, and where an arm of St Francis Xavier is still preserved and venerated) was a particularly important model. As Anthony Hutt points out it was designed by Vignola, the author of *The Five Orders of Architecture*, a work which has a profound influence on subsequent church building. Scrolls were used to link the high nave with the lower side aisles, as on a huge scale in the Se Cathedral. Towers flanking the west entrance were retained in Goan architecture, as in Portugal, long after they had been abandoned elsewhere. Interestingly, the destruction of the northern tower of the Se Cathedral by lightning returned the cathedral closer to what may have been its original Islamic model from the Iberian peninsula, the tower being modelled on the Islamic minaret.

The ornately gilded reredos, though usually on a much reduced scale, is typical of many of the Goan churches. Roman influence is clearly visible in one of the other great churches of Old Goa, the 17th-century Convent Church of St Cajetan taking St Peter's Rome as its model. Despite the reduced scale, recent restoration has highlighted the intrinsic quality of the building. Both its Michaelangelo-inspired façade and its interior, based on the form of a Greek cross with a central cupola, are strikingly effective. The evident importance of barrel vaulting, itself a reflection of the Roman arch dating back to the period of the Roman Empire, gives St Cajetan's a unique feel.

In the second half of the 18th century Rococo features began to be expressed in a new bout of church

Wayside cross

Margao

building. Indian architects played a significant part in decoration, especially of the reredos and the pulpit. In *Golden Goa*, Dr José Periera lists five Goan churches as masterpieces of the Indian Baroque – the *Holy Spirit* (Old Goa) being the most sublime; *Holy Spirit* (Margao) the most magestic; the *Santana* (Talaulim) the most perfect; *St Stephens* (Santo Estevam, Jua Island) the most ornate, and the *Piedade* (Divar) as the most luminous.

Domestic architecture

In the early 18th century Goa benefited directly from the huge wealth Portugal gained from Brazil, and while the court prospered as a result so individual noble families became wealthy through trading links with other Portuguese possessions in Africa and in Macau. Landed Goan families began to build houses to express their status and wealth.

They borrowed some of the fundamental features from the coastal architecture of the Konkan, well adapted to the monsoon climate's demands for protection from torrential rainfall and powerful sun. The sloping roofs of red Mangalore tiles (augmented at times with disastrous aesthetic effects by modern corrugated iron) kept off the rain. Large reception rooms offered space and air for receiving guests, and the biggest houses had a private chapel (or *Oratory*) with carved wooden altar, gilded decoration, and painted ivory statues where Mass could be celebrated. Curved windows, sometimes filled not with glass but with translucent oyster shell (*nacre*) gave a "warm, filtered light" while also securing privacy. Central courtyards, another feature of Indian domestic architectural design, also gave families private space, although some of the new grand houses also had outward looking windows, in sharp contrast to the entirely inward looking courtyard houses of traditional Goan society. Verandas and balconies allowed families to enjoy cool shaded space. In many houses the entertaining rooms were all on the first floor, allowing any breezes to bring some freshness.

Unlike the great proliferation of highly ornate church building which in Portugal was funded largely by a flow of wealth from Brazil, Goa's élite (which was almost entirely Indian rather than Portuguese) prospered on locally created wealth, and built their new houses to reflect that increasing prosperity. They also took advantage of Portuguese trade with the east to provide Chinese ceramics for domestic use and eastern designs for wooden furniture, much of which was ultimately made in Goa by Indian craftsmen. Yet despite all the innovations Goan domestic architecture, even on the grandest scale, never entirely severed its links with earlier Hindu forms. One example was the universal practice of building private chapels, which as Hall points out can be seen as an extension of the Hindu tradition of every house having a shrine dedicated to the domestic deity. Outside the Old Conquests, domestic architecture retained even stronger links with Hindu traditional architecture of the coastal region and both to the north and south of Goa the housing in the border regions is almost indistinguishable from that of the neighbouring states of Maharashtra and Karnataka respectively.

Hindu temple building

The principles of religious building were laid down in the *Shastras*, sets of rules compiled by priests. Every aspect of Hindu, Jain and Buddhist religious building is identified with conceptions of the structure of the universe. This applies as much to the process of building – the timing of which must be undertaken at astrologically propitious times – as to the formal layout of the buildings. The cardinal directions of north, south, east and west are the basic fix on which buildings are planned. The east-west axis is nearly always a fundamental building axis. George Michell suggests that in addition to the cardinal directions, number is also critical to the design of the religious building. The key to the ultimate scale of the building is derived from the measurements of the sanctuary at its heart. Indian temples were nearly always built to a clear and universal design, which had built into it philosophical understandings of the universe.

Cosmology

This cosmology, of an infinite number of universes, isolated from each other in space, proceeds by imagining various possibilities as to its nature. Its centre is seen as dominated by **Mount Meru** which keeps earth and heaven apart. The concept of *separation* is crucial to Hindu thought and social practice. Continents, rivers and oceans occupy concentric rings around the mountain, while the stars encircle the mountain in another plane. Humans live on the continent of **Jambudvipa**, characterized by the rose apple tree (*jambu*). The *shastras* show plans of this continent, organized in concentric rings and entered at the cardinal points. This type of diagram was known as a mandala. Such a geometric scheme could be subdivided into almost limitless small compartments, each of which could be designated as having special properties or be devoted to a particular deity. The centre of the mandala would be the seat of the major god. *Mandalas* provided the ground rules for the building of stupas and temples across India, and gave the key to the symbolic meaning attached to every aspect of religious buildings.

Temple design

Hindu temples developed characteristic plans and elevations. The focal point of the temple lay in its sanctuary, the home of the presiding deity, known as the womb-chamber (*garbagriha*). A series of doorways, in large temples leading through a succession of buildings, allowed the worshipper to move towards the final encounter with the deity himself and to obtain *darshan* – a sight of the god. Both Buddhist and Hindu worship encourage the worshipper to walk clockwise around the shrine, performing *pradakshina*. In contrast to the extraordinary profusion of colour and life on the outside, in most Hindu temples the interior is dark and cramped but here it is believed, lies the true centre of divine power.

Temple development in Goa

While some of the key principles underlying Hindu temple architecture remain the same in Goan temples the differences are striking, and the outward forms are wholly distinctive and unique. Both in design and in decoration many Goan temples, most of which are 18th century or later, have borrowed liberally from both Muslim and Christian architecture. The transformation was initiated by the Maratha leader Sivaji, who rebelled against the Muslim political dominance of Maharashtra and

Mandala

encouraged the development of a new temple style. The changes he introduced were subsequently developed into the Goan style. It took advantage of some features of Muslim architecture with which Sivaji was familiar in towns like Bijapur, including minarets, cusped arches and domes, or the beautifully curved *bangla* roofs loved by the Mughals. The Marathas also introduced long open pavilions in front of the temple, supported by columns, and what has become one of Goan temples' most distinctive features, the tall and often octagonal lamp towers or *deepmal* or *deepstambha*. Hutt writes that the "concept of the pillar with lamps on it as an offering to the deity is one of extreme antiquity, but seems to have been particularly developed at this period by the Marathas." These large pagoda-like structures are peculiar to Goa and some suggest the influence of Western church ideas concerning the place of worship.

Goan architects also added a drum tower, a 'room' with a pyramidal tiled roof *nagarkhana* (or *naubatkhana*) where temple musicians would sit above the entrance gateway. Another distinctive feature was the prominent *tulsi vrindavana*(basil enclosure), which was similar in principle to the humbler container which is an integral part of Goan Hindu domestic architecture. The *tulsi*, which is believed to have many mystical properties, is widely associated with Krishna and Lakshmi. The 'enclosure' next to a temple would sometimes assume monumental proportions, and adopt features imitating the more commonly seen piazza crosses in front of churches.

In place of the pyramidal or curving towers that signal the *garbagriha* (main shrine) in most Hindu temples, Goan temples are uniquely surmounted by the kind of dome unknown in the pre-Muslim period. However, Gomes Pereira suggests that

Hindu temple

Elevation

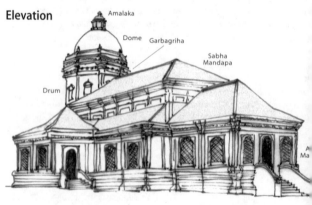

Plan

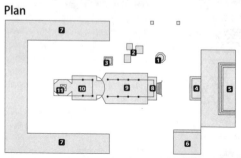

1 Deepmal (lamp tow...
2 Subsidiary shrines
3 Tulsi Vrindavana (basil enclosure)
4 Nagarkhana (drum t...
5 Temple tank
6 Ratha (temple car) s...
7 Agrashala (pilgrim rest rooms) & administrative offi...
8 Porch
9 Sabha Mandapa (ha...
10 Ardha Mandapa
11 Garbagriha (sanctu...

Goan architects went still further by introducing fundamentally European concepts into their temples. Classical styles, taking as their models churches in Old Goa like the Se Cathedral and Our Lady of Divine Providence gave both classical scales and the specific feature of the dome. The typical Goan temple comprised a regular series of features. The entrance porch would have an arch, sometimes surmounted by a dome. Inside, the pillared hall (*mandapa*), which could be regarded as similar to the nave of a church, was topped by a steep-pitched tiled roof, while the sanctuary itself was crowned by a dome which would sometimes sit over a European drum and be topped by a lantern.

Goan temples have other features distinguishing them from conventional Hindu temples. The interior is usually relatively open and light, even airy, in contrast to the dark stillness which pervades the sanctum of most temples in the rest of India. Decoration and embellishments in some of the temples are also of alien origin, imported glass chandeliers and tiles being particularly favoured.

The full distinctiveness of Goa's Hindu temples can only be appreciated in their context. Often set in the heart of lush valleys surrounded by dense greenery, instead of proclaiming themselves like the great hill top temples of peninsular India, Goa's temples are often completely hidden from view until the last moment. The temple tank provides not only the means of ritual cleansing but a beautifully cooling stretch of fresh water, usually close to the temple entrance. The pilgrim or worshipper is thus presented with an element of surprise up to the moment of entry, where at festivals the welcoming lamps flicker in the lamp tower and across the compound.

Muslim religious architecture

Although the Muslims adapted many Hindu features, they also brought totally new forms. Their most outstanding contribution, dominating the architecture of many north Indian cities, are the mosques and tomb complexes (*dargah*). The use of brickwork was widespread, and they brought with them from Persia the principle of constructing the true arch. Muslim architects succeeded in producing a variety of domed structures, often incorporating distinctively Hindu features such as the surmounting finial. By the end of the great period of Muslim building in North India in 1707, the Muslims had added magnificent forts and palaces to their religious structures. Both were testaments to imperial splendour, a statement of power as well as of aesthetic taste. Although Goa's Hindu temples reflected Muslim influence, true Islamic building can only be seen by travelling over the Ghats into Karnataka. Belgaum's fort and mosques are the nearest examples of the true Muslim peninsular styles.

Background

Culture

People

Despite over four centuries of Portuguese dominance, earlier characteristics of Goa's population are still obvious. While during the Inquisition the Portuguese made systematic efforts to wipe out all social traces of the earlier Hindu and Muslim cultures, many of their features were simply modified to conform to external Catholic demands. Thus even in the Old Conquest areas the predominantly Catholic community is still divided along much earlier caste lines.

The four major varna groups of Hindus, the Brahmins or priestly caste, Kshatriyas (warriors), Vaishyas (merchants) and Sudras (agriculturalists) retained their designations in only slightly modified form. Thus according to the People of India project of India's Anthropological Survey, the different sub-castes of the Brahmin community in Goa merged into the single Catholic Saraswat group, the Vaishya sub-castes merged into one, the Charddo Catholic community, and the remainder became Catholic Sudras. There was a small community of Catholic Mestiços, most having left Goa for Portugal after Liberation. Today the two highest Catholic castes, the Brahmin and Charddo Catholics, have become a single group, inter-marrying and generally occupying high positions in society. Catholic Sudras, who include the Christian fishing communities, remain separate.

The Catholics are sub-divided into a number of occupational groups. In Salcete, Ponda and Quepem, for example the Carpenter group (Thovoi) is common, and many continue to depend on making small items of furniture or decorative images for Church buildings. Along the coast the Catholic Kharvi, or fishermen, claim to be Goa's original inhabitants. While their surnames – Rodrigues, Costa, Souza, Dias, Pereira – have all been adopted from the Portuguese they are direct descendants of the Hindu fishing communities of the coast.

Unlike the Christian communities, the Hindu castes are still sub-divided along their original occupational lines. Thus the Brahmin community includes the Chitpavan Brahmins, present throughout Goa, originally as priests. Most claim Marathi as their mother tongue although many also speak Konkani, and they are strictly vegetarian. The Daivadnya Brahmins in contrast are largely goldsmiths, taking the name Shett. Unlike the Chitpavan Brahmins they are not vegetarian, eating fish, mutton and chicken but abstaining from beef, pork and buffalo. They have strong cultural links with Maharashtra.

One of the most remarkable communities among the Hindus is that known today as the **Gomantak Maratha Samaj**. The group belongs to the former *devdasis*, dancing women and prostitutes who had been dedicated to temples and the service of their deities. Ancient Hindu scriptures (the *Puranas*) had suggested that the most beautiful girls should be dedicated to temple service, and that they should be considered of high social status. In the social uplift movement of the 1940s and 1950s which sought to improve conditions for the devdasi community a number of different groups came together in the Gomantak Maratha Samaj. Among them were the *devlis*, who had been responsible for lighting the temple lamps or working as temple attendants, and the *Chedvaan*, *Bandi* and *Farjand* groups, who had been dependent on landlords.

Before independence all large temples had a priest (*pujari*), lamplighters (*jyotkar*), musicians and people who recited religious songs (*kirtankars*), and groups of temple girl dancers (*bhavins*). It was the children of this last group who formed the distinct *devli* community, remaining under the control of the trustees (*mahajans*) of the temple. Other members of this community include the *kalavants*, who claimed descent from the mythical *apsaras* or divine dancers and singers, and *bandes* (meaning literally 'bound up') who were tied to landlords as maids and concubines.

There are also the tribal groups such as the *Gavdes* and *Kunbis*. Gavdes were originally nomadic hunters and fishermen who worshipped natural elements, while the Kunbis usually worked on the land and herded animals on the hillsides and lived in villages with mud and thatch huts. Some continue to wear traditional tribal dress. Kunbi women can be identified by row upon row of bead necklaces and copper bangles covering their arms from wrist to elbow and their long well-oiled hair coiled up into a distinctive shape.

Language

Indian languages come in a seemingly baffling variety, many with their own scripts. Goa is located precisely on the dividing line which separates the Indo-European languages of North India from the Dravidian languages of the south.

The roots of nearly all the North Indian languages can be traced back to **Sanskrit** which originated with the Indo-Aryan pastoralists from Central Asia who moved into India from 2000 BC onwards. By sixth century BC Sanskrit had become the dominant language of North India. The Muslims brought Persian into South Asia as the language of the rulers, and like Sanskrit before it, and English from the 18th century onwards, Persian became the language of the numerically tiny but politically powerful élite across the sub-continent.

Out of the interaction between the Persian of the court and the native Sanskrit-based language developed Hindustani, separately identified as Hindi and Urdu. In the centuries which followed the major regional languages of North India developed, including **Marathi**, the language of Maharashtra, itself a sister language of **Konkani** spoken in Goa.

In sharp contrast, the dominant language of Karnataka, the state which borders Goa to the east and south, is **Kannada**, one of the four Dravidian languages (the others being Tamil in Tamil Nadu, Malayalam in Kerala and Telugu in Andhra Pradesh). Each has its own script. All the Dravidian languages were influenced by the prevalence of Sanskrit as the language of the ruling and educated élite, although Tamil, which has a literature going back over 2,000 years, was least affected. Kannada was clearly established by AD 1000.

Portuguese was widely spoken until 1961 and even today many of the older generation can speak it, but Marathi and Konkani remained important.

Konkani was introduced as the language of instruction in Church primary schools in 1991 and was added to the list of recognized languages in the Indian Constitution in August 1992. Nonetheless, very few government primary schools teach in Konkani compared with over 800 that use Marathi, but the issue is still contentious. Hindi is increasingly spoken with the influx of non-Goan employees in hotel resorts. English and Hindi are widely used on road signs, bus destinations and tourism-related notices. In rural areas, however, Konkani predominates.

It is impossible to spend even a short time in India without coming across several of the different scripts that are used. The earliest ancestor of scripts in use today was Brahmi, in which Asoka's famous inscriptions were written in the third century BC. Written from left to right, a separate symbol represented each different sound. For

Scripts

about a thousand years the major script of northern India has been the Nagari or Devanagari, which means literally the script of 'the city of the gods'. Hindi and Marathi join Sanskrit in their use of Devanagari. In Goa, you are likely to come across widespread use of Hindi, and the Roman script for English. Although **Konkani** is written both in **Roman** and **Devanagari** scripts, it is the latter which has now become the official script for the language.

Numerals Many of the Indian alphabets have their own notation for numerals. This is not without irony, for what in the western world are called 'Arabic' numerals are in fact of Indian origin. In some parts of the sub-continent, local numerical symbols are still in use, but by and large you will find that the Arabic number symbols, familiar in Europe and the West, are common and in general use in Goa.

Music and dance

Goans are noted at home and abroad for their love of music. Although Indian classical music is performed and Goa has a rich heritage of folk music and dance, Goan popular music reflects modern western popular influences.

Indian music can trace its origins to the metrical hymns and chants of the *Vedas*, in which the production of sound according to strict rules was understood to be vital to the continuing order of the Universe. Over more than 3,000 years of development, through a range of regional schools, India's musical tradition has been handed on almost entirely by ear. The chants of the **Rig Veda** developed into songs in the **Sama Veda** and music found expression in every sphere of life, closely reflecting the cycle of seasons and the rhythm of work.

Over the centuries the original three notes, which were sung strictly in descending order, were extended to five and then seven and developed to allow freedom to move up and down the scale. The scale increased to 12 with the addition of flats and sharps and finally to 22 with the further subdivision of semitones. Books of musical rules go back at least as far as the third century AD. Classical music was totally intertwined with dance and drama.

At some point after the Muslim influence made itself felt in the north, North and South Indian styles diverged, to become Carnatic (Karnatak) music in the South and Hindustani music in the north. However, they still share important common features: *svara* (pitch), *raga* (the melodic structure), and *tala* or *talam* (metre).

Hindustani music Hindustani music probably originated in the Delhi Sultanate during the 13th century, when the most widely known of North Indian musical instruments, the *sitar*, was believed to have been invented as well as the small drums, the *tabla*. The other important northern instruments are the *stringed sarod*, the reed instrument *shahnai* and the *wooden flute*. Most Hindustani compositions have devotional texts, though they encompass a great emotional and thematic range.

The essential structure of a melody is known as a *raga* which usually has five to seven notes, and can have as many as nine or even twelve. The music is improvised by the performer within certain governing rules and theoretically thousands of ragas are possible though only about a hundred are performed. Ragas have become associated with particular moods and specific times of the day.

Veena

Western influences

The party scene, to some synonymous with Goa, drew hundreds of westerners to beach venues near Anjuna and further north from the 1960s. Psychedelic lights, thunderous beats, spectacular fire juggling were all part of all night raves. Initially this was welcomed by many villagers who cashed in on an alien "cultural" graft by providing essential services to a fun seeking crowd. Party organisers, DJs, beach shack café and bar owners and anyone with cheap rooms to let benefited. Goa Trance music captured the western pop culture imagination and young people flocked to Goa's beaches to dance their nights, and sleep their days, away. The local chai ladies set up their stalls and earned a few rupees while some policemen exploited their power and made a handsome packet on the side. A few scapegoats were sent to prison for years for flouting Indian law which imposes severe penalties for the possession of drugs.

Impromptu parties, advertised on the grapevine, have become more restricted to the Christmas/New Year period. The music has become louder and more intrusive, enough to cause increasingly strong local protest. This has put pressure on the government to take steps to allow only venues away from built-up areas, to put a ceiling on the decibel levels and to curtail the hours of night revelling. More recently, the scene had shifted from Goa and was to be found more readily in Gokarna and Hampi in neighbouring Karnataka, but there too, public opinion is making an impact.

Contemporary South Indian music is traced back to Tyagaraja, Svami Shastri and Dikshitar, three musicians who lived and worked in the 18-19th centuries. They placed more emphasis on extended compositions than Hindustani music. Perhaps the best known South Indian instrument is the stringed *veena*, the flute being commonly used for accompaniment along with the violin (played rather differently to the European original), an oboe-like instrument called the *nagasvaram* and the drums, *tavil*.

Carnatic (Karnatak) music

India is rich with folk dance traditions. The rules for classical dance were laid down in the **Natya shastra** in the second century BC. It is still one of the bases for modern dance forms, although there are many regional variations. The most common sources for Indian dance are the epics, but there are three essential aspects of the dance itself, *Nritta* (pure dance), *Nrittya* (emotional expression) and *Natya* (drama). Like the music with which it is so closely intertwined, dance has expressed religious belief and deep emotion. Goa has its own folk dance traditions.

Dance

The religious influence in dance was exemplified by the tradition of temple dancers, *devadasis*, girls and women who were dedicated to the deity in major temples to perform before them. In South and East India there were thousands of *devadasis* associated with temple worship, though the practice fell into widespread disrepute, being associated with prostitution, and was banned in independent India. In Goa, in addition to girls and women who became *devadasis*, widows who escaped *sati* often sought refuge in temples and joined that group and subsequently became temple prostitutes. The practice of singing and dancing in the temples was expected in conjunction with serving influential and high caste members of the Hindu community sometimes as mistresses. The Portuguese codified the laws and customs relating to *devadasis* (both male and female) in the early 19th century.

Cinema

The hugely popular Hindi film industry comes mainly out of this tradition of larger-than-life productions with familiar story lines performed as escapist entertainment for the community. The stars lead fantasy lives as they enjoy cult status with a following of millions. It is not surprising that should they choose to turn their hand to politics, they find instant support in an unquestioning, adoring electorate. The experience of a Bollywood film is not to be missed - at least once in your life. Television has made a visit to a cinema redundant though it's always easy to find one in any sizeable town; the gaudy posters dominate every street scene. Be prepared for a long sitting with a standard story line, set characters and lots of action as the typical multi-million rupee blockbusters attempt to provide something to please everybody. Marathon melodramas consist of slapstick comedy contrasted with tear-jerking tragedy, a liberal sprinkling of moralizing with a tortuous disentangling of the knots tied by the heroes, heroines, villains and their extended families. The usual ingredients are the same: shrill Hindi "film music", unoriginal songs mouthed to the voice of playback artistes, hip-jerking dancing by suggestively clad figures which lack all subtlety when it comes to sexual innuendo, honeymooning couples before a backdrop of snowy mountains, car chases and violent disasters - these will keep you enthralled for hours. On a serious note, there are ample examples of truly brilliant works by world-class Indian film makers (Satyajit Ray, Rithwik Ghatak, Shyam Benegal, Aparna Roy to name a few) but they are not usually box office successes or made for popular consumption so they have to be sought out.

Religion

The visitor's first impression of the religion of Goa's peoples is likely to be highly misleading. Most books about Goa give prominence to the Portuguese Christian legacy. To all appearances the drive from the airport to Panaji or south to any of the coastal resorts might appear to confirm that the state is predominantly Christian. Stunningly bright white painted churches dominate the centre of nearly every village, most with the heritage of the Portuguese influence stamped on every feature. Some are modern, suggesting the continuing life of the overwhelmingly Roman Catholic Christian community. Yet while in the area of the Old Conquests, including Bardez in the north, Mormugao and Tiswadi, and southwards into Salcete, where tens of thousands of people were indeed converted to Christianity, the Zuari River represents a great divide between Christian and predominantly Hindu Goa. Today about 70 percent of the state's population is Hindu, and there is also a small but significant Muslim minority. Other minority groups are also found, notably Sikhs and Jains, though in far smaller numbers than elsewhere in India.

The misleading first impressions are easily reinforced by the lack of obviously recognizable Hindu buildings on the main tourist routes. Only when you get to Ponda or into the rural areas of the interior do you find significant Hindu temples, and these are mainly the product of the 18th and 19th centuries. Indeed, their curious blend of Muslim, Christian and Hindu features testifies to the distinctive influences on Hinduism in Goa over the last four centuries. For while nowhere in India is it possible to define a 'pure' Hinduism, either in terms of belief or practice, in Goa the interaction between the communities has blended features of each of the major religions. Thus it is no accident, that the only Hindu temple with a design rooted in the traditions of the peninsula, is that of Tambdi Surla. Deep in the forest and close to the border of Karnataka, and almost as far as it is possible to be from the Christianizing influences of the West or the Muslim routes into Goa of military and political control. It survived as it were by default.

But if there is only limited structural evidence of Hinduism's influence, the daily life of many Goan communities reflects the strong mutual respect for each other's traditions which is common. Village festivals are often shared, deities or saints are venerated by both communities, and mutual respect for each other's religious beliefs is shown at all levels of Goan society. This is not to say that there are no tensions between the communities, but many Goans will say that these have been created artificially by outsiders. Yet if the people of Goa show hybrid versions of each of the major religions, the roots of each are nonetheless clearly discernible, and it is necessary therefore to appreciate the fundamental characteristics of each in its Goan context.

Hinduism

While some aspects of modern Hinduism can be traced back more than 2,000 years before the birth of Christ, other features are recent. As early as the sixth century BC the Buddhists and Jains had tried to reform the religion of Vedism (or Brahmanism) which had been dominant in some parts of South Asia for 500 years. Great philosophers such as Sankaracharya (seventh and early eighth centuries AD) and Ramanuja (12th century AD) then transformed major aspects of previous Hindu thought.

Background

Key ideas A number of ideas run like a thread through intellectual and popular Hinduism. One recurring theme is 'vision', 'sight' or 'view'.

Darshan is used to describe the sight of the deity that worshippers hope to gain when they visit a temple or shrine. Equally it may apply to the religious insight gained through meditation or prayer.

The four human goals Many Hindus also accept that there are four major human goals; material prosperity (artha), the satisfaction of desires (kama), and performing the duties laid down according to your position in life (dharma). Beyond those is the goal of achieving liberation from the endless cycle of rebirths into which everyone is locked (moksha). It is the search for liberation that major schools of Indian philosophy have devoted most attention. Together with dharma, it is basic to Hindu thought. Dharma, an essentially secular concept, represents the order inherent in human life. The Mahabharata lists 10 embodiments of dharma, including truth, self-control, endurance, and continence. These are inseparable from five patterns of behaviour: non-violence, an attitude of equality, peace and tranquillity, lack of aggression and cruelty, and absence of envy.

Karma The idea of karma – 'the effect of former actions' – is central to achieving liberation. As C Rajagopalachari put it: "Every act has its appointed effect, whether the act be thought, word or deed. The cause holds the effect, so to say, in its womb. If we reflect deeply and objectively, the entire world will be found to obey unalterable laws. That is the doctrine of karma".

Rebirth The belief in the transmigration of souls (samsara) in a never-ending cycle of rebirth has been Hinduism's most distinctive and important contribution to Indian culture. The earliest reference to the belief is found in one of the Upanishads, around the seventh century BC, at about the same time as the doctrine of karma made its first appearance.

Ahimsa Belief in transmigration probably encouraged a further distinctive doctrine, that of non-violence or non-injury – ahimsa. The belief in rebirth meant that all living things and creatures of the spirit – people, devils, gods, animals, even worms – possessed the same essential soul.

Worship

The abstractions of philosophy do not mean much for the millions of Hindus living across South Asia today, nor have they in the past. The Hindu gods include many whose origins were associated with the forces of nature, and Hindus have revered many natural objects. Mountain tops, trees, rocks and above all rivers, are regarded as sites of special religious significance.

In Goa veneration of the tulsi (basil) plant is illustrated by the profusion of tulsi enclosures in front of houses and in temples. Stutley and Stutley recount how in one myth, when Krishna was chasing a nymph she changed herself into a tulsi plant, perhaps contributing to the widely held belief in its wide-ranging powers. Its religious virtues are summed up in the expression: "In its roots are contained all places of pilgrimage; its centre contains all the deities, and its upper branches all the Vedas." In addition to warding off mosquitoes and being an air purifier the tulsi is effective in warding off death, even being an antidote to snake venom. With all these desirable attributes it is not surprising that the herb should play such an important role in Hindu rituals from birth to death.

For most Hindus today worship (often referred to as 'performing **puja**') is an integral part of their faith. The great majority of Hindu homes will have a shrine to one of the deities. Individuals and families will often visit shrines or temples, and on special occasions will travel long distances to particularly holy places such as Varanasi. Goa's temples similarly are centres of periodic pilgrimage and of special festivals.

The popular devotion of simple pilgrims of all faiths in South Asia is remarkably similar when they visit shrines, whether Hindu, Buddhist or Jain temples, the tombs of Muslim saints or even churches such as Bom Jesus in Old Goa, where St Francis Xavier lies entombed. Perhaps Goa's most famous shrine at which both Christians and Hindus worship is the Church of St Jerome in Mapusa, better known as the Milagres Church, Our Lady of Miracles.

The Hindu Trinity

Popularly *Brahma* is interpreted as the creator in a trinity alongside *Vishnu* as preserver and *Siva* as destroyer.

In the literal sense the name Brahma is the masculine and personalized form of the neuter word Brahman. In the early *Vedas* Brahman represented the universal and impersonal principle which governed the Universe. Gradually, as Vedic philosophy moved towards a monotheistic interpretation of the universe and its origins, this impersonal power was increasingly personalized. In the *Upanishads* Brahman was seen as a universal and elemental creative spirit. Brahma, described in early myths as having been born from a golden egg and then to have created the Earth, assumed the identity of the earlier Vedic deity Prajapati and became identified as the creator.

Brahma

It is from Brahma that Hindu cosmology takes its structure. The basic cycle through which the whole cosmos passes is described as one day in the life of Brahma – the *kalpa*. It equals 4,320 million years, with an equally long night. One year of Brahma's life – a cosmic year – lasts 360 days and nights. The universe is expected to last for 100 years of Brahma's life, who is currently believed to be 51 years old.

By the sixth century AD Brahma worship had effectively ceased – before the great period of temple building, which accounts for the fact that there are remarkably few temples dedicated to Brahma, the most famous one being at Pushkar in Rajasthan. Goa is thus highly unusual in also having a Brahma temple at Carambolim. Nonetheless images of Brahma are found in most temples. Characteristically he is shown with four faces (each facing a cardinal direction).

Sarasvati, Brahma's consort, has survived into the modern Hindu world as a far more important figure than Brahma himself. In popular worship Sarasvati represents the goddess of education and learning, worshipped in schools and colleges with gifts of fruit, flowers and incense. She represents 'the word' itself, which began to be edified as part of the process of the writing of the *Vedas*, which ascribed magical power to words. Normally white coloured, riding on a swan and carrying a book, Sarasvati is often shown playing a *vina*. She may have many arms and heads, representing her role as patron of all the sciences and arts.

Vishnu is seen as the God with the human face, sometimes presented as the god of creation or preservation. From the second century a new and passionate devotional worship of Vishnu's incarnation as Krishna developed in South India. By 1000 AD Vaishnavism became closely associated with the devotional form of Hinduism preached by **Ramanuja**, whose followers spread the worship of Vishnu and his 10 successive incarnations (*avatars*) in animal and human form. For Vaishnavites, God took these different forms in order to save the world from impending disaster. AL Basham has summarized the 10 incarnations (see table).

Vishnu

By far the most influential incarnations of Vishnu are those in which he was believed to take human form, especially as **Rama** (twice) and **Krishna**. In the earliest stories about Rama he was not regarded as divine. Although he is now seen as an earlier incarnation of Vishnu than Krishna, he was added to the pantheon very late, probably after the Muslim invasions of the 12th century AD. Rama (or Ram – rhyme with *calm*) is a powerful figure in contemporary India, and for Goans Parasurama, Vishnu's sixth incarnation, is responsible for the creation of Goa itself. He had come to free the world by fighting the all-powerful king of the Kshatriyas. After his triumph he flung his axe from the top of the Sahyadri Range far out to sea and then commanded the sea to withdraw so that he could perform the most powerful of sacrifices, the Yajna. Thus Goa was created, pure, virgin land.

Commonly represented as Vishnu's wife, **Lakshmi** is widely worshipped as the goddess of wealth. Earlier representations of Vishnu's consorts portrayed her as **Sridevi**, often shown in statues on Vishnu's right, while **Bhudevi**, also known as Prithvi, who represented the earth, was on his left. Lakshmi is popularly shown in her own right as standing on a lotus flower, although eight forms of Lakshmi are recognized.

Siva Siva is interpreted as both creator and destroyer, the power through whom the universe evolves. He lives on Mount Kailasa with his wife **Parvati** and two sons, the elephant-headed **Ganesh** and the six-headed **Karttikeya**. Siva is also represented in Shaivite temples throughout India by the linga, literally meaning 'sign' or 'mark', but referring in this context to the phallus. The linga has become the most important symbol of the cult of Siva. Although Siva is not seen as having a series of rebirths, like Vishnu, he nonetheless appears in very many forms representing different aspects of his varied powers. In Goa his most common names are Nagesh, Mangesh or Saptakoteshwara. As Betall, who is shown naked with human skulls round his neck and covered in serpents, he is widely feared in Goan villages as having power over evil spirits. Other common names for Siva include: **Chandrasekhara**, **Mahadeva** and **Nataraja**, the Lord of the Cosmic Dance. Siva is normally accompanied by his 'vehicle', the bull (*nandi* or *nandin*). **Nandi** is one of the most widespread of sacred symbols of the ancient world and may represent a link with **Rudra**, who was sometimes represented as a bull in pre-Hindu India. Strength and

Vis hnu, preserver of the Universe

Krishna, eighth and most popular incarnation of Vishnu

Vishnu's ten incarnations

Name	Form	Story
1 Matsya	*Fish*	*Vishnu took the form of a fish to rescue Manu (the first man), his family and the Vedas from a flood.*
2 Kurma	*Tortoise*	*Vishnu became a tortoise to rescue all the treasures lost in the flood, including the divine nectar (Amrita) with which the gods preserved their youth. The gods put Mount Kailasa on the tortoise's back, and when he reached the bottom of the ocean they twisted the divine snake round the mountain. They then churned the ocean with the mountain by pulling the snake, raising the nectar, the other treasures, and the Goddess Lakshmi, Vishnu's consort.*
3 Varaha	*Boar*	*Vishnu appeared again to raise the earth from the ocean's floor where it had been thrown by a demon, Hiranyaksa. The story probably developed from a non-Aryan cult of a sacred pig.*
4 Narasimha	*Half-man, half lion*	*Having persuaded Brahma to promise that he could not be killed either by day or night, by god, man or beast, the demon Hiranyakasipu then terrorized everybody. When the gods pleaded for help, Vishnu appeared at sunset, when it was neither day nor night, in the form of a half man and half lion and killed the demon.*
5 Vamana	*A dwarf*	*Bali, a demon, achieved supernatural power by asceticism. To protect the world Vishnu appeared before him in the form of a dwarf and asked him a favour. Bali granted Vishnu as much land as he could cover in three strides. Vishnu then became a giant, covering the earth in three strides. He left only hell to the demon.*
6 Parasurama	*Rama with the axe*	*Vishnu was incarnated as the son of a Brahmin, Jamadagni as Parasurama killed the Kshatriya king for robbing his father. The king's sons then killed Jamadagni, and in revenge Parasurama destroyed all male kshatriyas (warrior caste), after 21 attempts.*
7 Rama	*The Prince of Ayodhya*	*As told in the Ramayana, Vishnu came in the form of Rama to rescue the world from the dark demon, Ravana. His wife Sita is the model of patient faithfulness while Hanuman is the monkey-faced god and Rama's helper.*
8 Krishna	*Charioteer of Arjuna. Many forms*	*Krishna meets almost every human need, from the mischievous child, the playful boy, the amorous youth to the Divine.*
9 The Buddha		*Probably incorporated into the Hindu pantheon in order to discredit the Buddhists, dominant in some parts of India until the sixth century AD. An early Hindu interpretation suggests that Vishnu took incarnation as Buddha to show compassion for animals and to end sacrifice.*
10 Kalki	*Riding on a horse*	*Vishnu's arrival will accompany the final destruction of this present age, Kaliyuga, judging the wicked and rewarding the good.*

Background

virility are key attributes, and pilgrims to Siva temples will often touch the Nandi's testicles on their way into the shrine.

Other Hindu deities

Ganesh Of thousands of Hindu deities, Ganesh is one of Hinduism's most popular gods. He is seen as the great clearer of obstacles. Shown at gateways and on door lintels with his elephant head and pot belly, his image is revered across India. Meetings, functions and special family gatherings will often start with prayers to Ganesh, and any new venture, from the opening of a building to inaugurating a company will not be deemed complete without a Ganesh puja.

Nagas & Naginis The multiple hooded cobra head often seen in sculptures represents the fabulous snake gods, the Nagas, though they may often be shown in other forms, even human. Statues of divine Nagas are usually placed on uncultivated ground under trees in the hope and belief, as Masson-Oursel puts it, that "if the snakes have their own domain left to them they are more likely to spare human beings". The Nagas and their wives, the Naginis, are often the agents of death in mythical stories.

Ganesh, bringer of prosperity

Parvati, daughter of Parvata and wife of Siva

Siva , as Nataraj, Lord of the Dance

Hindu society

Dharma is seen as the most important of the objectives of individual and social life. But what were the obligations imposed by *Dharma*? Hindu law givers, such as those who compiled the code of *Manu* (AD 100-300), laid down rules of family conduct and social obligations related to the institutions of caste and jati which were beginning to take shape at the same time.

Although the word caste was given by the Portuguese at the end of the 15th century AD, the main feature of the system emerged at the end of the Vedic period. Two terms – varna and jati – are used in India itself, and have come to be used interchangeably and confusingly with the word caste. **Caste**

Varna, which literally means colour, had a fourfold division. By 600 BC this had become a standard means of classifying the population. The fair-skinned Aryans distinguished themselves from the darker skinned earlier inhabitants. The priestly varna, the Brahmins, were seen as coming from the mouth of Brahma; the Kshatriyas (or Rajputs as they are commonly called in northwest India) were warriors, coming from Brahma's arms; the Vaishyas, a trading community, came from Brahma's thighs, and the Sudras, classified as agriculturalists, from his feet. Relegated beyond the pale of civilized Hindu society were the untouchables or outcastes, who were left with the jobs which were regarded as impure, usually associated with dealing with the dead (human or animal) or with excrement.

Jati is the group to which the great majority of Indians put themselves into rather than one of the four varna categories. There are thousands of different jatis across the country. Many used to be identified with particular activities, and occupations used to be hereditary. Caste membership is now decided simply by birth. Although you can be evicted from your caste by your fellow members, usually for disobedience to caste rules such as marriage, you cannot join another caste, and technically you become an outcaste.

The Dalits Gandhi spearheaded his campaign for independence from British colonial rule with a powerful campaign to abolish the disabilities imposed by the caste system. Coining the term *harijan* (meaning 'person of God'), which he gave to all former outcastes, Gandhi demanded that discrimination on the grounds of caste be outlawed. Lists – or 'schedules' – of backward castes were drawn up during the early part of last century in order to provide positive help to such groups. The term *Harigan* itself has now been widely rejected by many former outcastes as paternalistic and as implying an adherence to Hindu beliefs which some explicitly reject, and today many have adopted the secular term 'dalits' – the 'oppressed'.

Affirmative action Since 1947 the Indian government has extended its positive discrimination (a form of affirmative action) to scheduled castes and scheduled tribes, particularly through reserving up to 50 percent of jobs in government-run institutions and in further education leading to professional qualifications for these groups, and members of the scheduled castes are now found in important positions throughout the economy.

While for its secular life, in common with the rest of India, Goa follows the Gregorian calendar, for Hindus much of religious and personal life follows the Hindu calendar (see also page 42). This is based on the lunar cycle of 29½ days, but the clever bit comes in the way it is synchronized with the Gregorian solar calendar of the west by the addition of an 'extra month' (*adhik maas*), every two and a half to three years. **Hindu calendar**

Background

The four stages of life

Popular Hindu belief holds that an ideal life has four stages: that of the student, the householder, the forest dweller and the wandering dependent or beggar (sannyasi). These stages represent the phases through which an individual learns of life's goals and how to achieve them.

One of the most striking sights today is that of the saffron clad sannyasi (sadhu) seeking gifts of food and money to support himself in the final stage of his life.

There may have been sadhus even before the Aryans arrived. Today, most of these have given up material possessions, carrying only a strip of cloth, a staff (danda), a crutch to support the chin during meditation (achal), prayer beads, a fan to ward off evil spirits, a water pot, a drinking vessel, which may be a human skull and a begging bowl. You may well see one, almost naked, covered only in ashes, on a city street.

Hindus follow two distinct eras. The *Vikrama Samvat* which began in 57 BC (and is followed in Goa), and the *Salivahan Saka* which dates from 78 AD and has been the official Indian calendar since 1957. The *Saka* new year starts on 22 March and has the same length as the Gregorian calendar. In most of South India, the New Year is celebrated in the first month, *Chaitra* (corresponding to March-April), while in North India (and Tamil Nadu) it is celebrated in the second month of *Vaishakh*. The year itself is divided into six seasons: *Vasant* (spring), *Grishha* (summer), *Varsha* (rains), *Sharat* (early autumn), *Hemanta* (late autumn), *Shishir* (winter).

Hindu and corresponding Gregorian Calendar months

Chaitra	March-April	*Ashwin*	September-October
Vaishakh	April-May	*Kartik*	October-November
Jyeshtha	May-June	*Margashirsha*	November-December
Aashadh	June-July	*Poush*	December-January
Shravan	July-August	*Magh*	January-February
Bhadra	August-September	*Phalgun*	February-March

Hindu literature

Sanskrit was the first all-India language. Its literature has had a fundamental influence on the religious, social and political life of the entire region. Its early literature was memorized and recited, and it is still impossible to date with any accuracy the earliest Sanskrit hymns. They are in the Rig Veda, which probably did not reach its final form until about the 6th century BC, but the earliest parts of which may go back as far as 1300 BC – approximately the period of the fall of Mycenean Greece in Europe.

The Vedas   The Rig Veda is a collection of 1,028 hymns, not all directly religious. Its main function was to provide orders of worship for priests responsible for the sacrifices which were central to the religion of the Indo-Aryans. Two further texts that began to be created towards the end of the period in which the Rig Veda was being written down, the Yajurveda and the Samaveda, served the same purpose. A fourth, the Atharvaveda, is largely a collection of magic spells.

The Brahmanas   Central to the Vedic literature was a belief in the importance of sacrifice. At some time after 1000 BC a second category of Vedic literature, the Brahmanas, began to take shape. Story telling developed as a means to interpret the significance of sacrifice. The most famous and the most important of these were the Upanishads, probably written at some time between the 7th and 5th centuries BC.

The Brahmanas gave their name to the religion emerging between the 8th and 6th centuries BC, Brahmanism, the still distant ancestor of Hinduism. Two texts from about this period remain the best known and most widely revered epic compositions in South Asia, the Mahabharata and the Ramayana, known and loved by Hindus in every town and village in India. Dating the Mahabharata is problematic as the details of the great battle recounted in the Mahabharata are unclear. Tradition puts its date at precisely 3102 BC, the start of the present era, and also suggests that the author of the poem was a sage named Vyasa. Evidence suggests however that the battle was fought around 800 BC, at **Kurukshetra**. It was another 400 years before priests began to write the stories down, a process which was not complete until 400 AD. The Mahabharata was probably an attempt by the warrior class, the Kshatriyas, to merge their brand of popular religion with the ideas of Brahmanism. The original version of the Mahabharata was probably about 3,000 stanzas long, but it now contains over 100,000 – eight times as long as Homer's Iliad and the Odyssey put together.

The Mahabharata

The battle was seen as a war of the forces of good and evil, the **Pandavas** being interpreted as gods and the **Kauravas** as devils. The arguments were elaborated and expanded until about the 4th century AD by which time, as Shackle says, `Brahmanism had absorbed and set its own mark on the religious ideas of the epic, and Hinduism had come into being'. A comparatively late addition to the Mahabharata, the Bhagavad-Gita is the most widely read and revered text among Hindus in South Asia.

Good & evil

The Ramayana Valmiki is thought of in India as the author of the second great Indian epic, the Ramayana, though no more is known of his identity than is known of Homer's. Like the Mahabharata, it underwent several stages of development before it reached its final version of 48,000 lines.

The Ramayana

Sanskrit was always the language of the court and the élite. Other languages replaced it in common speech by the 3rd century BC, but it remained in restricted use for over 1,000 years after that period, essentially as a medium for writing. The remarkable Sanskrit grammar of Panini helped to establish grammar as one of the six disciplines essential to pronouncing and understanding the texts of the Vedas properly, and to conducting Vedic rituals. The other five were phonetics, etymology, meter, ritual practice and astronomy. Sanskrit literature continued to be written long after it had ceased to be a language of spoken communication. One of the `nine gems' of Chandragupta II's court, and one of India's greatest poets, **Kalidasa**, contributed to the development of Sanskrit as the language of learning and the arts. Vatsyana's Kamasutra not only explores the diversity of physical love but sheds light on social customs. In architecture the Nagara and Dravida styles were first developed. The Brahmins also produced theses on philosophy and on the structure of society, but these had the negative effect of contributing to the extreme rigidity of the caste system which became apparent from this period onwards. Literally `stories of ancient times', the Puranas are about the three major deities, Brahma, Vishnu and Siva. Although some of the stories may relate back to real events that occurred as early as 1500 BC, they were not compiled until the Gupta period in the 5th century AD. Margaret and James Stutley record the belief that "during the destruction of the world at the end of the age, Hayagriva is said to have saved the Puranas. A summary of the original work is now preserved in Heaven!" The stories are often the only source of information about the period immediately following the early Vedas. The Stutleys go on to say that each Purana was intended to deal with five themes: "the creation of the world (sarga); its destruction and recreation (pratisarga); the genealogy of gods and patriarchs (vamsa); the reigns and periods of the Manus (manvantaras); and the history of the solar and lunar dynasties". The tradition of writing in Sanskrit in the courts of India continued until the Muslims replaced it with Persian.

Sanskrit literature

Christianity

Although the Portuguese brought Roman Catholicism to Goa in the 16th century, Christians probably arrived in India during the first century after the birth of Christ. There is evidence that one of Christ's Apostles, **Thomas**, reached Kerala on the west coast of India in 52 AD, only 20 years after Christ was crucified. He settled in Malabar and then expanded his missionary work to China. It is widely believed that he was martyred in Tamil Nadu on his return to India in 72 AD, and is buried in Mylapore, in the suburbs of modern Chennai (Madras).

Christian origins

Until the arrival of the Portuguese most Goans were either Hindu or Muslim. However, within 50 years of the Portuguese arrival Christian influence became a force to be reckoned with. The Jesuit, St Francis Xavier, landed in Goa in 1542, and in 1557 Goa was made an Archbishopric. Despite his brief stay, he left an indelible imprint on Goa's religious life.

The Jesuits set up the first printing press in India in 1566 and began to print books in Tamil and other Dravidian languages by the end of the 16th century. The **Reformation** which took place in Europe from the 16th century onwards resulted in the creation of the Protestant churches, which reasserted the authority of the Bible over that of the church. By virtue of the Portuguese Catholic control Goa remained isolated from the developments through which Protestant missions subsequently worked extensively in other parts of India.

Although Goa remained almost entirely within the **Catholic realm** the influence of Catholicism varied sharply through time and in different parts of the Portuguese ruled territory. And, as Norma Alvares has written, "initially, despite their Christian skins, the Catholics remained furtive Hindus". The Inquisition was directed against this "unholy tendency" of these early converts to retain clandestinely their links with the Hindu faith. Certain phenomena, like caste, the Inquisition was unable to change. The Goan church eventually came to crystallize that institution in the form of the "*confrarias*".

The **Inquisition**, which lasted from 1560 to 1812, represented the most intensive, long term attempt to impose Catholic orthodoxy on the large newly converted Christian population. Because of the enormous lengths to which the courts of the Inquisition went to establish any heresy, its effective writ was geographically restricted to the area of closest Portuguese control – the Old Conquests – 'Ilhas' (comprising Tiswadi), Bardez and Salcete (including present day Mormugao). Every two or three years the Inquisition held great public trials with executions of the proven infidels. Here, not surprisingly, large scale conversions took place, and this area today retains by far the largest proportion of the Christian population.

Christian belief

Christian theology had its roots in Judaism, with its belief in one God, the eternal Creator of the universe. Judaism saw the Jewish people as the vehicle for God's salvation, the 'chosen people of God', and pointed to a time when God would send his Saviour, or Messiah. Jesus, whom Christians believe was 'the Christ' or Messiah, was born in the village of Bethlehem, some 20 km south of Jerusalem. Very little is known of his early life except that he was brought up in a devout Jewish family. At the age of 29 or 30 he gathered a small group of followers and began to preach in the region between the Dead Sea and the Sea of Galilee. Two years later he was crucified in Jerusalem by the authorities on the charge of blasphemy – that he claimed to be the son of God.

Christians believe that all people live in a state of sin, in the sense that they are separated from God and fail to do his will. They believe that God is personal, 'like a father'. As God's son, Jesus accepted the cost of that separation and sinfulness himself through his death on the cross. Christians believe that Jesus was raised from the dead on the third day after he was crucified, and that he appeared to his closest followers. They believe that his spirit continues to live today, and that he makes it possible for people to come back to God.

The New Testament of the Bible, which, alongside the Old Testament, is the text to which Christians refer as the ultimate scriptural authority, consists of four 'Gospels' (meaning 'good news'), and a series of letters by several early Christians referring to the nature of the Christian life. Roman Catholics also believe in the divine authority of the Pope as supreme head of the church and of the bishops and priests.

Christian worship

Most forms of Christian worship centre on the gathering of the church congregation for praise, prayer and the preaching of God's word, which usually takes verses from the Bible as its starting point. Different denominations place varying emphases on the main elements of worship, but in most church services today the congregation will take part in singing hymns (songs of praise), prayers will be led by the priest or minister of the congregation, readings from the Bible will be given and a sermon preached. For many Christians the most important service is Mass (Catholic) or the act of Holy Communion (Protestant) which celebrates the death and resurrection of Jesus in sharing bread and wine, which are held to represent Christ's body and blood given to save people from their sin. Although Christian services may be held daily in some churches most Christian congregations in Goa meet for worship on Sunday, and services are held in Konkani and in English. They are open to all.

Islam

Islam reached Goa both by land and sea. Since before the birth of Christ, Goa, along with other ports along the west coast of India from Surat in the north to Cochin in the south, was on the Arab sea trading route to Southeast Asia and China. When the Arab world converted to Islam in the seventh century AD many of the traders based in these Indian settlements followed suit. However, Goa was never more than a relatively minor port on this route and the size of the Muslim community was much smaller than in Kerala to the south. Relations with neighbouring Hindus were generally good, Hindu rulers often giving grants of land to Muslim traders or help in building mosques. Indeed, Hutt records that when Goa was captured by the Muslim ruler of Honavar to the south the 10,000 Hindu inhabitants were moved out of the town centre but were allowed to remain in the suburbs.

Subsequently Islam played a very different part in Goa's history. From the 13th century Turkish power brought Islam to India from the northwest. Mahmud of Ghazni stormed into Punjab, defeating the Rajput rulers in 1192. Within the next 30 years Turkish Muslim power stretched from Bengal in the east to Madurai, in modern Tamil Nadu, in the south. On their way south the Muslims followed the path taken by generations of their predecessors who had migrated into the 'Deccan' (meaning simply "south"). A chain of Muslim kingdoms was established on the landward side of the Ghats who contested for power with each other and with the Hindu state of Vijayanagar. Some of the Muslim kingdoms retained important links with Persia and with the Arab world, and sea ports on the west coast became an important avenue for military supplies, especially horses, both for the Hindu Vijayanagar Empire and the Muslim courts. Even in the 15th and 16th centuries business was business.

The five pillars of Islam

In addition to the profession of faith ("There is no God but Allah...") there are four further obligatory requirements imposed on Muslims. Daily prayers are prescribed at daybreak, noon, afternoon, sunset and nightfall. Muslims must give alms to the poor. They must observe a strict fast during the month of Ramadan. They must not eat or drink between sunrise and sunset. Lastly, they should attempt the pilgrimage to the Ka'aba in Mecca, known as the Hajj. Those who have done so are entitled to the prefix Hajji before their name.

Islamic rules differ from Hindu practice in several other aspects of daily life. Muslims are strictly forbidden to drink alcohol (though some suggest that this prohibition is restricted to the use of fermented grape juice, that is wine, it is commonly accepted to apply to all alcohol). Eating pork, or any meat from an animal not killed by draining its blood while alive, is also prohibited. Meat prepared in the appropriate way is called Halal. Finally, usury (charging interest on loans) and games of chance are forbidden.

The early Muslim rulers looked to the Turkish ruling class and to the Arab caliphs for their legitimacy, and to the Turkish élite for their cultural authority. From the middle of the 13th century, when the Mongols crushed the Arab caliphate, the Delhi sultans were left on their own to exercise Islamic authority in India, a role which was taken over from the 16th to the 18th centuries by the Mughals who shaped the greatest of the Muslim led empires.

Muslim beliefs

The beliefs of Islam (which means 'submission to God') could apparently scarcely be more different from those of Hinduism. Islam, often described as having "five pillars" of faith (see box), has a fundamental creed; 'There is no God but God; and Mohammad is the Prophet of God' (*La Illaha illa 'Ilah Mohammad Rasulu 'Ilah*). One book, the Qur'an, is the supreme authority on Islamic teaching and faith. Islam preaches the belief in bodily resurrection after death, and in the reality of heaven and hell.

The idea of heaven as paradise is pre-Islamic. Alexander the Great is believed to have brought the word into Greek from Persia, where he used it to describe the walled Persian gardens that were found even three centuries before the birth of Christ. For Muslims, Paradise is believed to be filled with sensuous delights and pleasures, while hell is a place of eternal terror and torture, which is the certain fate of all who deny the unity of God.

Islam has no priesthood. The authority of religious scholars Imams, learned men, judges etcetera, collectively referred to as the *Ulema*, derives from social custom and from their authority to interpret the scriptures, rather than from a defined status within the Islamic community. Islam also prohibits any distinction on the basis of race or colour, and there is a strong antipathy to the representation of the human figure. It is often thought, inaccurately, that this ban stems from the Qur'an itself. In fact it probably has its origins in the belief of Mohammad that images were likely to be turned into idols.

Mohammad and Muslim sects

Mohammad was born into a semi-priestly family of Mecca around 570 AD. At the age of 40 he received the first revelations of the Qur'an and began preaching. His message, however, angered powerful community leaders and traders and he was forced to flee to Medina; this date was named the *Hijra* and marks the beginning of the Islamic calendar. The faith Mohammad founded incorporated aspects of the

religious customs practised by the Arabs included the pilgrimage to the Ka'ba in Mecca which was believed to have been established by Adam.

During the first century after Mohammad's death Islam split into two sects which were divided on political and religious grounds, the Shi'is and Sunni's. The religious basis for the division lay in the interpretation of verses in the Qur'an and of traditional sayings of Mohammad, the *Hadis*. Both sects venerate the Qur'an but have different *Hadis*. They also have different views as to Mohammad's successor.

The **Sunni's** – always the majority in South Asia – believe that Mohammad did not appoint a successor and that Abu Bak'r, Omar and Othman were the first three caliphs (or vice-regents) after Mohammad's death. Ali, whom the Sunni's count as the fourth caliph, is regarded as the first legitimate caliph by the Shi'is, who consider Abu Bak'r and Omar to be usurpers. While the Sunni's believe in the principle of election of caliphs, **Shi'is** believe that although Mohammad is the last prophet there is a continuing need for intermediaries between God and man. Such intermediaries are termed *Imams* and they base both their law and religious practice on the teaching of the Imams.

The two major divisions are marked by further sub-divisions. The Sunni Muslims in India have followers of the Hanafi, Shafei, Maliki and Hanbali groups, named after their leaders. Numerically one of the smallest groups in South Asia is that of the Ismailis, who regard their leader, the Aga Khan, as their spiritual head.

Muslim year

The **Islamic calendar** begins on 16 July 622 AD. This was the date of the Prophet's migration (*Hijra*) from Mecca to Medina (in modern Saudi Arabia), and the year is denoted as 1 AH (Anno Hijrae).

The year is divided into 12 lunar months, alternating between 29 and 30 days, making a year of 354 or 355 days. The first month of the year is *Moharram*, followed by *Safar*, *Rabi-ul-Awwal*, *Rabi-ul-Sani*, *Jumada-ul-Awwal*, *Jumada-ul-Sani*, *Rajab*, *Shaban*, *Ramadan*, *Shawwal*, *Ziquad* and *Zilhaj*. The Islamic festivals, often linked to the sighting of the new moon, fall on different dates each year according to the Gregorian (solar) calendar of 365 days; they move 10 or 11 days earlier each year (see page 42 for further details).

Background

Buddhism

Despite its inaccessible location, at least after 250 BC Goa was home to Buddhist communities in the foothills of the Western Ghats. Emperor Asoka is believed to have sent a missionary monk Dharmarak to the area and another monk Punna is thought to have preached Buddhism in Zambaulim in Sanguem. Today Buddhism is practised mainly on the margins of the sub-continent, from Ladakh, Nepal and Bhutan in the north to Sri Lanka in the south. Although there are approximately five million Buddhists in Maharashtra, most are very recent outcaste Hindu converts, the last adherents of the early schools of Buddhism having been killed or converted by the Muslim invaders of the 13th century.

Buddhists developed cave sites as monasteries or temples such as at Arvalem in Bicholim, Khandepar in Ponda and Rivona in Sanguem. However, they have none of the exceptional murals and rock carvings found at Ajanta and Ellora in Maharashtra, north of Goa, or in Sigirya in Sri Lanka, and are comparatively small and insignificant. The presence of Buddhist monks in the 11th century at the court of Jayakeshi I of the Kadamba Dynasty is recorded in Sanskrit texts a century later. However, the stronger influences of Shaivism and Vaishnavism during Kadamba rule in Goa virtually eradicated Buddhism (and Jainism) from the area. Today there are fewer than 400 Buddhists in the whole of Goa.

The Buddha's Four Noble Truths

The Buddha preached Four Noble Truths: that life is painful; that suffering is caused by ignorance and desire; that beyond the suffering of life there is a state which cannot be described but which he termed nirvana; and that nirvana can be reached by following an eightfold path.

The concept of nirvana is often understood in the west in an entirely negative sense – that of 'non-being'. The word has the rough meaning of 'blow out' or 'extinguish', meaning to blow out the fires of greed, lust and desire. In a more positive sense it has been described by one Buddhist scholar as "the state of absolute illumination, supreme bliss, infinite love and compassion, unshakeable serenity and unrestricted spiritual freedom". The essential elements of the eightfold path are the perfection of wisdom, morality and meditation.

The Buddha's life

Siddharta Gautama, who came to be given the title of the Buddha – the Enlightened One – was born a prince into the warrior caste in about 563 BC. He was married at the age of 16 and his wife had a son. When he reached the age of 29 he left home and wandered as a beggar and ascetic. After about six years he spent some time in Bodh Gaya. Sitting under the Bo tree, meditating, he was tempted by the demon Mara with all the desires of the world. Resisting these temptations he received enlightenment. These scenes are common motifs of Buddhist art.

The next landmark was the preaching of his first sermon on 'The Foundation of Righteousness' in the Sarnath deer park near Varanasi. By the time he died the Buddha had established a small band of monks and nuns known as the *Sangha*, and had followers across North India. His body was cremated, and the ashes, regarded as precious relics, were divided up among the peoples to whom he had preached.

From the Buddha's death – or *parinirvana* – to the destruction of Nalanda (the last Buddhist stronghold in India) in 1197 AD, Buddhism in India went through three phases. Not mutually exclusive, they were followed simultaneously in different regions.

Hinayana 'The Little Way' insists on a monastic way of life as the only path to achieving *nirvana*. The Hinayana school of Theravada Buddhism is practised in Sri Lanka where it was introduced by Emperor Asoka's son, Mahinda in the first century BC, as well as in Myanmar and Thailand.

Mahayana 'The Great Way' believed in the possibility of salvation for all, practising a far more devotional form of meditation. The **Bodhisattvas**, saints who were predestined to reach the state of enlightenment through thousands of rebirths, gained prominence. The Buddha is believed to have passed through numerous existences in preparation for his final mission.

Vajrayana 'The Diamond Way' resembles magic and yoga in some of its beliefs. The ideal is to be 'so fully in harmony with the cosmos as to be able to manipulate the cosmic forces within and outside himself'. It had developed in the North of India by the seventh century AD, matching the parallel growth of Hindu Tantrism and is practised in the Himalaya.

Buddhist belief

Buddhism is based on the Buddha's own preaching. He developed his beliefs in reaction to the Brahmanism of his time, rejecting several of the doctrines of Vedic

Background

religion: the Vedic gods, scriptures and priesthood, and all social distinctions based on caste. However, he did accept the belief in the cyclical nature of life, and that the nature of an individual's existence is determined by a natural process of reward and punishment for deeds in previous lives – the Hindu doctrine of karma (see page 244). In the Buddha's view, though, there is no eternal soul.

Buddhism's decline

The decline of Buddhism in India probably stemmed as much from the growing similarity in the practice of Hinduism and Buddhism as from direct attacks. However, the Muslim conquest dealt the final death blow, being accompanied by the large-scale slaughter of monks and the destruction of monasteries. Without their institutional support Buddhism faded away.

Jainism

Like Buddhism, Jainism started as a reform movement of the Brahmanic religious beliefs of the sixth century BC. Its founder was a widely revered saint and ascetic, Vardhamma, who became known as Mahavir – 'great hero'. Mahavir was born in the same border region of India and Nepal as the Buddha, just 50 km to the north of modern Patna, probably in 599 BC. His family, also royal, were followers of an ascetic saint, Parsvanatha, who according to Jain tradition had lived 200 years previously.

Unlike Buddhism, Jainism never spread beyond India, but it has survived continuously into modern India, claiming four million adherents, though there are fewer than 500 in Goa itself.

Jain beliefs

Jains (*Jina*, literally meaning 'descendants of conquerors') believe that there are two fundamental principles, the living (*jiva*) and the non-living (*ajiva*). The essence of Jain belief is that all life is sacred, and that every living entity, even the smallest insect, has within it an indestructible and immortal soul. Jains developed the view of *ahimsa* – often translated as 'non-violence', but better perhaps as 'non-harming'.

Unlike Buddhists, Jains accept the idea of God, but not as a creator of the universe. They see him in the lives of the **24 Tirthankaras** (prophets – or literally 'makers of fords' – across the spiritual journey over the river of life), or leaders of Jainism, whose lives are recounted in the Kalpsutra – the third century BC book of ritual. **Mahavir** is regarded as the last of these great spiritual leaders. Much Jain art details stories from these accounts, and the Tirthankaras play a similar role for Jains as the Bodhisattvas do for Mahayana Buddhists.

The **five vows** may be taken both by monks and by lay people: Not to harm any living beings (Jains must practise strict vegetarianism – and even some vegetables, such as potatoes and onions, are believed to have microscopic souls); To speak the truth; Not to steal; To give up sexual relations and practice complete chastity; To give up all possessions – for the *Digambara* sect that includes clothes.

Jain sects

Jains have two main sects, whose origins can be traced back to the fourth century BC. The more numerous **Svetambaras** – the 'white clad' – concentrated more in eastern and western India, and the **Digambaras** – or 'sky-clad' – who on occasions go naked and are now concentrated in South India.

Background

Economy

Goa is one of India's most prosperous states. Its economy has been boosted both by remittances from Goans working abroad and by the inflow of foreign exchange from tourism. Goans have scattered around the world, not only to Europe and the United States, but also to the Middle East and the Gulf States. They continue to play a crucial role in the economic development of the state and have contributed to the sharp rise in land prices through their interest in hotel and other tourism related development.

Industry & exports Goa's manufacturers produce fertilizers, sugar, textiles, chemicals, iron pellets and pharmaceuticals. Rice is the staple product with fruit, salt, coconuts, pulses and betel (areca nut) also produced. The principal exports are coconuts, cashew, fruit, spices, manganese and iron ores, bauxite, fish and salt.

Fishing For villages the length of India's west coast fishing has provided the basic source of livelihood for generations. It remains important today, but changing technology has brought mixed blessings. The rapid increase in deep sea trawler fishing has brought competition for inshore fishermen which is arousing increasing hostility. Locally caught fish continue to be sold in the markets, but many Goan fishermen are increasingly fearful that they will be unable to continue to survive by fishing alone and so an increasing number are using their boats for tourism during the season.

Tourism Tourism plays an important role in the economy and saw rapid growth in the early '90s, though towards the end of the millennium the numbers stabilized. From 200,000 visitors in 1975 the figure reached over 1,100,000 in 1997, of which about 15 percent were foreigners. Direct charter flights from Europe have given a boost and the new civilian airport planned will address the demand for easier direct access.

The private sector provides the bulk of tourist facilities and services and is responsible for most of the accommodation with even modest householders benefiting by taking in paying guests. Although tourism brings money into the Goan economy, there is considerable opposition to the expansion of facilities for tourists. Some Goans criticize the Government's expansion plans as bringing little benefit to the local economy, while threatening to damage traditional social and cultural values. The spread of hippy colonies in the late 1960s and 1970s was deeply resented by some, and more recently the rapid development of power, including plans to generate nuclear power on the coast south of Panaji, have raised protests. Tourism has also fuelled heavy immigration from other states, mainly the rural poor from Karnataka, traders from Kashmir and hotel staff from elsewhere in India.

The State Government is keen to stress that tourism to Goa should remain within limits so that the environment and ecology are not sacrificed. It has concentrated on improving road networks, increasing water supply and waste disposal to tourist areas. The number of well maintained 'Sulabh' pay toilets in heavily used tourist spots is being increased.

The vast majority of foreign visitors (95 percent, as compared to 77 percent of domestic tourists) stay on the coastal belt, the wonderful beaches being the main attraction that draws them to this part of India. The authorities are keen to see that the rest of the state which has different architectural, cultural and scenic attractions, opens

Background

Official name	*The Republic of India*
National anthem	*Jana Gana Mana*
Constitution	*Democratic republic*
National flag	*A horizontal tricolour with equal bands of saffron, white and green from top to bottom. At the centre is an Asoka wheel in navy blue.*
Goa statistics	*Area: 3,800 sq km (1991 Census). **Population**: 1,170,000 (Urban 41%, Scheduled Castes 2%, Scheduled Tribes 1%). **Birth rate**: Rural 15:1,000, Urban 16:1,000. **Death rate**: Rural 8:1,000, Urban 7:1,000. **Literacy**: 75.5% (M84%, F67%). **Religion**: Hindu 66%, Muslim 5%, Christian 29%.*
India statistics	*Area: 3,287,000 sq km. **Population**: 1 billion (2000). **Annual increase**: 18,000,000. **Birth rate**: Rural 34:1,000, Urban 27:1,000. **Death rate**: Rural 12:1,000, Urban 7:1,000. **Infant mortality rate**: Rural 105:1,000, Urban 62:1,000. **Literacy**: 52% (M 64%, F 39%). **Religion**: Hindu 82.4% (Scheduled Castes: 139,000,000; Scheduled Tribes: 69,000,000); Muslim 11.7%; Christian 2.3%; Sikh 2.2% , Buddhist 0.8%; Jain 0.4%.*

up to tourists. It has already taken steps to improve facilities at Old Goa, one of the premier places to visit away from the coast. It hopes to encourage watersports and has also earmarked three old forts (the Aguada plateau, Reis Magos and Cabo de Rama) for restoration and development by providers of quality accommodation and sports facilities which will attract the higher spending foreigner.

Air transport through direct charter flights from Europe to the naval airport at **Transport** Dabolim has brought great benefits. The State Government is now keen to have a civilian airport to cope with the growing demands of international tourists and is awaiting clearance on a site in North Goa, at Mopa in Pernem.

While Goa has become far easier to reach from Europe, communications internally and with the rest of India are also improving rapidly. New State Highways are planned to connect Mormugao to Chorlem and Pernem to Polem, though these have been long promised and as yet very slow to be built. Many estuaries have now been bridged, transforming travel by road along the coast. The Zuari bridge at Cortalim has however had major problems (possibly affected by salinity) with the superstructure cracking. Light vehicles continue to cross the bridge but heavy vehicles face a lengthy diversion via Ponda. Improved ferry ramps and new ferries will be in place before repair work begins. Work on the bridge across the Chapora estuary (Siolim-Chopdem) has begun but completion seems a distant dream. The fast and comfortable a/c **catamaran** service which operated between Goa and Mumbai has been suspended for the time being. The **Konkan Railway** between Mumbai and Mangalore has put Goa firmly on the rail map. Other long-distance rail connections have also been improved in the last year.

Background

Footnotes

8

Footnotes

Glossary

Words in *italics* are common elements of words, often making up part of a place name

A

aarti (arati) Hindu worship with lamps

acharya religious teacher

Adinatha first of the 24 Tirthankaras, distinguished by his bull mount

agarbathi incense

Agni Vedic fire divinity, intermediary between gods and men; guardian of the SE

agrashala pilgrim resthouse

ahimsa non-harming, non-violence

ambulatory processional path

amrita ambrosia; drink of immortality

Ananta a huge snake on whose coils Vishnu rests

anna (ana) one sixteenth of a rupee (still occasionally referred to)

antaralaya vestibule between the temple hall and the sanctuary

apsara celestial nymph

apse semi-circular plan, as in apse of a church

architrave horizontal beam across posts or gateways

ardha mandapam chamber in front of main hall of temple

Ardhanarisvara Siva represented as half-male and half-female

Arjuna Hero of the Mahabharata, to whom Krishna delivered the Bhagavad Gita

arrack alcoholic spirit fermented from potatoes or grain

Aruna charioteer of Surya, the Sun God; Red

Aryans lit. 'noble' (Sanskrit); prehistoric peoples who settled in Persia and N India

asana a seat or throne

ashram hermitage or retreat

atman philosophical concept of universal soul or spirit

atrium court open to the sky in the centre In modern architecture, enclosed in glass

avatara incarnation of a divinity

ayah nursemaid, especially for children

B

bagh garden

baksheesh tip

balcao shaded wide verandah of a Goan house

bandh a strike

bandhani tie dyeing (W India, Rajasthan)

bania merchant caste

barrel-vault semi-cylindrical shaped roof or ceiling

Baroque (style) 17th century Italian, bold, exuberant, ornate decoration

bas-relief carving of low projection

basement lower part of walls, usually adorned with decorated mouldings

basti Jain temple

bazaar market

begum Muslim princess; Muslim woman's courtesy title

Bhagavad-Gita Song of the Lord; section of the Mahabharata

bhai brother

Bhairava Siva, the Fearful

bhakti adoration of a god or goddess

bhang Indian hemp

Bharata half-brother of Rama

bhavan building or house

bhumi 'earth'; refers to a horizontal moulding of a shikhara

bidi (beedi) tobacco leaf cigarette

Brahma Universal self-existing power; Creator in the Hindu Triad

Brahman (Brahmin) highest Hindu (and Jain) caste of priests

Brahmanism ancient Indian religion, precursor of modern Hinduism

Buddha   The Enlightened One; founder of Buddhism

bund   an embankment

burqa   an over-dress worn by Muslim women observing purdah

C

cantonment   planned military or civil area in town

capital   upper part of a column

catamaran   log raft, logs (*maram*) tied (*kattu*) together (Tamil)

cave temple   rock-cut shrine or monastery

chai   tea

chakra   sacred Buddhist wheel of the law; also Vishnu's discus

Chamunda   terrifying form of the goddess Durga

Chandra   Moon; a planetary deity

chapatti   unleavened Indian bread cooked on a griddle

charka   spinning wheel

charpai   'four legs' – wooden frame string bed

chattra   ceremonial umbrella on stupa (Buddhist)

chaudi   town square

chaukidar   night-watchman; guard

chauth   25% tax raised for revenue by Marathas

chhatri   umbrella shaped dome or pavilion

choli   blouse

chowk   (chauk) a block; open place in a city where the market is held

circumambulation   clockwise movement around a shrine

clerestory   upper section of the walls of a building which allows light in

cloister   passage usually around an open square

Communidade   village assembly/committee

corbel   horizontal block supporting a vertical structure or covering an opening

cornice   horizontal band at the top of a wall

crenellated   having battlements

crore   10 million

cruzado   Portuguese gold coin

cupola   small dome

D

daal   lentils, pulses

dado   part of a pedestal between its base and cornice

dahi   yoghurt

dais   raised platform

dak bungalow   rest house for officials

dak   post

dargah   a Muslim tomb complex

darshan   (darshana) viewing of a deity

darwaza   gateway, door

Dasara   (dassara/dussehra/dassehra) 10 day festival (September-October)

deepmal   (deepstambha) temple lamp tower

Devi   Goddess; later, the Supreme Goddess

dhansak   Parsi dish made with lentils

dharamshala   (dharamsala) pilgrims' rest-house

dharma   moral and religious duty

dhobi   washerman

dholi   swinging chair on a pole, carried by bearers

dhoti   loose loincloth worn by Indian men

dhow   Arab triangular-sailed trading ship

digambara   lit. 'sky-clad'; Jain sect in which the monks go naked

dikpala   guardian of one of the cardinal directions mostly appearing in a group of eight

Diwali   festival of lights (October-November)

dosa   thin pancake

double dome   composed of an inner and outer shell of masonry

dupatta   long scarf worn by Punjabi women

Durga   principal goddess of the Shakti cult

durwan   watchman

dwarpala   guardian deities at temple doorways (on silver doors of sanctuary)

E

ek   the number 1, a symbol of unity

F

faience   coloured tilework, earthenware or porcelain

festa   Christian saint's day

feni   spirit distilled from palm sap or juice of the cashew apple

fidalgo   Upper class Portuguese noble

filigree   ornamental work or delicate tracery

finial   emblem at the summit of a stupa, tower, dome, or at the end of a parapet

frieze   horizontal band of figures or decorative designs

G

gable   end of an angled roof

gaddi   throne

gadi/gari   car, cart, train

Ganapati   see Ganesh

Gandharva   semi-divine flying figure; celestial musician

Ganesh   (Ganapati) elephant-headed son of Siva and Parvati

Ganga   goddess personifying the Ganga river

ganja   Indian hemp

garbagriha   lit. 'womb-chamber'; a temple sanctuary

garh   fort

Garuda   Mythical eagle, half-human Vishnu's vehicle

Gaunkar   settler in Goan village

ghat   hill range, hill road; landing place; steps on the river bank

ghazal   Urdu lyric poetry/love songs, often erotic

ghee   clarified butter for cooking

giri   hill

godown   warehouse

Gopala   (Govinda) cowherd; a name of Krishna

Gopis   cowherd girls; milk maids who played with Krishna

gopuram   lit. 'cow gate'; gateway tower in Hindu temple

gram   chick pea, pulse

Greek cross   cross where each are is the same length

gulal   red colour (powder) thrown when celebrating Shigmo

gumbaz   (gumbad) dome

gur   palm sugar

guru   teacher; spiritual leader, Sikh religious leader

H

Haj   (Hajj) annual Muslim pilgrimage to Mecca

halwa   a special sweet meat

Hanuman   Monkey devotee of Rama; bringer of success to armies

harem   women's quarters (Muslim), from 'haram', Arabic for 'forbidden by law'

Hari   Vishnu Harihara, Vishnu- Siva as a single divinity

Hasan   the murdered eldest son of Ali, commemorated at Muharram

hat   (haat) market

hathi   (hati) elephant

hidalgo   Portuguese nobleman

Hiranyakashipu   Demon king killed by Narasimha

Holi   spring festival (February-March)

hookah   'hubble bubble' or smoking vase

hundi   temple offering

Hussain   the second murdered son of Ali, commemorated at Muharram

I

icon   statue or image of worship

Id   principal Muslim festivals

Idgah   open space for the Id prayers

idli   steamed rice cake (Tamil)

imam   Muslim religious leader

imambara   tomb of a Shiite Muslim holy man; focus of Muharram procession

Indra   King of the gods; God of rain; guardian of the East

Inquisition   special courts to test the Faith and punish deviation from Catholic orthodoxy

Ishana   Guardian of the North East

Ishvara   Lord; Siva

J

jaggery   brown sugar, made from palm sap

jali   lit. 'net'; any lattice or perforated pattern

jamb   vertical side slab of doorway

Jami masjid   (Jama, Jumma) Friday

mosque, for congregational worship

jataka stories   accounts of the previous lives of the Buddha

jaya stambha   victory tower

-ji   (jee) honorific suffix added to names out of reverence and/or politeness; also abbreviated 'yes' (Hindi/Urdu)

Jina   lit. 'victor'; spiritual conqueror or Tirthankara, after whom Jainism is named

K

Kailasa   mountain home of Siva

Kali   lit. 'black'; terrifying form of the goddess Durga, wearing a necklace of skulls/heads

Kalki   future incarnation of Vishnu on horseback

kalyanmandapa   marriage hall

kameez   women's shirt

kapok   the silk cotton tree

karma   impurity resulting from past misdeeds

Kartikkeya/Kartik   Son of Siva, God of war

keystone   central wedge-shaped block in a masonry arch

khadi   woven cotton cloth made from home-spun cotton (or silk) yarn.

khana   suffix for room/office/place; also food or meal

kharif   monsoon season crop

kohl   antimony, used as eye shadow

Krishna   8th incarnation of Vishnu

kshatriya   Hindu warrior caste, second after brahmins

Kubera   Chief yaksha; keeper of the treasures of the earth, Guardian of the North

kumar   a young man

Kumari   Virgin; Durga

kumbha   a vase-like motif, pot

kumhar   (kumar) potter

kund   lake, well or pool

kurta   Punjabi shirt

kutcha   (cutcha) raw; crude; unpaved; built with sun-dried bricks

L

lakh   100,000

Lakshmana   younger brother of Rama

Lakshmi   Goddess of wealth and good fortune, consort of Vishnu

lassi   iced yoghurt drink

lathi   bamboo stick with metal bindings, used by police

lingam   (linga) Siva as the phallic emblem

Lingaraja   Siva worshipped at Bhubaneswar

lintel   horizontal beam over doorway

lunette   semicircular window opening

lungi   wrapped-around loin cloth, normally checked

M

madrassa   Islamic theological school or college

mahamandapam   large enclosed hall in front of main shrine

maha   great

Mahabharata   Sanskrit epic about the battle between the Pandavas and Kauravas

Mahadeva   lit. 'Great Lord'; Siva

mahal   palace, grand building

maharaja   great king

maharani   great queen

maharishi   (Maharshi) lit. 'great teacher'

Mahavira   lit. 'Great Hero'; last of the 24 Tirthankaras, founder of Jainism

Mahayana   The Greater Vehicle; form of Buddhism practised in East Asia, Tibet and Nepal

Mahisha   Buffalo demon killed by Durga

Maitreya   the future Buddha

makara   crocodile-shaped mythical creature symbolizing the river Ganga

makhan   butter

mandala   geometric diagram symbolizing the structure of the Universe

mandapa   columned hall preceding the temple sanctuary

mandir   temple

mangesh   a form of Siva in Goa

Manueline   after King Manuel (1495-1521), ornate entrances and twisted piers often seen in Portuguese churches

Marathas   17th/18th century Maharashtrian power which challenged the Mughals and the British for supremacy in India

marg   wide roadway

masjid   lit. 'place of prostration'; mosque

mata   mother

math   Hindu religious seminary

maund   measure of weight, normally 40 seers

maya   illusion

memsahib   married European woman, term used mainly before Independence

Mestiços   of Portuguese-Indian parentage

mihrab   niche in the western wall of a mosque

mitthai   Indian sweets

Mohammad   'the praised'; The Prophet; founder of Islam

moksha   salvation, enlightenment; lit. 'release'

mridangam   musical instrument, barrel-shaped drum

mudra   symbolic hand gesture

Muharram   period of mourning in remembrance of Hasan and Hussain, two murdered sons of Ali

mullah   religious teacher (Muslim)

Mulattos   of Portuguese-African parentage

mundkars   tenants

mural   wall decoration

N

Naga   (nagi/nagini) Snake deity; associated with fertility and protection

nagara   city, sometimes capital

nagar khana   drum house; arched structure or gateway for musicians (also naubat khana)

nallah   (nullah) ditch, channel

namaaz   Muslim prayers, worship

namaste   common Hindu greeting (with joined palms) translated as: 'I salute all divine qualities in you'

Nandi   a bull, Siva's vehicle and a symbol of fertility

Narayana   Vishnu as the creator of life

nata mandapa   (nat-mandir; nritya sala) dancing hall in a temple

Nataraja   Siva, Lord of the cosmic dance

natya   the art of dance

navagraha   nine planets, represented usually on the lintel or architrave of the front door of a temple

Navaratri   lit. '9 nights'; name of the Dasara festival

nave   central section in a church separating aisles from the choir

nawab   prince, wealthy Muslim, sometimes used as a title

niche   wall recess containing a sculpted image or emblem, mostly framed by a pair of pilasters

nirvana   enlightenment; lit. 'extinguished'

niwas   small palace

O

obelisk   tapering and usually monolithic stone shaft

oriel   projecting window

P

padma   lotus flower, Padmasana, lotus seat; posture of meditating figures

paisa   (poisa) one hundredth of a rupee

palanquin   (palki) covered litter for one, carried on poles

pan   leaf of the betel vine; sliced areca nut, lime and other ingredients wrapped in leaf for chewing

panchayat   a 'council of five'; a government system of elected councils

pandal   marquee made of bamboo and cloth

pandit   teacher or wise man; a Sanskrit scholar

pankah   (punkha) fan, formerly pulled by a cord

parapet   wall extending above the roof

Parinirvana   the Buddha's state prior to nirvana, shown usually as a reclining figure

parishads   political division of group of villages

Parsi   (Parsee) Zoroastrians who fled from Iran to W India in the 9th century to avoid persecution

parterre   level space in a garden occupied by flower-beds

Parvati   daughter of the Mountain; Siva's consort

Pashupati   lit. 'Lord of the Beasts'; Siva

pediment   mouldings, often in a triangular formation above an opening or niche

pendant   hanging, a motif depicted upside down

peon   servant, messenger (from Portuguese *peao*)

piazza cross   cross in the church square

pice   (old form) 1/100th of a rupee

pietra dura   inlaid mosaic of hard, semi-precious stones

pilaster   ornamental small column, with capital and bracket

pipal   Ficus religiosa, the Bodhi tree

pir   Muslim holy man

podium   stone bench; low pedestal wall

porch   covered entrance to a shrine or hall, generally open and with columns

portico   space enclosed between columns

praça   open square/area in a town

pradakshina patha   processional passage

prasadam   consecrated temple food

puja   ritual offerings to the gods; worship (Hindu)

pujari   worshipper; one who performs puja (Hindu)

pukka   lit. 'ripe' or 'finished'; reliable; solidly built

Puranas   lit. 'the old'; Sanskrit sacred poems

purdah   seclusion of Muslim women from public view (lit. 'curtains')

purnima   full moon

qibla   direction for Muslim prayer

Quran   holy Muslim scriptures

R

rabi   winter/spring season crop

Radha   Krishna's favourite consort

raj   rule or government

raja   king, ruler

Rajput   dynasties of western and central India

Rama   Seventh incarnation of Vishnu

Ramayana   Sanskrit epic – the story of Rama

Ramazan   (Ramadan) Muslim month of fasting

rani   queen

rath   chariot or temple car

Ravana   Demon king of Lanka; kidnapper of Sita

reredos   screen behind an altar

rickshaw   3-wheeled bicycle-powered (or 2-wheeled hand-powered) vehicle

rishi   'seer'; inspired poet, philosopher

rupee   unit of currency in India

sabha   columned hall (sabha mandapa, assembly hall)

sacristy   place in church where vestments and vessels are kept

sadar   (sadr/saddar) chief, main

sadhu   ascetic; religious mendicant, holy man

sahib   title of address, like 'sir'

Saiva   (Shaiva) the cult of Siva

sal   hardwood tree of the lower slopes of Himalayan foothills

salaam   lit. 'peace'; greeting (Muslim)

salwar   (shalwar) loose trousers (Punjab)

samadhi   lit. 'concentrated thought', 'meditation'; a funerary memorial

sambar   lentil and vegetable soup dish, accompanying main meal (Tamil)

samsara   transmigration of the soul

sanyasi   wandering ascetic; final stage in the ideal life of a man

saranghi   small four-stringed viola shaped from a single piece of wood

Saraswati   wife of Brahma and goddess of knowledge

sarod   Indian stringed musical instrument

sarvodaya   uplift, improvement of all

sati   (suttee) a virtuous woman; later applied to the act of self-immolation on a husband's funeral pyre

Sati   wife of Siva who destroyed herself by fire

satyagraha   'truth force'; passive resistance

seer   (ser) unit of weight equal to about 1 kg

sepoy   (sepai) Indian soldier, private

seva   voluntary service

Shakti   Energy; female divinity often associated with Siva

shamiana   cloth canopy

Shankara   Siva

sharia   corpus of Muslim theological law

shastras   ancient texts setting norms of conduct for temple architecture

shastri   religious title (Hindu)

shehnai   (shahnai) Indian wind instrument similar to an oboe

Shesha (Sesha) serpent who supports Vishnu

shikhara (sikhara) curved temple tower or spire

shloka (sloka) Sanskrit sacred verse

shri (sri) honorific title, often used for 'Mr'; repeated as sign of great respect

sindur vermilion powder often used in temple ritual

singh (sinha) lion; also Rajput caste name adopted by Sikhs

Sita Rama's wife, heroine of the Ramayana epic

sitar classical Indian stringed musical instrument with a gourd for soundbox

Siva The Destroyer among Hindu gods

Sivaratri lit. 'Siva's night'; festival (February-March) dedicated to Siva

soma sacred drink mentioned in the Vedas

stambha free-standing column or pillar, often with lamps or banners

stucco plasterwork

sudra lowest of the Hindu castes

Sulabh washed clean (toilets with attendants)

sultan Muslim prince (sultana, wife of sultan)

Surya Sun; Sun God

svami (swami) holy man; also used as a suffix for temple deities

svastika (swastika) auspicious Hindu/Buddhist emblem

swadeshi home made goods

swaraj home rule

swatantra freedom

syce groom, attendant who follows a horseman or carriage

T

tabla a pair of drums

tahsildar revenue collector

takht throne

taluk (a) administrative subdivision

tamasha spectacle, festive celebration

tandava dance of Siva

tank lake created for irrigation; in temple architecture a masonry-lined body of water, often with stepped sides

tapas (tapasya) ascetic meditative self-denial

tempera distemper; method of mural painting by means of a 'body,' such as white pigment

tempo 3 wheeler vehicle

terracotta burnt clay used as building material

thali South and West Indian vegetarian meal

tiffin snack, light meal

tika (tilak) vermilion powder applied by Hindus to the forehead as a symbol of the divine; auspicious mark on the forehead; now often simply decorative

tikka tender pieces of meat, marinated and barbecued

tirtha (teertha) sacred water

Tirthankara lit. 'ford-marker'; the title given to 24 religious teachers worshipped by Jains

topi (topee) pith helmet

torana gateway with two posts linked by architraves

Trimurti Triad of Hindu divinities, Brahma, Vishnu and Siva

trisul the trident chief symbol of the god Siva

tulsi sacred basil plant

tulsi vrindavan basil enclosure

tympanum triangular space within the cornices of a pediment

U

Uma Siva's consort in one of her many forms

untouchable 'outcastes', with whom contact of any kind was believed by high caste Hindus to be defiling

Upanishads ancient Sanskrit philosophical texts, part of the Vedas

ur village (Tamil)

ustad master

uttarayana northwards

V

vaddo (wado) ward, village 'area'

vaisya the 'middle-class' caste of merchants and farmers

Valmiki sage, author of the Ramayana epic

Vamana dwarf incarnation of Vishnu

Varaha boar incarnation of Vishnu

varna 'colour'; social division of Hindus into Brahmin, Kshatriya, Vaishya and Sudra

Varuna Guardian of the West, accompanied by Makara (see above)

Vayu Guardian of the North-West; wind

vault arched roof (wood, stone or brick)

Veda (Vedic) oldest known Hindu religious texts

Vedanta the final parts of the Vedic literature

verandah enlarged porch in front of a hall

vilas house or pleasure palace

vimana towered sanctuary containing the cell in which the deity is enshrined

vina (veena) plucked stringed instrument, relative of sitar

Vishnu a principal Hindu deity; creator and preserver of universal order

vyala leogryph, lion-like sculpture

W

-wallah suffix often used with a occupational name, eg rickshaw-wallah

yagasala hall where the sacred fire is maintained and worshipped; place of sacrifice

yagya (yajna) major ceremonial sacrifice

Yaksha (Yakshi) a demi-god, associated with nature in folk religion

yali hippopotamus-like creature in the ornamentation of Chalukyan temples

Yama God of death, judge of the living; guardian of the south

yantra magical diagram used in meditation; machine

yatra (jatra) pilgrimage

yoga school of philosophy concentrating on different mental and physical disciplines (yogi, a practitioner)

yoni a hole in a stone, symbolising the vagina or female sexuality

Z

zenana segregated women's apartments

Eating out

Eating out in India is normally cheap and safe but menus can be dauntingly long and full of unfamiliar names. North Indian dishes are nearly universal. Outside their home states regional dishes are normally only served in specialist restaurants.

Pronounce

ā as in ah *ī as in bee*
ō as in oh *u as oo in book*
nasalized vowels are shown as an un etc
Note *These marks to help with pronunciation do not appear in the main text.*

Useful words in Konkani
Goan Dishes

Ambot tik *a hot, sour curry made with shark, squid or ray and eaten with rice*
Apa de camarão *a spicy prawn-pie with flour crust*
Balchão *a preparation of red masala and onions used as a sauce for prawns or king-fish (also meat). A less common dish, notleast because it is made without coconut and served with bread*
Caldo/Caldinha *delicately spiced light fish curry*
Cafrial *meat marinated in pepper and garlic and braised over a slow fire*
Chouriço *Goan sausage made of pork pieces stuffed in tripe, boiled or fried with onions and chillies; often eaten stuffed into bread*
Feijoada *Haricot bean (feijão) stew; sometimes served with chouriço*
Guisado *tomato based soup*
Kishmaur *ground, dried shrimp mixed with shredded coconut and chopped onion - an accompaniment*
Recheiado *usually a whole fish, cut in half, served with a hot masala sauce*
Seet corri *fish curry with coconut rice*
Soupa de carne *spicy soup made with meat and rice stock*
Sorpotel *a highly spiced dish of pickled pig's liver and heart, seasoned with vinegar and tamarind; perhaps the most famous of Goan meat dishes!*
Vindaloo *spicy pork or beef, marinated in garlic, wine vinegar and chillies (elsewhere in India `vindaloo' often refers to a hot, spicy curry)*
Xacutti *(`shakooti') hot chicken or meatdish prepared with coconut, pepper and star anise (fr chacontine)*

Goan Bread

Goan bread is good and there are pleasant European style biscuits

Undo *a hard crust round bread*
Kankonn *hard and crispy and shaped like a bangle; often dunked in tea*
Pāo *crusty bread rolls, soft inside*
Pollee *like a chapatti, often stuffed with vegetables*
Sannan *Goan version of idli made with ground rice, coconut and fermented palm sap (toddy)*

Goan Sweets

Sweets are sometimes too sweet for the Western palate

Alebele *a sweet pancake with coconut filling*
Bebinca *a layered coconut pancake and jaggery delicacy made with egg yolks, coconut milk, sugar, nutmeg and ghee*
Bolinhas *small semolina cakes*
Doce *fudge-like sweet made with nuts and milk*
Dodol *a mix of jaggery and coconut with rice flour/semolina and nuts*
Neuro *semi-circular pastry*

Useful words in Hindi

dāl *lentils, beans*
ghī *clarified butter*
gosht, mās *meat, usually mutton*
jhinga *prawns (Bengali chingri)*
macchli *fish*
makkhan *butter*
murgh *chicken*
murgh *chicken*
panīr *drained curds (cubes or pieces)*
sabzī *vegetables*
āloo *potato*
baingan *aubergine*
band gōbi *cabbage*
bhindi *okra, ladies' fingers*
gājar *carrots*
khumbhi *mushroom*
lauki *green gourd*
matar *peas*
piāz *onion*

phool gōbi   cauliflower
sāg   spinach
saym   green beans

Methods of preparation

Many items on restaurant menus are named according to well-known methods of preparation, roughly equivalent to terms such as 'Provençal' or 'sauté'.

bhoona   in a thick, fairly spicy sauce
do piaza   with onions (added twice during cooking)
jhāl frāzi   spicy, hot sauce with tomatoes and chillies
kebab   skewered (or minced and shaped) meat or fish; a dry spicy dish cooked on a fire
kìma   minced meat (usually 'mutton')
kofta   minced meat or vegetable balls
korma   in fairly mild rich sauce using cream /yoghurt
masālā   marinated in spices (fairly hot)
madras   hot
makhani   in butter rich sauce
mughlai   rich North Indian style
nargisi   dish using boiled eggs
peshwari   rich with dried fruit and nuts (Northwest Indian)
tandoori   baked in a tandoor (special clay oven) or one imitating it
tikka   marinated meat pieces, baked quite dry
vindaloo   hot and sour Goan meat dish using vinegar

Ordering a meal

A thāli for which you might pay Rs 15 (in small dhabas) to Rs 50, is usually the cheapest way of eating; the menu is fixed but refills are normally offered. You will be expected to eat with your fingers although a spoon is usually available. When ordering from a menu, you might like to try some 'bread' and/or rice, a vegetable and/or meat curry, bhāji, dāl, raita and pāpad. It is perfectly acceptable to order as little as some bread or rice and a vegetable dish or dāl. Sweets are an extra. Gulāb jāmun, rashmalāi and kulfi are popular. The Bengali mishti doi is not to be missed.

Typical dishes

Regional dishes are described in their appropriate sections. Coastal and riverine areas often have a wide range of specialist seafood.

aloo gobi   dry potato and cauliflower with cumin
aloo, matar, kumbhi   potato, peas, mushrooms in a dryish mildly spicy sauce
bhindi bhaji   lady's fingers fried with onions and mild spices
dāl makhani   lentils cooked with butter
dum aloo   potato curry with a spicy yoghurt, tomato and onion sauce
kìma mattar   mince meat with peas
matar panìr   curd cheese cubes with peas and spices (and often tomatoes)
nargisi kofta   boiled eggs covered in minced lamb, cooked in a thick sauce
rogan josh   rich, mutton/ beef pieces in creamy, red sauce
sāg panìr (pālak panìr)   Drained curd sautéd with chopped spinach in mild spices

Rice

Chāwal   plain boiled rice
biriyāni   partially cooked rice layered over meat and baked with saffron.
pulao/ pilau   fried (and then boiled) rice cooked with spices (cloves, cardamom, cinnamon) with dried fruit, nuts or vegetables. Sometimes cooked with meat, like a biriyāni

Roti – breads

chapāti (phoolka, roti)   thin, plain, wholemeal unleavened bread cooked on a tawa (griddle), usually made from ātā (wheat flour). Makkai-ki-roti is with maize flour. Soft, thicker version of poori, made with white flour
nān   oven baked (traditionally in a tandoor) white flour leavened bread often large and triangular; sometimes stuffed with almonds and dried fruit
parāthā   fried bread layered with ghì (sometimes cooked with egg or stuffed with potatoes)
poori   thin deep-fried, puffed rounds of flour (Bengali loochi, Punjabi bhaturā)

Accompaniments

achār pickles (usually spicy and preserved in oil)

chutnī often fruit or tomato, freshly prepared, sweet and mildly spiced

dahī plain yoghurt

papad, pappadom deep fried, pulse flour wafer rounds

raita yoghurt with shredded cucumber, pinapple or other fruit, or bundi (tiny batter balls)

Sweets

These are often made with reduced/ thickened milk, drained curd cheese or powdered lentils and nuts. They are sometimes covered with a flimsy sheet of decorative, edible silver leaf

barfī fudge-like rectangles/ diamonds

khīr, payasam, paesh thickened milk rice/ vermicelli pudding

gulāb jāmun dark fried spongy balls, soaked in syrup

halwa rich sweet made from cereal, fruit, vegetable, nuts and sugar

kulfi cone-shaped Indian ice cream with pistachhios/ almonds, uneven in texture

jalebi spirals of fried batter soaked in syrup

laddoo lentil based batter 'grains' shaped into orange rounds

rasgulla (roshgulla) balls of curd in clear syrup

rasmalāi spongy curd rounds, soaked in sweetened cream and garnished with pistachio nuts

Snacks

bhāji, pakora vegetable fritters (onions, potatoes, cauliflower, aubergine etc) deep-fried in batter

chāt sweet and sour cubed fruit and vegetables flavoured with tamarind paste and chillis

chanā choor, chioora ('Bombay mix') lentil and flattened rice snacks mixed with nuts and dried fruit

dosai South Indian pancake made with rice and lentil flour; served with a mild potato and onion filling (masala dosai) or without (ravai or plain dosai)

idli steamed South Indian rice cakes, a bland breakfast food given flavour by its spiced accompaniments

kachori fried pastry rounds stuffed with spiced lentil/ peas/ potato filling

samosā (Bengali shingārā) cooked vegetable or meat wrapped in pastry circle into 'triangles' and deep fried

vadai deep fried, small savoury lentil 'doughnut' rings. Dahi vada - similar rounds in yoghurt

Drinks

chai tea boiled with milk and sugar

doodh milk

kāfi ground fresh coffee boiled with milk and sugar

lassi North Indian cool drink made with yoghurt and water, salted or sweetened

nimboo pāni refreshing drink made with fresh lime and water, chilled bottled water, added salt or sugar syrup but avoid ice. Also, fresh lime soda

pāni water

Footnotes

Useful Konkani words and phrases

Travellers in the 'tourist' areas of Goa can quite easily get by without any knowledge of Konkani or Hindi. Learning and using a few local words, as needed, when visiting a foreign country is always received warmly.

Pronounce

ā *as in* **ah**   ī *as in* **bee**
ō *as in* **oh**   u *as oo in* **book**
ū *as in* **hub**
t *and* d *are usually* **soft (dental)** *eg* dī *as in* **thee**
j *is often pronounced like* **z**
nasalized *vowels are shown as* añ, iñ, em̄ ,em̄, *etc (Place names often end with a nasal vowel eg Pern***em***)*
NB *These marks to help with pronunciation in this section do not appear in the main text*

Useful words and phrases

Hello
 Hullo
How are you?(m)
 Tūñ kosso assa?
How are you?(f)
 Tūñ kosheam̄ (girl)/ koshi (woman) assi?
My name is ...
 Mhūjem nāoñ...
Cheers!
 Viva!
Good-bye!
 Barem̄!/Adeūs!
Pardon?
 Kite-m mhalle-m?
Sorry
 Tchūk zāli
Thankyou
 Deo barem̄ korūñ!/obrigād
May I take a photo?
 Photo kadum̄?
Yes/No
 Hoi/ Na
I
 haoñ
you
 tūñ
we
 ami
clean
 līmp/sāf
closed
 bandh
dirty
 sooj

drink
 pio-mche-m̄/pioñk
food
 khānem̄
fruit
 pholl
cashew
 kazū
coconut
 nāll
green coconut
 ādsar
mango
 ambō
orange
 laranja
pineapple
 ananas
good
 bare-m
hot (temp)
 hūñ
hot (spicy)
 tikh
meal
 jevonn
shop
 dūkān
water
 ūdak
what?
 kitem̄?
when?
 kenna?
where?
 khaiñ
which?
 khaiiñchem̄?
who?
 konn?
why?
 kityāk?

Health

medicine
 awkhad
Please get a doctor
 Matso dotorac affoi
I have a fever
 Mhaka zor āila

I feel unwell
  Haoñ baro nā
I have a tummy ache
  Marjay pottan charpta
I have diarrhoea
  Maka bhairī zalya

Hotel

I want a room please?
  Mhaka yek room zai mellat?
... with a toilet?
  Rooman mhaka toilet zai?
What is the room rate?
  Roomacheṁ bhade-m kitte-m?
I'd like to see it
  Mhaka room dekhūñ zai
... larger room
  ... whodlō room
Please clean the room
  Matso room sāf kor
There is no hot water/soap
  Rooman gorom udak/sabu nā

Restaurant

Menu please
  Matso menū dī
Bill please
  Matshe-m bill dī
I'll have this
  Haoñ heṁkhatañ
A bottle of water
  Ūdkachi yek bātli
Not chillies please
  Mhaka tikh naka
No ice/sugar please
  ... burf naka/sākhar naka
Sugar and milk please
  Matsi sākhar āni dūdh dī
spoon/fork/knife
  tchomchō/kanttō/sourī

Shopping

How much is this?
  Yay kitlay poishay?
I'll have this
  Haoñ heṁghetañ
Too much
  Ekdom mharaog
Make it cheaper!
  Matsheṁ ūnnay kor
... a bigger one?
  Whodleṁassa?
... a smaller one?
  Lhañ assa?
... another one like this?
  Asleṁ anik assa?
Receipt please
  Receipt dī

I don't want it
  Mhaka naka teṁ

Travel

I need a taxi
  Mhaka taxi zāi
Can I share a taxi?
  Taxi bhāgak koruñya?
How much to Colva?
  Colwa kitlay podtollay?
Where is the Bus Station?
  Bus Station khaiñ assa?
When does the Bus leave?
  Bus kenna sūttally?
Next bus?
  Dūsri bus kenna?
How far is Panaji?
  Poñnji kithli poiss assa?
How long (will it take)?
  Kithlō wogauth?
Have I/we reached Panaji?
  Poñnji powlay?
I want to hire a cycle
  Mhaka yek cycle bhadyak zai

Time and day

now attañts
morning sakāl
afternoon donpara
evening sānz
night rāt
at night ratīñ
today āz
tomorrow fālya-m
yesterday kāl

Sunday Āi-tār
Monday Somār
Tuesday Mungllār
Wednesday Būdhwār
Thursday Birestār
Friday Sūkrār
Saturday Shenwār

Numbers

1 yek
2 dōñ
3 tīn
4 chār
5 pānts
6 so
7 sāt
8 ātth
9 nnov
10 dhā
20 wīss
100 shumber
1,000 hazār

Footnotes

Hindi words and phrases for places outside Goa

Pronounce

ā as in ah   *ī* as in bee
ō as in oh   *u* as oo in book
nasalized vowels are shown as *aṇ uṇ* etc
Note *These marks to help with pronunciation do not appear in the main text.*

Useful words and phrases

Hello, good morning, goodbye
  namaste
Thank you/ no thank you
  dhanyavād or shukriyā/ nahīṇ'shukriyā
Excuse me, sorry
  māf kījiye
Yes/ no
  jī hāṇ / jī nahīṇ
Never mind/ that's all right
  koi bāt nahīṇ
What is your name?
  āpkā nām kyā hai?
My name is ....
  merā nām .... hai
Do you speak English?
  āp ko angrezī ātī hai?
a little
  thorī -sī
Pardon?
  phir batāiye
How are you?
  kyā hāl hai?
I am well, thanks, and you?
  maiṇ thīk hūṇ, aur āp?
Not very well
  maiṇ thīk nahīṇ hūṇ
Where is the ....?
  ....kahāṇ hai?
Who is ....?
  .... kaun hai?
What is this?
  yeh kyā hai?

Shopping

How much is this?
  iskā kyā dām hai?
That is very expensive!
  bahut mahangā hai!
Make it a bit cheaper!
  thorā kam kījiye!

Hotel

What is the room charge?
  kirāyā kitnā hai?

Please show the room
  kamrā dikhāiye
Is there an air-conditioned room?
  kyā a/c kamrā hai?
Is there hot water?
  kyā kamre meṇ garam pānī hai?
... a bathroom/ fan/ mosquito net
  ....bathroom/ pankhā/ machhar dānī
Is there a large room?
  barā kamrā hai?
It's not clean
  sāf nahīṇ hai
Please clean it
  sāf karwā dījiye
Are there clean sheets/ blanket?
  sāf chādareṇ/ kambal haiṇ?
This is OK
  yah thīk hai
Bill please
  bill dījiye

Travel

Where's the railway station?
  railway station kahāṇ hai?
How much is the ticket to Agra?
  Agra kā ticket kitne ka hai?
When does the Agra bus leave?
  Agra bus kab jāegī?
How much?
  kitnā?
Is it far?
  bahut door hai?
left/ right
  bāieṇ/ dāhinā
go straight on
  sīdhā chaliye
nearby
  nazdīk
Is it near the station?
  station ke pās hai?
Please come at 8
  āth bajai ānā
slowly
  dhire
quickly
  jaldi
stop
  rukiye

Restaurants

Please show the menu
  menu dikhāiye

No <u>chillis</u> please
 <u>mirch</u> nahĩn dālnā
....<u>sugar/ milk/ ice</u>
 chĩnĩ/ doodh/ baraf....
A bottle of water please
 ek botal pāni dĩjiye
sweet/ savoury
 mĩthā/ namkĩn
spoon, fork, knife
 chamach, kān̠tā, chhurĩ

Time and days

now abhĩ
morning suba
afternoon dopahar
evening shām
night rāt
today āj
tomorrow/ yesterday kal/ kal
day din
week haftā
month mahĩnā
year sāl

Sunday ravivār
Monday somvār
Tuesday mangalvār
Wednesday budhvār
Thursday vĩrvār
Friday shukravār
Saturday shanivār

Numbers

1 ek
2 dō
3 tĩn
4 chār
5 pānch
6 chhai
7 sāt
8 āth
9 nau
10 das
11 gyāra
12 bārāh
13 terāh
14 chaudāh
15 pandrāh
16 solāh
17 satrāh
18 athārāh
19 unnĩs
20 bĩs
100/ 200 sau/ do sau
1,000/ 2,000 hazār/ do hazār
100,000 lākh

and aur
big barā
café/ food stall dhābā/ hotel
chemist dawāi kĩ dukān
clean sāf
closed band
cold thandā
day din
dirty gandā
English an̠grezi
excellent bahut achhā
food/ to eat khānā
hot (spicy) jhāl, masāledār
hot (temp) garam
luggage samān
medicine dawāi
newspaper akhbār
of course, sure zaroor
open khulā
post office dāk khānā
police station thānā
road rāstā
room kamrā
shop dukan
sick (ill) bĩmār
silk reshmĩ/ silk
small chhotā
that woh
this yeh
town shahar
water pānĩ
what kyā
when kab
where kahān̠/ kidhar
which/who kaun
why kiun̠
with ke sāthh

Fruit (phal)

apple seb
banana kelā
coconut nāriyal
green coconut dāb
lemon nimbu
lychee lichi
mango āmb
orange santrā
pineapple anānās

Basic vocabulary

These are used locally though often pronounced differently (eg daktar, haspatāl): airport, bank, bathroom, bus, doctor, embassy, ferry, hotel, hospital, juice, police, restaurant, station, stamp, taxi, ticket, train.

278

Index

282

Map index

Shorts

Special interest pieces on and about Goa

Footnotes

Will you help us?

We try as hard as we can to make each Footprint Handbook as up-to-date and accurate as possible but, of course, things always change. Many people write to us - with corrections, new information, or simply comments.

If you want to let us know about an experience or adventure - hair-raising or mundane, good or bad, exciting or boring or simply something rather special - we would be delighted to hear from you. Please give us as precise information as possible, quoting the edition number (you'll find it on the front cover) and page number of the Handbook you are using.

Your help will be greatly appreciated, especially by other travellers. In return we will send you details about our special guidebook offer.

Write to Elizabeth Taylor
Footprint Handbooks
6 Riverside Court
Lower Bristol Road
Bath
BA2 3DZ
England
or email info@footprintbooks.com

Sales & distribution

Footprint Handbooks
6 Riverside Court
Lower Bristol Road
Bath BA2 3DZ England
T 01225 469141
F 01225 469461
E Mail info@
footprintbooks.com

Australia
Peribo Pty
58 Beaumont Road
Mt Kuring-Gai
NSW 2080
T 02 9457 0011
F 02 9457 0022

Austria
Freytag-Berndt Artaria
Kohlmarkt 9
A-1010 Wien
T 01 533 2094
F 01 533 8685

Reiseladen
Dominikanerbastei 4
A-1010 Wien
T 0222 513 8936
F 0222 513 893619

Belgium
Craenen BVBA
Mechelsesteenweg 633
B-3020 Herent
T 016 23 90 90
F 016 23 97 11

Canada
Ulysses Travel Publications
4176 rue Saint-Denis
Montréal
Québec H2W 2M5
T 514 843 9882
F 514 843 9448

Caribbean
Kingston Publishers
10, LOJ Industrial Complex
7 Norman Road
Kingston CSO
Jamaica
T 001876 928 8898
F 001876 928 5719

Europe
Bill Bailey
16 Devon Square
Newton Abbott
Devon TQ12 2HR. UK
T 01626 331079
F 01626 331080

Denmark
Kilroy Travel
Skindergade 28
DK-1159 Copenhagen K
T 33 11 00 44
F 33 32 32 69

Nordisk Korthandel
Studiestraede 26-30 B
DK-1455 Copenhagen K
T 3338 2638
F 3338 2648

Scanvik Books
Esplanaden 8B
DK-1263 Copenhagen K
T 33 12 77 66
F 33 91 28 82

Finland
Akateeminen Kirjakauppa
Keskuskatu 1
FIN-00100 Helsinki
T 09 12141
F 09 121 4441

Suomalainen Kirjakauppa
Koivuvaarankuja 2
01640 Vantaa 64
F 08 52 78 88

France
L'Astrolabe
46 rue de Provence
F-75009 Paris 9e
T 1 42 85 42 95
F 1 45 75 92 51

VILO Diffusion
25 rue Ginoux
F-75015 Paris
T 01 45 77 08 05
F 01 45 79 97 15

Germany
GeoCenter ILH
Schockenriedstrasse 44
D-70565 Stuttgart
T 0711 781 94610
F 0711 781 94654

Brettschneider
Fernreisebedarf
Feldkirchnerstrasse 2
D-85551 Heimstetten
T 089 990 20330
F 089 990 20331

Geobuch Gmbh
Rosental 6
D-80331 München
T 089 265030
F 089 263713

Gleumes
Hohenstaufenring 47-51
D-50674 Köln
T 0221 215650

Globetrotter Ausrustunge
Wiesendamm 1
D-22305 Hamburg
F 040 679 66183

Dr Götze
Bleichenbrücke 9
D-2000 Hamburg 1
T 040 3031 1009-0

Hugendubel Buchhandl
Nymphenburgerstrasse
D-80335 München
T 089 238 9412
F 089 550 1853

Kiepert Buchhandlung
Hardenbergstrasse 4-5
D-10623 Berlin 12
T 030 311880

Greece
GC Eleftheroudakis
17 Panepistemiou
Athens 105 64
T 01 331 4180-83
F 01 323 9821

India
Roli Books
M-75 GK II Market
New Delhi 110048
T (011) 646 0886
F (011) 646 7185

Israel
Geographical Tours
8 Tverya Street
Tel Aviv 63144
T 03 528 4113
F 03 629 9905

Italy
Librimport
Via Biondelli 9
I-20141 Milano
T 02 8950 1422
F 02 8950 2811

Kenya
Textbook Centre
Kijabe Street
PO Box 47540
Nairobi
T 2 330340
F 2 225779

Netherlands
Nilsson & Lamm bv
Postbus 195
Pampuslaan 212
N-1380 AD Weesp
T 0294 494949
F 0294 494455

Norway
Schibsteds Forlag A/S
Akersgata 32 - 5th Floor
Postboks 1178 Sentrum
N-0107 Oslo
T 22 86 30 00
F 22 42 54 92

Tanum
PO Box 1177 Sentrum
N-0107 Oslo 1
T 22 41 11 00
F 22 33 32 75

Olaf Norlis
Universitetsgt 24
N-1062 Oslo
T 22 00 43 00

Pakistan
Pak-American Commercial
Zaib-un Nisa Street
Saddar
PO Box 7359
Karachi
T 21 566 0418
F 21 568 3611

South Africa
Faradawn CC
PO Box 1903
Saxonwold 2132
T 011 885 1787
F 011 885 1829

South America
Humphrys Roberts
Associates
Caixa Postal 801-0
Ag. Jardim da Gloria
06700-970 Cotia SP
Brazil
T 011 492 4496
F 011 492 6896

Southeast Asia
APA Publications
38 Joo Koon Road
Singapore 628990
T 865 1600
F 861 6438

Spain
Altaïr
Balmes 69
08007 Barcelona
T 93 3233062
F 93 4512559

Bookworld España
Pje Las Palmeras 25
29670 San Pedro Alcántara
Málaga
T 95 278 6366
F 95 278 6452

Libros de Viaje
C/Serrano no 41
28001 Madrid
T 01 91 577 9899
F 01 91 577 5756

Sweden
Hedengrens Bokhandel
PO Box 5509
S-11485 Stockholm
T 8 6115132

Kart Centrum
Vasagatan 16
S-11120 Stockholm
T 8 111699

Lantmateriet Kartbutiken
Kungsgatan 74
S-11122 Stockholm
T 08 202 303
F 08 202 711

Switzerland
Artou
8 rue de Rive
CH-1204 Geneva
T 022 311 4544
F 022 781 3456

Office du Livre OLF SA
ZI 3, Corminboeuf
CH-1701 Fribourg
T 026 467 5111
F 026 467 5466

Schweizer Buchzentrum
Postfach
CH-4601 Olten
T 062 209 2525
F 062 209 2627

Travel Bookshop
Rindermarkt 20
Postfach 216
CH-8001 Zürich
T 01 252 3883
F 01 252 3832

USA
NTC/ Contemporary
4255 West Touhy Avenue
Lincolnwood
Illinois 60646-1975
T 847 679 5500
F 847 679 2494

Footnotes

Footnotes

Footnotes

Footnotes

Footnotes

Footnotes

Footnotes

Footprint travel list

Footprint publish travel guides to over 120 countries worldwide. Each guide is packed with practical, concise and colourful information for everybody from first-time travellers to travel aficionados . The list is growing fast and current titles are noted below. For further information check out the website **www.footprintbooks.com**

Andalucía Handbook
Bali & the Eastern Isles Hbk*
Bangkok & the Beaches Hbk*
Bolivia Handbook
Brazil Handbook
Cambodia Handbook
Caribbean Islands Handbook
Chile Handbook
Colombia Handbook
Cuba Handbook
Dominican Republic Handbook*
East Africa Handbook
Ecuador & Galápagos Handbook
Egypt Handbook Handbook
Goa Handbook
India Handbook
Indian Himalaya Handbook*
Indonesia Handbook
Ireland Handbook
Israel Handbook
Jordan Handbook*
Jordan, Syria & Lebanon Hbk
Laos Handbook
Libya Handbook*
Malaysia Handbook
Myanmar Handbook
Mexico Handbook
Mexico & Central America Hbk
Morocco Handbook
Namibia Handbook
Nepal Handbook
Pakistan Handbook
Peru Handbook

Rio de Janeiro Handbook*
Scotland Handbook
Singapore Handbook
South Africa Handbook
South American Handbook
South India Handbook*
Sri Lanka Handbook
Sumatra Handbook
Thailand Handbook
Tibet Handbook
Tunisia Handbook
Venezuela Handbook
Vietnam Handbook

* available autumn 2000

In the pipeline – Turkey, London, Kenya, Rajasthan, Scotland Highlands & Islands, Syria & Lebanon

Also available from Footprint
Traveller's Handbook
Traveller's Healthbook

Available at all good bookshops

Map 1

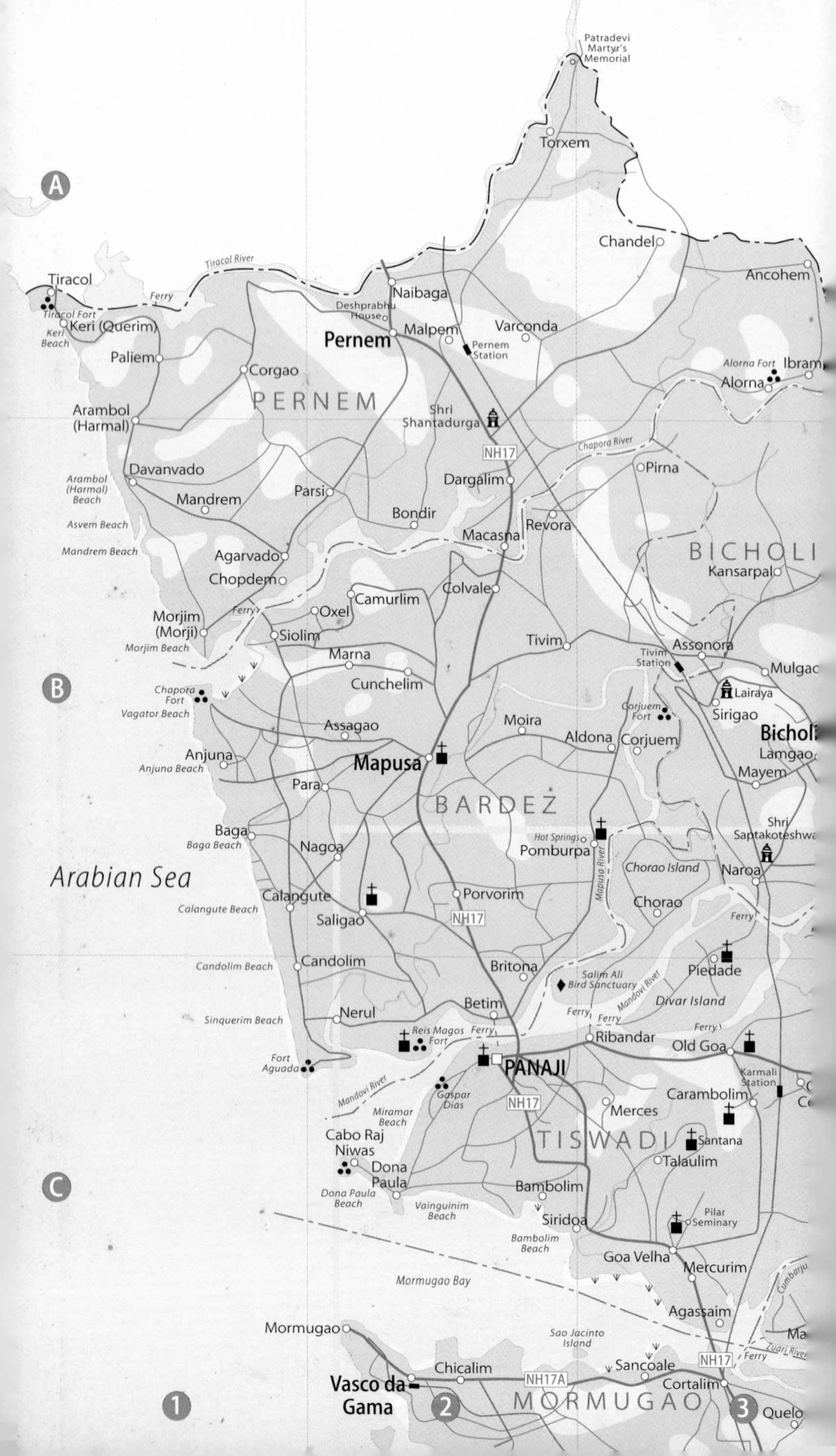

Map 1

A

B

C

1

2

3

Patradevi Martyr's Memorial

Torxem

Chandel

Ancohem

Tiracol
Tiracol River
Ferry
Tiracol Fort
Keri Beach
Keri (Querim)

Naibaga
Deshprabhu House
Malpem
Varconda

Pernem
Pernem Station

Alorna Fort
Ibram
Alorna

Paliem

Corgao

PERNEM

Shri Shantadurga

NH17

Chapora River

Pirna

BICHOLI

Kansarpal

Arambol (Harmal)

Davanvado

Arambol (Harmal) Beach

Mandrem

Parsi

Bondir

Dargalim

Macasna

Revora

Asvem Beach

Mandrem Beach

Agarvado

Chopdem

Camurlim

Oxel

Colvale

Tivim

Tivim Station

Assonora

Mulgac

Morjim (Morji)

Morjim Beach

Ferry

Siolim

Marna

Cuncheliim

Moira

Aldona

Corjuem

Corjuem Fort

Lairaya

Sirigao

Bicholi

Chapora Fort

Vagator Beach

Assagao

Lamgao

Mayem

Anjuna

Anjuna Beach

Para

Mapusa

BARDEZ

Shri Saptakoteshwa

Baga

Baga Beach

Nagoa

Pomburpa

Hot Springs

Chorao Island

Naroa

Arabian Sea

Calangute

Porvorim

Mapusa River

Chorao

Ferry

Piedade

Calangute Beach

Saligao

NH17

Britona

Salim Ali Bird Sanctuary

Divar Island

Candolim

Candolim Beach

Nerul

Betim

Mandovi River

Ferry

Ribandar

Ferry

Ferry

Old Goa

Karmali Station

Sinquerim Beach

Reis Magos Fort

Ferry

Fort Aguada

Mandovi River

Gaspar Dias

PANAJI

Carambolim

Ce

Cabo Raj Niwas

Miramar Beach

Dona Paula

Dona Paula Beach

Merces

NH17

Santana

Talaulim

Bambolim

TISWADI

Vainguinim Beach

Siridoa

Bambolim Beach

Pilar Seminary

Mercurim

Goa Velha

Cumbarju

Mormugao

Mormugao Bay

Agassaim

Ma

Sao Jacinto Island

Sancoale

NH17

Ferry

Zuari River

Vasco da Gama

Chicalim

NH17A

Cortalim

Quelo

MORMUGAO

N

0 km 3
0 miles 3

MAHARASHTRA

KARNATAKA

A

B

C

SATARI

damarg

Ponsuli

Iverm
Curdo

Golauli

Ambacho Gol

Gululem

Gonteli

Porlem

Codal

Shri
Brahma

Nanorem

Sarvona

Zormen

Carambolim

Map 2

Shri
Rudreshwar

Sanquelim

Carapur

Arvalem

Onda

Bondir

vam

Pissurlem

Sonal

Valpoi

Amone

Marcela

Vaguriem

Ansolem

Velguem

Cuntol

arjua

Betqui

Nahus

Caranzol

Orgao

Surla

nastari

Volvoi

Velgeum

Birondem

Siranguli

Querim

Ananta

Assodem

im

Savoi Verem

Govanem

Mangesh

Bamboi

Gangem

Toldem

Mardol

Priol

Usgaon

Bondla
Wildlife
Sanctuary

Udolxem

Balcornem

shi-
asimha-

NH4A

Khandepar

Pascoal

Codar

Tisk

Sancordem

Surla

Farmagudi

Curti

Ganesh

adoro

gesh &
akshmi

Ponda

Betora

Darbandora

Queula

Shri Shantadurga

4

5

6

Kudne River

Valvanti River

Khandepar River

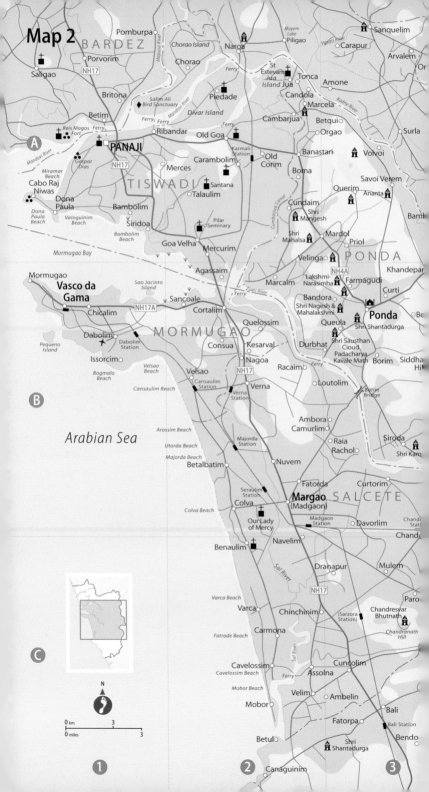

Map 3

SALCETE

Benaulim
Navelim
Madgaon Station
Chandorgoa Station
Chandor
Xelde
Dranapur
Mulem
Nirmal Nagar
Paroda
Varca Beach
Varca
Chinchinim
(Sarzora Station)
Chandreshwar Bhutnath
Quepen
NH17
Carmona
Chandranath Hill
Gaoker Kumberwa
Fatrade Beach
Cavelossim
Cungolim
Sal River
Cavelossim Beach
Ferry
Assolna
Mobor Beach
Velim
Ambelin
Bali
Mobor
Bali Station
Fatorpa
Bendordem
Betul
Shri Shantadurga

Canaguinim
Morpirla
Vellawunda
Quedem
QUEPE
Cabo de Rama Fort
Molorem
Padi
Cola (Kola)
Gocolc
NH17
Saleri
Barcem
Xele
Agonda
Gullem
An
Agonda Beach

Arabian Sea

Palolem
Nagorcem
Canacona Island
Palolem Beach
Chaudi
Colomb Beach
Canacona Station
Kindelbaga
Rajbag Beach
Ferry
Talpona

Galgibaga
Ferry
Mashen
NH17
(Lol Stat
Lo

Tanos

N

0 km   3
0 miles   3

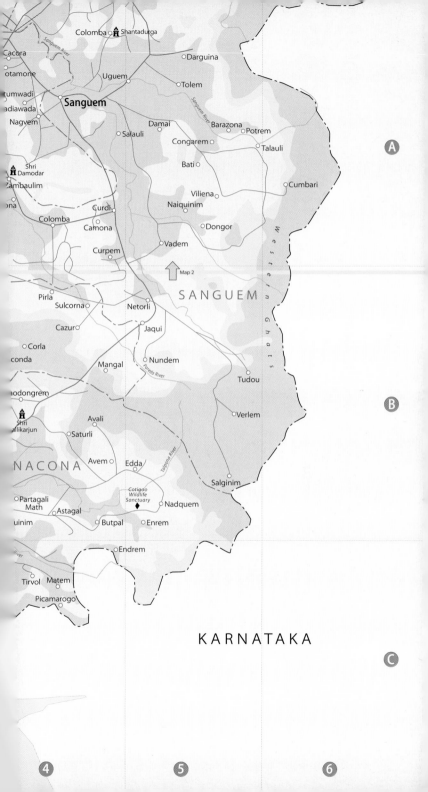

What the papers say

"I carried the South American Handbook in my bag from Cape Horn to Cartagena and consulted it every night for two and a half months. And I wouldn't do that for anything else except my hip flask."
Michael Palin

"Footprint's India Handbook told me everything from the history of the region to where to get the best curr
Jennie Bond, BBC correspondent

"Of all the main guidebook series this is genuinely the only one we have never received a complaint about."
The Bookseller

Awards
Wanderlust Readers' Award for Top Guidebook Series
Bronze Award

Literati Club
Outstanding Achievement

Mail order
Available worldwide in good bookstores, Footprint Handbooks
can also be ordered directly from us in Bath, via our website
or from the address on page 2.

Website
www.footprintbooks.com
Take a look for the latest news, to order
a book or to join our mailing list.